Henry Eyster Jacobs

Annotations on the Epistles of Paul to the Romans and I. Corinthians

Chaps. I-VI

Henry Eyster Jacobs

Annotations on the Epistles of Paul to the Romans and I. Corinthians *Chaps. I-VI*

ISBN/EAN: 9783337020804

Printed in Europe, USA, Canada, Australia, Japan

Cover: Foto ©Lupo / pixelio.de

More available books at **www.hansebooks.com**

THE LUTHERAN COMMENTARY

A PLAIN EXPOSITION OF THE

Holy Scriptures of the New Testament

BY
SCHOLARS OF THE LUTHERAN CHURCH IN AMERICA

EDITED BY
HENRY EYSTER JACOBS

Vol. VII.

New York
The Christian Literature Co.
MDCCCXCV

ANNOTATIONS

ON THE

EPISTLES OF PAUL

TO THE

ROMANS AND
I. CORINTHIANS, Chaps. I.–VI.

BY

HENRY E. JACOBS, D.D., LL.D.

Professor of Systematic Theology, Lutheran Seminary, Philadelphia, Pa.

New York
The Christian Literature Co.
MDCCCXCVI.

COPYRIGHT, 1896,
BY
THE CHRISTIAN LITERATURE COMPANY.

INTRODUCTION.

The Epistle to the Romans is one of the few books of the New Testament, whose genuineness has never been called in question by any critic of standing. The Tübingen school accepted it, with the two Epistles to the Corinthians and the Epistle to the Galatians, as undoubtedly Pauline. Irenæus, Clement of Alexandria and Tertullian quote from it as an Epistle of Paul. It is acknowledged as such by the Gnostics, Basilides, Valentinus, Heracleon, Epiphanes and Theodosius. It is only in respect to the closing chapters, that we find any doubts entertained concerning the integrity,—and that upon entirely insufficient grounds, of which the chief is that the salutations are entirely too numerous to individuals in a church at a place where the Apostle had never been. "The best refutation is a consecutive reading of chapters xii.-xvi. by a reader who does not start with a pedantic theory of what Paul *ought* to have related, or alluded to, or discussed" (MOULE).

No intimation is given in the New Testament of the origin of the church at Rome. It appears clear, however, that when this Epistle was written, it had been in existence for many years, ch. 1:8-13; 13:11, 15. The Jewish population of Rome, it is well known from Philo and Josephus, had become numerous. "Strangers of Rome," Acts 2:10, were among the multitude present on the

Day of Pentecost. Among the three thousand converts, we may believe, were some who became the nucleus of the Roman congregation. They may have gained converts from among their Jewish brethren. The persecution, when Stephen died, that scattered the church at Jerusalem, Acts 8 : 1, probably increased the number of Christians at Rome.

With the freedom of movement belonging to the times, many of the Gentiles converted by St. Paul at different places, probably had moved thither. The general dissatisfaction with the heathen religions that had prepared the way at Rome for the conversion of many heathen to Judaism, operated still more effectually in affording the occasion for many conversions to Christianity. With a nucleus thus formed, the church at Rome seems to be already strong. Composed preponderantly of Gentiles, although including many Jews, it belonged to the domain of the Apostle to the Gentiles. The Greek names in the salutations, the Greek names of the early bishops, the continuance of Greek as the ecclesiastical language for centuries, the Greek inscriptions on the tombs of Christians in the catacombs, confirm the Greek character of the early church at Rome. It was a church chiefly of strangers in the world's capital. Acts 28 : 21, 22 clearly shows that it was scarcely known among the Jews in Rome.

The early tradition (Dionysius, Irenæus, Eusebius, Jerome) that ascribes the founding of the church to Peter during the reign of Claudius (A. D. 41-54) abounds in difficulties that are irreconcilable with the facts recorded in Acts. For example, it reports that Peter founded the church at Rome after founding that at Antioch; but, according to Acts 11 : 19, sqq., he did not found the church at Antioch. There is no allusion to Peter either in this Epistle, or in the Epistles written by Paul from Rome. Besides Paul expressly disclaims building upon another man's foundation, ch. 15 : 20. The Roman church must have had its origin chiefly, even though indirectly, in the missionary activity of Paul.

The time of its composition is agreed upon with almost entire unanimity. It was the last of the four Epistles (Galatians, 1 and 2 Corinthians, Romans), written during his Third Missionary Journey in the Spring of 58 or 59 A. D., just before starting for Jerusalem, where he was imprisoned and whence he was sent to Rome. Phœbe, deaconess of the church at Cenchrea, the eastern harbor of Corinth, was about going to Rome. In the house of Gaius, ch. 16: 23, a Corinthian Christian, whom Paul had baptised, he wrote this letter, through Tertius as his amanuensis, for transmission to Rome.

In determining its main purpose, it is difficult to distinguish between what belongs to the human author and the providential place this Epistle was intended by a Higher Power to occupy. The Apostle could not have been conscious of the far-reaching significance of this Epistle for the future of the Church. No peculiar circumstances in the Roman church could have called forth the Epistle. The mere mention of the two words " Rome " and " Christianity " suggests thoughts that rise above all merely local and temporal limitations. As the Apostle of the Gentiles, it was Paul's mission to raise the preaching of the Gospel above all merely national circles, and to proclaim it to the whole world, of which Rome was the capital. " It breathes the spirit of a truly imperial ambition." Understanding, with a truly military insight, the strategic importance of cities, Paul seeks to strengthen the position of Christianity in Rome for the conquest of the whole world. Throughout his ministry, his gaze was ever steadfastly fixed on Rome. "I must also see Rome," were his words, Acts 19 : 21. All his other work he seems to regard only preparatory to what was to be done at Rome.

The epistle discusses, therefore, the principles that underly this thought of the world-embracing influence of the church at Rome. The thoughts here recorded are not new to the Apostle. They are the mature product of his most profound reflections in his solitary journeys and voyages, and in his efforts to bring the knowledge of Christ to men of all nationalities and of all classes and conditions of life. As at Rome all meet, so at the very idea of Rome, these thoughts are focussed, and flow forth in a continuous discourse by an inner necessity of his nature, impelled and guided by the inspiration of the Holy Spirit.

Starting with the statement of the design of his Apostleship to bring "all the nations" into obedience to the faith, ch. 1 : 5, he expounds the theme of "THE UNIVERSALITY OF THE GRACE OF GOD IN CHRIST."

After an *Introduction* (ch. 1 : 1-15), the theme is announced, and the argument proceeds: I. All alike under condemnation (1 : 18—3 : 20). II. All alike are offered Justification by Faith (3 : 21—5 : 21). III. The Universality of grace, no apology for sin (6 : 12—8 : 39). IV. Relation of this doctrine to Judaism (9 : 1—11 : 36). V. Practical Exhortations (12 : 1—15 : 13). VI. Personal Matters, 15 : 14—16 : 27.

LITERATURE.

The following commentaries have been freely used in the preparation of this volume.

ALFORD, HENRY : *The Greek Testament, with a Critical*

and Exegetical Commentary. Sixth edition, London, Oxford and Cambridge. I. 1871. Anglican. Learned, judicious and to the point.

ANSELM : *Enarrationes in Epistolam ad Romanos.* In Vol. II. *Opera Omnia,* Cologne, 1712. Patristic. Condenses results of his predecessors, avoiding many of their aberrations. Frequently striking and suggestive.

BALDUIN, FREDERICK : *Commentarius in Omnes Epistolas Pauli.* Frankfort on the Main, 1664. Balduin was Professor and general Superintendent at Wittenberg. B. 1575, d. 1627. The treatment is exhaustive and discriminating, although scholastic in form. Each section of the epistle is discussed under the following heads : (1) Analysis. (2) Paraphrase. (3) Theological questions. (4) Theological aphorisms. The more we have studied this commentary, the greater has been our admiration.

BENGEL, JOHN ALBERT : *Gnomon.* Translation of Vincent and Lewis, Philadelphia, 1862. Too well known to need characterization.

BESSER, WILLIAM F. : *Bibelstunden.* The exposition of Romans fills two volumes. (Halle, 1861.) A series of expository lectures based on very thorough studies, and extensive reading of exegetical, homiletical and devotional literature. Combines solidity with deep spirituality. Especially valuable for its numerous quotations. Lutheran to the core.

BROWN, DAVID : *Handy Books for Bible Classes; The Epistle to the Romans.* Edinburgh, without date. An excellent outline of the argument, from the Calvinistic standpoint. The same author has published a valuable exposition in the JAMESON, FAUSSET AND BROWN series of Commentaries.

CALOVIUS, ABRAHAM : *Biblia Illustrata.* Vol. IV., Dresden and Leipsic, 1719. Includes and criticises the exposition of Grotius. A work of stupendous industry and sober judgment. Particularly valuable for its long and thorough excursuses. The exegesis of Calovius is always running into Dogmatics and Polemics; but it dare not be ignored by any scholar who aims at thoroughness. He was Professor at Wittenberg, and the foremost Lutheran controversialist of his age.

CALVIN, JOHN: *In Novum Testamentum Commentarii.* Edited by Tholuck. Berlin, 1834. Calvin's great strength was as an exegete. A model of clearness and acuteness, that deserves far more attention than is usually given it.

CHALMERS, THOMAS: *Lectures on the Epistle to the Romans.* New York, 1843. Expository Lectures of extraordinary diffuseness. Argumentative throughout. Chalmers was the great theologian and religious leader of the Free Church of Scotland. Calvinistic.

GIFFORD, E. H.: Romans in *Speakers' Commentary.* New York, 1881. Based on Meyer and Philippi. Anglican.

GODET, F.: *Commentary on Romans.* Translated from the French by Rev. A. Cusin. Revised and edited by Talbot W. Chambers, New York, 1889. One of the most readable commentaries ever published, combining thoroughness of exegetical investigation and scientific method with theological insight, clear and almost popular style, and great practical force. Avoids diffuseness and keeps close to the argument, with occasional scintillations of thought and pointed remarks showing the genius of the author. Calvinistic.

HODGE, CHARLES: Commentary. New Edition. Philadelphia, 1883. Sober and theological. Represents mild Calvinism.

HUNNIUS, ÆGIDIUS: *Thesaurus Apostolicus, complec-*

tens Commentarios in omnes Novi Testamenti Epistolas. Wittenberg, 1705. Hunnius was Professor at Marburg and Wittenberg. B. 1550, d. 1603. First gives an analysis, and then deduces theological topics from each verse. Mild in temper, but most decided in its Lutheran position.

LIDDON, H. P.: *Explanatory Analysis.* London, 1893. A posthumous work of the greatest Anglican theologian of this century. It was first printed for use in the class room. The work is done with the greatest minuteness, and presents the thoroughly logical character of Paul's treatment, as it is found nowhere else. He acknowledges Meyer's suggestions as the source of his elaboration, but also uses Philippi freely. Accompanied by many illustrations and references of great value, especially from classical and patristic sources, and translated German works. While there is little original work done, the book, by its striking methods, marks an advance in the presentation of the subject. The great defect is the lack of acquaintance with Luther, Melanchthon and Calvin, and in fact with all the theology of the Reformation, which it shows. This results in a misunderstanding of the doctrine of justification. See especially on p. 85, where faith is represented as justifying simply as "the initial act of union with God." In justice to Dr Liddon it must be said that he did not publish his commentary, partly because he was dissatisfied with the treatment of the first portion of the book.

LUTHARDT, C. E.: *Die Lehre von den letzten Dingen.* Leipzig, 1861. Contains an exegetical treatment of Chap. 11: 11-32.

Kurzgefasster Commentar zu den heiligen Schriften. Edited by Strack and Zöckler. Commentary on Romans. Nördlingen, 1887. A compact summary of results.

MELANCHTHON, PHILIP: *Annotationes* (1529, 1530, 1539); *Commentarii* (1532, 1540, 1544); *Enarratio* (1556, 1558, 1561). Constantly uses the text as a starting-point for discussion of dogmatical and ethical questions. Abounds in happy definitions. Introduction especially important. Too frequently runs into diffuse discussions. These three works are contained in Vol. XV. of the *Corpus Reformatorum*, Halle, 1848.

MEYER, H. A. W.: Commentary, translated from the German by Moore and Johnson. Edited by Dickson and Dwight. New York, 1884. See WEISS, B.

MOULE, H. C. G.: *The Cambridge Bible for Schools. The Epistle to the Romans*. Cambridge, 1892. A very modest, but most scholarly and judicious volume. We have never referred to it without profit. The same author has written the volume on Romans in *The Expositor's Bible*, but has not reached the standard of his smaller book.

OLSHAUSEN, H.: Biblical Commentary, translated from the German. Edinburgh, 1849.

PHILIPPI, F. A.: Commentary, translated from the German by Banks. Two volumes, Edinburgh, 1878, 1879. The most thorough of the entire list, presenting the most complete development of Paul's arguments from the standpoint of a well-trained and well-balanced theologian, who knows how to avail himself of the best exegetical results. Philippi seems to owe most to Calovius, as Calovius does to Balduin.

SANDAY, W., AND HEADLAM, A. C.: A critical and exegetical commentary (International Critical Commentary). New York, 1895. This most recent of the commentaries exhibits the fruits of very extensive research, and much versatility of learning. But it is intensely disappointing because of its intentional avoidance of the theological arguments, although there is some valuable material belonging properly to *Dogmengeschichte* introduced. The unity of the Epistle falls to pieces by the exaggeration of critical methods. There is a good criticism of Commentaries, which omits Philippi; although the work is indebted to Philippi in its free use of Gifford, who highly appreciates and with proper acknowledgment appropriates material from the former Lutheran professor at Rostock.

STUART, MOSES: *Commentary.* Andover, 1835. Congregationalist. A grammatical commentary, with extensive use of the German apparatus of the period.

THOLUCK, A.: *Commentary.* Translated into English by Rev. R. Menzies. Philadelphia, 1844.

WEISS, BERNHARD: Sixth edition of Meyer, Göttingen, 1881. A thorough revision, amounting almost to an independent work. Combines the merits of Meyer as a grammatical exegete and repository of results of previous exegetes, with a more thorough insight into Paul's theological reasoning.

Besides the above, we have also looked into the commentaries of Chrysostom, Fritzsche, Rückert, Lange, Shedd and the Synopses of Poole and Starke. We regret that "Notes on the Epistles of St. Paul from Unpublished Commentaries," London and New York, 1895, by the late Bishop LIGHTFOOT, came to us too late to be of service on Romans.

ANNOTATIONS ON
THE EPISTLE TO THE ROMANS.

I. PREFACE (1-17).

1. *Salutation* (1-7).

An expansion of the ordinary greeting with which letters began (Acts 23 : 26), first by describing who the author is and what is his message (1-6), then describing those to whom he writes (7a), and then extending the ordinary greeting, so as to comprise every blessing which is to be desired by one Christian for another (7b).

> 1-7. Paul, a servant of Jesus Christ, called *to be* an apostle, separated unto the gospel of God, which he promised afore by his prophets in the holy scriptures, concerning his Son, who was born of the seed of David according to the flesh, who was declared *to be* the Son of God with power according to the spirit of holiness, by the resurrection of the dead; *even* Jesus Christ our Lord, through whom we received grace and apostleship, unto obedience of faith among all the nations, for his name's sake: among whom are ye also, called *to be* Jesus Christ's: to all that are in Rome, beloved of God, called *to be* saints: Grace to you and peace from God our Father and the Lord Jesus Christ.

Ver. 1. **Paul** is his Roman name. The Hebrew "Saul" designated him as a Jew. When he comes forth from Judaism to proclaim the Gospel to all nations, the very change of name indicates the wider compass of his thought and work. He sinks his nationality in the use of a name belonging to the vocabulary of the language of the world. It occurs first in Acts 13 : 9 with the account of the beginning of Paul's missionary activity as the Apostle to the Gentiles. The inference seems a very remote one that traces the name to a memorial of the conversion of Æmilius Paulus (Acts 13 : 12). **A servant.** Not descriptive of the general relation of a believer to Christ, as in 1 Cor. 7 : 22 ; Eph. 6 : 6; but, as in Ps. 105 : 6, 42 ; Josh. 1 : 1 ; Isai. 20 : 3 ; Acts 4 : 29; 16 : 17 ; Rev. 15 : 3, of a special relation in which the general duty of submission is concentrated and intensified. In the O. T., the ordinary designation of prophets is that of " the servant of God," or " the servant of the Lord ; " in the N. T., that of Apostles is just as frequently " the servant of Jesus Christ." This substitution at once suggests Christ's divine nature. **Called to be an apostle** designates the specific form of the service. " An Apostle is a person immediately called by God to teach the Gospel, furnished with an infallible testimony, and having a universal vocation, so that he can teach in every place " (MEL.). For proofs of Paul's apostleship, see Acts 9 : 6, 15 ; 22 : 21 ; 26 : 16-18 ; Gal. 1 : 1, 12. The call is emphasized to indicate that the office was no self-chosen one. God has placed him there, and, hence, it is solely for God that he speaks. **Separated,** i. e. from the great body of believers and from all other occupations, to this particular work. It cannot refer to God's election, which would require a different word in Greek, or to his consecration with Barnabas as a missionary. The reference is to the Providential guidance which has prepared him for the work and placed him in it. **Unto the Gospel.** Unfettered, therefore, by the restrictions and limitations of the Law. He has a higher standpoint and a wider outlook. **Of God** i. e. God is its author, Christ is its theme.

Ver. 2. **Promised afore,** indicating the inner and substantial harmony of Law and Gospel. The latter is nothing new, but is the substance of the testimony of the Old Testament from the beginning. **By his prophets.** (Cf. Acts 10 : 43.) The reference is not limited to the authors of O. T. prophetical books; it embraces all who prophesied, including Moses, Samuel, David, etc. " It is not wonderful that his feelings rise at the thought of being the principal instrument of a work thus predicted " (GOD.).

Ver. 3. **Concerning his Son.** This is to be connected with " promised afore." " Son " cannot be limited to a title of the Messiah, in the light of such passages as ch. 8 : 3, 32 ; Gal. 1 : 16 ; 4 : 4 ; Col. 1 : 13 sqq. ; Phil. 2 : 6 sqq., but clearly refers to the " only begotten Son " (John 1 : 14). **Born of the seed of David.** In fulfilment of Jer. 23 : 15 ; Ps. 132 : 11. This occurred through his birth of Mary (Gal. 4 : 4). **According to the flesh,** i. e. His human nature, in all its parts, came by descent from David.

Ver. 4. **With power** limits " Son of God." " The powerful Son of God " (MEL.), contrasting the weakness of the human, with the strength of the divine, since, by His human nature, He was subject to pain and death. **Spirit of holiness.** This is very naturally interpreted as His divine nature, since the Holy Spirit is never so designated elsewhere, and because of the parallel clause of preceding verse. On the other hand, the interpretation of LUTHER and CALVIN, which interprets it as " the Holy Spirit," is in harmony with the Apostle's argument by which he rises from the consideration of the letter to that of the spirit. The Holy Spirit, whose power is displayed in the resurrection (ch. 8 : 11), dwelling in believers, is the source of their freedom and the ground and proof of the universality of divine grace. " The

Spirit of God was given after Christ's ascension, whence He sanctifies Christians and glorifies Christ in all the world as the Son of God "(LUTHER). **By the resurrection of the dead.** Not by the " resurrection from the dead," but by the fact that the dead are raised. The resurrection of Christ is both proof of this, and the assurance and power of the resurrection of all others (John 11 : 25; Rom. 8 : 11; 1 Cor. 15 : 12). The resurrection then declares that Christ is the Almighty Son of God (Ps. 2 : 7). **Jesus Christ our Lord.** This Son of God is none other, he says, than Jesus whom we have known historically, and whom we have recognized as the Messiah and our Lord.

Ver. 5. **Through whom** indicates that the blessings mentioned come through Christ's mediation. **Grace and apostleship.** The former designates gifts received by Paul in common with all other believers, viz., the divine grace of which he became partaker, when called and converted on the way to Damascus (1 Cor. 15 : 10); the latter refers to the particular office with which he was entrusted and the extraordinary gifts with which it was furnished. Paul's apostleship was not confined to the Gentiles; it embraced also "the children of Israel" (Acts 2 : 15). **Unto obedience of faith.** The aim of the apostleship is to bring men to faith, and, through faith, to make them obedient to the Gospel. Faith here means confidence in the truth of the divine message which is sent through the Apostle. Such faith will produce obedience when this apostolic message is delivered. **Among all the nations.** The Gospel demands an obedience as universal as that demanded by the Empire of which Rome was the capital. Here we have the claim of an imperial dominion for Christianity, coextensive with the race. **For his name's sake.** The name of Christ will be magnified by this obedience. (Cf. Acts 9 : 15 ; 15 : 26; 21 : 13 ; 2 Thess. 1 : 12.)

Ver. 6. **Among whom.** A clear proof that the church of Rome was composed principally of Gentiles. **Called to be Jesus Christ's**, or "the called," of God, "who belong to Jesus Christ." On this account, Paul demands of them a hearing.

Ver. 7. **All in Rome**, whether of Jewish or Gentile origin. **Beloved, called,** restrictive of "all," indicating those who have appropriated to themselves God's universal love, and have accepted the call. Called out of the world, they have been separated from it, and have been consecrated to God's service, **called to be saints. Grace to you,** etc. An expansion and interpretation of the Christian greeting, as in Acts 15 : 23 ; James 1 : 1. Grace is the unmerited favor of God bestowed on man, which when appropriated becomes in man an active principle of salvation, progressively freeing him from all evil, and building him up in the new life in Christ. **Peace** is the repose of the soul in God following the appropriation of grace. Benedictions are regularly without the verb. They are not mere wishes, but actually convey what they announce. Hence the verb to be supplied must be both optative and indicative. **God and the Lord Jesus Christ.** (Cf. 1 Cor. 1 : 3 ; 2 Cor. 1 : 2 ; Gal. 1 : 3 ; Eph. 1 : 2 ; Phil. 1 : 2 ; Col. 1 : 2 ; 1 Thess. 1 : 1 ; 2 Thess. 1 : 1 ; 1 Tim. 1 : 2 ; 2 Tim. 1 : 2 ; Tit. 1 : 4 ; Phil. 3 ; James 1 : 1 ; 2 Pet. 1 : 1, 2.) Not so much a distinction of persons in the Trinity, as a reference to different periods in the Plan of Redemption ; first, as hidden within God, and, then, as manifested in the Person and Work of Christ. **Christ** is the official name of the incarnate Son of God. The thought begins with God as unincarnate, and proceeds to God as incarnate.

2. *Personal Introduction* (8-15).

Paul begins nearly all his letters by expressing his gratitude to God for the faith of his readers, and assuring them of his desire to be with them.

8-15. First, I thank my God through Jesus Christ for you all, that your faith is proclaimed throughout the whole world. For God is my witness, whom I serve in my spirit in the gospel of his Son, how unceasingly I make mention of you, always in my prayers making request, if by any means now at length I may be prospered by the will of God to come unto you. For I long to see you, that I may impart unto you some spiritual gift, to the end ye may be established; that is, that I with you may be comforted in you, each of us by the other's faith, both yours and mine. And I would not have you ignorant, brethren, that oftentimes, I purposed to come unto you (and was hindered hitherto), that I might have some fruit in you also, even as in the rest of the Gentiles. I am debtor both to Greeks and to Barbarians, both to the wise and to the foolish. So, as much as in me is, I am ready to preach the gospel to you also that are in Rome.

Ver. 8. **First** points to an implied "secondly" in ver. 10. "First, I give thanks." "Secondly, I make request." The ardor of the Apostle's thought leads to a change of construction, by the time he reaches ver. 10, that occasions a suppression of the "secondly." **My God.** (Cf. Acts 27 : 23.) His personal life is so thoroughly grounded in his relations to God, that the candid expression of his deepest feeling is accompanied by the confession of that which is its center, viz., that God is his God. The possessive pronoun indicates the apprehension of faith. (Cf. John 20 : 28.) "In the words 'My God,' he sums up all his *personal* experiences of God's fatherly help, in the various circumstances of his life, and particularly in those of his apostleship" (GOD.). **Through Jesus Christ.** "As a Christian, he thanks his God, as one who takes out of the gracious hand of Christ all that God gives, and returns to the same hand all that he offers God (Col.

3 : 17; Heb. 13 : 15) " (BESS.). **Your faith**, i. e. the strength and quality of their faith. They have risen above the external, the visible, the transient. **Is proclaimed.** Literally " is being proclaimed." **Throughout the whole world.** Hyperbole, for " far and wide throughout the Roman Empire "; but only however where there are Christians. (Cf. 1 Thess. 1 : 8–10.)

Ver. 9. **God is my witness.** The appeal to God is explained either by the fact that it was surprising that he should be so deeply interested in a congregation which he had never visited, or to give additional assurance of his interest to those who might have thought that, since he had never visited it, the Apostle to the Gentiles had heretofore been indifferent to the congregation in the world's metropolis. With WEISS, we cannot regard this an oath in the proper sense of the term. **Serve in my spirit.** Ground of his appeal to God. None but God knows; for his worship is not a merely external one, but the intimate communion of his spirit with God. **In the Gospel**, in preaching the Gospel. Beneath all his outward activity as missionary and preacher, there is not only the constant sense of the divine presence, but also the joyful service of his heart, by which he seeks only that which will most please God. **How unceasingly.** Not the fact of his intercessions, but the strength of the love that prompts the intercessions, is here declared. " The thanksgiving with which he begins this epistle is a flame of the fire which burns without quenching upon the altar of prayer in his Christian heart " (BESS.). **My prayers.** Special seasons of prayer.

Ver. 10. **By the will of God to come.** " I must see Rome," was a settled conviction of Paul (Acts 19 : 21). " God bends His almighty will to the prayers of His children; and Paul at last reached Rome " (BESS.). Comp.

Acts 27 : 14. But his prayer to be prospered, so as to reach Rome, was answered in a way that he had not anticipated.

Ver. 11. **I long.** From the fulness of "grace and apostleship," ver. 5, with which he is endowed, he longs to communicate to the Romans all that his personal presence could give beyond that of his written word. As ver. 15 indicates that his great object is to preach the Gospel at Rome, not any apostolic miraculous gift (1 Cor. 14), but every such blessing as attends this preaching must be understood by **some spiritual gift.** "In his apprehension, all such instruction, comfort, joy, strengthening, etc., as are produced by means of his labors, are regarded not as procured by his own human individuality, but as a result which the Holy Spirit works by means of him—the gracious working of the Spirit whose organ he is" (MEY.). "The living voice of the teacher is more effectual to teach and strengthen, than reading in his absence what he has written" (HUNN.).

Ver. 12. **That I with you may be comforted.** The greatest of the Apostles who had enjoyed the revelations of the celestial Paradise (2 Cor. 12 : 2-4), longs for the blessings that the presence with him of the humblest of the Roman Christians can bestow. His gifts and work react upon himself. Whatever he gives to others comes back to him increased abundantly. The word means both "comfort" and "exhort." Christian perfection is not found in monastic seclusion or any ascetic isolation from others, but is more and more nearly approached as the faith of Christians is stimulated and encouraged by that of their brethren.

Ver. 13. **I would not have you ignorant.** The question naturally was asked why if Paul took such an interest in the Roman Church, he had not visited it earlier. This is his answer. **Was hindered.** (Cf ch. 15 : 22.) Paul's plans for his missionary journeys were not made by divine inspiration. God's will as to whither he should go was often unknown until the time came. **Some fruit.** The true aim of the preaching of the Gospel. "Therefore let the ambitious display of learning and talent be far distant from the ministers of the Church, and especially from their sermons" (HUNN.). **The rest of the Gentiles.** This leaves no doubt that the Church of Rome was composed chiefly of Gentiles.

Ver. 14. **I am debtor,** because of God's appointment (Acts 26 : 17 sqq.; 1 Cor. 9 : 16). The commission to preach the Gospel he calls in 1 Tim. 1 : 14 "the good deposit" (R. V. marginal reading). **To Greeks and to Barbarians,** the two classes into which Gentiles were divided. Paul was no debtor to the Jews (Gal. 2 : 7). The Greeks designated all other nations as barbarians. The Roman Christians may have been composed chiefly of Greeks. Besides, inasmuch as the Romans absorbed Greek culture and used the Greek language, they would naturally be included among the Greeks rather than among the barbarians. **Wise and unwise,** i. e. the educated and uneducated, suggested by the contrast between Greeks and barbarians, but not necessarily coextensive, since there were also Greeks who were uneducated.

Ver. 15. **So,** viz. as a debtor. **As much as in me is.** "For my part." Always ready, the determination of the time when he is to visit Rome belongs to God. **At Rome also.** It was no small undertaking to proclaim the Gospel at the world's capital, with all its power and culture and wealth and social forces antagonizing this word. Paul realized fully the gravity of the situation, as may be learned from Acts 28 : 15.

THE THEME STATED:

THE UNIVERSALITY OF GRACE.

16-17. For I am not ashamed of the gospel : for it is the power of God unto salvation to every one that believeth; to the Jew first, and also to the Greek. For therein is revealed a righteousness of God by faith unto faith: as it is written, But the righteous shall live by faith.

Ver. 16. **I am not ashamed.** The first part of this verse closes the preceding paragraph, which was devoted partially to answering the charge that he had been deterred from visiting the Roman church by his dread of the issues which he would there be compelled to face. The preaching of the Gospel is the very last thing in the world of which he has reason to be ashamed. " The Gospel is calculated to provoke not shame, but enthusiasm " (LIDD.). **For it is the power of God.** This introduces the real theme. It is power in and through which God works (1 Cor. 1 : 18 ; Eph. 6 : 17; 1 Thess. 2 : 13; Is. 55 : 11 ; Rom. 10 : 17). In this, it is contrasted with human wisdom, which, even in its highest stage, can never attain what is accomplished by the Gospel. " Its specific effect is faith, i. e. man's trust in Christ for salvation " (WEISS). **Unto salvation.** The forces of nature are powers of God, but for other ends. The Law is God's power ; but only to condemn (2 Cor. 3 : 9). Salvation must be understood here both in the negative and the positive sides. Begun in this life, in deliverance from God's wrath, it is completed in the future life, in deliverance from sin, pain and death. **To every one that believeth.** " Faith is the condition of the saving effect of the Gospel, which is itself conditioned by the divine power of the Gospel ; the hand of the beggar, which receives the gift of God after it has been opened and made capable of receiving by the Giver; for by nature, this beggar has a lame hand" (BESS.). "As was admirably said by a poor Bechuana: 'It is the hand of the heart'" (GOD.). **To the Jews first,** etc. Both Jew and Gentile are saved upon the same terms and in the same way. The historical priority of the offer of salvation to the Jews, in accordance with God's divinely instituted order, indicating an original difference of rank, no longer avails. The period of that priority and rank has passed; and there is no longer any warrant for Jewish particularism and exclusiveness. The Gospel is now for all alike.

Ver. 17. Explanation as to how the Gospel exerts its saving power. **Therein** refers to Gospel as distinguished both from nature and from the Law. Even the elements of "Gospel" found in the Old Testament prophets seem excluded here. The previous testimony through the prophets is but the promise of a way to be opened hereafter, not the glad news of the opening itself accomplished" (PHIL.). **Is revealed.** Made known, and, when made known, offered. The complete realization of what is revealed is not attained until the revelation is appropriated; then with the knowledge attained through experience, it seems almost as though the revelation had never been made before. **A righteousness of God.** Not an attribute of God, as in 3 : 5, but the righteousness which God gives man, the righteouness that comes from God and that avails with God. "Paul calls the righteousness of faith the righteousness of God, because God has originated and prepared it, reveals and bestows it, approves and crowns it (2 Pet. 1 : 1). To it is opposed men's *own* righteousness (Rom. 10 : 3). We ourselves are called the righteousness of God (2 Cor. 5 : 21)" (BENG.). **By faith unto faith.** "The righteousness availing before God is revealed, as coming from faith, unto faith. Faith is the condition, even as it is the organ apprehending righteousness" (PHIL.). "Only to one who believes what the Gospel says is the righteousness offered therein, revealed as actually present, while it remains a concealed and unrevealed benefit, and therefore as good as not present, to one who does not accept the message of salvation" (WEISS). Faith being the means of apprehending this revelation, it may be said to be revealed by faith. This revelation, however, is made in order that faith should receive it. Faith reveals. Then faith applies what faith has revealed; and, in applying, still more is revealed. Everything depends on faith. It is the beginning, the middle and the end of all spiritual life. **As it is written.** The quotation is made in order to show that there is no antagonism to its teaching. This is also its doctrine. **The righteous shall live by faith** (Habak. 2 : 4). Righteous by faith, he lives by faith. The spring of his life, even after he has been justified, is in supernatural and not mere natural sources. He lives because by faith the Gospel is a living power within him. Faith is no mere intellectual act, but it is the self-surrender of man with all that he is and has and loves and desires and thinks to God. The righteous man lives by his faith, solely because, in this way, the righteousness of God, just described, becomes his. With his self-surrender to God, the power of God is appropriated, and becomes within him a new spring of life. Righteous by faith indicates justification; living by faith, regeneration and sanctification.

PART I.

ALL MEN ALIKE UNDER CONDEMNATION
(1 : 18—3 : 20).

SECTION I.—THE STATE OF HEATHENISM (1 : 18-32).

For all men, grace is needed; because, by nature, all are without righteousness. The alternative is plain: "The righteousness of God" (ver. 17), or "the wrath of God" (ver. 18). The one means life; the other, death. A continuous revelation of wrath has marked the history of the race. Here and there, signal displays of this wrath break forth in the lives of nations and individuals, pointing to a severer punishment on the Day of Judgment. The entire course of Heathenism is downward, until it sinks into crimes that violate even nature. This descent is partially a judgment inflicted upon them for disregard of God's claims. The restraints removed, they sink whither their desires tend.

"The argument of this section may be thus stated: Major premiss: Whoever sins incurs the judgment of God, from which he can be delivered only by the righteousness of God (2 : 1-16).

"Minor premiss: But the heathen, although taught by Nature and Conscience (1 : 18-32), and the Jews, although possessing the Mosaic Law (2 : 17—3 : 8), have sinned by falling short of, or contradicting their respective standards of righteousness.

"Conclusion: Therefore, as the Old Testament had

already proclaimed, ' all the world is brought under the judgment of God' (3 : 19), and accordingly needs this righteousness (3 : 9–20) " (LID.).

18–23. For the wrath of God is revealed from heaven against all ungodliness and unrighteousness of men who hold down the truth in unrighteousness; because that which may be known of God is manifest in them; for God manifested it unto them. For the invisible things of him since the creation of the world are clearly seen, being perceived through the things that are made, *even* his everlasting power and divinity; that they may be without excuse: because that, knowing God, they glorified him not as God, neither gave thanks; but became vain in their reasonings, and their senseless heart was darkened. Professing themselves to be wise, they became fools, and changed the glory of the incorruptible God for the likeness of an image of corruptible man, and of birds, and fourfooted beasts, and creeping things.

Ver. 18. **The wrath of God.** A necessary inference from the love of God. It is " only the love of the holy God to all that is good, in its energy against all that is evil " (WEISS). " If God is not angry with the ungodly and unrighteous, He does not love the godly and righteous; for in matters that are diverse, he must be moved towards both sides or towards neither " (LACTANTIUS, *De ira Dei*, 5 : 9). **Is revealed,** viz. in the history of the heathen world, and in signal punishments inflicted upon other transgressors, pointing forward to the Judgment Day (ch. 2 : 5). **From heaven.** As the abode of God, the source whence this wrath proceeds. (Comp. Ps. 2 : 4, 5; Dan. 5 : 5 sq.; 2 Thess. 1 : 7 sq.) The universality of its range is also suggested. **Ungodliness,** against the First; **unrighteousness,** against the Second Table. **Who hold down.** Violence is done conscience. Known truth is intentionally disregarded and suppressed. **In unrighteousness.** Their wrongdoing to their fellow-men corrupts, suppresses, paralyzes the truth with respect to God. The root of the intellectual error is in the heart.

Ver. 19. **That which may be known.** Clearly: All

that can be or that is known without a supernatural revelation. It is not God's fault that they are without the knowledge which others have. **It is manifest.** Note the contrast between this word referring to the natural, and **is revealed** of ver. 18 referring to the supernatural, knowledge of God. (See Acts 14 : 17; 17 : 26 sq.) **In them,** i. e. in their consciousness, or in their hearts (ch. 2 : 15; Gal. 1 : 16). **God manifested it,** viz. by the knowledge impressed upon the heart, and inferred from the contemplation of nature.

Ver. 20. **The invisible things of him.** His invisible attributes. **Since the creation.** Ever since there was an intelligent mind to observe the outward world, the inference is irresistible. **Are clearly seen.** God can be known, then, so far as He reveals Himself. The innate knowledge of God (ch. 2 : 15) is called into activity and consciousness by the contemplation of an external world. **Even his everlasting power and divinity.** The first thought suggested by Nature is that of power, and this power is inevitably referred to a cause, which is recognized first as "Almighty," and then by a necessary inference as "Eternal," since the one attribute implies the other. " Divinity " is " the sum total of that which God is as a Being possessed of divine attributes " (MEYER), " the sum total of qualities in virtue of which the creative power can have organized such a world" (GODET). **That they may be without excuse,** i. e. that they may not plead any lack of evidence, as an excuse. Godet well notes that Paul, unlike some to-day, does not disparage Natural Theology, and regards this as a proof of the Apostle's breadth of mind and heart—" the first basis of his universalism," in connection with his proof of the universalism of sin and of grace.

Ver. 21. **Because** qualifies "without excuse." **They**

glorified him not, etc. He has made himself known, in order, when known, to be contemplated and loved. He is not only to be known, but, when known, to be thankfully recognized and worshipped as God. **As God,** i. e. with a true conception of what God is, regulating their thoughts of God, according to the standard of the revelation which God had given. (Comp. John 1:14; 4:24.) **Became vain.** Where this adoration is wanting, the knowledge given deteriorates. The unused talent is taken away. "Knowledge of God has its permanent root only in communion with Him" (PHIL.). Having neglected to set God before it, as the supreme object of its activity, the understanding was reduced to work *in vacuo;* it peopled the universe with fictions and chimæras" (GOD.). All relations thus become confused and perverted. "If I know not God, I know not myself" (VILM.). **Darkened.** The moral sense became weakened and diseased, and conscience was rendered an uncertain guide.

Ver. 22, 23. **Professing themselves to be wise.** The nearest example was the Greeks, among whom Paul was then living at Corinth. Beyond them the characterization includes also the representatives of all heathen religions (Egyptian, Indian, etc.), and extends to all forms of knowledge, that desert Revelation and seek to treat of God solely from natural reasoning. **They became fools.** The very climax of this folly being idolatry (Jer. 10:14 sq.). He does not attack their philosophy or learning; but shows that when not consecrated to the service of God, the most highly educated become guilty of the very greatest absurdities. **Changed the glory.** (Comp. Ps. 106:20.) The glory is here the sum of the attributes of God as revealed to man. See "divinity" (ver. 20). **For the likeness of an image,** i. e. they changed that which is real and substantial for a mere likeness, and this likeness, that not even of a man, but of the image of a man, etc. A likeness formed after a pattern or model in the mind of the artist. The gods of Greece and Rome were grotesque exaggerations of men (anthropomorphic polytheism). Those of Egypt, India, etc., afford illustrations of the worship of animals, as the bull, the ibis, the cat, the crocodile, etc. (therianthropic polytheism). A complete perversion of Nature as God created it. Man, created after the image of God, makes himself the model according to which to make for himself gods. Man, created to be lord of the animal creation (Ps. 8 : 7-9), degrades himself by worshipping this creation that God intended to serve him. These hallucinations of religious insanity are at the same time an outrage upon Nature itself. Heathenism is neither the original condition of the race, nor a higher stage in its development. "The history of religions, thoroughly studied as it is now-a-days, fully justifies Paul's view. It shows that the present heathen people of India and Africa, far from rising of themselves to a higher religious state, have only sunk, age after age, and become more and more degraded. It proves that at the root of all pagan religions and mythologies, there lies an original Monotheism" (GOD). The process seems to be as follows: First, faith in God, in the sense of a loving self-surrender and cheerful obedience to Him, and the apprehension of the Unseen, Eternal and Infinite, departs. Man has no longer the power to grasp the unity of God. The seeming contradictions in the conception of God become inexplicable, and he seeks relief either in dualism or in the hypothesis of a plurality of gods. Dualism or Polytheism entering, the thought of an Infinite and Supreme Being vanishes, since this can be held only by Monotheism. The gods then are brought within the sphere of the finite. If finite, then to them may be ascribed the weaknesses of men. Human and then bestial forms are made their symbols, or are regarded as temporarily inhabited by them. Finally, in the popular mind, they are regarded and worshipped as though real gods.

24-32. Wherefore God gave them up in the lusts of their hearts unto uncleanness, that their bodies should be dishonoured among themselves: for that they exchanged the truth of God for a lie, and worshipped and served the creature rather than the Creator, who is blessed for ever. Amen.

For this cause God gave them up unto vile passions: for their women changed the natural use into that which is against nature: and likewise also the men, leaving the natural use of the woman, burned in their lust one toward another, men with men working unseemliness, and receiving in themselves that recompense of their error which was due.

And even as they refused to have God in *their* knowledge, God gave them up unto a reprobate mind, to do those things which are not fitting; being filled with all unrighteousness, wickedness, covetousness, maliciousness; full of envy, murder, strife, deceit, malignity; whisperers, backbiters, hateful to God, insolent, haughty, boastful, inventors of evil things, disobedient to parents, without understanding, covenant-breakers, without natural affection, unmerciful: who, knowing the ordinance of God, that they which practise such things are worthy of death, not only do the same but also consent with them that practise them.

Ver. 24. **God gave them up**, etc. It is the divine order that sin shall be punished by sin. " Wherewithal a man sinneth, by the same also shall he be punished" (Wis. 11 : 16). While not the author of sin, He has established such a connection between sinful acts, that, when His Spirit is withdrawn, the natural consequence of one sin is another sin. " The curse of an evil deed is that it must continually bring forth evil." With the communion with God broken, and the conception of the spirituality of God weakened or effaced, man is urged chiefly by material wants and sensual instincts. The root of all true morality is religion. When this root is cut, a certain external morality may remain for a time, as a remnant of their former state, as flowers may seem fresh for some hours after they have been plucked; but such morality gradually vanishes, and, in this moral insanity, even unnatural crimes result. Dishonoring God, they dishonor themselves. As the knowledge of God recedes, the degradation deepens.

Ver. 25. **For that they exchanged,** or "seeing that they were such as exchanged." The verse is parenthetical, assigning the reason for the severe judgment just mentioned. **The truth of God** means the truth concerning God. **A lie.** Their false worship. **Worshipped and served.** The former refers to that which is inward; the latter to that which is outward. **The creature rather than the Creator.** They started with the intention or, at any rate, the profession of using the creature only as an image of the Creator; but the result is that the Creator is supplanted by the creature. **Blessed forever.** A doxology called forth by his indignation at the dishonor done God, as though he would do all in his power to make up for this offence committed by others (Comp. Rom. 11 : 36; Gal. 1 : 5.)

Ver. 26, 27. Where the whole life is a lie, and the creature takes God's place, everything else may be expected to be turned from its proper use. These verses contain a more specific statement of what is affirmed in a general way in ver. 24. The picture is a revolting one. Paul endeavors to suppress nothing. His object is to show the odiousness of sin, and the degradation into which a godless life descends. "In stigmatizing sins, we must often call a spade a spade. The unchaste usually demand from others an absurd modesty" (BENGEL). Every student of the Greek and Roman classics can find abundant evidence in these writers for the truth of these statements. The moral sense was so blunted that the unnatural relations were often openly acknowledged. The shamelessness of the Emperors Tiberius and Nero may be especially mentioned. Grotius, after citing numerous passages from the Greek and Latin writers, adds : " All things at Rome were full of such examples. The cultured world had become a second Sodom ; looking with indulgence upon the characteristic sin of Sodom." **Vile passions,** stronger than " lusts " of ver. 24, indicating that they had become the slaves of sensuality. **Their women.** The Greek uses the word " females," instead of " women ; " since the truly womanly character is gone, and " the simple physical allusion to sex comes exclusively to view " (PHIL.). For the same reason, ver. 27, in the Greek, has " males " instead of men. The vice of the women, as the more shameful perversion of nature, is stated first. **Recompense of their error.** The error was idolatry, consequent upon forgetfulness of God. The recompense was the degradation to which they were subjected, by these vices and the other sins which inevitably followed. " The noblest creature of God sinks to the very lowest, when it attempts to exalt itself above the Creator " (BESS.). " Is not **leaving the natural use** in various ways, in eating and drinking, clothing and dwelling, trade, etc., in all estates and spheres of life, a sign of the present time ? " (BESS.)

Ver. 28. In the original, there is a contrast between **refused to have** and **reprobate** inexpressible in a translation. It might be approximately rendered in both places by **rejected.** Rejecting God, God left them to the control of a mind without His wisdom and guidance. " As thou treatest God, God treateth thee." **In their knowledge.** The word is emphatic, meaning practical or experimental knowledge. **Not fitting,** i. e.

beneath the dignity of man, things which would be abhorrent to man's mind, if this had not been perverted.

Ver. 29-32 give a catalogue of sins defining "those things which are not fitting" of the preceding verse. Beyond a progress from more general to special sins, any classification cannot be made with certainty. Some are manifestly associated because of paranomasia. Classifications are attempted by BENGEL, LANGE, MEYER and VILMAR. One of the most recent is by LIDDON, viz. "1. Four general forms of evil. 2. Seven anti-social sins; five in feeling and two in language; both being especially hateful to God. 3. Three sins of self-assertion. 4. Six sins against natural principles on which society is based." "Paul evidently lets his pen run on, as if he thought that of all the bad terms that should present themselves, none would be out of place or exaggerated" (GOD.).

Ver. 29. **Unrighteousness** heading the list, embraces all that follow. **Wickedness** = good for nothing. **Covetousness** lust for money. **Maliciousness**—taking pleasure in doing wrong. **Envy, murder,** joined together in Greek because of their similar sound. **Strife** the outward manifestation of envy. **Deceit.** (Comp. Juvenal, Satire 2: "What am I to do at Rome? I cannot lie.") **Malignity.** "The disposition which judges everything on the worse side" (ARISTOTLE, Rhetoric, II : XIII.) It is prompted by a love of mischief.

Ver. 30. **Whisperers**—secret slanderers. **Backbiters**—calumniators of all kinds, with special reference, probably, to informers who ruined others by espionage and false reports. **Hateful to God.** Whether this or the marginal reading "haters of God" be correct, depends upon the accent of the Greek word. If the reading here followed be accepted, it must be explained as a parenthetical clause introduced to indicate that the sins just mentioned in an especial way brought down God's wrath. **Insolent**= (*hybristas*). The word means "one who, uplifted with pride, either heaps insulting language upon others, or does them some shameful act of wrong" (THAYER). Paul applies it to his conduct to the Church, prior to his conversion (1 Tim. 1 : 13). Aristotle defines *hybris* as "the doing and saying those things about which the person who is the subject of this treatment has feelings of delicacy," entirely for the sake of the mortification which the person who is wronged receives. **Inventors of evil things**, such as new refinements of vicious pleasures or new cruelties.

Ver. 31. **Without understanding**, i. e. with respect to spiritual and religious things, and, therefore, they are incapable of discriminating between right and wrong. The similarity of sound (paranomasia) in the Greek, determines the close connection of this word with that which follows. **Covenant-breakers.** Those upon whose most solemn pledges no reliance can be placed. **Without natural affection.** The bonds of relationship no longer establish a claim. Parents disregard children, and children parents. There is no family-feeling.

Unmerciful: Illustrated by gladiatorial shows, sanguinary combats of wild beasts, "innocent martyrs burning to death in their shirts of pitchy fire," and the numerous cruelties connected with Roman slavery.

Ver. 32. **Who,** i. e. their character is such that, although they know God's ordinance, etc. **Ordinance**=sentence. What intensifies the guilt is that these sins are committed in the very face of the clearest and deepest knowledge (the word is emphatic), that God's judgment is impending, and God is openly defied. **Consent.** The guilt of the person who approves the sin of another, is greater than that of the one who himself commits the sin; for the former cannot plead the heat of passion that moves the latter. The contrast between **practice** and **do** occurs also in ch. 2 : 3; 7 : 15; 13 : 4; John 3 : 20. The former refers more to a habit; the latter to a result. The former, to the direction of the activity towards a particular purpose; the latter to its accomplishment.

Ample illustrations of this degradation of Heathenism, with references to the classical and patristic writers where they are presented, may be found in such readily accessible books as DE PRESENSEE'S *The Ancient World and Christianity*, Book V., Ch. II.; STORR'S *Divine Origin of Christianity*, Lecture VIII.; FARRAR'S *Early Days of Christianity*, Ch. I.; and his *Witness of History to Christianity*, Ch. IV.; *Seekers after God*, Ch. III.; UHLHORN'S *Christian Charity in the Ancient Church*, Ch. I.: "A World without Love"; TRENCH'S *Hulsean Lectures*, etc. Of cotemporary descriptions, the most noted is that of Seneca, the tutor of Nero: "All things are full of iniquity and vice. More crime is committed than can be remedied by restraint. We struggle in a huge contest of criminality; daily the passion for sin is greater, the shame of committing it is less. . . . Wickedness is no longer committed in secret; it flaunts before our eyes, and has been sent forth so openly into public sight, and has prevailed so completely in the breast of all, that innocence is not rare, but non-existent" (*De Ira*, II. 8).

SECTION II.—THE LAW UNIVERSAL: SIN AND JUDGMENT INSEPARABLE (ch. 2 : 1-16).

The Apostle uses the black picture he has drawn of the fate of the heathen in their forgetfulness and independence of God, as a means to excite in others the consciousness of sin and of the need of grace. The method is similar to that pursued by Nathan in 2 Sam. 12 : 1-7, differing only in that there a parable, whereas here a real statement of facts, is given. While his intention is to make the application to the Jews, ver. 17, he leads to this by an argument of universal force. Not all Gentiles were guilty of the precise forms of sin detailed in the preceding chapter. Among them were some of rigid external morality, whose protests against current vices were heard. To them as well as to Jews belongs this appeal. Mere civil righteousness, without the grace of God, is of no avail. The germs of the sins just described are in the heart, and need only favorable circumstances to develop the entire career of crime. All alike are beneath God's judgment and God's wrath. The possession of the Law by the Jews affords no immunity from this judgment.

1-16. Wherefore thou art without excuse, O man, whosoever thou art that judgest : for wherein thou judgest another thou condemnest thyself; for thou that judgest dost practise the same things. And we know that the judgment of God is according to truth against them that practise such things. And reckonest thou this, O man, who judgest them that practise such things, and doest the same, that thou shalt escape the judgement of God? Or despisest thou the riches of his goodness and forbearance and longsuffering, not knowing that the goodness of God leadeth thee to repentance ? but after thy hardness and impenitent heart treasurest up for thyself wrath in the day of wrath and revelation of the righteous judgment of God; who will render to every man according to his works : to them that by patience in well-doing seek for glory and honour and incorruption, eternal life : but unto them them that are factious, and obey not the truth, but obey unrighteousness, *shall be* wrath and indignation, tribulation and anguish, upon every soul of man that worketh evil, of the Jew first, and also of the Greek ; but glory and honour and peace to every man that worketh good, to the Jew first and also to the Greek : for there is no respect of persons with God. For as many as have sinned without law shall also perish without law : and as many as have sinned under law shall be judged by law ; for not the hearers of a law are just before God, but the doers of a law shall be justified : for when Gentiles which have no law do by nature the things of the law, these, having no law, are a law unto themselves; in that they shew the work of the law written in their hearts, their conscience bearing witness therewith, and their thoughts one with another accusing or else excusing *them ;* in the day when God shall judge the secrets of men, according to my gospel, by Jesus Christ.

Ver. 1. **Wherefore** refers to what has just been said. The person addressed also knows what is stated in ver. 32. **Without excuse,** because of sin against light and knowledge. **O man.** Slightly reproachful. (Comp. Luke 12 : 14; ch. 9 : 20.) The word *anthrope* refers to any member of the human race, whether man or woman, Jew or Greek. It prepares the way for a direct appeal to the Jew, ver. 17, under a general charge of universal application. **Judgest . . . judgest.** A. V. brings out more clearly the contrast in the original. The second "judge" is a stronger term than the first. (Comp. 1 Cor. 11 : 32.) **The same things.** Not necessarily in all their details, but those of essentially the same moral character. (Comp. John 8 : 7.)

Ver. 2. **According to truth,** the standard of the divine judgment. It deals with naked facts, and is, therefore, absolutely impartial.

Ver. 3. " Do you expect that in your case a special exception is possible?" Some Jews seemed to think so (Matt. 3 : 8, 9; Luke 3 : 8). But the question is not restricted to Jews. " Do you think, because of your better moral knowledge, or external morality covering a heart longing to commit similar crimes, or your connection with a godly ancestry or with the chosen people, that you will be exempt from judgment? If so, you presume on God's goodness. Can this be so ? "

Ver. 4. **Or despisest thou?** To use the goodness of God as a palliative to soothe conscience when it reminds of sin, is to abuse and trifle with God's unspeakable kindness and love. Such conduct is no better than the weak indulgence with which men often pass by crimes that they ought to punish. **The riches.** A favorite word of Paul, to express the abundance and value of God's blessings (ch. 9 : 23 ; 11 : 33), and especially in Ephesians, "riches of grace" (Eph. 1 : 2 ; 2 : 7); "riches of glory" (Eph. 3 : 16). **Goodness** in the sense of kindness, mildness, gentleness; see the corresponding adjective in Matt. 11 : 30. See TRENCH, *Synonyms*, Part II., p. 58 sqq. **Forbearance**=the holding back of wrath and punishment. In classical Greek, the word means "a truce." See TRENCH, ib., p. 15 sq. It is of a more temporary character than **long-suffering,** which is "goodness, face to face with moral evil for long periods of time" (LIDDON). By the presumption referred to in the preceding verse, man intentionally interrupts the execution of the purposes of God's goodness. **Leadeth thee.** God leads or draws. Nevertheless man resists and declines to follow. God forces none. Grace is always resistible. God allows man to thwart His plans of love. Even some ultimately condemned are "being led" towards repentance (Matt. 23 : 37). **Repentance.** (See comments on Matt. 3 : 2.) Punishment is deferred not to render you careless concerning your sins, but to lead you to abhor them.

Ver. 5. **After:** "In virtue of," " because of." **Hardness,** insensibility to all God's favors. **Impenitent heart,** i. e. one which, notwithstanding God's leading and drawing, has not come to repentance. **Treasurest for thyself wrath.** Man's resistance of divine grace does not place him where he would have been, if grace had never come to him. Every privilege bestowed brings a corresponding responsibility. The rejection of the riches of goodness, etc., has as its consequence " a treasure of wrath."

The resistance of God's grace from day to day gradually accumulates a vast store of wrath for the time of reckoning (Deut. 32 : 34 sq.). **In the day of wrath :** A condensed construction for "which is to be paid in the day of wrath." The *Dies iræ* of Thomas Celano, "That day of wrath, that dreadful day," was suggested by this verse. The repetition, "wrath," "wrath," adds to the earnestness and terror of the warning. "Why have many no sense of wrath? Because the day of wrath has not yet come" (BENGEL). **Revelation,** viz. "day of the revelation." The judgment of God is passed upon them already. Only as yet it is concealed; but a day is coming when it will be unveiled. All shall see and hear and know it. **Just judgment** points back to the thought of ver. 2. If the judgment be just, there will be impartiality. All must be treated alike.

Ver. 6. **According to his works.** At the very head of the Epistle, whose especial aim it is to show that salvation is all of grace, Paul gives this testimony concerning works. Sinful deeds merit punishment; good works merit no reward. "They justify not a man; but show that a man is justified already before God" (LUTHER). Hence men will be recompensed "according to their works, not according to the merits of their works, nor on account of their works" (CALOV.). "In the Last Judgment, good works are to be produced as a testimony of faith, according to which testimony, the Son of God will pronounce His sentence" (HUNNIUS). In this place, it may be noted that the Apostle is not treating of justification, but of the inevitable consequences of sin; nevertheless, the incidental allusion to a double reward is in no way inconsistent with the doctrine fully explained afterwards. A reward of merit is one thing; a reward of grace is quite another. (See APOLOGY, 153 sq.)

Any attempt to use this verse in support of any claim for human merits that will be recognized and rewarded on the Day of Judgment, loses sight of the entire argument which is here being unfolded. The principle of reward is laid down, together with the proof that in no one is it fulfilled; hence the universality of condemnation which has called forth the universality of grace as embodied and proclaimed in a universal Gospel.

Ver. 7. **Patience in well-doing.** Lit. "Patience of a good work," conceiving of all the good works of a godly life collectively as one good work. Patience or persistence in this, defying opposition, deterred by no threats or dangers, allured from its path by no temptations, joyfully suffering all losses to attain its end, is the work of one who is on the way to life eternal. Such a soul is sustained by high ideals. The only real **glory and honor** are joined with **incorruption** (1 Cor. 15 : 42 ; 1 Pet. 1 : 4); hence these ideas are heavenly, and not earthly. "In discoursing of things to come, being unable to describe them, he calls them 'glory and immortality'" (CHRYSOSTOM), words often combined to indicate the heavenly sphere (1 Pet. 1 : 7 ; 2 Pet. 1 : 17 ; Heb. 2 : 7).

Ver. 8. **Factious.** In other places in the N. T., the word refers to intriguing partisanship (2 Cor. 12 : 20; Gal. 5 : 20; Phil. 1 : 16; 2 : 3; James 3 : 14, 16). As it indicates here the opposite of "patience in well-doing," the main thought must be "self-seeking," in contrast with self-denial.

"The incessant plotting for material earthly advantage or superiority, as distinct from the repose of a soul satisfied with and at peace with God, is here meant. The Jewish spirit of faction was constantly opposing its

self-seeking to the Gospel, Acts 13 : 45; 18 : 12; Gal. 4 : 17; 6 : 12; 1 Thess. 2 : 14" (LIDDON).
Obey not the truth. The consequence and manifestation of their factiousness. The truth here means revealed truth. **Obey unrighteousness.** All forms of sin (1 John 5 : 17). The word is used here in a general sense, as in Luke 13 : 27, for offences against both tables of the Decalogue and not specialized, as in ch. 1 : 18 for those against the Second Table. **Wrath and indignation.** The stronger word comes last. Wrath notes the temper or disposition as it gradually grows under the provocations given; indignation, the outburst which at last follows when the measure of iniquity is full. The change in construction is significant. In ver. 7 "eternal life" is the object of God's gift; but here "wrath and indignation," being nominatives, are not brought by God, but come as the direct result of man's own course of conduct.

Ver. 9. **Tribulation and anguish.** The former, the pressure of a crushing burden; the latter, the straitness and helplessness of confinement. "When, according to the ancient law of England, those who wilfully refused to plead had heavy weights placed upon their breasts, and so were pressed and crushed to death, this was literally *thlipsis* (tribulation). When Bajazet, having been vanquished by Tamerlane, was carried about in an iron cage, this was *stenochoria*" (TRENCH, II. 22). First, the weight of the wrath of God; then "the wringing of the heart under the punishment it produces" (GOD.). **Upon every soul of man.** The soul is put for the person. The Apostle thus lays emphasis upon the individualizing of the punishment, since "the soul forms the central point of the life of each individual" (WEISS, Bib. Theol. I. 123). **Worketh evil.** A more intensive word is here used than in "worketh good" of ver. 9. The possibilities of "working out" evil are greater than those of working good. **To the Jew first.** As the bestowal of grace (ch. 1 : 16), so also the infliction of wrath. The Jew, in both cases, is first. Exalted privileges bring corresponding responsibilities, and, if despised, entail greater penalties (Matth. 11 : 22; Luke 12 : 48).

Ver. 10. **Glory and honor.** They find that for which they have sought (ver. 7). **Peace** is added as the blessing which man enjoys in receiving glory and honor. **Worketh good.** The difference between this and the word used in preceding verse is almost that which may be found between "working out" and "working at." **To the Jew first,** etc. A universal law is here laid down. "By these words, Paul includes all Jews and Gentiles, even those who had died before the coming of Christ" (BESSER). The one obeyed the truth given in revelation and lived in hope of the coming Christ. The other followed the traces of truth declared by his conscience, and, like Ruth and Naaman and the wise men of the East, were led to Christ. We cannot demand of the heathen any higher degree of knowledge as to what was involved in the promise concerning the coming Christ, than was sufficient for the salvation of the patriarchs, whose faith of what God meant by His promises was most dim and obscure. "The Last Day will make it manifest that in ways, concealed to our eyes, God has sent a ray of Gospel light into the dark soul of every heathen, and that those who have not excluded this ray he has placed under grace enabling them to do good, and to forsake evil. We do no violence to the text when, among believers in Christ, we seek first of all for Jews, but also for Gentiles, who on the Day of Judgment will appear as those who have done good. The close of this chapter (ver. 29) shows clearly that by the words "who worketh good" something is expressed that is not a matter of thought and without reality, but that has been brought to realization by God's spirit and grace " (BESSER). (See notes on ch. 10: 14-19.)

Ver. 11. **No respect of persons.** This uniformity of treatment is determined by the absolute justice of God. A just judge looks only at the case. The ancients symbolically expressed this principle by the bandage over the eyes of the Statue of Justice. Whatever the nationality, birth, station, attainments, wealth of those to be judged, all must be treated precisely alike. In the determination of the verdict, the personal factor in the criminal must be entirely excluded. To have respect to persons is frequently condemned in Holy Scripture (Deut. 1 : 17 ; 2 Chr. 19 : 7 ; Prov. 24 : 23 ; James 2 : 1). This was the lesson Peter learned (Acts 10 : 34,35). MELANCHTHON'S application to the universality and particularity of grace is noteworthy: " Respect of persons is to give equal things to unequals or unequal things to equals. Justice is equality, proportioned according to a measure or standard. A judge is just when he observes the standard equally, punishes the guilty and defends the innocent. Accordingly when it is said that there is no respect of persons with God, we ascribe to God the praise of righteousness and equality. God is universally angry with sin in man, and universally receives all fleeing to the Mediator. This standard he has established in his most wise and most just counsel, and wants it to be immovable. Paul, accordingly, says : ' God will have all men to be saved,' i. e. According to the standard that He has fixed, He is equal to all. It is His will that all be saved, but many, by their own fault, do not receive the offered benefit. This is a great and necessary consolation, because in the minds of all men there is great alarm on account of the imagination that there is inequality in

God. Men often exclaim: 'Even though God receives others; nevertheless you are not in that number. Could not so powerful a Lord reject whom He pleased?'" (*Enarratio*, A. D. 1556).

Ver. 12. **Law** refers here to any written revelation of God's will. The principle is laid down that it is not the possession of a written revelation that saves, or the lack of one that condemns. The application of this principle leads of course to the thought of the Mosaic law, as the written revelation which Israel had and in which it boasted. For the different uses of the word "law," see GIFFORD (Speaker's Commentary, Romans, Introduction, pp. 41–48). **Perish without law**, being judged, as ver. 15 shows, by the standard of the unwritten law. They perish as the natural result of their continuance in sin. Their destruction does not come by an act of God interrupting the regular order, as is salvation (1 : 16). Their eternal death is the fruit of their sinful estate. **Under law.** Literally "in," i. e. within the sphere in which the law's demands are clearly revealed. **Judged** means more than "perish." Besides the consequences of their other sins, the still greater guilt has been incurred of resisting the means provided for leading them to repentance.

Ver. 13 shows why the mere possession of a written revelation cannot save. **Not the hearers of a law**, i. e. the Jews who heard the law read every Sabbath in their synagogues (John 12 : 34; Acts 13 : 15; 15 : 21; 2 Cor. 3 : 14). **Shall be justified**, i. e. accounted and pronounced righteous. God's rule is here given, without reference to the question whether there be any in whom it is fulfilled. Chapter 3 : 20 declares that in no case is this realized. After stating the standard of the law, he proceeds to show that it is not attained, in order to enforce his theme of the universal need of grace.

Ver. 14. **For when Gentiles.** The absence of the article shows that like the opposite instances of crime among the heathen recorded in ch. 1, the case is not universal. Occasional instances among the Gentiles here establish a principle. The argument is that, if mere hearing of a law were to justify, even then the Jews would not claim it as their exclusive prerogative. For while the Gentiles are without a written revelation, the lives of *some among them* clearly show the presence of an inner law that guides them. " For example, Neoptolemus in Philoctetes, when he refuses to save Greece at the expense of a lie; or Antigone, when she does not hesitate to violate the temporary law of the city, to fulfil the eternal law of fraternal love: or Socrates, when he rejects the opportunity of saving his life by escaping from prison, in order to remain subject to magistrates " (GOD.). It is not meant that they do all that the law requires, but that the external conduct of these rare examples in certain cases is inexplicable, except upon the theory of an inner law. "'Are you aware,' said Socrates, 'that there are inner laws?' 'You mean those,' said Hippias, ' that are in force about the same matters everywhere.' 'Can you affirm, then, that men made such laws.' 'I believe that it was the Gods who made these laws for men.'" (XENOPHON, Memorabilia, IV. 4.) **A law unto themselves,** i. e. their moral nature supplies the place of the revealed law. Paul uses here an expression of Aristotle: "Against such there is no law" (comp. Gal. 5 : 23); "for they themselves are a law" (Politics, III. XIII. 14). "Being a law to himself" (Nic. Ethics, IV. 14). This verse which was used by Pelagius against Augustine does not declare that any heathen was ever justified by his conformity to the law. The occasional and fragmentary obedience only indicated that the law was present, but not that it in any way approached the standard of fulfilment which was demanded.

Ver. 15. **The work of the law,** viz. that which the law produces among Jews, the knowledge of right and wrong. **Written in their hearts.** The writing of the Mosaic law on two tables furnishes the illustration concerning this, properly speaking, unwritten law. **Their conscience bearing witness therewith**=Their consciousness of the moral character of their acts. "Conscience gives witness to the inner law in man, impels and directs man to act according to that law (the so-called precedent conscience), judges his doings according to this law, and reflects his actions and his circumstances in the light of this law (the subsequent conscience)" (LIDDON). **Their thoughts one with another.** When conscience is roused to activity, all the processes of a court of justice occur within man's own mind. Man discusses within himself his guilt or innocence. His consciousness of his want of conformity with the law presses upon him, and he seeks for excuses and sits in judgment upon their validity. This occurs too among the heathen even in the midst of the depravity which is described in such dark colors in ch. 1. **Accusing** coming first shows that this is the principal, and **excusing** the subordinate office of conscience among the heathen. The accusations preponderate.

Ver. 16. **In the day,** etc. Some connect this directly with ver. 12; others, with ver. 13, regarding the intervening verses parenthetical. BENGEL connects it with " show " in ver. 15, which would change the tense of the verb here. It is better to regard it as summing up this part of the argument, and qualifying the entire preceding paragraph from ver. 6, as though Paul had written : " All of which shall be made manifest in the day," etc. **The**

day is the Judgment Day (1 Cor. 1 : 8; 5 : 5; 2 Cor. 1 : 14; especially Acts 17 : 31). **According to my Gospel.** The Gospel here stands for the entire revelation of God in Christ, as Paul preached it (Gal. 1 : 16; Eph. 3 : 9). The universality of grace and universality of judgment belonged together. Grace presupposes judgment. The distinctive feature of the declaration of coming judgment by the Gospel is the fact that Jesus Christ is the Judge (John 5 : 22; Acts 10 : 42; 17 : 31; 1 Cor. 4 : 5). Coming judgment was acknowledged in some way by all men. It was taught by the inner law. But judgment by Christ is the doctrine of the Gospel.

SECTION III.—THE STATE OF THE JEWS (2 : 17—3 : 8).

The preceding section has been a skilful transition, preparing the way for proving that the Jews also are under condemnation. The first part of this section simply states more clearly and pointedly what has thus been already proved.

1. *Examination of the Boast which the Jews make concerning their Possession of the Law* (17-24).

<small>17-24. But if thou bearest the name of a Jew, and restest upon the law, and gloriest in God, and knowest his will, and approvest the things that are excellent, being instructed out of the law, and are confident that thou thyself art a guide of the blind, a light of them that are in darkness, a corrector of the foolish, a teacher of babes, having in the law the form of knowledge and of the truth ; thou therefore that teachest another, teachest thou not thyself ? thou that preachest a man should not steal, dost thou steal ? thou that sayest a man should not commit adultery, dost thou commit adultery? thou that abhorrest idols, dost thou rob temples? thou who gloriest in the law through thy transgression of the law dishonourest thou God? For the name of God is blasphemed among the Gentiles because of you, even as it is written.</small>

Ver. 17. **But if.** The reading of the best Mss. The

second member (apodosis) of this interrogatory conditional sentence, begins in ver. 21: "If thou bearest the name, etc., how is it that thou that teachest another, teachest not thyself?" Before the sentence can be completed, the matters in which the Jew prided himself are first stated in general (ver. 17, 18), and then those in which he contrasted himself with, and exalted himself over others (ver. 19, 20). **The name of a Jew.** Hebrew indicates the language, Jew the nationality, and Israelite the theocratic privileges of the people. The national feeling has absorbed that of religion, and the two are identified in the mind of the Jews, whom Paul addressed. Pride in the national name is indicated in ver. 28; 9:9; Gal. 2:15; Rev. 2:9; 3:9. The real honor of the Jewish nation was that it was the bearer of the promise concerning Christ, and from it came our Lord's humanity (Heb. 7:14). "Without the kernel, Christ, the name Jew is an empty nut." **And restest upon the law.** A still greater gift than the name Jew. But even in his high regard for the Mosaic law, he has begun to forget that his chief prerogative was the covenant made with Abraham, and that the law was given solely through that covenant. **Boastest in God,** i. e. of the peculiar relations in which the Jew stood to God, as exclusively the covenant God of Israel. The Gentiles were "without God" (Eph. 2:12).

Ver. 18. **Knowest his will.** The emphasis is on the knowing. Not obedience, but knowledge is the great boast of the Jew. **Approvest the things that are excellent.** Another translation is: "Dost distinguish the things that differ." The Jew prided himself on recognizing by very intuition what was good. "He, at any rate, knew a good thing whenever he saw it." This skill he ascribed to his thorough instruction in the law, the Greek for **instructed** being the word from which catechism is derived.

Vers. 19, 20. Now come the points in which the Jew contrasts himself with and exalts himself above others. In his opinion, the Gentiles are "blind," "in darkness," "foolish," "babes," while he is "a guide," "a light," "a corrector," "a teacher." All this he claims for himself because he has in the law not only the truth itself, "but besides the exact formula, by means of which he can convey this truth to others" (GOD.). GIFFORD gives an excellent illustration from the sermons of the Rabbi Artemon (1873): "If the earth is to be full of the knowledge of the Lord as the waters cover the sea, it must be through our agency. We must infuse that knowledge; we possess the best materials for instruction, and we must make it a duty and a glory to enlighten the world."

Ver. 21, 22. Then comes the arraignment. "The Apostle turns to strike" (JOWETT). Conceding the high estimate which the Jew puts upon the law, he proceeds to test the Jews according to this standard. The first question contains the general charge of universal unfaithfulness. Then follow, as illustrations, specific examples of the manner in which some adherents of Rabbinism did not teach themselves. It must not be imagined that he charges all with being guilty of each specific sin. Two of them are sins against the Second Table. In mentioning them, Paul has clearly Ps. 50 : 16-18 in mind. From them, he proceeds to the First Table. **Rob temples.** The primary reference is to the violation of Deut. 7 : 25, 26 : "Dost thou who art so rigid in thy rejection of idolatry, as to treat all idols as an abomination, bringing defilement on them who touch them (comp. 1 Macc. 1 : 54), use them for purposes of gain, when heathen temples are open to thee, or thou art a receiver of what is taken therefrom?" Well-known cases were probably in mind. Acts 19 : 37 implies that such offences were not rare. The fundamental and universally applicable charge is that of a purely mercenary service of God, which was ready to bend every rule of life, even those most sacred, to motives of purely temporal gain, Such Jews had no hesitancy, like some Christians, it is said, of modern times, to speculate in idols. All scruples, which the law of which they boasted suggested, were readily disposed of.

Ver. 23 sums up the entire paragraph. **Who gloriest in the law** sums up verses 17-20. **Dost thou dishonor** sums up verses 21-22.

Ver. 24. Two O. T. passages in the Apostle's mind in this very free citation, which is rather an adaptation than a formal quotation, viz.: the LXX. of Is. 52 : 5 and Ezek. 36 : 21-23. The application, however, differs from that originally made where the oppression of the Israelites causes them to fall into disesteem, and, then, contempt passes over from them to the God whom they worship. The principle there, as here, is that whatever dishonor befalls Israel, affects the estimate in which the God of Israel is held by the Gentiles.

2. Examination of the Jewish Boast concerning Circumcision (ver. 25-29).

25-29. For circumcision indeed profiteth, if thou be a doer of the law: but if thou be a transgressor of the law, thy circumcision is become uncircumcision. If therefore the uncircumcision keep the ordinances of the law, shall not his uncircumcision be reckoned for circumcision? and shall not the uncircumcision which is by nature, if it fulfil the law, judge thee, who with the letter and circumcision art a transgressor of the law? For he is not a Jew, which is one outwardly, neither is that circumcision, which is outward in the flesh: but he is Jew, which is one inwardly; and circumcision is that of the heart, in the spirit, not in the letter; whose praise is not of men, but of God.

Ver. 25 anticipates the objection that this argument would overthrow the value of circumcision. The answer is that circumcision was intended as an aid in keeping the law and to those keeping the law. It was a testimony of God's grace to the individual Israelite, introducing him into the paths of obedience and sustaining him therein. In breaking the law, the covenant thus established was broken, and its promises frustrated by those not fulfilling its conditions. "The general principle must be applied to all external forms of worship, that they profit not for the work done (*ex opere operato*), nor merit the forgiveness of sins, but that they please in those who are righteous. This is applicable not only to the Levitical services, but also to external works and ceremonies in the Church" (MELANCHTHON). (Comp. 1 Cor. 7 : 19.) Illustrations of this extravagant estimate of circumcision are not rare. Thus PHILIPPI and MEYER quote Rabbi Berechias: "Lest heretics and apostates and godless Israelites may say: Since we are circumcised we will not descend to hell, what does God do? He sends an angel, and removes their circumcision, so that they descend to hell." Another statement is: "Circumcision is equivalent to all the commandments that are in the law." **Circumcision profiteth,** viz. as a seal of the righteousness by faith (Rom. 4 : 11), and a pledge of God's promise concerning a future Messiah. **If thou be a doer of the law.** Circumcision presupposes a fulfilment of the law. The circumcised man must fulfil the law, or be justified by a satisfaction for his sin. Otherwise, the rite is of no value.

Ver. 26 recurs to the thought of ver. 14. **The uncircumcision** -uncircumcised persons. In so far as Gentiles keep the law, their obedience is just as pleasing to God as though they were circumcised. The time has not yet come in this Epistle to deduce what is undoubtedly a perfectly legitimate inference, that if Gentiles **keep the ordinances of the law,** this proves that the righteousness of Christ has been made theirs and justifies as fully as though they were circumcised. From the legal standpoint, everything is determined by man's obedience or disobedience; from the evangelical standpoint, everything is determined by the obedience of Christ. Circumcision thus sinks into a matter of minor importance.

Ver. 27. The **uncircumcision which is by nature,** viz. those born Gentiles and who do not become Jews. The verse shows that circumcision, instead of benefitting, only increases the guilt of the disobedient. To sin notwithstanding the possession and knowledge of the written word (**letter**), and the seal, in circumcision, of God's promise and loving aid, only adds to the transgression and condemnation. There are heathen whose exemplary lives condemn not only Jews, but also Christians. But in saying that, without circumcision, some heathen are better than many Jews who are circumcised, the Apostle does not teach that any Gentiles without Christ are justified before God. The main argument of the Epistle must be kept in view, which such an inference would directly contradict. **If it fulfil the law** refers, then, both to the relative obedience of the heathen in some external matters, and to the fruits of the new life in converted and regenerated heathen. Neither justify; but both judge the circumcised transgressor of the law.

In verses 28, 29, he explains why this is so. **One outwardly,** i. e. one merely by circumcision, profession, observance of external religious duties, etc. **Outward in the flesh,** a still more specific reference to birth and circumcision. **One inwardly,** i. e. it is the secret, inner life that makes the true Jew. The relation to God is determined, not by what is external, but by what is internal and spiritual. The service of God is a spiritual service (John 4 : 23, 24). **Circumcision of the heart** was an expression familiar to readers of the O. T. (Lev. 26 : 41; Deut. 10 : 16; Jer. 4 : 14; Ezek. 44 : 9). It means the purifying of the inner life from everything immoral and unclean. **In the spirit.** Not man's spirit, but "by the Holy Spirit" (OSIANDER, GROTIUS, PHILIPPI, BESSER, MEYER, WEISS, GODET, HODGE, LIDDON, LUTHARDT). "Spiritual circumcision is nothing but faith which the Holy Ghost works in hearts" (LUTHER). This interpretation is based upon the contrast here made between spirit and letter, as in ch. 7 : 6; 2 Cor. 3 : 6. "The notion that the possession of the Holy Spirit could not be ascribed to believers of the O. T. is refuted at once by Ps. 51 : 12. Whoever, with Luther, in most intimate experience, simply sees in the Psalms the liturgy of all saints, and has drunk the richest of spiritual comfort in time of trial, will be unable again to sympathize with views of the O. T. and its worthies so full of dishonor" (PHILIPPI). Nevertheless it is only in the N. T. where this is completely fulfilled. **Whose praise.** The praise for all whereof the Apostle has just spoken. **Of God.** Therefore, real, not seeming; permanent, not temporary; estimated not by human, but by divine standards (Matt. 6 : 6. Comp. 1 Cor. 4 : 5).

We do not understand this passage to mean that the godly Gentile, who has been regenerated of the Holy Spirit, is really a spiritual Jew; but that the true Jew is one who uses his external advantages and continues to avail himself of the peculiarities and prerogatives of his race, in entire subordination to his inner and higher spiritual life. He aims solely that God's purposes in giving him a place among Jews may be attained. He therefore is the true Jew, while that member of his race, who is scrupulous in his observance of all Judaic rites, but knows nothing more or that is deeper or beyond, has ceased to be a Jew Of course, the premises are here stated, which lead soon to the conclusion that national distinctions have been abolished. This, however, belongs to a later stage of the argument, and would not harmonize with the statement of the prerogatives of Israel that still remain to be given in the next chapter.

3. *Objections Answered* (ch. 3 : 1-8).

1-8. What advantage then hath the Jew? or what is the profit of circumcision? much every way: first of all, that they were intrusted with the oracles of God. For what if some were without faith? shall their want of faith make of none effect the faithfulness of God? God forbid: yea let God be found true, but every man a liar; as it is written,
  That thou mightest be justified in thy words,
  And mightest prevail when thou comest into judgment.
But if our unrighteousness commendeth the righteousness of God, what shall we say? Is God unrighteous who visiteth with wrath? (I speak after the manner of men.) God forbid: for then how shall God judge the world? But if the truth of God through my lie aboundeth unto his glory, why am I also still judged as a sinner? and why not (as we be slanderously reported, and as some affirm that we say), Let us do evil, that good may come? whose condemnation is just.

(*a.*) *The blessings of the covenant being spiritual, what advantage then was there in external connection with Israel?*

Ver. 1. **What advantage then?** Throughout this Epistle, Paul often argues with an imaginary opponent. He starts difficulties which he then immediately answers. The difficulties are doubtless those which had been felt by him, as he passed through the struggles whereby, as a zealous advocate of Rabbinism, he was led to Christianity. We enter into his own mind; and hear the questions of Paul the Jew, and the answers of Paul the Christian. Nor must we forget that what was argued by him within, was also argued by him without. His own former difficulties were re-echoed, wherever he found intelligent Jewish opponents. The subject is a live one, on which he is always thinking, and conversing with himself. **Then** points back to the two preceding verses. The objection raised is: "If the blessings of the covenant be wholly internal, since no one is a true Jew, unless he be such internally, there are no advantages whatever belonging to external connection with the Jewish people. God has not in any way caused them to differ from the Gentiles." **What is the profit of circumcision?** This question only intensifies the former. It was not birth, but covenant relations to God conferred in circumcision that gave the Jew his prerogatives. Is all this nothing? It is as though "in our day a nominal Christian, when put face to face with God's sentence were to ask what advantage accrues to him from his Creed and Baptism, if they are not to save him from condemnation" (GOD.).

Ver. 2. **Much every way.** An answer to both questions. **First of all.** Of the numerous advantages that might be mentioned, it is sufficient for him to mention but one. **Oracles of God.** There is a possible reminiscence here of Stephen's discourse (Acts 7 : 38. Comp. Heb. 5 : 12; 1 Pet. 4 : 11). The "oracles" were the utterances or declaration of the will of God. The highest prerogative of Israel, says Paul, was in its being made the organ for the communication of revelation, and thus for the preparation of salvation for the whole world. As this revelation has its centre in redemption, the "oracles" refer particularly to the promises concerning Christ.

This becomes manifest from ver. 3, where the disposition of faith or lack of faith towards these oracles shows that their chief contents were what was to be believed. (Comp. 9 : 4.) These promises were contained not only in the prophets (Acts 3 : 24), but also in the Pentateuch. Nevertheless the law is not excluded. The time has not come in the argument for the Apostle to enter into an enumeration of the contents of revelation. **They were instrusted with,** for themselves and for the world. A great privilege, but imposing a corresponding responsibility. This prerogative of Israel is celebrated in Ps. 147 : 19, 20.

(*b.*) *But, says the objector, your argument denies the value of a supernatural revelation, unless it be received by faith. As, however, the great body of Jews believed not, the possession of these oracles gave the Jews no advantage* (ver. 3, 4).

Ver. 3. **Shall their want of faith?** He answers the objection by a question. The thought is that God has His purposes to fulfil through Israel, that can be thwarted through no interference of man. If some of the nation, even the majority, withstand God's will, His purposes shall surely reach their end through those still remaining faithful. Men may separate and exclude themselves from the saving order; but they cannot hinder its progress. In all ages, an unbroken line of witnesses is maintained, through whom God's promises are ripening for fruition. This thought is expounded in chapters 9, 11. " The divine promises confer everlasting salvation upon Jews who believe, and to them circumcision is a sacrament confirming the promises. Do you think that God will withdraw His promise, and not stand by His covenant with Israelites, because, by unbelief, some repel these heavenly blessings?" (L. OSIANDER).

Ver. 4. **God forbid.** Lit. "Be it not so." An expression, like a corresponding one in Hebrew (Gen. 44 : 17 ; Josh. 22 : 29 ; 1 Sam. 20 : 2), used to express the abhorrence with which the mere suggestion of God's unfaithfulness is repelled. Often used in this Epistle. **Let God be true.** The truest of men will be found false, before the least untruth can be ascribed to God. "The truth of God is first completely realized in the fulfilment of His promises" (WEISS). His truth is the only truth. All truth in man comes from God. **Every man a liar.** Man becomes a liar not only by not fulfilling his promises, but also by not doing his duty, i. e. neglecting his obligations and thus denying God. Man is false to himself in his assumed independence of God. The expression occurs in the LXX. of Ps. 116 : 11. Wherever, then, a covenant is broken, it is man, and not God who breaks it. An appeal is made to Ps. 51 : 4, to show that wherever there may be a question concerning the faithfulness of God, God will always be shown in the end to be victor. **Thou mightest be justified,** viz. proved to be righteous. "There are two classes of men. One confesses with David that **God is true,** just and holy: the other says : 'Thy word is not true. We are not blind,'" etc. (LUTHER, on Ps. 51 : 4). **In thy words ;** i. e. "All thy words proved to be true." **Prevail when thou comest unto judgment ;** i. e. Gain the suit whenever thou art made a defendant in man's court ; vindicated in every contest in which men complain of injustice. The righteousness of God is displayed the more vividly by its contrast with man's unrighteousness.

(*c.*) *God's righteousness being brought into clearer light by man's sin, God, therefore, says the objector, cannot punish what contributes only to His glory.*

Ver. 5. The unrighteous Jew is represented as pleading, that, whatever may be his sins, God loses nothing thereby, since the Apostle himself has just suggested in ver. 4 that every sin is overruled to God's glory. In repeating the question. **Is God then unrighteous,** he seems almost ashamed to mention it, apologizing for it in the words : **I speak after the manner of men.** Thus he indicates that it is frivolous, and scarcely worthy of notice. The application of the word *unrighteous* to God is revolting to the Christian heart, nevertheless as it is a question that he knows is and will be occasionally raised, an answer must be given.

Ver. 6. **God forbid.** See on ver. 4. **How shall God judge the world?** God's judgment of the world is assumed as needing no proof. But as there is to be such a judgment, there is no place for the argument suggested in the preceding verse. If God cannot punish that which He uses to advance His glory, then " He must entirely abdicate His office as Judge of all the earth " (MOULE); since every sin, those of Gentiles as well as those of Jews, He uses to advance His glory. It is a proof of the glory of God's wisdom and power, that, without diminishing the guilt of the offender, and notwithstanding the offender's most strenuous efforts to the contrary, God uses man s acts to promote ends far different from what man intended. The sinner deserves no thanks for the good that, contrary to his intention, comes out of his sin.

Ver. 7-8. The Apostle, with great logical skill, carries this argument of disobedient Israelites to its inevitable conclusion. " Why, if this be true," he says, " if it be true, that God will reward with His favor sins that He has turned to His glory, then it becomes our duty to sin all we can ! The more, the better ! " This just inference carries with it the refutation of the premises on which it is based. All responsibility is at an end. Its absurdity is so self-evident, that he only states it, leaving the consciences of the readers to give the answer. He adds only to the exposure of this thoroughly immoral theory the expression of his intensest indignation : **Whose condemnation is just.** Even at that early period, the preaching of the doctrine of the free grace of God in Christ was maligned, as a preaching of immorality. The very same false principle, which these teachers of the law laid to the charge of Christianity, St. Paul here shows pervaded their conduct and even their argument against Christianity. The condemnation is not a mere word of Paul, but of the Holy Ghost speaking through Paul. " Notwithstanding its temporary application to the Jewish people, this passage has a real permanent value. It has always been sought to justify the greatest crimes in history by representing the advantages in which they have resulted to the cause of humanity. There is not a Robespierre who has not been transformed into a saint in the name of utilitarianism. But to make such a canonization valid, one would require to begin by proving that the useful result sprang from the evil committed as its principle. Such is the teaching of Pantheism. Living Theism, on the contrary, teaches that this transformation of the bad deed into a means of progress is the miracle of God's wisdom and power, continually laying hold of human sin, to derive from it a result contrary to its nature " (GOD.).

SECTION IV.—SIN AND RUIN UNIVERSAL (3 : 9–20).

The charge is summed up, as applicable to Jew and Greek alike, and is supported by the Old Testament Scriptures.

9–19. What then? are we in worse case than they? No, in no wise: for we before laid to the charge both of Jews and Greeks, that they are all under sin; as it is written,
> There is none righteous, no, not one;
> There is none that understandeth,
> There is none that seeketh after God;
> They have all turned aside, they are together become unprofitable;
> There is none that doeth good, no, not so much as one:
> Their throat is an open sepulchre;
> With their tongues they have used deceit:
> The poison of asps is under their lips:
> Whose mouth is full of cursing and bitterness:
> Their feet are swift to shed blood;
> Destruction and misery are in their ways;
> And the way of peace have they not known:
> There is no fear of God before their eyes.

Now we know that what things soever the law saith, it speaketh to them that are under the law; that every mouth may be stopped, and all the world may be brought under the judgement of God:

Ver. 9. **Are we in worse case?** The word used in the Greek here occasions much difficulty, although the context, and especially the answer to the question, leave little doubt as to the meaning. A. V. gives: "Are we better than they?" This the American revisers insist should be retained. The English revisers prefer: "Are we in worse case?" with the marginal reading: "Do we excuse ourselves?" "Are we in worse case?" is explained as the interrogation of a Gentile. But the text speaks of no Gentile, and all the questions treated are those of Jews. As PHILIPPI argues, the middle voice must be regarded as used here with a slightly modified force for the active. The Jew then is regarded as asking the question: "Have we any advantage for ourselves? Is the privilege of advantage to us?" That is, with all the advantages which the possession of the oracles of God have given, has our use of them been such that we are morally the better for it? However great may be the divergence of interpreters concerning the meaning of the verb, all agree on the meaning of the application and answer: **No, in no wise,** i. e. we have no excuse to offer. All are involved in the same guilt and ruin. **We before laid to the charge.** It is Paul who has made this charge. He uses "we," as authors are wont to do. The charge was made concerning the Jews in ch. 2 : 1 sqq., and concerning the Gentiles in ch. 1 : 18 sqq. **Under sin,** not simply "sinful," but "in absolute subjection to the power of sin" (Comp. ch. 7 : 25; Gal. 3 : 22). The various sins of Jews and Gentiles enumerated were simply the breaking forth of the one sin that pervaded all, and that expressed itself in one form in one, and in another form in another. "The most virtuous heathen and the most devout Jew were justly chargeable with a wicked heart" (BESSER).

Ver. 10-18. Scripture proofs. Even an inspired Apostle supports his position at every step by an appeal to Holy Scripture. Vers. 10-12 support the general charge; ver. 13-18 give specific cases.

Ver. 10. **As it is written.** MICHAELIS and MOULE regard the remaining words of the verse as not a quotation, but only as the statement of the proposition which he assumes in the succeeding paragraph to prove. The variation from Ps. 14 : 2 is consistent, however, with Paul's mode of quoting O. T. texts. Conscious of the inspiration of the Holy Spirit, he is not bound to the painful accuracy of a mere copyist, or to the exactness of an uninspired man in citing Scripture. His variations are inspired interpretations. **There is none righteous.** Upon this principle he changes "doeth good" into "righteous," since the defect with respect to the doing of good was due to the lack of righteousness. If the words of the Psalmist, "There is none that doeth good," are true, the inference is clear, "There is none righteous." But the universal need of righteousness is the theme of this part of the Epistle. **No, not one.** An addition of the LXX., transferred from Ps. 14:3. It individualizes the statement, and declares that there is no exception.

Ver. 11. **None that understandeth.** (See also ch. 1:31.) The conditional form of Ps. 14:2, which becomes negative by the answer in the succeeding verse, is at once put into the negative form by Paul. The change goes beneath the outward life, to its dispositions and motives. The darkening and perversion of the intellect, because of sin, are here described. (Comp. 1 Cor. 2:14; Eph. 4:18.) "The Scriptures deny to the understanding, heart and will of the natural man all aptness, skill, capacity and ability in spiritual things, to think, to understand, begin, will, undertake, do, work or concur in working anything good and right as of itself" (FORMULA OF CONCORD, p. 554). **None that seeketh after God.** The cause of the lack of understanding is due to the determination of man's will against God. Seeking comprises desire, worship, obedience.

Ver. 12. "He says: **They all** have turned aside in order to include those also who seem especially to draw near to God.... They who sin openly are less harmful than hypocrites who not only do not themselves believe, but who try to persuade others that nothing that is said concerning the wicked and godless pertains to them" (LUTHER). **Together,** "to comprehend the entire class of the godless, both those showing by manifest sins that they are godless, and those who, by a fair outward appearance cover their wickedness" (LUTHER). **None--no, not one.** "A universal negative, corresponding to the universal affirmative that precedes" (LUTHER).

The above section most clearly presents the doctrine

of Original Sin, and precisely meets the arguments of the Roman Catholic opponents of the Augsburg Confession, in their criticism of its definition of Original Sin. Compare the chapter of the APOLOGY, which explains the substance of this paragraph: "In the Scriptures, righteousness comprises not only the Second Table of the Decalogue, but the First also, which teaches concerning the fear of God, concerning faith, concerning the love of God. . . . Therefore, the ancient definition, when it says that sin is the lack of righteousness, not only denies obedience with respect to man's lower powers, but also denies the knowledge of God, confidence in God, the fear and love of God, or certainly the power to produce these affections" (pp. 78 sq.).

Ver. 13. **Their throat.** The Greek word is *larynx*, the throat as an organ of speech; not pharynx, the organ for swallowing. **An open sepulchre.** As the sepulchre when opened emits pestilential vapors, so whenever they open their mouths, their speech is corrupt and corrupting, "false doctrine, Epicurean speeches, blasphemy, slander, obscenity," etc. (L. OSIANDER). **With their tongues,** etc. "The sugared tongue which charms you like a melodious instrument" (GOD.). The imperfect tense shows that the deceit is one habitually practised (Ps. 5:9). **Poison of asps** (Ps. 140:3). Honey and venom are artfully combined. While they flatter, the concealed fangs are full of poison, ready to be injected at the opportune moment.

Ver. 14. **Whose mouth,** etc., shows that, however sweet and charming may be their speeches, back of the smoothness of the tongue, there is nothing but bitterness. Whenever they speak out candidly, they are full of complaints, malignity, defiance (Ps. 140:3).

Ver. 15. **Swift to shed blood.** As before we have had

sin as manifested in speech, so here we have it manifested in deed. Quotation from Is. 7 : 8. Under the impulse of some overpowering passion, covetousness, lust, revenge, etc., they are eager to take the lives of any who obstruct their way to the object they have in view. Whether they be unoffending, or even their benefactors, matters not. There is no respect for the value of life. There seems to be even a delight in such crimes. Murder may become a pastime. Those whose tastes are warlike and chafe for the summons to battle, fall under this description.

Ver. 16. **Destruction.** Literally, "Breaking," **and misery.** The former refers to the ruin with which their track is strewn. Carnage and rapine reign everywhere. The latter refers to the sorrow which this brings, the groans of the dying, the cries of the orphaned and widows, the lingering death of the wounded, the pangs of poverty and want. History abounds in illustrations. Wherever they go, they transform fruitful fields into a wilderness (Joel 2 : 3). This is the reverse of Ps. 84 : 6.

Ver. 17. **The way of peace.** That, namely, which brings peace and happiness to their fellow-men. Always quarrelling, and influenced in all things by purely selfish motives, they do not know how to do a disinterested act to benefit others. The root of all peace with our fellow-men must be peace with ourselves; the root of all peace with ourselves is peace with God. LUTHER (on Ps. xiii.), with his deeply spiritual insight traces this absence of peace to the absorption of the soul in the world of sense. Their interests rest entirely in constantly changing phenomena. There is no substance on which their hearts can be anchored. "Whithersoever their affairs are carried they are carried with them," "they cannot find peace since they seek it in things which from their very nature cannot abide." They know not the cross. *Via crucis, via pacis.*

Ver. 18. **No fear of God.** This sums up all and explains all. (From Ps. 36 : 2.) "The fear of God" is a well-known O. T. expression (Ps. 111 : 10; Prov. 1 : 7, 9, 10; Is. 11 : 2) for the practical recognition of man's true relations to God in all the events and acts of life. (Comp. Acts 9 : 31.) "All men begotten according to the common course of nature are born with sin, that is, *without the fear of God*" (AUG. CONF., Art. II.). Not servile, but filial fear is here meant, which has its roots in love and faith. (See Gen. 22 : 12.) Such is the sad condition of a life sundered from communion with God.

Ver. 19. **Now we know,** etc. The self-righteous Jew being ready to meet this argument by exclaiming that the picture is true to the life of the Gentiles, Paul anticipates him by urging that, however applicable this may be to the Gentiles, the condemnation recorded in the Law must be for those to whom the Law came. The indictment is, therefore, brought against the Jews. Of them, then, none is righteous, no, not one. The charge is a sweeping one. The whole world is beneath God's judgment. All humanity is alike under condemnation. **The law saith.** Here the word of God recorded in the Old Testament. (Comp. 1 Cor. 14 : 21; John 10 : 34; 12 : 34; 15 : 25.) It is called "the Law," because the Mosaic Law is a most important portion of it, but especially " because everything in Scripture that serves to bring men to a knowledge of their sins is Law" (WEISS). Law as distinguished from Gospel. **Under the law.** (Comp. on ch. 2 : 12.) **Every mouth may be stopped,** i. e. may be deprived of every plea or excuse (Job 5 : 16; Ps. 107 : 42). **Under the judgment,** the word refers to one who in an action at law has lost his case.

CONCLUSION OF ARGUMENT OF PART I.—ALL UNDER
CONDEMNATION.

20. Because by the works of the law shall no flesh be justified in his sight: for through the law *cometh* the knowledge of sin.

Ver. 20. **Because**; i. e. Every mouth will be stopped, none can offer any excuse, and the whole world will be guilty, because, with no other supernatural revelation than that of the law, there can be no justification. **Works of the law** are those prescribed by and wrought under the constraint of the law, " such as man can do, when he has no other help than the law " (GOD.). The statement is true also of the good works of the regenerate; they cannot justify. But to introduce this here would be foreign to the argument Paul is now presenting. He is showing what man is without the Gospel. " As long as man does the works because they are commanded, from fear of punishment or desire for reward, he is under the law, and his works are properly called by St. Paul ' works of the law.'" (FORMULA OF CONCORD). " The work of the law is whatsoever a man doeth or can do of his own free will " (LUTHER). The entire contest is violated by interpreting "law " as referring to the Ceremonial Law. The offences specified in the arraignment of both Jews and Gentiles were against the Moral Law. In no law whatever, ceremonial or moral, can justification be found. **No flesh.** Human nature universally corrupted and enfeebled by sin is powerless. **Justified.** (Comp. on ch. 2:13.) **Knowledge of sin.** The law is the standard of right. Whatever fails to comply with the law, is therefore sin (1 John 3:4). " Sin is lawlessness " (R. V.). The fuller the knowledge of the standard, the greater therefore the knowledge of the failure to reach the standard. The contrast becomes the more manifest, when the objects, "man" and "the law," are placed side by side. The law is the rule which measures man's life. Growth in the knowledge of the law is, therefore, constantly attended by an ever increasing deepening of the sense of sin, and overwhelming consciousness of sin and ruin. "God published the law, to show us how far we are from true godliness and righteousness, that we might cast away all hope of our righteousness and merits, and flee to Christ" (OSIANDER).

Thus closes the first part of the Epistle. The theme is the universality of the grace of God. The first part of the argument is the universal need of grace. This has been shown, first, by the failure of the Gentiles, and, secondly, by the failure of the Jews, to attain righteousness before God. But all mankind being comprised under these two classes, all have the same want. By nature, they are beneath the judgment of God, who is justly offended because of their sins, and neither by nature, nor the law, can they be restored to God's favor.

5

PART II.

ALL ALIKE ARE OFFERED JUSTIFICATION BY FAITH IN CHRIST (3 : 21 — 5 : 19).

SECTION I.—THE NEW WAY OF LIFE IN CHRIST INTENDED FOR ALL MEN—A BRIEF SUMMARY OF THE PLAN OF SALVATION (3 : 21-31).

21-31. But now, apart from the law, a righteousness of God hath been manifested, being witnessed by the law and the prophets, even the righteousness of God through faith in Jesus Christ unto all them that believe; for there is no distinction; for all have sinned, and fall short of the glory of God; being justified freely by his grace through the redemption that is in Christ Jesus: whom God set forth *to be* a propitiation, through faith, by his blood, to shew his righteousness, because of the passing over of the sins done aforetime, in the forbearance of God; for the shewing, *I say*, of his righteousness at this present season; that he might himself be just, and the justifier of him that hath faith in Jesus. Where then is the glorying? It is excluded. By what manner of law? of works? Nay: but by a law of faith. We reckon therefore that a man is justified by faith apart from the works of the law. Or is God *the* God of Jews only? is he not *the* God of Gentiles also? Yea, of Gentiles also: if so be that God is one, and he shall justify the circumcision by faith, and the uncircumcision through faith. Do we then make the law of none effect through faith? God forbid: nay, we establish the law.

Ver. 21. **But now** marks the time. In these latter days of Gospel grace, as contrasted with the preceding period of Heathenism and Judaism. (Comp. Gal. 4 : 4; Eph. 3 : 5; ch. 16 : 26.) **Apart from the law.** Without reference to any conditions or requirements of the law. In contrast with "through the law" of the preceding verse. Our fulfilment of the law has nothing whatever to do with the righteousness that is provided for us. This is described as **the righteousness of God,** i. e. a righteousness prepared and bestowed by God, as contrasted with one earned by man's obedience. (See on ch. 1 : 17.) **Hath been manifested,** i. e. revealed in Christ (Col. 1 : 26), so that all may see and hear it. **Being witnessed by the law,** etc. It is nothing new; but was long foretold in all parts of the Old Testament (comp. ch. 1 : 2); nevertheless has been heretofore a mystery (ch. 16 : 26). Notice the two-fold use of law in this verse: "Apart from the law" refers to law as distinguished from the Gospel; "Witnessed by the law" refers to the Gospel promises in the Old Testament. Christ is the key to the interpretation of the Old Testament. What it meant was only dimly apprehended until Christ came.

Ver. 22. The Apostle recurs to the theme of the Epistle in ch. 1 : 16, 17. The righteousness prepared by God; and made man's, when accepted by the faith or self-surrender of the heart of Christ, is offered universally on the sole condition of faith. Unbelievers are condemned because of their refusal to accept this righteousness. "Only unbelief damneth" (LUTHER). **No distinction.** Whatever the distinctions among men, they alike need righteousness, and this righteousness has been provided for all alike in Christ. " A mountain-top differs in level from a mine floor; but it is as impossible to touch the stars from the mountain as from the mine " (MOULE). As universal as is man's ruin, is God's gracious provision and offer. They who decline being saved as sinners are excluded from the benefits of our Lord's redeeming work (Matt. 9 : 13). Nor, on the other hand, is there any sin whose guilt is beyond the provisions of redemption (1 Tim. 1 : 15).

Ver. 23. **All have sinned.** The tense here is important,

which both A. V. and R. V. have failed to observe. The meaning is not: "All have sinned," but that, at some definite point in time past, "all sinned." (See ch. 5:12.) The American revisers propose in the margin the true rendering. "The sin of each one is presupposed as an historical fact in the past, whereby the sinful state is occasioned" (WEISS). Since there is no righteousness that avails before God, except such as is perfect and complete, a single sin committed during his life would forever prevent justification on the ground of the law of the one who sinned. But since this has occurred, at some time or other, with all, none can be justified by the law. We regard this statement, however, as reaching back still further to the sin of Adam. **Fall short.** In consequence of this sin, they fail to attain the standard of righteousness which God has prescribed. **Glory of God,** viz. the glory which God bestows upon man, the holiness, righteousness and purity in which man was created and which God wants to see restored in man. To be accounted righteous before God is the highest glory of which man is capable.

Ver. 24. **Being justified freely.** This is an explanatory statement confirming what immediately precedes. The thought is: "And if they are to be justified, they must, therefore, be justified freely." The universality of the act of sin and of the sinful state, is followed by the declaration of the universality and equality of the terms and conditions of deliverance from it. The mode of justification is **freely,** i. e. without anything in man to deserve it (Matt. 10:8; 2 Thess. 3:8; 2 Cor. 11:7); the origin is **by his grace,** i. e. God's favor towards those deserving only His wrath, and the means, **the redemption which is in Christ Jesus.** In all passages referring to Justification, Redemption means purchase by the payment of a price. A comparison with synonymous expressions clearly proves this (1 Cor. 6 : 20 ; 7 : 23 ; Gal. 3 : 13 ; Pet. 20 : 28). The price is mentioned in Matt. 20 : 28 ; 1 Tim. 2 : 6, and especially in Eph. 1 : 7. All are slaves under sin, and cannot be liberated except at a price no less costly than that of the life of the Son of God. "Such is the wrath of God that it can be appeased by no victim except only by the death of His Son" (MELANCHTHON). "Who hath redeemed me, a lost and condemned creature," etc. (SMALL. CAT.; 1 Pet. 1 : 18 sq.). Thus, in one sense, justification is not free ; an ample price has been paid for it by the sufferings and death of Christ. But it is free to us, since this price is not paid by us, but has been paid by the Son of God Himself.

Ver. 25. **Set forth.** The alternate translation in margin "purposed" is equally well supported by Scriptural usage. It is the same word that is used for "purposed" in ch. 1 : 13. (Comp. Eph. 1 : 9.) The thought then becomes that of the predetermination or predestination of Christ as the sacrifice for sin, as in 1 Pet. 1 : 20. But, as CALVIN remarks, "if we adopt the other interpretation, the argument remains the same, viz. that God, in His own time, publicly presented Him whom He had purposed should be Mediator." CALOVIUS correctly combines both. "The *prothesis* [purpose, setting forth] occurred in God's eternal counsel (1 Pet. 1 : 20), in the oracles of the prophets and the types of the O. T. (Rev. 13 : 8), in the sending and setting forth of Christ as Mediator (1 Tim. 4 : 10), and in the preaching of the Gospel, whereby He was clearly set forth to all as the true Mercy Seat, so that whoever embrace it by faith obtain forgiveness of sins and grace." **To be a propitiation.** The Greek word is that used in the LXX. for Mercy Seat (*Kapporeth*), the lid of the ark of the Covenant, sprinkled once a year with the blood of atonement (Lev. 16 : 13-16; Heb. 9 : 5). The idea of covering inherent in the word is not that of a covering of the ark, but of the covering of the sins there made. Hence it is to be understood as meaning "the instrument of atonement." (See OEHLER'S O. T. *Theology*, Transl. pp. 253-257.) It set forth the fact "that the God who dwells in the midst of His people can only commune with them in virtue of an atonement offered to Him, but that He is also a God who can be reconciled." When Paul calls Christ the Mercy Seat he means that, in Christ all that is fulfilled which the Mercy Seat had foreshadowed. So ORIGEN, CHRYSOSTOM, THEODORET, LUTHER, L. OSIANDER, GROTIUS, CALO-VIUS, BENGEL, THOLUCK, OLSHAUSEN, PHILIPPI, BESSER, DELITZSCH, CREMER, LIDDON, GIFFORD, etc., understand this passage. The objections of MEYER, HODGE, STUART, ALFORD, BROWN, LUTHARDT, MOULE, SANDAY, etc., are chiefly: 1. As the High Priest sprinkled the Mercy Seat, this would necessitate us to think of Christ as sprinkling Himself with His own Blood. 2. The Mercy Seat was concealed from the sight of the people. The first is answered by the argument of the Epistle to the Hebrews that Christ is both High Priest and sacrifice (Heb. 7 : 27). The second is answered by the contrast between the Old and New Testaments. The Mercy Seat of the O. T. was accessible only once a year, and then only to the High Priest; that of the N. T. is for all times and peoples. Other objections are stated and answered at length by PHILIPPI, and with less fulness by GIFFORD in *The Speaker's Commentary*.

Instead of "Mercy Seat," some propose to translate the word by "Propitiator" or "Reconciler." There is no example, however, of the word being used with respect to persons. Others propose "Propitiation" in the sense of "a propitiatory sacrifice." This also is without the support of any example. For this, another word is used in 1 John 2:2. The Greek *hilasterion*, here used, does not mean sacrifice. The suggestion is contrary also to the analogy of faith. God is nowhere said in Scripture to present or offer a sacrifice; the sacrifice must be offered to God. "Christ presented Himself to God an expiatory sacrifice (Heb. 9:14, 28; Eph. 5:2; John 17:19), but not, God offered or presented Him to mankind in sacrifice" (Phil..). Here, God sets forth, i. e. presents Christ to the world as its true and all-availing Mediator. He is the Mercy Seat or Propitiatory.

Through faith, by his blood. Preferable to Marg. and A. V., "faith in His blood." The clauses are correlative, and each limits "Mercy Seat." It is only *through faith* that man makes the Mercy Seat, i. e. Christ, his own. But the Mercy Seat in itself is of no avail. To reconcile with God, it must be sprinkled with blood. Christ is no Mediator and Saviour apart from His suffering and death. The Cross is the centre of every Christian life. A suffering, bleeding, dying Jesus is the sum and substance of the Gospel. *Sanguis Christi, Christi evangelium.* No reconciliation with God is to be found in Jesus as a holy example or a pure teacher. If our sins are to be blotted out, we need His Blood (1 John 2:2).

To show his righteousness. The death of Christ manifests not only God's love, but also His justice. This justice could be satisfied in no other way than by the death of His Son. It is startling testimony to the awful significance of sin, and the earnestness of God against it! The complete acquiescence of the sufferer in the justice of the penalty which he bears is an additional exhibition of the divine righteousness.

Because of gives the reason why this manifestation of

His righteousness was necessary. The A. V. is here entirely at fault. **The passing over of the sins done aforetime in the forbearance of God.** Here again the A. V. entirely misleads. " Passing over " (*paresis*) of sins is very plainly different from their forgiveness (*aphesis*). The sins that were passed over were not forgiven. Reference is made to what is taught in Acts 17 : 30. For many long ages before Christ there had been no supernatural interference with the course of sin which the world had been pursuing. Death indeed prevailed, and, from time to time, signal judgments descended upon nations and individuals. Nevertheless these were only reminders of the claims of divine justice, and in no way commensurate with the guilt of the crimes committed. Lest, then, His long forbearance might be construed as indifference to sin (Ps. 50 : 21 ; Ecc. 8 : 11), God shows once for all the extent of His wrath by letting the punishment for sin fall upon His Son when He stands in the place of a sinful world. Nor must it be forgotten that God's delay in punishing the godless before Christ was due to the atonement which, although to be offered in the future, was to Him who sees the end from the beginning an ever-present reality.

BESSER says that this verse contains three thoughts : " Blood," " Faith," and " Righteousness."

Ver. 26. **For the shewing** resumes the thought of " to shew " of ver. 25, and depends on " set forth." **At this present season,** i. e. the time of Christ's advent, which is pre-eminently the Day of Salvation. A contrast between the times of the Old and the New Testaments is implied. **That he might be just,** dependent on " set forth " of ver. 25, repeats the thought just stated, in order to combine it with another. **And the justifier of him.** " We have here the greatest paradox of the Gospel; for in the *law*,

God is seen as *just and condemning*; in the *Gospel*, He is seen as *just and justifying* the sinner" (BENGEL). "The highest revelation of God's grace is also the highest revelation of His righteousness" (BESSER). His justice does not exclude His mercy; nor His mercy His justice. The blood sprinkled on the Mercy Seat proclaims His justice; the Mercy Seat sprinkled with blood His mercy. Even in the forgiveness of sins, the justice of God is asserted and vindicated: "The Cross puts the holy God on His throne, rebellious man in the dust" (GOD.). "'Just in punishing' and 'merciful in pardoning' men can understand; but 'just in justifying' the guilty startles them" (BROWN). **That hath faith in Jesus**, viz. who, by faith, makes this revelation of the justice and mercy of God in Jesus his own, recognizes himself as the lost and condemned creature who needs a redeemer, and, having found this redeemer in Jesus Christ, acknowledges and owns Him as his Lord. Faith in Jesus is the entire, unreserved, self-surrender of the heart to Jesus. It is not a work of man arising from the exercise of his own powers in response to the word of God, but it is a work throughout of the Holy Ghost (1 Cor. 12 : 3).

"Stop here for a moment, dear Christian, and look into the divine work of Justification, as the Apostle has presented it in the three verses, 24-26. From beginning to end, it is the work of God, without any aid or co-operation on our part. God's grace and God's righteousness kiss one another in redemption through the blood of Christ, and this redemption has purchased for us sinners the gift of righteousness in the forgiveness of sins. But you ask, whether the reception of this gift may not perhaps depend upon our co-operation? No. For this comes through faith, and faith, the trust of the heart in God's promise, or the taking possession of the divine gift and grace, is not our work, but the gracious work of God in us (Eph. 2:8-10). 'I believe that I cannot by my own reason or strength believe in Jesus Christ my Lord or come to Him,' etc. Because it is the nature of faith to banish all trust in our own works and nature, and to surrender itself entirely to the grace of God in Christ Jesus, it avails for justification. This it does, not as a virtuous, meritorious work (man is justified *through* faith, not *because of* faith), or because good and precious works follow that please God (for it is Christ received by faith, and not the fruit of faith that justifies man). The works of the faith of saints are indeed good; but the best of them is not good enough to avail before God as a foundation, or a partial foundation, for justification. Hence the Apostle insists that the article concerning justifying faith must not be commingled with that concerning the powers of sanctification, which are active in the believer. The consolation offered by the Gospel to a poor sinner is dependent upon our making the faith whereby we are justified the same that it is according to the Apostolic doctrine, viz. the taking to ourselves of the righteousness that has been completed for us in Christ Jesus" (BESSER).

Ver. 27. **Where then is the glorying?** A question of triumph. The argument is so complete! If man's justification depends entirely upon the justifying grace of God, and this is given solely because it has been purchased by the blood of Christ, man has nothing pertaining to his natural life whereof to boast. **By what manner of law?** Law does not mean here a positive enactment, but "according to what rule," "upon what principle," "by what system," as in ch. 7:21; 8:2; 9:31; 10:31; James 2:12. As such the Gospel, while not "the law," is "**a law**," since its blessings are bestowed upon the sole condition of faith. It is God's order to impart His righteousness through faith, which He also bestows according to a mode of working which He has revealed. All that faith does is only to receive what God provides; and yet even this receptive power of faith is a result of the work of grace within us.

Ver. 28. **We reckon therefore.** The weight of manuscripts, and the opinion of both TISCHENDORF and WESTCOTT and HORT, are on the side of the marginal reading: "For we reckon." This, then, introduces a summary of the entire preceding argument, as proving what has just been stated in ver. 27. **A man.** A general term for any member of the human race. It is used in contrast to Jew and Gentile in the next verse. It must not be forgotten that the doctrine of Justification by Faith has been introduced by the Apostle in support of what is his main theme, viz. the universalism of the Gospel. **Is justified by faith**, i. e. by merits of Christ received by faith, as has been just explained. Luther's addition of "alone" (not original with Luther, but found in the Nürenberg German Bible of 1483 and a Geneva Italian Bible of 1476 (see PHILIPPI), does not belong properly to a translation, although it is completely justified by the context. For if justification be not by faith alone, works must have something to do with our justification. Nevertheless the Apostle has just said that the law of works has nothing to do with justification, and in the next clause "**apart from the works of the law**" he repeats the statement. The entire doctrine of this verse, in its various relations, is most clearly stated in the *Formula of Concord:* "A poor sinful man is justified before God, i. e. absolved and declared free and exempt from all his sins, and from the sentence of well-deserved condemnation, and adopted into sonship and heirship of eternal life, without any merit or worth of his own, also without all preceding, present or subsequent works, out of pure grace, alone because of the sole merit, complete obedience, bitter suffering, death and resurrection of our Lord Christ, whose obedience is reckoned to us for righteousness. The treasures are offered us by the Holy Ghost in the promise of the holy Gospel; and faith alone is the only means whereby we lay hold upon, accept and apply and appropriate them to ourselves" (p. 571). The attempt to limit these works to those of the unregenerate, is sufficiently met by the illustration of Abraham, commented upon in the succeeding chapter.

Ver. 29. **Or is God the God of Jews only.** This may be rendered more idiomatically: "Does God belong only to the Jews?" He would assuredly be only a Jewish God, if obedience to the Jewish law were the sole condition of Justification.

Ver. 30. **If so be that God is one.** Monotheism, says Paul, is at stake in this argument. If you make God a Jewish God, then the Gentiles are right in making gods for themselves. **He shall justify** indicates the uniform application of redemption under the Gospel dispensation. **The circumcision by faith.** If Jews are to be justified— and many of them shall be—this will occur only by faith. The circumcised are not excluded, but circumcision has no effect upon justification. **The uncircumcision through faith.** We are not persuaded by MEYER that the variations "by faith" and "through faith" are accidental. There are no accidents in Paul's style. "Never did jeweller chisel his diamonds more carefully than the Apostle does the expression of his thoughts" (GOD.).

The difficulty of determining the reason of the distinction is indeed great. "**By**," "out of," indicates *origin;* "through" indicates *instrument.* CALVIN suggests that Paul means that the difference between the two is as small as there is between being justified by faith or through faith. But the omission of the article in the former clause and its introduction in the latter is also significant. The marginal reading is true to the original when it gives us: "He shall justify the circumcision *out of faith* and the uncircumcision *through the faith.*" Hence we believe there is much force in the explanation of LIDDON: "It was the development of the subjective faith of the Jews which would lead to their justification; it was the objective faith of Christendom, of which as yet they knew nothing, which would be the means of justifying the Gentiles."

Ver. 31. **Make the law of none effect.** The objector whose voice has been heard so often throughout what precedes, comes forward again. Why, he says, if the law has nothing to do with our justification, you might as well deny its obligation and divine authority. Not at all, says Paul. **Nay, we establish the law.** We only place the law in its true place. Its office is to convict of sin (ver. 20). It leads to Christ and the Gospel (Gal. 3 : 24). From faith comes the new obedience, when, with faith, love, the fulfilling of the law, enters (ch. 13 : 10). " Faith fulfils all laws; works fulfil not a tittle of the law" (LUTHER). The truest friends and champions of the law, those who actually and not merely seemingly fulfil it, are found only where the plan of salvation in Christ has been appropriated and prevails.

SECTION II.—THE NEW WAY OF LIFE IN CHRIST AN OLD WAY. JUSTIFICATION BY FAITH UNDER THE OLD TESTAMENT (ch. iv.).

Abraham's Example (vers. 1-5).

1-5. What then shall we say that Abraham, our forefather according to the flesh, hath found? For if Abraham was justified by works, he hath whereof to glory; but not toward God. For what saith the scripture? And Abraham believed God, and it was reckoned unto him for righteousness. Now to him that worketh, the reward is not reckoned as of grace, but as of debt. But to him that worketh not, but believeth on him that justifieth the ungodly, his faith is reckoned for righteousness.

Ver. 1. **What then shall we say?** A frequent phrase of Paul (3:5; 6:1; 7:7; 8:31; 9:14). The reading of A. R. V. is preferable: **That Abraham our forefather hath found according to the flesh,** i. e. What blessings did Abraham obtain according to his own natural powers, in contrast with the workings of divine grace? "What has Abraham found by his own labor?" Some find in this appeal proof that the majority of the Roman Church were Jews. But in 1 Cor. 10:1, Paul writes to the Corinthian Church, which was chiefly Greek, concerning the children of Israel as "our fathers." He writes from the standpoint of a Christianized Jew, just as when he says "What shall we say?"

Ver. 2 assumes that Abraham was **justified by his works.** His works fulfilled all the conditions that man's standard of righteousness could require. "He had many excellent and heroic virtues, and undoubtedly surpassed all men of his age in wisdom and every kind of virtues. These Paul does not despise, but he says that they cannot be set over against the wrath and judgment of God" (MEL.). The thought is: "Wherein Abraham was justified by works, he has whereof to glory. But he has nothing whereof to glory before God. Therefore he was not justified before God." Had Abraham been justified before God by works, his service of God would have been mercenary. All the charm of his obedience would be gone. Then comes the implied application: "If, then, even Abraham was not justified before God by works; much less, they who boasted of him as their father."

Ver. 3. **Abraham believed God.** "The firm apprehension of a promise is called faith. It justifies, not as our work, but as God's. For a promise is a divine gift and thought, whereby God offers us something. It is not a work of ours, whereby we do something for God or give something to God, but we receive it from God, and that too only by His mercy. . . . Faith alone apprehends the promise, believes God when He promises, reaches forth the hand and receives when God offers. This is the peculiar office of faith. Love, hope, patience have other works to do. They do not apprehend the promise, but they obey commandments. They hear God ordering and commanding; they do not hear God promising. This faith does" (LUTHER on Gen. 15 : 6). **It was reckoned unto him for righteousness.** The inability of Abraham to find justification by works is confirmed by Scripture (Gen. 15 : 6). The word "reckon" or "impute" excludes the idea of any inherent merit or righteousness. There was no righteousness or merit in his faith; for then faith would be only a work of another kind. When Abraham believed, God treated him precisely as though he were righteous. The promise, through faith in which Abraham entered into a state where he was thus graciously treated, was that of the coming Messiah (Gen. 15 : 5). What that promise contained, he apprehended very feebly; but there was a complete self-surrender of his will to the word of God. Faith is a relation, an attitude, a temper, a disposition of man towards God. It contains within itself the readiness to receive with joy whatever God may reveal, and to do or suffer with joy whatever God may appoint. Abraham was reckoned righteous by being brought into such thoroughly receptive relations to God, that all the blessings that God had to give were made his in advance.

Ver. 4. **Not as of grace, but as of debt.** An inference from the Old Testament testimony. If by works Abraham had been justified, why would the statement be that "the reward was reckoned"? For if it came by works, this was nothing more than Abraham deserved. The very thought of "grace," in connection with God's dealings with Abraham, shows that he receives what he has not earned. God treats him as though he possesses that which he does not have. **But as of debt.** If justification be by works, we make God our debtor.

Ver. 5. **To him that worketh not,** i. e. to one whose good works are not wrought for the purpose of obtaining justification through them; one who does not endeavor to purchase justification by his works. "The man who has obtained justification may be looked upon as in possesssion of a title-deed, which secures to him a right to God's favor. The question is, How comes he into possession of this title-deed? Did he work for it, and then receive it as a return for his work? No, he did not work for it; and thus it is that justification is to him who worketh not—that is, he did nothing antecedent to his justification to bring this privilege down upon him; and it is a contradiction to allow that it is by doing anything subsequent to justification that he secures this privilege, for it is secured already " (CHALMERS). **But believeth on him that justifieth.** His faith does not lay hold of just anything. It is not mere belief in the goodness of God; but it is trust in God as justifying those who, if justice, without mercy, were enforced could not be justified. On the one hand, it is confidence in the free promise of God; on the other hand, it is complete self-surrender of the heart and life to One whom, in the promise, man has learned to trust. "Believing on Him" means more than regarding His word as true; it designates a personal relation. **The ungodly.** A very forcible word, meaning, in the original, one guilty of open and flagrant sin. An extreme case is taken, such as is not found in Abraham, to show how a godly life has nothing whatever to do with justification. **His faith is reckoned for righteousness.** Manifestly not because the faith has any merits; for faith is pure receptivity. Faith cannot exist without an object. Not even in thought can we separate faith from its object. When anything of value, therefore, is ascribed to faith, it belongs to the object which faith apprehends and contains. Receiving God's promise by faith, the promise of God with respect to him is realized. Taking the merits of Christ as his own, as God extends them to him, these merits are reckoned as his. Faith is reckoned for righteousness; because faith takes to itself and by the grace of God keeps Christ's righteousness as its own.

David's Testimony (vers. 6-8).

6-8. Even as David also pronounceth blessing upon the man, unto whom God reckoneth righteousness apart from works, *saying*,
 Blessed are they whose iniquities are forgiven,
 And whose sins are covered.
 Blessed is the man to whom the Lord will not reckon sin.

Ver. 6. **Apart from works.** As "to reckon righteous" is the same as to justify, this verse, with the preceding, is the source of the formula: "Justification by faith without works," i. e. the works of believers have nothing whatever to do with their justification.

Ver. 7, 8. A quotation from Ps. 32:1, 2. This gives the negative, as ver. 3 gives the positive side of justification. Both go together. On the one hand, justification is treating man as though he were righteous; on the other, it is the passing by and not reckoning, i. e. the forgiving of sins. This quotation is intended to show that justification does not consist in the removal, but in the covering or hiding from sight of sin. However far sanctification may have progressed, sins always remain in this life. "When David, worn out by perpetual torture of conscience, breaks forth in this explanation, it is certainly from experience that he speaks; for he had served God already for many years. Having discovered, then, after his great progress, that all are miserable who are called to God's tribunal, he exclaims that there is no other way of obtaining happiness, than by the Lord's receiving us into grace by the non-imputation of our sins. Thus the imagination of those is refuted, who say that the righteousness of faith is only the beginning, and that by works believers obtain possession of righteousness, which they have acquired by no merits" (CALVIN). "Therefore, even though the converted and believing have incipient renewal, sanctification, love, virtue and good works, yet these neither can nor should be introduced into or confounded with the article of justification before God, in order that the honor which belongs to Him may remain with Christ the Redeemer, and, since our new obedience is incomplete, tempted consciences may have sure consolation" (FORMULA OF CONCORD, p. 576).

Neither the Circumcision of Abraham and David, nor their Observance of the Law, determined their Justification by Faith (vers. 9-18).

9-18. Is this blessing then pronounced upon the circumcision, or upon the uncircumcision also? for we say, To Abraham his faith was reckoned for righteousness. How then was it reckoned? when he was in circumcision or in uncircumcision? Not in circumcision, but in uncircumcision: and he received the sign of circumcision, a seal of the righteousness of the faith which he had while he was in uncircumcision: that he might be the father of all them that believe, though they be in uncircumcision, that righteousness might be reckoned unto them; and the father of circumcision to them who not only are of the circumcision, but who also walk in the steps of that faith of our father Abraham which he had in uncircumcision. For not through the law was the promise to Abraham or to his seed, that he should be heir of the world, but through the righteousness of faith. For if they which are of the law be heirs, faith is made void, and the promise is made of none effect: for the law worketh wrath; but where there is no law, neither is there transgression. For this cause *it is* of faith, that *it may be* according to grace; to the end that the promise may be sure to all the seed; not to that only which is of the law, but to that also which is of the faith of Abraham, who is the father of us all (as it is written, A father of many nations have I made thee) before him whom he believed, *even* God, who quickeneth the dead, and calleth the things that are not, as though they were.

Vers. 9, 10. "But," continues the Apostle, "some one may say that justification without works is a special privilege of the circumcised, since the O. T. passages, just cited, refer to Abraham and David." The answer begins by drawing a line of distinction between David and Abraham. "If David were the only one involved," the implication is, "this might be assumed as the basis of an argument." But with respect to Abraham, the case is not so clear. David was circumcised in infancy; Abraham, not until he was ninety-nine years old (Gen. 17:24). To which period of Abraham's life did this declaration concerning his justification belong? The answer is **Not**

in circumcision, but in uncircumcision. The declaration of Gen. 15:6 was made at least fourteen years before the institution of circumcision in Gen. 15.

Ver. 11. **The sign of circumcision,** i. e. circumcision as a sign. **A seal of the righteousness of faith,** i. e. of the righteousness of which faith has been made the possessor. In Abraham's case, therefore, circumcision was only a pledge of the justification which he had received years before; just as, under the New Testament, obedience to the new law and the new life, wrought by the indwelling of the Holy Spirit, are the seal of the righteousness of Christ which the believer has received. Thus circumcision was neither in itself an act which conferred irresistible grace for justification, nor was it valueless. It was an attestation of the divine assurance that Abraham was justified by grace through faith. Nor must this passage be regarded as teaching that, in all cases, justification preceded circumcision. **That he might be the father of all them that believe.** The divine intention, at the institution of circumcision, had in view a community of believers, collected from all nations (Gen. 18:18), independently of their relations to circumcision. The sole bond of union was their common faith, diffused from Abraham through the promise given him, which made him the true spiritual father of all believers (John 8:37, 39). **Though they be in uncircumcision,** i. e. faith, not circumcision determines the matter. **That righteousness might be reckoned,** i. e. "Who believe so as to receive the imputed righteousness of Christ."

Ver. 12. **The father of circumcision.** Abraham is the true father of circumcised believers. Their spiritual oneness with him is determined by their possession of faith, such as Abraham had before he was circumcised. **But who also walk in the steps of that faith.** Here the reference is made not merely to entrance into the covenant, but to persevering continuance in it. Even the once having the faith of Abraham is nothing, unless that faith be carried through the whole life. Thus the entire argument of these two verses becomes: The children of Abraham are: 1. All uncircumcised believers ("All them that believe, though they be in uncircumcision"). 2. All circumcised believers. 3. Both only as long as they believe. Thus circumcision has nothing to do with making valid the offer of justification. All depends on faith. Whatever value circumcision has, is as a means of strengthening faith, by the pledge of God's grace which it offers.

Ver. 13. **For** gives the reason why Abraham's fatherhood was more far-reaching than the sphere of circumcised believers, and that it excluded all circumcised unbelievers. **Not through the law**, i. e. through any definitely or elaborately arranged system of ordinances. While the Mosaic law is in mind, the application is still wider. According to Gal. 3:17, the law was 430 years later. **The promise** referred primarily to the land of Canaan (Gen. 15:18; 17:8, etc.). But a preceding promise indicated that its scope was still wider, and made Abraham and his seed **heir of the world**. It referred to the universal empire of the Messiah (Ps. 2:8), the sharing in it of all spiritual children of Abraham (Matt. 5:5), and beyond this, the new heavens and new earth (2 Pet. 3:13), with all that believers inherit in Christ (1 Cor. 3:22). The natural seed was the type of the spiritual; the earthly Canaan, the type of heavenly. **Through the righteousness of faith.** Because God found in him the righteousness which through faith He had given him.

Ver. 14. **If they which be of the law**, etc. This verse means: If man is to earn these things by conformity to law, why should mention of righteousness to be obtained in a different way have been made? What place is there for any promise of grace? The dilemma is: Either law or the righteousness of faith. Either law or promise. Admit the former, and you deny the latter. Salvation by the law and salvation by the promise are incompatible propositions (Gal. 3 : 18). **The promise, of none effect.** " For if the promise would require the condition of our merits and the law, it would follow, since we would never fulfil the law, that the promise would be useless " (APOLOGY, p. 90).

Ver. 15. **For the law worketh wrath,** i. e. A sinful man has neither hope nor help from the law. No grace is there (John 1 : 17). Its only effect upon a sinful man is to bring the inner sin out into open transgression, and thus to increase God's wrath against the sinner. " Thus the divine wrath has its differences of degrees. It rests upon the unconscious sinfulness of Adamitic human nature (Eph. 2 : 3; John 3 : 3). It is aggravated by the fact of sin against the natural perception of God and law of conscience (2 : 14, 15). It reaches its highest point when sin is developed as transgression of the law of God revealed from without " (PHILIPPI). **No law, no transgression.** He does not say, no sin. A transgression refers to a positive act in violation of a divine command or prohibition. The general corruption is, in a transgression, determined to a particular point. The argument means that the coming of law adds guilt for a positive transgression to that of the general guilt belonging to the person's sinful state.

Ver. 16. **For this cause,** i. e. there being no grace by the law. **It is of faith.** The promise of the inheritance is received by faith, belongs to faith. **According to grace,** i. e. that it may be bestowed entirely as a favor from

God, without regard to man's merit or worthiness, so that the thought of relation to the law may be completely excluded. **That the promise may be sure.** For if the fulfilment of the promise depend in any measure upon man's fulfilment of the law, it is rendered uncertain. "We never could determine when we would have sufficient merit" (APOLOGY). The question which naturally occurs whether the conditions of faith, then, do not interfere with the gratuity of the promise is well answered: "Although the promises of the Gospel are received by faith, and cannot be received otherwise than by faith, nevertheless, on this account, they do not cease to be gratuitous: first, because faith itself is a gift of God, and not our work, inasmuch as the Holy Ghost, through the word of the Gospel, enkindles faith in our hearts; secondly, because faith does not concur as a merit, the worth of which God regards, but only as an organ, as the hand of a beggar, which in receiving alms does not make these alms less of a gratuity" (GERHARD, L. T. 3 : 161). **All the seed,** i. e. all who believe. The next clause analyzes this into two classes, viz. first, **That which is of the law,** i. e. believers, who by birth and circumcision were once Jews, and, secondly, **That which is of the faith,** i. e. those who have not been Jews, and who, except on the ground of the promise of grace apart from the law, could have no hope whatever of the blessings of everlasting life. **Of the faith of Abraham.** Both such faith as Abraham had, and faith proceeding from and grounded in Abraham's faith, as the bearer to the world of the divine promise. **Father of us all** indicates the common ground on which, by faith, both Jew and Gentile stand. All the members of the Church at Rome had the same claim to this inheritance.

Ver. 17. **As it is written** (Gen. 17 : 5). This is "a

preaching of the Gospel beforehand " (Gal. 3 : 8). **Before him,** i. e. " the father of us all *before him,*" the same as though he had called Abraham the spiritual father of all nations. Abraham's spiritual children embraced representatives of all nations. Some were Abraham's children also by natural descent, sprung from his own body, " now as good as dead " (ver. 19). Others were made Abraham's children by God's special order and command—not by natural inheritance—but by the grace of Him who **calleth the things that are not as though they were.** The pledge of this introduction of Gentiles among the seed of Abraham was given in the fact that even Abraham's natural offspring in Isaac had become his in a supernatural way. The same grace operated in both cases. Why should it be regarded an impossibility for Gentiles to be spiritual children of Abraham, when the miracle of the birth of Isaac is regarded?

The Nature of Faith, as Illustrated by the Faith of Abraham (vers. 18-25).

18-25. Who in hope believed against hope, to the end that he might become a father of many nations, according to that which had been spoken, So shall thy seed be. And without being weakened in faith he considered his own body now as good as dead (he being about a hundred years old), and the deadness of Sarah's womb : yea, looking unto the promise of God, he wavered not through unbelief, but waxed strong through faith, giving glory to God, and being fully assured that, what he had promised, he was able also to perform. Wherefore also it was reckoned unto him for righteousness. Now it was not written for his sake alone, that it was reckoned unto him ; but for our sake also, unto whom it shall be reckoned, who believe on him that raised Jesus our Lord from the dead, who was delivered up for our trespasses, and was raised for our justification.

Ver. 18. **In hope,** i. e. a hope inspired by God's promise became the motive of his faith. **Against hope,** i. e. where all hopes according to the natural order were vain. The former refers to natural; the second, to supernatural hope. "For unless faith soar aloft on heavenly pinions, so as to look down upon all carnal sense, it will always stick in the mire of the world" (CALVIN). **To the end that he might.** This translation shows that the translators regard this as expressing the divine purpose in bestowing the faith. But we prefer to regard this clause as declaring what Abraham believed, viz. "He believed that he would become the father of many nations." The Greek construction is a peculiarly emphatic one to declare how he threw himself upon God's promise, away from self, and all else. That promise henceforth became the one determinative principle of his life.

Ver. 19. **He considered his own body.** The best manuscripts omit the negative found in A. V. In the popular understanding, the general sense does not vary. When the negative is accepted, the passage means he did not take the deadness of his body into the account. When omitted, the thought gains force. He is then regarded as reflecting on his age and the deadness of his body. When the promise was made, he did not forget this (Gen. 17 : 17), but declared it to God. But his word of seeming astonishment and his laugh came not from doubt, but from joy. He knew all this, says Paul, and yet he believed. "I think that Christ had in mind this very passage (Gen. 17 : 17), when he said (John 8 : 56): 'Your father Abraham rejoiced to see my day, and he saw it, and was glad.' For his falling on his face and laughing, as Christ explains, was only the expression of a soul overflowing with joy, in the fact that he now was certain that he would be the father, and Mary, the mother of Jesus Christ, through whom salvation and blessing would come to the whole world" (LUTHER). **The deadness,** etc. (Comp. Gen. 18 : 11.)

Ver. 20. **Looking unto the promise.** " Looking " is not in the Greek text, but is carried over in thought from " considered " of the preceding verse. **He Wavered not.** There was no hesitation or doubt. The word used also in ch. 14 : 23 ; Matt. 21 : 21 ; Acts 10 : 20 ; James 1 : 6, means literally to discriminate. "All this," the thought is, " made no difference, when he had an explicit promise from God. He did not stop to sift evidence concerning that of which God assured him." **Through unbelief.** He could not waver, since all vacillation comes from unbelief; and from this he was free. **Waxed strong,** i. e. His faith grew as it was exercised. **Giving glory to God.** " Glory is the sum of the attributes of God. To give glory is to ascribe to God His true character as the Almighty, the All-holy," etc. (LIDDON). " To God, he ascribed the *glory of truth*, for even should God promise what is impossible, he deceives no one ; and the *glory of power*, for since nothing is impossible to God, he was full of confidence that God would accomplish that which the natural order does not effect. These are the two fulcrums of faith ; and he who finally accepts them to the honor of God brings his faith into captivity to the obedience of Christ. It is a characteristic of all believers " (BALDWIN).

Ver. 21. **Being fully assured,** i. e. being perfectly certain. Same word in ch. 14 : 5 ; Col. 4 : 12, and corresponding noun in Col. 2 : 2 ; 1 Thess. 1 : 5 ; Heb. 6 : 11 ; 10 : 22. This was an important proof-text in the controversies against the decrees of Trent, in which the Roman Catholics deny that certainty is an attribute of justifying faith. The word here used excludes all doubt from faith. The older Protestant expositors refer to the etymology of the word as indicating the filling of the sails of a ship with wind. Thus GERHARD (L. T. 3 : 366):

"Ships which are borne along with full sails go towards the appointed place by the most direct course, hasten with utmost speed, never pause, nor look for rocks or shoals,—all of which may be most forcibly applied to faith firmly cleaving fast to the divine promises." GODET, however, makes a different application: "To fill a vessel to the brim. This word, used in the passive, applies to a man filled with a conviction which leaves no place in his heart for the least doubt." **What God had promised.** Faith is thus in its real nature a relation of a person to a Person. Whenever it appears as the acceptance of a statement, that statement is accepted solely because of Him who makes it. Faith is trust in God, which necessarily expresses itself in the acceptance of all that God teaches, and the self-surrender of the heart to all that God wills.

Ver. 22. **Wherefore,** i. e. Since there was such complete surrender to God of all that pertained to self, and such absolute reliance on God's promise. **It was reckoned.** The construction is impersonal. The meaning is: "He was reckoned righteous." "He was treated as though righteous." For explanation of the expression, see notes on ver. 3.

Ver. 23, 24. (Comp. Rom. 15 : 4.) **Shall be reckoned.** The Greek construction emphasizes the certainty of what is prophesied to take place.[1] All who believe shall, when they believe, find this righteousness imputed also to them. The object here is to show that the terms of salvation to believers under the present dispensation are identical with those in the case of Abraham. All are justified solely through faith in God's promise. The only difference is that the faith of Abraham was directed to

[1] *Mello* with the infinitive is used, in general, of what is sure to happen" (THAYER).

the future towards a coming Saviour, while that of those under the N. T. embraces a Saviour who has come and wrought complete redemption. Most that to him was a matter of expectancy is to us one of accomplished fact. **Who believe.** The present tense indicates that justification occurs *when* men believe. See *Augsburg Confession*, Art. iv.: " Men are justified freely for Christ's sake through faith, when they believe that they are received into favor and their sins forgiven for Christ's sake." **On him.** Faith is not simply a persuasion of the truth of an historical fact; but it is a relation of person to person. Back of the fact lies the Person whom the fact reveals. The same Person to whom Abraham looked for the fulfilment of the promise is the One whose power and faithfulness have been manifested to a later age in the resurrection of Christ, and upon whom, therefore, believers of the N. T. confidently rely. **That raised Jesus our Lord.** The resurrection is mentioned as attesting the completion of the redemption promised Abraham.

Ver. 25. **Delivered up.** A frequent expression for the surrender of the Son of God, as a victim for the sins of the world. In ch. 8 : 32, the Father is said to have delivered up the Son. In Gal. 1 : 4 ; 2 : 20, and Eph. 5 : 2, the Son is said to have given Himself for us. In Matt. 20 : 19 ; 27 : 2 ; Mark 15 : 10, etc., He is said to have been delivered by the Pharisees, elders, priests, etc., and in John 19 : 16 by Pilate. The harmony of the divine and human factors in the delivery of Christ to death is stated in Acts 2 : 23 and John 19 : 11. **For our trespasses.** Literally, " on account of our trespasses," in order that a satisfaction for them might be rendered and God's wrath propitiated. (Comp. John 1 : 29 ; Is. 53 : 6 ; 1 Pet. 2 : 24.) Abraham's faith in this delivery of Christ to death was confessed in his words on Mt. Moriah (Gen. 22 : 8). **For**

our justification. Literally, "on account of." As our sins caused His death, so *our justification caused His resurrection*. When our sins were not yet atoned for, and God's wrath was not yet appeased, He endured death and passed beneath God's wrath for our sakes. When the demands of the law were completely satisfied, and every sin had received the full penalty which it merited, and God's wrath was turned to love, justification was provided for us. Hence, because the work of redemption had reached its consummation, and there were no more sins for which an offering was to be made, he rose again "on account of our justification." Potential justification for all men is thus certified to by Christ's resurrection. "When the debtor is proved insolvent, his security is thrown into prison; but as soon as the latter succeeds in clearing the debt, the debtor is legally set free, and his security is liberated with him. We sin, He dies; we are justified, He lives again. So long as the security is in prison, the debt is not paid; the immediate effect of payment would be his liberation" (GODET). (Comp. 1 Cor. 15:17.) Another interpretation regards the Greek preposition *dia*, here used, as meaning "for" (so the A. V. and R. V.), and explains this clause as meaning that the resurrection of Christ was necessary in order to produce justifying faith in the hearts of men, the resurrection being the great argument in the Apostolic preaching to bring men to Christ. For it proves that the death of Christ was not that of a malefactor or of a misguided zealot, but a vicarious death for our sins; and thus renders the appropriation by faith of this death possible. "Without His resurrection, the atoning work of His death would have remained without subjective appropriation; His surrender for our transgressions would not have attained its end— our justification" (MEYER). While this explanation is the one more commonly given, and affirms a doctrine which is entirely in harmony with Scripture, nevertheless we cannot regard it as justifying the change in the meaning of the preposition *dia* from the sense used in the former clause.

If it be objected to the interpretation here accepted that justification for each believer begins, not from our Lord's death, but from the time that this death is appropriated by faith, the answer is correctly given: "The Apostle here states the ideal of the matter; he means not individual justification, but the work which forever secured justification for the believing Church. A close parallel is the *It is finished* (John 19:30). In the Divine Idea, every future believer was declared to be justified, through an accomplished Propitiation, when Jesus rose" (MOULE). We go even farther, and say that so far as God was concerned there was already at Christ's resurrection justification for all men; only this justification had afterwards to be appropriated by those to whom it would be applied and whom it would benefit.

SECTION III.—THE GOSPEL PROVISIONS FOR JUSTIFICATION, NOT TEMPORARY, BUT PERMANENT (5 : 1-21).

The harmony between the O. and N. T. has been established by the argument just given. The Apostle proceeds next to show that justification is not simply a matter of the present. He looks forward into the future, and declares the blessedness of the justified man both for time and eternity. As all humanity had fallen into sin, so complete deliverance for all humanity is provided through redemption in Christ.

(a.) The Security of the Justified Proved by an Argument from the Love and Mercy of God (vers. 1-11).

1-11. Being therefore justified by faith, let us have peace with God through our Lord Jesus Christ; through whom also we have had our access by faith into this grace wherein we stand, and let us rejoice in hope of the glory of God. And not only so, but let us also rejoice in our tribulations: knowing that tribulation worketh patience; and patience, probation; and probation, hope: and hope putteth not to shame; because the love of God hath been shed abroad in our hearts through the Holy Ghost which was given unto us. For while we were yet weak, in due season Christ died for the ungodly. For scarcely for a righteous man will one die: for peradventure for the good man some one would even dare to die. But God commendeth his own love toward us, in that, while we were yet sinners, Christ died for us. Much more then, being now justified by his blood, shall we be saved from the wrath of God through him. For if, while we were enemies, we were reconciled to God through the death of his Son, much more, being reconciled, shall we be saved by his life; and not only so, but we also rejoice in God through our Lord Jesus Christ, through whom we have now received the reconciliation.

Ver. 1. **Being therefore justified.** This connects with the last clause of preceding chapter, where justification is mentioned. At the same time, it brings the attention of the reader back to the main argument by which the universality of grace has been proved, viz. Justification by Faith. **By faith.** " Faith justifies, not by itself, by its own worth or value, or by moving God to justify the believer, but because, as an instrument or receptive means, it lays hold of the merit of Christ, in view of which God is moved to pardon and consider righteous, of His mere grace, the penitent sinner believing in Christ " (HOLLAZIUS). The meaning cannot be misunderstood, if the connection with preceding verse and the correct interpretation of the latter be kept in view. Chapter 4 : 25 treats of the provision of justification for mankind; this verse, of its subjective appropriation. By faith, man takes to himself and claims God's forgiving love. **We have peace.** Upon this translation, found in the A. V., the American revisers insist. The difference in the original depends only upon the question of a long or a short *o*. While the preponderance of manuscripts favors the R. V. "let us have peace," the change is inconsistent with the entire argument. This is no place for personal appeal and a practical application. Hence the greater number of expositors, including Philippi, Meyer, Weiss, Godet, etc., insist that, in this case, the testimony of the manuscripts is not determinative of the text. Internal evidence undoubtedly has its weight, especially when the variation of the text may be explained by the early liturgical use of the passage, in which the indicative might readily have given place to the subjunctive. The thought in this connection is not man's disposition towards God, but God's disposition towards man. God's anger is over, and He has towards the justified no thoughts but those of love. (Comp. Eph. 2 : 14, 16, 17.) No reference is made here to peace of conscience, which is designated "peace from God" (ch. 1 : 7), or "the peace of God" (Phil. 4 : 7), but never "peace with God." **Through our Lord Jesus Christ.** The whole argument is : God now is reconciled, not because of our works, but because of the righteousness of Christ, which through faith is ours.

The too much overlooked commentary of ANSELM brings out well the thought of the verse according to the contrast which Paul had in mind : "Justified by faith, let us have peace with God, which you do not have as long as you claim for yourselves a false justification, some by the law, others by the powers of the free will. It is as though he said : This dissent that you boast of your own merits, as though you were justified by yourselves, is against God. But justification which is of faith makes peace with God, because it expels the hostile presumption of human merits and humbly submits itself to God, acknowledging that we are saved solely by grace alone. We are justified by faith, and, nevertheless, gratuitously, because even faith is a gift of God."

Ver. 2. As ver. 1 treats of peace, this verse treats of hope. The grace or favor of God is far more than peace. It freely bestows all the blessings of everlasting life. It is here described as a state into which believers enter, and in which they stand; it is not therefore a merely transitory experience of God's love. **We have had our access.** Comp. this with the present tense of A. V. Emphasis is laid upon the fact that it is through Christ alone that the very first approaches of divine grace were enjoyed. The reference is to the past; when they became Christians, they had this access. The law did not begin the work, and Christ complete it; but before and without our fulfilment of the law, Christ brought this grace. The question has been earnestly discussed as to whether " access " be understood as transitive or intransitive. While the two meanings may be in a measure harmonized, the above explanation is given according to the view of those who take it transitively, as meaning " introduction " (THOLUCK, MEYER, WEISS, GIFFORD). The words are used in the classics " of the manœuvre by which an engine of war is brought close to the walls of a besieged city." But the intransitive meaning advocated here by PHILIPPI, CREMER, GODET, has equal weight of classical usage, where it is often applied to access to a king, and where such approach was made through a προσαγωγεύς, a word derived from this noun. **And we also rejoice.** Whether this reading or " let us rejoice " be correct, must be decided from the reading adopted in ver. 1. The American revisers and the

Authorized version prefer this reading. "And" connects "rejoice" with "we have peace with God" of preceding verse, the clause "by whom . . . stand" being parenthetical. Then the whole thought is justified by faith, with respect to the present we have peace, and with respect to the future "we **rejoice in hope.**" The word for "rejoice," or more properly "boast" or "glory." As BENGEL suggests the "glorying," excluded in 3 ; 27, is now admitted. There is no glorying by the Law, but there is by the Gospel. **The glory of God** is that which God has and believers are one day to share (John 17 : 22 ; 1 Thess. 2 : 12 ; Rev. 21 : 11 ; 2 Pet. 1 : 4 ; 1 John 3 : 2). (PHIL.)

Ver. 3. **And not only so,** i. e. we rejoice not only in hope, but even in the midst of tribulations. He writes from the consciousness of the seeming contradiction of this profusion of joy to a life full of toils and hardships, and especially of troubles that he is called upon to endure because of his testimony to the Gospel. But these, he answers, detract nothing from the blissfulness of his hope. While tribulations blight the hopes and end the boasting of the natural man, the Christion rejoices even though they fall heavily upon him (Matt. 5 : 10, 22 ; Acts 5 : 41 ; 1 Pet. 4 : 12 sq.). **In our tribulations.** In the preceding verse, he says "rejoice in hope." But in the Greek, different prepositions are used. We do not rejoice in tribulations, as we rejoice in (or as the Greek says "*upon*") hope. We rejoice upon hope, even in the midst of our tribulations, is the meaning. Hope underlies all the joy. Sustained, buoyed up by hope, we rejoice in our tribulations. **Patience.** The word here used is not the mere passive virtue of meek endurance, but the active one of perseverance under suffering and discouragement. In the natural man, tribulation, or even delay and opposition, produce impatience, and often a surrender of the good cause which they had espoused (Matt. 13:21).

Ver. 4. **Probation.** Lit. testing. (Comp. 2 Cor. 8:2.) We learn the preciousness and sustaining power of faith as we remain true to God amid our trials (1 Pet. 1:7). **Hope.** Because "as the Christian is tried, he is thrown forward for support upon the unseen future" (LID.). The reference must of course be to a still higher degree of hope. "Hope returns in a circle upon itself. Faith tested and approved, produces hope in enhancing and confirming it; for in the spiritual life, every enhancement and confirmation is at the same time a fresh act of production. Comp. John 2:11, where the faith of the disciples already existing is produced by the miracle of Jesus, in so far as by the miracle it is heightened and corroborated" (PHIL.). (See also James 1:12.)

Ver. 5. **And hope,** viz., the hope of God's glory, ver. 2, "the Christian hope which has its foundation in the consciousness of justification, and is, therefore, to be distinguished from all merely self-devised hope" (WEISS). **Putteth not to shame.** Does not disappoint. **The love of God.** Not our love to God, but God's love to us, as the succeeding verses clearly show. (Comp. 8:39; 2 Cor. 13:13.) Constantly experiencing new proof of this love, our hopes can never be disappointed. **Hath been shed abroad.** Poured out from heaven upon us, with the suggestion of the fulness and richness of the gift (Tit. 3:6). The result is the certainty of God's favor and everlasting life. With this love and certainty made ours, tribulations cannot be regarded evidences of God's wrath, but only of His love. **Through the Holy Ghost.** Hence it is not simply by an inference which we draw from the consideration of the facts of Redemption, that we are assured of this love, but by the agency of the Holy Ghost who accompanies our contemplation of the truth with His presence and working. (Comp. 8 : 16; 2 Cor. 1 : 22 ; Eph. 1 : 13.) **Which was given unto us.** Not an unnecessary clause, as might be inferred from its treatment by most expositors. The aorist participle refers to a gift made at a definite time in the past, viz. on the Day of Pentecost. The Holy Ghost given them abides in the Church forever (John 14 : 16). He is here on earth, attesting in men's hearts the wonders of God's love. They find their assurance of salvation not in ecstatic raptures, whereby they are raised to Heaven, but in the Word sealed by the Holy Spirit (10 : 6-8).

Ver. 6. **For.** A proof of this love of God is introduced. **While we were yet weak,** i. e. in our utter helplessness. **In due season.** At the proper time; either when our sins particularly needed it, or, more probably, as in 3 : 5, as appointed by God (Gal. 4 : 4). **For.** In behalf of. **The ungodly.** Those whose sins were particularly aggravating and deserving God's wrath. "Christ, the Son of God, was given, not for the righteousness of saints, but for the unrighteousness of sinners" (LUTHER). No contrast is intended here between different classes of men. The meaning is: "For all as ungodly," or "for us as ungodly." If we claim not to belong to the ungodly, we exclude ourselves from the benefits of Christ's death (Luke 5 : 31).

Ver. 7. **For scarcely.** A proof that God's love is without anything in human love with which to compare it. **A righteous man ... the good man,** The former is one careful to perform all duties required of him ; the latter delights to confer favors upon others. "The righteous man does what he ought, keeps within the limits assigned him, limits which he neither selfishly nor unselfishly transgresses, and gives to every one his due; the good man does as much as ever he can, and proves his moral quality by promoting the well-being of him with whom he has to do; accordingly here also the article is added to indicate a special relation between the persons spoken of" (CREMER). For the former it is scarcely conceivable that any one should be willing to die, although the possibility of death for the latter, under, however, very exceptional circumstances, is conceded.

Ver. 8. **But God commendeth**, i. e. proves **his own love**, as contrasted with the love that might lead to self-immolation for a good man. "The expression contrasts God's manner of loving with ours. God cannot look above Him to devote Himself, as we may, to a being of more worth than Himself. His love turns to that which is beneath Him (Is. 57:15)" (GOD.). **While we were yet sinners.** "Sinners" is in contrast with "the good man" of ver. 7. "Yet sinners" is in contrast with what by God's grace justified persons have now become. It means before we were forgiven or justified; before we had faith; before we had been introduced into the grace wherein we stand (ver. 2). **Christ**, viz. as God incarnate, seen and known of men. (See note on 1:7.) **Died for us.** No clearer statement than this could be given of the doctrine of a vicarious satisfaction for sin.

Ver. 9. **Much more.** An argument from the greater to the less. If God's love has been such as has been stated in ver. 8, there is nothing that we may not rely upon it to do; if, at such a sacrifice, He saved us from a greater ruin, we surely should not doubt His support and intervention in dangers far less imminent and circumstances far less extreme. The "much more" refers in thought to our assurance, not to salvation. **Being now justified by his blood.** In God's sight, therefore, no longer sinners, but cleansed from all sin (1 John 1:7), and having the righteousness of God (10:4). If God, then, so loved us when we were without righteousness, and were only sinners, much more may we be assured that the same love will complete our salvation, when we are freed from the guilt of sin, and are in God's sight the Holy One that Christ is. (Comp. 8:32.) "By His blood" recurs to redemption by Christ's death in vers. 6-8. **The wrath,** viz. that impending on the Day of Judgment (2:5, 6; 1 Thess. 1:10; 2 Thess. 1:8). **Through him,** i. e. through the efficacious work of the Risen and Ascended and Exalted Christ.

Ver. 10. **For if while we were enemies.** The same thought as in ver. 9. By its repetition in different words, it is interpreted. "Three stages are indicated, **enemies, reconciled, saved.** Divine love, which has brought us from the first to the second, will yet more certainly bring us from the second to the third" (GOD.). **Enemies.** Those beneath God's wrath; since the death of Christ overcame not man's enmity to God, but God's wrath toward man. **We were reconciled.** Rendered pleasing to God, a synonym for "justified" of the preceding verse. **By his life.** The death of Christ, our justification; the life of Christ, our sanctification and glorification (John 14:19; Gal. 1:20; ch. 8:34). If, when an enemy of God, He made provision for my forgiveness, surely, when forgiven, the power of Christ living in me will avail for the entire completion of the work of grace.

Ver. 11. **Not only so.** In concluding the paragraph, he sums up the argument, recurring in thought to vers. 1, 2. Not only are we justified; not only do we stand in a state of grace, **but we also rejoice** or "glory." **Through our Lord Jesus Christ . . . through whom,** i. e. Reconciled through Christ, we rejoice through Christ. In all the acts and states of the Christian life, the meditation of Christ is made prominent.

(*b*.) *The Relation to the Justified to Christ Illustrated by the Relation of the Race to Adam* (vers. 12–21).

A summary of the entire argument enforced by an exposition of the parallel between Adam and Christ. Death for the whole race came from the former. Salvation for the whole race is provided in the latter. The organic union between Adam and the race is replaced by an organic union between Christ and the justified.

12-21. Therefore, as through one man sin entered into the world, and death through sin; and so death passed unto all men, for that all sinned:— for until the law sin was in the world: but sin is not imputed when there is no law. Nevertheless death reigned from Adam until Moses, even over them that had not sinned after the likeness of Adam's transgression, who is a figure of him that was to come. But not as the trespass, so also *is* the free gift. For if by the trespass of the one the many died, much more did the grace of God, and the gift, by the grace of the one man, Jesus Christ, abound unto the many. And not as through one that sinned, *so* is the gift: for the judgement *came* of one unto condemnation, but the free gift *came* of many trespasses unto justification. For if, by the trespass of the one, death reigned through the one; much more shall they that receive the abundance of grace and of the gift of righteousness reign in life through the one, *even* Jesus Christ. So then as through one trespass *the judgement came* unto all men to condemnation; even so through one act of righteousness *the free gift came* unto all men to justification of life. For as through the one man's disobedience the many were made sinners, even so through the obedience of the one shall the many be made righteous. And the law came in beside, that the trespass might abound; but where sin abounded, grace did abound more exceedingly: that, as sin reigned in death, even so might grace reign through righteousness unto eternal life through Jesus Christ our Lord.

Ver. 12. **Therefore** directly connects with the two-fold mention of the mediation of Christ in ver. 11, and, as this concluded the argument begun in 1 : 17, it refers indirectly to the entire preceding discussion. **Through one man,** viz. Adam, ver. 14 (1 Cor. 15 : 22). No contradiction is thereby involved with 1 Tim. 2 : 14, where the diverse temptations of Adam and Eve are stated. Adam, not Eve, was the head of the race (1 Tim. 2 : 13 ; 1 Cor. 11 : 3). If, after Eve's fall, Adam had not fallen, the propagation of the race from another mother whom God could have provided might have followed. It was, therefore, not Eve's, but Adam's conduct under temptation that determined the future of the race. **Sin** cannot be limited to a sinful act, but includes everything in state or act, not conformable to God's will " (1 John 3 : 4).[1]

Entered into the world, viz. the world of men (John 3 : 16 ; Heb. 10 : 5 ; 1 Tim. 1 : 15), i. e. it began to exist and to do its work among men. **Death through sin.** Death exists in three forms, viz. *Spiritual death*, or the separation of the soul from God (1 John 3 : 14 ; Eph. 2 : 1), *physical or temporal death*, or the separation of the soul from the body, and *eternal death*, or the eternal separation of body and soul from God in the world to come (Rom. 1 32 ; 2 Cor. 2 : 16 ; Rev. 2 : 11). But all really constitute but one death at three different stages. All alike enter humanity with Adam's sin. Eternal death is the consummation of spiritual and temporal death. But as the form in which death forces itself upon our attention

[1] "ἡ ἁμαρτία denotes (1) *sin as an act*, which signification is the only one belonging to ἁμάρτημα, Mark 3 : 28 ; 4 : 12 ; Rom. 3 : 25 ; 1 Cor. 6 : 18. So Matt. 12 : 31 ; Acts 7 : 60 ; 2 Cor. 11 : 7 ; James 1 : 15. But without doubt, 'ἡ ἁμαρτία signifies also (2) *sin as a propensity*, an inner principle, a power ruling over man. So Rom. 7 : 8 ; 9 : 17, 23. Finally, 'ἡ ἁμαρτία denotes (3) *sin as the synthesis* of the propensity and the act. So John 1 : 29 ; Rom. 3 : 20 ; 4 : 8 ; 1 Cor. 15 : 56 ; 2 Cor. 5 : 21 : 2 Thess. 2 : 3, etc. In the present passage, then, we are naturally led to include under it everything which this expression can denote according to the teaching of Scripture, and of the Apostle. . . . The sinful condition of the world, with all sinful acts issuing therefrom, is contemplated as an abstract unity " (PHIL.).

most constantly is that of temporal death, the allusion here is particularly to that. The argument is to prove that the reign of sin is coextensive with that of death. Constant observation proving the universality of temporal death, the inference is that sin is equally universal. The significance of death here is entirely in its relations to man. Through sin, death entered humanity which had been created immortal. **And so,** i. e. because of this connection between sin and death. **Passed unto.** Lit. "went through," "pervaded" all humanity. **For that.** The rendering "in whom," "through whom," "on account of whom," while doctrinally correct, is exegetically inadmissible. The reference is causal: "Because all sinned." "The question is not about the particular sin of individuals; in Adam's sin, all have sinned, as all died in Christ's death for their salvation" (BENGEL). The tense in Greek signifies an act committed at a definite time in the past, and not one that continues to be repeated. Once for all, the sin was committed. Even those yet to be born sinned in Adam, because they were in Adam.

The sentence is complete. The construction, begun with the "as," is broken off by the current of thought being diverted into another channel. But the idea in the Apostle's mind when he begins finds ultimate expression in vers. 18, 19.

Ver. 13. **Until the law,** i. e. up to the time when the law was given, even before the law was. The law, as the next verse clearly shows, is the law of Moses. In this verse the word "law" is used in two different senses. Before, through Moses, that which is peculiarly known as "law" was given, sin existed. But if **sin is not imputed when there is no law,** and, nevertheless, the reign of death proves that sin has been imputed, it is manifest that another law existed prior to that of Moses—a law so universal that its range of obligation must be coextensive with the dominion of death. Death is the evidence of sin. But sin is the evidence of law. Death, therefore, is the proof of the existence of law. All die; all, therefore, have broken the law. This has occurred, as ver. 12 shows, by the one sin of Adam in his violation of the law given in Paradise. Another powerful blow to Jewish particularism, with its claims to special consideration because of its relations to Moses, as though there were no law but that of Moses.

Ver. 14. **Nevertheless death reigned.** " No sovereign has had so many subjects " (BENGEL). **Even over them that had not sinned after the likeness of Adam's transgression,** i. e. with the same conscious array of the will of an individual against a specific divine command. ("Who of us with his teeth destroyed the forbidden fruit in Paradise?"—ZWINGLI, *Ratio Fidei*). "It is not to be denied that death is the wages of every sin. But it is proved that the first cause of sin was the first sin. This has destroyed us, just as the robber who has plundered his victim, after having murdered him, is punished for the murder, and yet he did not rob with impunity, since the punishment of the robbery was merged in that of the murder; but, as compared with the punishment of murder, it was scarcely taken into account " (BENGEL). The sin of Adam is the root and source of all other sins. All others are simply the result and full fruitage of that one sin which all committed in Adam. **Who is a figure of him that was to come.** Thus the opinion that Adam is a type or figure of each of his descendants, as they successively came under temptation to sin, is repudiated. Adam's fall is not an object-lesson, showing how all others are led astray. But the figure or type in Adam is far different. Adam is the type of Christ. Nevertheless, we must be careful in tracing the real points of comparison; since every figure applies only in part. Adam and Christ are alike in their universal relation to humanity. The fall of Adam brought death to all men; the work of Christ provided life for all men (1 Cor. 15 : 22).

Ver. 15. **But not as the trespass.** The point of comparison having been stated, those of contrast are next given. The agreement lies in the relation which, in both cases, "the one" bears to "the many." But there is a marked difference in what is accomplished by the relation. The one brought death; the other brings life. For the death of the one, a remedy is provided, affording complete deliverance. The life of the other can be interrupted by no power sufficient to overcome it. **The gift by the grace of the one man,** etc., cannot be wrested from those who by faith cleave to Christ. All the power of God is exerted to counteract the work of the one, but not of the other. **The one man, Jesus Christ.** The human nature is emphasized; since apart from His humanity, Christ is not Mediator. (Comp. 1 Tim. 2 : 5.) Besides the unity, or, to use a modern term, the solidarity of humanity is found in its two heads, the unity of death in Adam, and of life in Christ. **Abound,** viz. given beyond all measure and comparison. **Unto the many.** "The many" in both clauses declares that the gift of God's grace is, in its provisions, coextensive with man's sin. That only the justified obtain and enjoy this gift, ver. 16, is not due to any defect in God's provision, but solely to the unwillingness of a portion of humanity to appropriate what God offers.

Ver. 16. **And not as through one that sinned,** viz. Adam. While the one sin of one man brought death to all, the many sins of the many men are forgiven, so far as God's provision and offer are concerned, by the free gift of God in Christ. In the preceding verses, the contrast had been between Adam and Christ. Here the contrast changes. It is between the one sin of Adam, and the many sins of his posterity; as they are viewed from the standpoint of the provisions of divine grace. " Far richer is grace than sin; since grace abolishes many sins, original and actual, and however atrocious. Since, then, grace is richer than sin, we ought to know that no sins are so atrocious as to be beyond the amplitude of divine grace " (MEL.).

Ver. 17. **For if by the trespass of the one.** This verse shows the extensive, as ver. 16 had shown the intensive, superiority of grace. It transfers the workings of divine grace to the eternal world by contrasting the reign of death over men, ver. 14, with the reign of believing and justified men over death. **They that receive the abundance.** In ver. 15, the abundance was shown to have been acquired once for all. The present participle here used indicates that men, one by one, through a period of time, successively avail themselves of "the abundance," or, in other words, **the gift of righteousness,** i. e. righteousness bestowed as a free gift. **Shall reign in life,** i. e. life eternal. (Comp. 8:17; 2 Tim. 2:12; Rev. 20:5.) The argument may be summarized: "Adam possessed a finite righteousness and a conditional promise of eternal life; Christ brought an infinite righteousness, and the free gift of eternal life itself. Adam committed *one* sin, and, in virtue of this, incurred the penalty of death; Christ atoned for *many* sins, and not merely abolished death, but planted life in its stead" (PHIL.). (Comp. 2 Tim. 1:10.)

Vers. 18, 19 summarize the argument begun in ver. 12. The italics in our translation obscure the contrast. The suppression of the verb makes a tabular exhibition the most literal translation.

Unto all men
- Through one trespass.=To condemnation.
- Through one act of righteousness.= To justification.

The **one act of righteousness** is defined in ver. 19 as **the obedience of Christ,** which is fully explained in Phil. 2 : 8. Our justification is found not simply in the sufferings of Christ, but in His active obedience to the law. The sufferings and death of Christ are not merely passive. Christ suffered by His own act of self-surrender (John 10 : 18). Our old theologians have, therefore, said : "The active obedience of Christ is passive ; and His passive obedience is active."

All men, co-extensive in both clauses, as in ver. 15. In both cases, the act is directed towards all. Through Christ's obedience, all have potential justification unto life. Even though some do not accept, justification is provided for all. Even CALVIN : " He makes grace common to all, because it is set forth, not because it is actually extended to all ; since Christ suffered for the sins of the whole world, and, by the kindness of God, He is offered to all without distinction ; and, nevertheless, not all apprehend Him." **Of life.** Justification brings life ; and that, too, eternal life. (Comp. 1 John 5 : 11, 12.)

Ver. 19. **Shall the many be made righteous.** This describes the appropriation of justification, as the preceding verse did its preparation. Justification was provided for man in the past ; but the appropriation of this obtained and provided justification is, for the great mass of the race, in the future. The reference is to the succession of believers individually realizing the gift of justification. **Be made** literally means " Be set down as," and, therefore, " be regarded," " be declared," " be treated as." No argument can be drawn from this passage to prove that justification is a process whereby man becomes inherently righteous. The Greek word, as well as the entire argument, is against such suggestion.

Ver. 20. **And the law.** The argument being concluded in ver. 19, it is applied to that of which the Jew boasted. As is usual in this Epistle, he advances in his mind an objection. If everything centre upon Adam and Christ, the thought is, What then is the significance of Moses? If the ruin, wrought by Adam, can be repaired only through Christ, what is the use of the Mosaic law? The answer is, that the law, coming to those ruined and enfeebled by sin, cannot repair the ruin and restore man to primitive righteousness. To righteous men, the law has other uses; but as long as men are unreconciled to God through Christ, its office and effect are only to increase the malady. Hence it **came in beside,** i. e. it has an entirely subordinate place, it is only an auxiliary to faith, since it prepares for faith, by imparting the knowledge of sin. **That the trespass might abound.** The word "trespass" being used in the preceding verses (vers. 15, 17, 18), with especial reference to the sin of Adam, must have the same meaning here. The effect of the law is only to multiply the trespass of Adam in his descendants. It offers the occasion for the inner corruption inherited from Adam to express itself in numberless forms. The state of sin comes forth into positive acts, as man is brought into contact with the law. The disease is brought to the surface. " Here, then, the subject is not the final purpose in view, but only the mediate purpose, because the chief point was to insist that the law was in no wise a medium of righteousness, but only a means of enhancing unrighteousness" (Phil.). The law brings the disease to that critical stage in which the remedy is sought and unerringly applied. "Things had to become worse to the human family, before they could become better" (Lid.). **Where sin abounded**, i. e. the locality or sphere where this occurred, primarily in Israel, and then, as the argument shows, throughout humanity. **Did abound more exceedingly.** The verb here used has the force of a superlative, while that of the preceding clause is comparative.

Ver. 21 makes what has preceded still more explicit. **Sin reigned in death.** Since, in death, the power of sin culminates. (Comp. 6:23.) The reign of death, ver. 14, is a reign of sin. **Grace reign . . . unto eternal life.** The progressive stages of the reign of grace are here suggested. Its goal is eternal life. But the reign of grace begins already here. This occurs, however, **through righteousness**, viz. the application of the righteousness of Christ. Grace being imparted thus through the righteousness of Christ, and this righteousness having as its ultimate end eternal life, this eternal life must, therefore, come, neither in whole, nor in part, through the law, but solely and entirely through Jesus Christ. Compare the close of the explanation of the Third Article of the Creed in Luther's Small Catechism.

This is, thus, a triumphant conclusion to the entire thought of the chapter. The reign of sin, coming from Adam, has been shown to be inferior to the reign of grace coming from Christ. The law, with its particularism, is far inferior to the Gospel with its universalism.

PART III.

THE UNIVERSALISM OF GRACE, NO APOLOGY FOR SIN (6 : 1—8 : 39).

SECTION I.—SALVATION BY GRACE AFFORDS THE HIGHEST INCENTIVE TO MORALITY (6 : 1-14.)

1-11. What shall we say then? Shall we continue in sin, that grace may abound? God forbid. We who died to sin, how shall we any longer live therein? Or are ye ignorant that all we who were baptized into Christ Jesus were baptized into his death? We were buried therefore with him through baptism into death : that like as Christ was raised from the dead through the glory of the Father, so we also might walk in newness of life. For if we have become united with *him* by the likeness of his death, we shall be also *by the likeness* of his resurrection ; knowing this, that our old man was crucified with *him*, that the body of sin might be done away, that so we should no longer be in bondage to sin ; for he that hath died is justified from sin. But if we died with Christ, we believe that we shall also live with him ; knowing that Christ being raised from the dead dieth no more ; death no more hath dominion over him. For the death that he died, he died unto sin once : but the life that he liveth, he liveth unto God. Even so reckon ye also yourselves to be dead unto sin, but alive unto God in Christ Jesus. Let not sin therefore reign in your mortal body, that ye should obey the lusts thereof : neither present your members unto sin *as* instruments of unrighteousness ; but present yourselves unto God, as alive from the dead, and your members *as* instruments of righteousness unto God. For sin shall not have dominion over you : for ye are not under law, but under grace.

Ver. 1. **What shall we say then? Shall we continue in sin,** etc. The law, it has just been proved, is entirely subordinate to the Gospel. The Apostle now anticipates the charge which always appears where the doctrine of justification by faith alone is taught, that this doctrine encourages indifference with respect to the duties assigned us by the law. The abundance of offences, we have just been told (5 : 20), only increases the reign of grace. If this be so, then the thought is natural that one may as well sin for the sake of advancing the glory of God. The Apostle next shows how entirely contradictory such course would be to the very nature of the Christian life.

Ver. 2. **God forbid.** (Comp. note on 2 : 4.) **We who died to sin.** The reference in the next verse to Christ's death, and the repetition of "died unto sin" in ver. 10, fix the meaning as that of participation in Christ's death. Not merely then : "We who have been liberated from sin," or "We in whom the life-communion with sin has been destroyed," but rather : "We, who on the Cross of Christ experienced the full bitterness and entire penalty of sin, and who were thus raised above and beyond it." The tense in the Greek shows that the allusion is to a specific point of past time. This time is that of regeneration and justification, which in ver. 3 is connected with baptism. **How shall we any longer live?** An exclamation of surprise, that they who have been redeemed, and have entered into the enjoyment of these blessings of redemption, should in any way be influenced by the power from which they have been redeemed! **Therein,** i. e. in sin, as the element of our life. It is one thing, because of the weakness of the flesh, and against the prevailing temper of the life, to sin; it is another, to live in sin. Life in sin refers to the condition of the heart and mind and will, determining the entire conduct, so that every act of those living such life is only sin. Life in sin is absolutely incompatible with faith in Christ. Man cannot at the same time be dead to sin and live in sin. If he live in sin, the benefits of Christ's death are not appropriated, and are, therefore, to him of no avail.

Ver. 3. This he supports by an appeal to Christians because of their baptism. **We who were baptised into Christ Jesus.** Baptism brings us into life-communion with Christ; it spiritually incorporates us with Him, so that thenceforth we are His members. Brought thus into communion with His life, we also share in all the power and efficacy of His death, the culmination and goal of His redemptive work. **Were baptised into his death.** The full force of this is explained by vers. 9, 10. All that Christ's death has purchased, all that His life has merited, become the property of those who live in the grace of their baptism. "It is just as if, at that moment, Christ suffered, died and were buried for such a man, and as if such a man, suffered, died and were buried with Christ" (BENGEL). On the relation between baptism and the preached word, PHIL.: "The word that goes before baptism offers to all collectively the gracious gifts which baptism conveys to the particular definite individual. Faith before baptism accepts for itself also the gift promised in the Word to all; faith, in and after baptism, accepts the blessing given by God Himself to it specially."

Ver. 4. **We were buried, therefore, with him through baptism and death.** Burial is the surest proof of death. The thought is: we became as truly partakers of His death, as though we had been buried with Him in the same tomb. As in baptism by immersion the person was buried beneath the water, so, by the grace of the Holy Spirit working in baptism, he was made truly participant of all Christ's sufferings, dying with Christ, buried with Christ, and thus with Christ dead to all the temptations of the world, the flesh and Satan, and superior to all the penalties of the violated law. As the eye and ear of the dead are insensible to the sights and sounds of the world about them, so, in so far as the blessings of baptism have been appropriated by the baptized person, and he lives in the grace of his baptism, is he dead to sin and all its allurements. **As Christ was raised from the dead.** Even the death of Christ had the resurrection in view as its goal. (Comp. 4 : 25.) So also the work of grace does not end with the believer's death to sin; but this death to sin looks forward to a higher, holier and brighter life. The forgiveness of sins and the favor of God, all that is implied in justification, have the Christian's complete sanctification as their crown and goal. **Through the glory of the Father.** The glory of God is the sum of the perfections of God, "the aggregate of all His attributes according to their undivided, yet revealed fulness" (UMBREIT), "the fulness of all that is good in God, all His redeeming attributes" (CREMER). Here "the collective perfections of the Father, chiefly His omnipotence (1 Cor. 6 : 14; 2 Cor. 13 : 4; Eph. 1 : 19), raised Jesus from the dead" (LID.). (Comp note on 4 : 21.) The Father is especially mentioned, not to exclude the Son —since He arose also in His own power (John 10 : 18)— but because the Father suggests at once the secret, invisible fulness of the Godhead, and the Son, the manifestation, in time, of God's hitherto hidden perfections. (Comp. John 1 : 18.) So also He comes to judge in the glory of the Father (Matt. 16 : 27; Mark 8 : 38; Luke 9 : 26). **In newness of life,** i. e. "a new kind of life." As our Lord assumed a new mode of life after His resurrection, so, with regeneration, believers enter into a new mode of life, and exercise the powers of this new mode of life in their daily conduct.

Ver. 5. **United with him by the likeness.** The marginal reading is preferable: "United with the likeness."

The literal rendering is "grown together to," "become incorporate with," "vitally connected with; not implanting, but coalescence is the idea" (MOULE). **The likeness of his death** is baptism; the **likeness of his resurrection** is the spiritual life of believers, and also their bodily life, so far as pervaded by the resurrection life of Christ. Incorporation with Christ means, first, death with Christ, and, then, participation in the fulness of His life. The practical reference here necessarily emphasizes the new spiritual life that pervades believers, as manifested in the daily renewal; but it is still more comprehensive, since it looks forward also to the resurrection-life of the regenerate man.

Ver. 6. **Knowing this,** i. e. "As those who know." **Our old man.** "Man, as he is from Adam, sinful, guilty, fallen from God, judged by God, without spiritual life, brought under the dominion of the flesh." (Comp. Eph. 4 : 22; Col. 3 : 9.) It is called "old" from the standpoint of one who has been regenerated and is experiencing the renewal of the spirit (2 Cor: 5 : 17). **Was crucified.** Christ assumed our sin. When He was crucified, our sin, or our old sinful self, was crucified with Christ. " But what happened on the cross for the whole world is personally applied through baptism (vers. 3, 4) to every one baptized, in order that he may appropriate it by faith and be saved" (BESSER). "If St. Paul's language seems exaggerated, it is because we who were baptized as unconscious infants can hardly realize what Baptism was to the adult believer in the Apostolic age" (GIF.). But while our sin or sinful self was thus crucified on the cross of Christ, and, in our baptism, this crucifixion was applied to us, nevertheless sin is not entirely destroyed. The old Adam still lives, but in decrepitude and daily process of death. **Body of sin.** Another vivid figure. **All sins proceeding from the old man are regarded as constituting an organized body with various members,** as in Col. 3 : 5. The collective mass of sins of various kinds constitutes the one body. The use of " body " in its literal sense in ver. 12 presents no real difficulty to this interpretation. Some regard this as referring to the body as the chief source and seat of sin ; but this view conflicts with scripture, which traces sin to the corrupt heart, i. e. the perverted spiritual nature of man. The figure here is similar to that by which man's sinful nature is termed flesh (John 3 : 6 ; Rom. 7 : 5 sqq.). Thus the doctrine is forcibly taught that redemption and justification have as one of their ends the believer's complete sanctification. **Done away.** The word thus rendered is used by St. Paul twenty-five times. It means " rendered powerless," " made of none effect " (ch. 3 : 3, 31), but not absolutely annihilated. **No longer be in bondage to sin.** Once captives, we were completely under its power. But our master, " our old man," has been crucified and is paralyzed. We have escaped. The body of sin has been deprived of its power. As freemen, we have been raised to a higher sphere, and, certainly, will not think of returning to our former bondage.

Ver. 7. The argument continues to explain how every claim that sin can make upon its former subjects who have died with Christ has been met. Dying with Christ, the wages of sin, death (ver. 23), have been fully paid by them. In His death, therefore, they are **justified from sin,** i. e. freed from the guilt and punishment of sin ; and, in this freedom from guilt and punishment, they have also attained freedom from the dominion of sin. "As respects the past, he is justified from the guilt of sin ; as respects the future, from its dominion" (BENGEL).

Ver. 8. **If we died with him,** i. e. on the cross and in

our baptism (see note on ver. 6), **we shall also live with him.** This is not to be limited to everlasting life. In fact, that is not what is chiefly meant. The entire context shows that the reference here is mainly to the Christian life on earth, the life of Christ in the believer (Gal. 2 : 20), and the life of the believer in Christ (Col. 3 : 3. Comp. John 4 : 4). Partaker of Christ's death, he also shares in all the energy and activity and purity of Christ's resurrection-life.

Ver. 9. **Knowing that,** i. e. because we know. The ground of our confidence that we shall live with Christ is our knowledge that, by His resurrection, Christ entered into a sphere forever beyond the reach of death. **Dieth no more.** The resurrection-life of Christ was not a temporary matter, but a permanent condition. He rose from the dead, never again, like Lazarus or the young man at Nain, to subject Himself to the power of death, but to be forever its Master. The inference is that he who has risen with Christ, as long as he shares in the same death and resurrection, is forever the master of death and Hell and sin and all their powers. **No more hath dominion,** i. e. rules or lords it over him no longer. Absolutely speaking, death never had dominion over Him (John 10 : 17, 18 ; Acts 2 : 24). He became subject to death in the humiliation whereby He became obedient to the law (Phil. 2 : 8). But with this state of humiliation over, He remains forever the conqueror and lord of death.

Ver. 10. **The death** (lit. "that which") **he died, he died unto sin.** This means that every claim that could be made by sin has been satisfied. Sin demanded death ; death was endured. All the punishments of sin are included in the one word "death." All these penalties having been borne, He is now dead to sin forever. Nothing more can be exacted. In dying **"once for all"** (comp.

Heb. 7:27; 9:12; 10:10; 1 Pet. 3:18) on account of sin, He died forever to sin. If, then, we have died with Christ (ver. 8), we have also, in Christ's death, satisfied all the demands of the law, and are forever raised above all penalties that sin may threaten. **The life that he liveth**, then, is no longer occupied with any conflict with sin and death. The humiliation has been succeeded by the exaltation to God's Right Hand, where, in His humanity, He enjoys the presence of the Father, as it was not enjoyed while He abode visibly among men (John 17:5; Acts 7:55). The service of God through death and as the bearer of sin, has been succeeded by what is God's service in its higher form, viz. eternal life-communion with the Father, uninterrupted and unobscured by any claim that sin could make upon Him, as man's surety.

Ver. 11. **Even so reckon ye also yourselves**, etc. This is the natural inference from vers. 8-10. Made partakers of Christ, in Him we have died to sin; in Him, even though the complete fulfilment of the promise is yet in the future, we have been quickened to the higher life in the Father, in which Christ lives at the Right Hand of God. The word "reckon" urges believers to recall and acknowledge what, by God's grace, they have become.

Ver. 12. **Let not sin, therefore, reign.** We cannot altogether banish or expel sin, for it remains with us and in us as long as we live, but we can prevent it from reigning, or getting the upper hand. **In your mortal body.** "Body" cannot be regarded otherwise than in the literal sense. It is mentioned not because it is, above the soul, the seat of sin, but since bodily sins are the first to be noticed, and, in them, sin assumes its most concrete and vivid form. He who begins the struggle against bodily sins soon finds that their roots lie much deeper than the body. It is the perversion of the bodily appetites by an unholy will and the lack of restraint upon them by a holy will, that occasion bodily sins. This body is called "mortal," since its destruction by sin is inevitable. Thus far, but no farther, can sin still exert its power on him who lives in life-communion with Christ. By resisting sin, the soul rises victorious above the reign of death, even though, in the conflict, it loses its body. The child of God should, therefore, rule and subdue that power which cannot, except by his own consent, destroy his soul. **Lusts thereof** refers to the perversion of the bodily appetites caused by indwelling sin. As the suggestions of evil arise, they must be repelled and suppressed. A large part of the Christian warfare consists in this internal struggle.

Ver. 13. **Present**, i. e. place at the disposal of. **Members** are the various bodily organs. (Comp. ch. 3 : 13–15.) **Instruments.** Better as in margin: "Weapons." Sin is regarded as a ruler engaged in warfare, using as weapons for his unrighteous deeds the organs of man's body, now the eye, now the ear, and then the hand or the foot, etc. The contrast is more far-reaching. **Present yourselves**, i. e. your entire personality with all its powers and gifts and functions. **Alive from the dead**, viz. because of the new spiritual life, resulting from union and life-communion with Christ, His resurrection-life. (Comp. Rom. 8: 10, 11.) **Your members.** Every bodily organ and endowment are intended for the service of God.

Ver. 14. The possibility of such service is here shown to rest upon the sustaining and invigorating and ever efficient power of divine grace. **Sin shall not have dominion over you**, viz. as long as this union and life-communion with Christ continue (John 10 : 28). **Under law.** (Comp. Gal. 4 : 21.) As long as one is under law, successful resistance to sin and successful efforts to do God's will are impossible. "Conscience, fettered and terrified by the law, hates the Judge; conscience, set free through grace, loves the Reconciler" (PHIL.). Only as we receive Christ and the Holy Spirit is it that any inner and spiritual obedience to the law becomes possible. This is what is meant by being **under grace.** Comp. MELANCHTHON in *Apology*, chapter " Of LOVE and the Fulfilling of the Law," and the *Formula of Concord*, " Of the Third Use of the Law." See also LUTHER, Introduction to Romans. " By 'being without law,' he does not mean that we should have no law or that every one should do as he pleases, but ' to be under the law ' is when we are occupied with the works of the law without grace. But grace makes us love the law; so that there is no more sin present, and the law is no more against us, but is at one with us."

SECTION II.—RELATION OF SALVATION BY GRACE TO THE LIFE OF BELIEVERS ILLUSTRATED (6: 15—7 : 6).

(*a.*) *From Slavery* (6 : 15-23).

15-23. What then? shall we sin, because we are not under law, but under grace? God forbid. Know we not, that to whom ye present yourselves *as* servants unto obedience, his servants ye are whom ye obey; whether of sin unto death, or of obedience unto righteousness? But thanks be to God, that, whereas ye were servants of sin, ye became obedient from the heart to that form of teaching whereunto ye were delivered; and being made free from sin, ye became servants of righteousness. I speak after the manner of men because of the infirmity of your flesh: for as ye presented your members *as* servants to uncleanness and to iniquity unto iniquity, even so now present your members *as* servants to righteousness unto sanctification. For when ye were servants of sin, ye were free in regard of righteousness. What fruit then had ye at that time in the things whereof ye are now ashamed? for the end of those things is death. But now being made free from sin, and become servants to God, ye have your fruit unto sanctification, and the end eternal life. For the wages of sin is death; but the free gift of God is eternal life in Christ Jesus our Lord.

Ver. 15. What then? shall we sin, etc. The transfer of believers from the sphere of the law to that of grace, having been shown to be the very ground upon which they are to successfully resist sin, the Apostle recurs to the very common and superficial objection, noted in 6:1, which he has now completely overthrown, that the preaching of grace encourages sin. The assumption of these objectors is directly contrary to what has just been taught.

Ver. 16. To whom ye present yourselves as servants, his servants ye are. This verse explains the connection between acts and states of servitude. The Kingdom of God and that of Satan are exclusive and antagonistic. A state of indifference and neutrality, with occasional acts of compliance, now to the one side, and then to the other, for the purpose of maintaining and declaring independence, is, therefore, impossible. No acts of liberty in human life are isolated; they determine the future. He who deliberately does sin a service, loses his freedom and becomes the slave of sin. He who obeys God, acknowledges, in his very act of obedience, God's claims, and subjects himself to God's will. All must be **servants whether of sin or of obedience, unto death,** i. e. eternal death, as the goal of the service of sin. **Obedience** refers, as in Acts 1:5 and 16:26, to the "obedience of faith." "It is faith in the Gospel which the Apostle here designates by the word 'obedience.'... Every time the Gospel is preached to the sinner, he is challenged to decide between the obedience of faith or the carnal independence of sin" (GOD.). **Righteousness** refers here to inherent righteousness, moral purity, the fruits of the Spirit, as the result of justifying faith and the indwelling of Christ. Eternal life and eternal holiness are inseparable. The inference is that the reign of grace is a reign of holiness.

Ver. 17. **Thanks be to God that whereas,** etc. The great change that has occurred in the Roman Christians as the consequence of their acceptance of the doctrine of grace, calls forth the Apostle's expression of thanksgiving. **Ye became obedient** expresses not simply an act, but a habit of obedience. **From the heart.** As in Matt. 18 : 35, "not by constraint." "The good are good from the heart, and good voluntarily" (BENGEL) (Heb. 8 : 10). "From the heart," therefore, as the characteristic of obedience under grace, is opposed both to legal obedience, and also to the obedience offered sin by a bad conscience and an enslaved will. **That form of teaching,** viz. the Gospel in its strictest sense, the doctrine of a Crucified, Risen, Ascended Saviour, and the free forgiveness of sins, as the fruit of His meritorious work for all who believe. **Whereunto ye were delivered,** viz. by the grace of God. They could not have obeyed the Gospel but for the regenerating grace which attended and wrought through the word as preached. The power to believe must first be wrought by God, or man is helpless. "Elsewhere the Scriptures speak of the doctrine as given to us (2 Peter 2 : 21; Jude 3). Paul changes this into another expression, in order to proclaim the glory of the divine efficacy of the Gospel" (BESSER).

Ver. 18. **Being made free,** viz. from slavery to sin. **Ye became servants of righteousness.** Literally: "Ye were enslaved to righteousness." The Christian is not without law; but his law is the law of grace. He obeys, not from an external, yet none the less truly and completely from an inner constraint, i. e. from the necessities of a nature in which the ever living, ever active Spirit of God dwells and works. So far as the work of grace has taken possession of his heart, he cannot sin (1 John 3 : 9). A familiar Collect (Common Service, Gen. Coll. 87) well expresses this thought : " Whose service is perfect freedom " ; the Latin still more emphatically : *Cui servire est regnare*. The highest degree of freedom is that of such elevation above sin and temptation, that, like God and the holy angels, there is no longer any danger of a fall. Not to serve righteousness is to lose freedom.

Ver. 19 begins with an apology for using such a term as " servant " or " slave," to describe the relation of a Christian to his Master. The figure, he feels, introduces elements into the conception of this service, that should be separated from it. The service is inner, joyous, free ; that of the slave is external, forced, mechanical,—the hands act, while the heart rebels. He uses this figure because there is no better at hand. Like every true teacher, he accommodates himself to **the infirmity of your flesh.** What he means by the figure is to insist that they yield to God a service no less devoted than that which they have heretofore given to sin. **Uncleanness.** Moral defilement, a wrong which man commits against himself. **Iniquity.** Lit. " lawlessness," against God. **Unto iniquity** designates degrees. **Unto sanctification.** The reference is not to the gradual process of purification from sin, but to the goal of perfect and complete holiness.

Ver. 20 contains a slight irony. The natural man boasts much of his freedom. The Apostle shows the kind of freedom the natural man has to boast of, viz. freedom **in regard to righteousness,** while actually a slave of sin !

Ver. 21, 22, contrast the results of the service of sin with those of the service of righteousness. LUTHER, MELANCHTHON, PHILIPPI, GODET, TISCHENDORF, etc., divide the sentence in ver. 21 somewhat differently, viz. **What**

fruit had ye then? Was it in those things whereof ye are now ashamed? That is, they had nothing to show for all the efforts of their past lives, except those things of which they are now ashamed. The answer to the question as punctuated by W. H. and by both A. V. and R. V. is "Nothing whatever." This is implied also in Luther's interpretation. **The end,** as in ver. 18, the "goal" or "final result." In such course of life everything tends towards death. The immediate effect of these things is shame; their ultimate end, eternal death. On the other hand, the service of righteousness has, as its more immediate effect, sanctification, and, as its final goal, eternal life. (Comp. ver. 19.)

Ver. 23. Two masters ask our service, sin and God. Only one, i. e. sin, pays **wages.** In but one sphere can man earn or merit anything, and that is in the service of sin. But its wages is **death.** If merit determine our future, we can secure it only by a life of sin, with perdition as its reward. God pays no wages. His servants receive the results of their service, not for merit, but only as a **free gift.** Their service and obedience of God come not from their own powers, but are themselves fruits of the Holy Spirit dwelling in justified man.

"Thus the unseparable connection of justification and sanctification, which forms the basis and fundamental view of this chapter, reappears at its end. He that is justified by faith in Christ has eternal life as God's gracious gift; and inasmuch as sanctification is simply the subjective development of the objective gift of justification, **eternal life** remains even for the sanctified what it was at first, **the free gift of God,** whose possession he does not first earn by means of sanctification, but only awaits, and, when he has attained the end of sanctification, actually receives" (PHIL.).

(b.) *Illustration from Marriage* (7 : 1–6).

The inconsistency of a life of sin by a justified person is illustrated by the marriage relation.

1–6. Or are ye ignorant, brethren (for I speak to men that know the law), how that the law hath dominion over a man for so long time as he liveth? For the woman that hath a husband is bound by law to the husband while he liveth; but if the husband die, she is discharged from the law of the husband. So then if, while the husband liveth, she be joined to another man, she shall be called an adulteress: but if the husband die, she is free from the law, so that she is no adulteress, though she be joined to another man. Wherefore, my brethren, ye also were made dead to the law through the body of Christ; that ye should be joined to another. *even* to him who was raised from the dead, that we might bring forth fruit unto God. For when we were in the flesh, the sinful passions, which were through the law, wrought in our members to bring forth fruit unto death. But now we have been discharged from the law, having died to that wherein we were holden; so that we serve in newness of the spirit, and not in oldness of the letter.

Ver. 1. **I speak to men that know the law.** This is not addressed exclusively to Jews in the Roman Church, but, as the original shows, to all to whom he writes the epistle. In the assemblies of the early Christians, Gentiles as well as Jews, the law was read. As in 6 : 14, the reference is to the Mosaic **law**. **Hath dominion over,** i. e. the claims of the law can be cancelled only by death. **Over a man,** i. e. every member of the human family.

Ver. 2. **For the woman that hath an husband.** The general principle having been stated, it is applied to a particular sphere. The marriage relation is permanent. Its obligations can be annulled only by death. Divorce is not here mentioned; since it is lawful only where a moral separation has already occurred by a criminal act of the other party—in this case, the husband, i. e. when he has already died to her as a husband. **She is discharged**

from the law, etc. In the death of her husband, she dies as a wife, the marriage is dissolved and she is free from all the obligations which her entrance into that estate imposed.

Ver. 3 simply carries out the thought of ver. 2. All marriage obligations being cancelled by the death of the other party to the contrast, the survivor is perfectly free to remarry. This second marriage is as pure and holy as if it were the first.

Ver. 4. **Wherefore, my brethren.** Now comes the application of the figure. The soul of the believer is compared to a woman living in a second marriage after the death of her first husband. The first husband was the law; the second is Christ. As the wife has died as a wife in the death of her husband, so the believer has died to the law in the death of Christ. The law has died to him, since, in the death of Christ, all the demands of the law have been satisfied (Col. 2 : 14). The death that Christ died to sin (6 : 10) was also a death to the law, since it was death to the law because of sin. This death was once for all. Every claim of the law was satisfied; there was no further obligation for whose discharge it could ask. By baptism (6 : 4) the Christian is brought into communion with this death. The death of Christ is made his death. Hence the significance of the passive construction: **Ye were made dead to the law.** The soul has lost its first husband; and all claims arising from that alliance are at an end. "The law had power over every man so long as it was alive; and its power went to the infliction of a grievous curse upon all, for all had broken it. But after it got its death-blow on the cross, this power ceased; and we became free from it—just as the woman is free from all the terror and all the tyranny of that deceased husband, who was wont to lord it, and, perhaps with justice, too, most oppressively over her. Thus ought we to hold ourselves as free from the whole might and meaning of that law, which has now spent its whole force, as an executioner, on that body by which the whole chastisement of our peace has been borne. When a sense of the law brings remorse or fearfulness into your heart, transfer your thoughts from it as now dead to Christ as your now living husband" (CHALMERS). Nowhere is the doctrine of the vicarious satisfaction of Christ more forcibly stated. **That ye should be joined unto another.** The soul now married to Christ heeds only His claims, and shares in no other life than His resurrection-life. **Bring forth fruit.** The works of the new obedience, the fruits of the Spirit (Gal. 5 : 22), are the issue of this marriage. The Christian's freedom from the constraint of the law does not elevate him above the obligation to produce the very works that the law requires. The difference is that now they are produced from an inner necessity of his nature ; now they proceed from love to Christ and the believer's union with Christ and the presence of the Holy Spirit. **Unto God.** Such fruit as pleases God.

Ver. 5. **When we were in the flesh.** This does not refer, as in Gal. 2 : 20, to the life of believers in the body, but, as in Rom. 8 : 8, 9, to the unregenerate nature (John 3 : 6). It is assumed that all believers were once "in the flesh." **The sinful passions.** Lit. "passions of sins," i. e. passions which lead to sinful actions. **Which were through the law.** They were excited to activity, but were not produced by the law. The dominant evil desire is roused to action by the commands and prohibitions of the law. (Comp. vers. 7, 8.) **Wrought,** i. e. were active. **In our members,** every sinful desire having its particular bodily organ through which to work. **Unto death.** Life in the flesh tends only to death. It is not improved by hearing the law, or by its endeavors to fulfil the law. As long as regeneration is absent, the preaching of the law renders matters only worse. The argument shows that the proposed way of salvation through the law has but one end, viz. death.

Ver. 6. **But now we have been discharged from the law.** This is explained by ver. 4. **So that we serve.** Freed from the law, we no less serve, but rather it is only now that we truly serve God. **In newness of spirit.** Impelled by a life-principle, previously absent, and of a nature entirely different from what had previously controlled man; for newness here means "of a new kind." More is meant than "a harmony between the inclinations and moral obligation"; for the discharge of duty has become the chief joy of the heart. What to the carnal man was **letter** is to the regenerate and spiritual man **spirit.** "The letter is the law considered not in itself, since, thus considered, it is spiritual and living (ver. 14; Acts 7 : 38), but in respect to the sinner, to whom it cannot give spirit and life, but leaves him to death, although he may meanwhile aim to do what the letter and its sound may command; so that the appearance and the name may remain, just as a dead hand is still a hand" (BENGEL). Applying this to the marriage illustration, the obedience of the letter is that of a slave who, with fear and aversion, obeys externally the master who has never won her love; the obedience of the spirit is that of the bride who, rejoicing in the love of her husband, makes his interests her first thought, and the furtherance of them the chief of all her pleasures.

SECTION III.—POWERLESSNESS OF THE LAW, BOTH
BEFORE AND AFTER JUSTIFICATION, TO SANCTIFY
(7 : 7–23).

This is intended to enforce the more remote argument, viz. that it is only through the Gospel with its doctrine of salvation by grace alone, that the holy life, which the advocates of Judaism so extol, is possible. In Chapter III. St Paul had taught that the law could not justify; here he teaches that it is just as powerless to sanctify. In proving that its office is not to sanctify, he explains what is its true function, viz., to detect and condemn sin.

(*a.*) *The Law and the Unregenerate* (vers. 7–13).

7–13. What shall we say then? Is the law sin? God forbid. Howbeit, I had not known sin, except through the law: for I had not known coveting, except the law had said, Though shalt not covet: but sin, finding occasion, wrought in me through the commandment all manner of coveting: for apart from the law sin *is* dead. And I was alive apart from the law once; but when the commandment came, sin revived, and I died; and the commandment, which *was* unto life, this I found *to be* unto death; for sin, finding occasion, through the commandment beguiled me, and through it slew me. So that the law is holy, and the commandment holy, and righteous, and good. Did then that which is good become death unto me? God forbid. But sin, that it might be shewn to be sin, by working death to me through that which is good;—that through the commandment sin might become exceeding sinful.

Ver. 7. **What shall we say then? Is the law sin?** The state of sin having been shown to be co-extensive with that of the law, the Apostle shows next, that this is entirely accidental, and does not occur on account of any identity between the law and sin. It is a consequence of man's fallen estate and of the corruption that prevents him from having any other than a perverted and vitiated relation to the law. The experience of every individual since Adam is that sin exists before the law approaches him. But **I had not known sin,** i. e. recognized it as sin. The unregenerate man, without the law, follows the impulses of his corrupt nature unrestrained except in so far as the weak voice of conscience at times may be heard. With the revelation of the law, conscience is quickened into activity and is supernaturally enlightened; then he perceives the wrong relations in which he stands to God. He had coveted habitually in obedience to the suggestions of the flesh. But it is only when the law comes to him and declares authoritatively "Thou shalt not covet" that he recognizes the impulse as coveting. He learns to know it by contrast. He recognizes the presence of a higher will opposing the hitherto uninterrupted sinful career of his life.

Ver. 8. But to this higher will the unregenerate man refuses to submit. He regards the interposition of this will as an entirely unwarrantable intrusion. Glorying in his imagined independence, he seeks to display it by acts of hostility to the law. **Sin, finding occasion,** i. e. Original sin, or the corruption of his nature, roused to sinful activity, when interrupted by the voice of the law, immediately covets all that it knows the law forbids. Wherever the law interposes a "shalt not," it opposes a "shalt." An illustration is given by AUGUSTINE in his *Confessions* of a sin of his boyhood: "The theft which I loved for the theft's sake. My pleasure was not in the pears; it was in the offence itself." Compare Ovid: *Nitimur in vetitum semper cupimusque negata* ("We ever strive for what is forbidden, and long for objects that are denied us"). The essence of every sin lies in the desire to be otherwise than God wants us to be. **Coveting** is sin in motion towards its end. **Apart from the law, sin**

is dead, i. e. is dormant or latent. "It flows along smoothly, until it is met by an impeding barrier, over which it leaps with tumultuous violence. Comp. 1 Cor. 15 : 56" (PHIL.).

Ver. 9. **I was alive.** Reference is made to the personal experience of the Apostle as the type of a general experience. **Alive** must be interpreted in connection with the word **dead** in ver. 8. Sin is there said to be dead, where it is only latent; so the Apostle was alive, when he lived in a state of unconsciousness as to the requirements and disclosures of the law. Note the contrast: When sin is dead, he is alive; when sin is alive, he is dead. A difficulty occurs in determining the time to which he refers. When was he **apart from the law?** Some understand him as recalling the life of childhood, when the meaning of the law is not yet recognized. Others refer it to the state of security in which he lived while occupied with merely external obedience to the law, and a revelation of its inner, spiritual nature was made, in the light of which it could readily appear as though he had been before without the law—so much more intense and searching was its light. Still others refer it to the experience frequently repeated in the lives of all children of God; for as spiritual sight increases, the demands of the law are constantly found to be more comprehensive, and, with every new discovery, there is a repetition of this experience. The meaning here is that once he had so inadequate a conception of what the law means and commands, that he was in no way conscious of its constraint. **When the commandment, came,** viz. "Thou shalt not covet," ver. 7. **Sin revived,** i. e. was excited to conscious activity. **I died** describes the sense of guilt and moral impotence that followed this discovery.

Ver. 10. **Unto life ... unto death.** The means given to lead to life becomes a means to bring death. Human corruption diverts the law from its proper sphere to a service foreign to that for which it was designed. **I found to be,** viz. when its true meaning became at last known. The very commandments on the observance of which I relied for salvation, I at last learned, in my sinful condition, could only condemn me.

Ver. 11. (Comp. ver. 8.) **Sin,** and, therefore, not the law, is the real cause of death. The law is only its **occasion,** as sin uses the law to induce men to disobey. The very barrier which the law erects against transgression is made the occasion of suggesting its commission. **Beguiled me.** An allusion to the temptation in Paradise (Gen. 3 : 1, 4, 5, 15 ; 1 Tim. 2 : 14).

Ver. 12. **Law** refers to the entire Mosaic code: **commandment** to each particular precept, and, in this case, that mentioned in ver. 7, as illustrating all. **Holy,** as the revelation of a holy God, manifesting His holy nature and will; **just,** as the correct standard of right; **good,** as an infallible exhibition of the life that pleases God and attains the highest happiness. He calls the law and its precepts *holy*, with respect to the efficient and material cause, because it has a holy author, and is itself destitute of every imperfection or impurity; he calls it *just*, with respect to its formal cause, because it is the norm of justice; he calls it *good*, with respect to its final cause, because it promises bodily and spiritual good to those who obey" (BALD.). "Luther once said that no apostle gave such hateful and reproachful names to the law, as did Paul; e. g. 'the strength of sin,' 'bringing forth fruit unto death,' 'the dead letter,' 'preaching of condemnation,' 'yoke of bondage,' 'weak and beggarly elements.' But these names are derived from the reckoning of perverted persons who abuse the law. But in this verse we hear what the law is, according to its glorious nature" (BESSER).

Ver. 13. Did then that which is good become death unto me? The law no more brings death than it brings sin. The real nature of sin becomes apparent in its use of what is good to work evil. It is as though a Bible or a communion vessel were used by a murderer to deal a fatal blow. The revelation of the character and will of the Holiest, made to impart holiness to His creatures, is used to increase their sin and condemnation. The holier the objects thus perverted, the greater the guilt and hatefulness of the subject perverting it. **Sin that it might be shown to be sin,** i. e. that its true character might be revealed, in all its deceitfulness, and enormity and atrocity and heinousness. **That sin might become exceeding sinful.** This occurs when the depravity of our nature comes forth into acts of positive transgression. The desire for what is contrary to God's will is bad enough; but when the desire is not suppressed, but is permitted to control the entire life, then sin becomes exceeding sinful.

(*b.*) *The Law and the Regenerate* (vers. 14–25).

14–25. For we know that the law is spiritual: but I am carnal, sold under sin. For that which I do I know not: for not what I would, that do I practise; but what I hate, that I do. But if what I would not, that I do, I consent unto the law that it is good. So now it is no more I that do it, but sin which dwelleth in me. For I know that in me, that is, in my flesh, dwelleth no good thing: for to will is present with me, but to do that which is good *is* not. For the good which I would I do not: but the evil which I would not, that I practise. But if what I would not, that I do, it is no more I that do it, but sin which dwelleth in me. I find then the law, that to me who would do good, evil is present. For I delight in the law of God after the inward man: but I see a different law in my members, warring against the law of my mind, and bringing me into captivity under the law of sin which is in my members. O wretched man that I am! who shall deliver me out of the body of this death? I thank God through Jesus Christ our Lord. So then I myself with the mind serve the law of God; but with the flesh the law of sin.

The meaning of this section has occasioned more discussion than probably any other portion of the Epistle. The Greek fathers and Augustine in his first period regard it as continuing the description of the struggle of the law with the unregenerate man contained in the preceding verses. Augustine in his later period, followed by the Reformers of both the Lutheran and the Reformed Churches, ascribes it to the struggle within the regenerate. The argument for the former interpretation is: 1. To say that the regenerate man is "sold under sin," is inconsistent with ver. 25. To say that the regenerate man is helpless to accomplish what, by the grace of God, he wills, overlooks the new powers bestowed in regeneration. On the other hand, the change of tense from the past to the present, and the impossibility of affirming of the unregenerate that they delight in the law of the Lord after the inward man, are conclusive that Paul confesses a conflict frequently repeated in his experience. The conclusion is that the law is so little adapted to communicate life, that even the regenerate man is conscious of a constant struggle against it. The dominion of sin is over; but the remnants of sin still present are excited by the proclamation of the law, and manifest, although in a feebler measure, the characteristics described in the preceding paragraph. As the remnants of sin or the powers of the new life assert themselves, and he concentrates his attention upon either, a double consciousness results, so that he can truly say here, **I am carnal, sold under sin,** and in ver. 25, "With the mind I serve the law of God," or in 8:2, that he is free from the law of sin and death.

Luthardt has found no less than one hundred and ten

passages in Luther where he thus treats this passage, e. g. on Gal. 5 : 17 : " Not only the sophists, but even some of the Fathers, attempt to excuse Paul. They deem it improper for an elect organ of Christ to be said to have sin. We put our faith in the words of Paul, in which he candidly confesses that he is sold under sin, etc. Here they answer that the Apostle is speaking in the person of the ungodly. The godless do not complain concerning rebellion, conflict, the captivity of sin, because sin effectually reigns in them; but for this reason, the complaint of Paul and of all saints is most true. They have done not only unwisely, but impiously, who have made the excuse that Paul and other saints are without sin. With this persuasion, proceeding from ignorance of the doctrine of faith, they have abolished the forgiveness of sins, and rendered Christ of none effect." Comp. SMALCALD ARTICLES, p. 329: " Paul (Rom. 7: 14–25) shows that he wars with the law in his members; and this, not by his own powers, but by the gift of the Holy Ghost that follows the remission of sin." FORMULA OF CONCORD, p. 555: " If now, in St. Paul and in other regenerate men, the natural or carnal free will, even after regeneration, strives against God's law, much more perverse and hostile to God's law and will will it be before regeneration."

The reference of this passage to a state of transition from the unregenerate to the regenerate state cannot be accepted, since, as long as man is unregenerate, it is impossible for him with his mind to serve the law of God.

Ver. 14. **For we know**, i. e. we Christians know what the natural man does not know (1 Cor. 2 : 14), **that the law is spiritual**. It goes deeper than the outward life. It is the revelation of God's will; and God is a spirit. It, therefore, requires an inner and spiritual obedience. "If the law were a bodily matter, we could satisfy it by our works. But since it is spiritual, no one can satisfy it, unless he do from the bottom of his heart all that he does. But such a heart is the gift only of the Holy Ghost" (LUTHER). This, men, without Christ, do not perceive, but "imagine that, by outward works, they can fulfil the law. . . . Hence Christ takes the law into his own hands, and explains it spiritually from Matt. 5 : 21 sqq.; Rom. 7 : 14, and 1 : 18" (FORM. OF CONCORD, p. 591). "He calls the law spiritual, not because, as Origen explained, the doctrine of the law has an allegorical and spiritual meaning; but, partly, because it has the Holy Ghost as its author; partly, because its commandments are spiritual, not according to man's determination, but as the expression of the exquisite will of God; *partly*, because it requires not so much external discipline, but man's spirit, i. e. his whole heart and mind; *partly*, because such perfection can be understood only by the spirit of God; *partly*, also because the blessings it promises to the obedient are spiritual" (BALD.). **I am carnal**, not "I was," but "I am." This he can say consistently even with the declaration of 8 : 9, that he is not in the flesh. The new spiritual insight communicated in regeneration, and increasing with sanctification, enables him more and more to see the real nature of the indwelling corruption that pervades and underlies all that he does and thinks. A few drops of aniline or of blood color a large amount of water and render it impure by penetrating every atom. The more deeply spiritual the believer, the more delicate is his sense of sin, and the more vivid his consciousness of its presence. In accordance with his carnal nature, he recognizes the tendency to look simply on outward compliance with the law, instead of on its spiritual demands. Just to the degree then that he recognizes himself as carnal, has he begun to be spiritual.

Sold under sin. This same delicate spiritual insight reveals to him the fact that in spite of his efforts, sin, assuming various forms, constantly asserts its power and defeats him. Thwarted and baffled in his efforts to yield God a perfectly pure and holy service, he confesses, in so far a bondage of the will that still remains from his former estate, even though viewed from another standpoint, and, with the sustaining power of God's grace taken into the account, he serves God in freedom (8:2). "This clause states what the flesh can do of itself. For by nature man is no less a servant of sin than are slaves who are bought and sold whom their masters abuse, like oxen or asses, according to their pleasure; so we are driven by the power of sin, so that all the mind and all the heart and all the deeds are disposed towards sin" (CALVIN).

Ver. 15. **For that which I do I know not.** A proof of this bondage. The slave obeys what his master commands without asking about the meaning or the consequences of his action. So the regenerate man sins, when the flesh, taking advantage of his partial ignorance, surprises him, and hurries him onward to obey impulse instead of God's will. He commits sin without knowing when he commits it that it is sin. He does much of which he disapproves and which he even loathes. The words of Ovid are often used to illustrate this verse:

> "*Video meliora proboque,*
> *Deteriora sequor.*"

("I see the better things, and approve of them; but I follow the worse.") **For not what I would, that do I practise.** "He never does what he wishes, because he never performs a perfectly pure act in perfectly holy love.

When he glances from the height of spiritual freedom, to which grace has raised him, down into the deep abyss of nature's sin, which is alluring and enticing, there attend him continually, along with the consciousness of inward strength and freedom, the sense of an alien power and bondage" (PHIL.). (Comp. Matt. 26:41.)

Ver. 16. **If what I would not, that I do.** The emphasis on "would not," i. e.: If my will is directed against that which I, nevertheless, do. **I consent unto the law.** He who inwardly loathes sin, and whose will is directed against sin, proves thereby the inner harmony of his mind with the law.

Ver. 17. **So therefore it is no more I that do it.** If a crowd be standing on the brink of a precipice, some one by pushing me may cause me to fall on a person, who, by my fall, is plunged into the abyss. If my will have done all in its power to avert this calamity, it would not be I, but another power that is responsible. So, if a man do not sin willingly and knowingly, but against his will and inmost desire, the power whence the sin comes must be foreign to his personality, deeply rooted though it is in his nature. Paul says this, not to excuse himself, but to show the great power of indwelling sin, which, against his most earnest efforts, nevertheless, asserts itself, and, every now and then, when he is off his guard, gains the upper hand. "Thus he divides himself as it were into spirit and flesh; in so far as he is spiritual and regenerate, he consents to the law, and wishes nothing that is prohibited in the law; in so far as he is carnal, sin works in him those things which are contrary to the law, and of which he himself disapproves. Sin, moreover, is said to work, just as the ear hears and the eye sees; for as the soul hears through the ear and sees through the eye, so the soul, through original sin or concupiscence, works those things in the regenerate that are not pleasing to the Spirit" (BALD.).

Ver. 18. For I know that in me, that is, in my flesh. This means, first, as Luther declares, that he and his flesh are one thing, i. e. the flesh is the man himself in so far as he is not yet perfectly renewed by divine grace. But it means, secondly, that he is more than flesh, since, beside the remnants of his corrupt nature, there is "an inward man" (ver. 22), or "mind" (ver. 22, 25). The unregenerate, however, are nothing but "flesh." **No good thing.** All that is in him from natural endowment is corrupt. There has been far more than a mere impairment of natural powers. **For to will is present with me.** The new life imparted in regeneration leads him to holy purposes. This will is directly ascribed in Phil. 2 : 13 to the working of God within him. **But to do that which is good.** Indwelling sin hinders the execution of what he resolves upon, so that no service is rendered God with that perfection and completeness which the law demands and he desires. The reality constantly falls short of his ideals. It is a conflict of the flesh with the Spirit (Gal. 4 : 17).

Vers. 19, 20, give emphasis to the thought by repeating what is substantially the same as ver. 15. A slight change occurs, however, in the use of "do not" with "good"; and of "practise" with "evil." It may be paraphrased: **The good which I would, I do not** carry to completion, **but the evil which I would not, that** I am working at, even when I am attempting to do good.

Ver. 21. I find then the law. "Law" often signifies the regular order in which events or experiences are found to occur. As we speak of "the laws of nature," so the Apostle describes his experience in this matter as so uniform, that it may be called a law, or principle, or rule. (So among others, PHILIPPI, GODET, WEISS, LUTHARDT.) As such, it is directly contradictory to the law of God. Instead of being able to yield to the law of God the obedience it demands, his life manifests the reign of another, and that of a hostile law, viz. that of the intrusion of evil into all his plans for good. **Evil is present,** i. e. every holy purpose is attended by a struggle. Every volition to do what is good is accompanied by the consciousness of the presence of indwelling sin, that attempts to dissuade and hinder.

Ver. 22. **I delight in.** Literally: "I delight with." A personification of the law. Whatever the law wants, says Paul, I am delighted with. Thus the entire harmony of his will with the law, is expressed. Not mere submission to the law, but positive delight in it is here confessed. **The inward man.** The inmost center of his being, "in his real personality." The context, however, shows that this personality is, in this case, that of a regenerate person. (Comp. 2 Cor. 4 : 16; Eph. 3 : 16 with Rom. 6 : 6; Eph. 4 : 22 ; Col. 3 : 9.) Ps. 119 has been cited as a fitting illustration of this verse, combining, as it does, delight in the law, with confessions of sinfulness and prayers for sustaining grace.

Ver. 23. **But I see a different law.** (Comp. ver. 21.) Not simply another law, but one of another kind. **In my members warring against the law of my mind.** The contrast is between what he is in his mind or heart, i. e. what he actually is, and what he sees in his life. As the "mind" refers to the very centre of his life, "the members" refer to what is more remote from his personality, viz. to the circumference of his life, self as it comes to expression in his relations to the outer world. (Comp. ver. 5 ; 6 : 13.) He does not say that this law originates or exists exclusively in his members, but, in the words,

"I see," declares that it is there that it forces itself upon his attention; in his bodily organism, and in that which most directly concerns it, sin issues from its inner depths to the surface. Not merely licentiousness, intemperance, gluttony, etc., are here meant, but the bodily sins stand for a class that comprehend also the array of reason against revelation, where the visible, tangible, material, and temporal are made the standards according to which to judge divine things. **Warring against.** More than attacking is here meant. The Greek word implies a long and protracted war, and means "to be in the field," "to be enlisted," "to be on a military expedition against." The law in the members is on a campaign against the law of the mind. **Bringing me into captivity.** Not the past, but the present, is here meant. Not that he had been made captive, but that the work continues, is the burden of his complaint. **Under the law of sin.** Four laws are here mentioned: The law of God, the law of sin, the law of the mind and the law in the members. But in the regenerate man, the law of God has become the law of the mind, while the law of sin and the law in the members coincide. Nevertheless the law of sin, while in the members, does not control the members of the regenerate, as the law of God controls his mind. There is, indeed, a law of sin in his members; but, as his body is the temple of the Holy Ghost (1 Cor. 3 : 16), another law works even in the members.

Ver. 24. **O wretched man that I am.** The exclamation of the regenerate man, called forth by the consciousness of the presence of indwelling sin. If the objection be urged that this is inconsistent with the consciousness of victory over death and sin, abounding in such passages as 5 : 1 sqq.; 8 : 1 sqq.; the answer is readily made that the Christian life abounds in such paradoxes. Our Lord's cry on the cross (Matt. 27:46), was not inconsistent with a sense of the presence and sustaining power of His Father even amidst what seemed to be His desertion. As the regenerate man looks upon himself as he is without the grace of God, and as there ever remains in him that which is not perfectly renewed, this must be always his cry. Never is his joy in deliverance by grace so great, or his thanksgivings so fervent, as when they directly succeed such a cry of profound misery over still present sin. **Who shall deliver me?** The question is asked not in ignorance, but because it points forward to an answer that shall place in his mouth the shout of triumph. **This body of this death.** Equivalent to "this mortal body." Not the material body exclusively, but the body and soul, as not yet perfectly sanctified, everything in man still subject to sin and death, and used by sin to separate man from God. In this work the body is especially employed, since, by its contact with the external world, it becomes the avenue through which temptations from without address us, and the organ whereby they are responded to from within.

Ver. 25. **I thank God through Jesus Christ our Lord.** The marginal reading of R. V., **But thanks be to God**, is adopted by the best editors (TISCHENDORF, and WESTCOTT and HORT), and has at least equal, if not great manuscript authority. The cry for deliverance prompted by the sense of sin is followed by the exclamation of gratitude at the remembrance of the deliverance which God's grace has actually brought. The Christian Life constantly advances with such alternations. The sense of spiritual poverty is succeeded by exultation over the riches we have in Christ. Those using the Common Service of the Lutheran Church in this country may be surprised to find in these two verses the thoughts of the responses that follow the Scripture Lessons at Matins and Vespers, "But

Thou, O Lord, have mercy upon us," "Thanks be to God." *So then*, etc., recapitulates the entire section from ver. 14. So far as "the flesh" still remains, viz. so far as his nature has not been entirely pervaded by the sanctifying influences of the Holy Spirit—but only so far—the regenerate man serves sin. The influences of the Spirit, however, having entirely taken possession of the centre of his life, so as to make his "mind" and his "inward man" (ver. 22) one and the same with "the new man," he has begun to serve God in joyous freedom; and this is the service of his real self.

SECTION IV.—THE COMPLETE VICTORY OF THE HOLY SPIRIT IN CHRISTIANS, A PLEDGE THAT MORALITY IS NOT IMPERILLED BY CHRISTIAN FREEDOM (ch. 8: 1-39).

SPENER has beautifully said: "If we compare the Holy Scriptures to a ring, I believe that Paul's Epistle to the Romans is the gem; and this reaches its culmination in the eighth chapter." A recent Calvinistic writer says: "In this surpassing chapter, the several streams of the preceding argument meet and flow in one 'river of the water of life, clear as crystal, proceeding out of the throne of God and of the Lamb,' until it seems to lose itself in the ocean of a blissful eternity" (BROWN).

(*a*.) *The Freedom of the Regenerate* (vers. 1-11).

1-11. There is therefore now no condemnation to them that are in Christ Jesus. For the law of the Spirit of life in Christ Jesus made me free from the law of sin and of death. For what the law could not do, in that it was weak through the flesh, God, sending his own Son in the likeness of sinful flesh and *as an offering* for sin, condemned sin in the flesh: that the ordinance of the law might be fulfilled in us, who walk not after the flesh, but after the spirit. For they that are after the flesh do mind the things of the flesh; but they that are after the spirit the things of the spirit. For the mind of the flesh is death; but the mind of the spirit is life and peace: because the mind of the flesh is enmity against God; for it is not subject to the law of God, neither indeed can it be: and they that are in the flesh cannot please God. But ye are not in the flesh, but in the spirit, if so be that the Spirit of God dwelleth in you. But if any man hath not the Spirit of Christ, he is none of his. And if Christ is in you, the body is dead because of sin; but the spirit is life because of righteousness. But if the Spirit of him that raised up Jesus from the dead dwelleth in you, he that raised up Christ Jesus from the dead shall quicken also your mortal bodies through his Spirit that dwelleth in you.

Ver. 1. **There is, therefore, now no condemnation.** Lit.: "No condemnation, now, therefore, to them," etc. Not a complete sentence, but an exclamation, condensing in a motto or shout of victory the substance of what had thus far been taught. **No condemnation.** (Comp. 5 : 16, 18.) Not "nothing worthy of condemnation," but "the sentence of condemnation does not belong or apply to them." (Comp. John 3 : 18.) **Therefore** points back to the thanksgiving, with which the preceding chapter ends. **Now** has a weak temporal allusion, viz. "under these circumstances," an implied contrast to the state prior to regeneration (ver. 2). **In Christ Jesus.** (Comp. 6 : 11.) The principal passage where this expression occurs is 2 Cor. 5 : 17. It means to be incorporated with Christ (Eph. 5 : 30), made one with Him, a member of His body. Christ is the element in which the Christian lives and moves; the ground in which his life is rooted, and whence it derives all its nourishment. "This occurs when Christians are introduced by baptism into a real life-communion with Christ. By this life-communion with Christ, they receive the power which delivers them from the service of sin" (WEISS).

Ver. 2. The Christian is even here on earth within the realm of life, and not that of death. **For the law of the Spirit of life.** "Law" as explained in notes on

7 : 21, 23. "Law of spirit of life," is the activity of the Holy Spirit within man (John 7 : 38, 39), working only because of the Atonement of Christ, and by applying to men the benefits of Christ; hence called "the Spirit of life **in Christ.**" **Made me free.** The tense refers to a definite point in the past. It cannot refer, therefore, directly to sanctification, or to justification, but to that which brings justification, viz. to the work of the Holy Spirit in bestowing faith, i. e. to regeneration. "The deliverance was effected as one act with the communication of the Spirit in baptism, which placed them in life-communion with Jesus. Progressive sanctification is the farther development and result of this act" (WEISS). **Law of sin and death** is one law. (Comp. 7 : 23.) "Death" is here added as the antithesis to "spirit of life." The inner principle of his nature is now the life-principle, proceeding from the Holy Spirit, instead of the death-principle which controlled his unregenerate condition.

Ver. 3. **For what the law could not do.** A contrast is here made between inefficiency of the law and the efficacy of the Gospel. "Law" is here used in its proper sense for the Moral Law. As in ch. 6 : 7, 10, 13, 14, he vindicates the law, ascribing its seeming weakness not to any defect inhering in the law, but to the impotence of man's nature, corrupted and enfeebled by inborn sin, i. e. **by the flesh.** (Comp. 7 : 18.) **God sending,** etc. This entire clause, and not merely "God," is in contrast with "the law" of the former clause. **His own Son** clearly implies the pre-existence of Christ (comp. Gal. 4 : 4 ; John 10 : 36; 17 : 3), and the peculiar love of the Father to Him who was sent. **In the likeness of sinful flesh.** Lit. : " In the likeness of the flesh of sin." If Paul had said : "in sinful flesh," he would have favored the

Ebionite error, which denied Christ's sinlessness. If he had said: "in the likeness of flesh," he would have taught Docetism, which denied the reality of the incarnation. But he here teaches that Christ truly assumed flesh, and that the flesh which he assumed was the likeness of sinful flesh (Hebr. 4 : 15). In this verse, "flesh" means the entire human nature (John 1 : 14; Rom. 1 : 3; 9 : 5). The comparison lies in that, although actually without sin, nevertheless He became, like sinful men, subject to suffering and death, the wages of sin. The sinless one is just as though He were a sinner (Phil. 2 : 7). "Every one condemned innocently appears in the likeness of a criminal, without himself being a criminal" (PHIL.). **For sin.** The design of the incarnation is to provide a remedy for sin. Were there no other, this passage would be sufficient to disprove the assertion, sometimes made, that the Son of God would have become incarnate, even though man had not sinned. **Condemned.** Not simply in word, but in act. The sentence has not only been passed, but has been executed. "Through His Son, who partook of human nature, but was without sin, God deprived sin (which is the ground of condemnation) of its power in human nature, broke its deadly sway, just as the condemnation and punishment of wicked men put an end to their power to injure or do harm" (THAYER). **In the flesh.** "The flesh was the sphere in which Christ gained the victory over sin, by overcoming every temptation to sin throughout his sinless life, and, therefore, in which also his actual condemnation of sin to powerlessness was accomplished" (WEISS).

Ver. 4 declares God's purpose in thus condemning sin. **That the ordinance** (marginal reading: "requirement") **of the law.** The reference is to man's conformity to God's demands. A contrast, as BENGEL remarks, with "condemned" (ver. 2). Expositors are divided as to whether Paul treats here of justification or of sanctification. The solution is that he declares all that the Gospel makes us in our relations to the law. Hence MELANCHTHON combines both: "This can be understood in a two-fold manner: 1. Of imputation because by faith, for Christ's sake, the law is fulfilled in us, viz. imputatively, i. e. by faith, for Christ's sake, we are accounted righteous, just as if we had satisfied the law. 2. Of the effect, viz. that newness of life may be begun in us by the gift of the Holy Spirit." **Who walk.** A description of the habitual external manifestation of an inner direction of heart, mind and purpose. **Not after** points to the governing rule or standard. **Flesh,** as in 7 : 18, and frequently elsewhere (see ver. 3), man's depraved nature, all in man that is unregenerate. **Spirit.** The American Revisers ask that this be spelled with a capital to make plain the reference to the Holy Spirit. If the reference be to the regenerate human spirit, this necessarily means that spirit, as the abode of the Holy Spirit, and the organ, through which He directs the life. Even then the Holy Spirit becomes the ultimate rule. " But here, as in a large majority of N. T. passages, the personal Divine Spirit is depicted, as in such a sense inhabiting and informing the regenerate human spirit, that He, rather than it, is regarded as the dominant rule and influence in the being. Thus, ver. 9, the regenerate are said to be ' in the Spirit,' not ' in the flesh,' not because their human spirits are in command of their being, but because *the Divine Spirit dwells in them* " (MOULE).

Ver. 5 divides mankind into two mutually exclusive classes. All are either unregenerate, viz. **after the flesh,** or regenerate, viz. **after the Spirit** (John 3 : 6). The unregenerate are determined in all their thoughts, aspirations and cares, solely by motives arising from a corrupt nature; while the regenerate, notwithstanding the fleshly element still within them, are determined by motives proceeding from the indwelling Spirit (ver. 9). No unregenerate man can be influenced by spiritual motives, or can seek after spiritual things. Man must be made spiritual, in order to live after the Spirit. (Comp. 1 Cor. 2 : 14.)

Ver. 6. **The mind of the flesh.** "The mind" is simply that which the flesh thinks. We often ask: "What is your mind concerning the matter?" Here, then, we do not find the intellectual faculty, or that which perceives, judges and thinks, but the object or result of this activity. In classical Greek, the word is frequently used for "high and noble feeling." "The thought is that human righteousness, philosophy, jurisprudence, etc., yea, even the law of God, as reason, without the Holy Spirit, regards them, and tries to conform to them, are death" (MELANCHTHON). **Death,** both as tending to death, and belonging to the sphere of spiritual death, or alienation from God. **The mind of the spirit,** i. e. the thoughts and purposes wrought in man by the Holy Spirit. **Is life and peace,** i. e. it is the beginning of the Kingdom of God in man, which is "righteousness, peace and joy in the Holy Ghost" (Rom. 14 : 17. Comp. ver. 2).

Ver. 7. **Because** gives the reason why the flesh, by its efforts, can attain no other result than death. **The mind of the flesh is enmity against God,** i. e. all that the unregenerate man thinks, purposes, judges, decides, is pervaded by his hatred of God. **For it is not subject,** i. e. the flesh is not subject. **Neither indeed can be.** A complete refutation of any imagination concerning the freedom of the will in spiritual things. As long as the flesh prevails, man cannot yield obedience to the law.

Submission to the law, true obedience from the heart, can come only through regeneration. Until man is regenerate, the law, instead of aiding, only increases his guilt as shown above (7 : 10, 13).

Ver. 8. **They that are in the flesh** differs from "after the flesh" of ver. 5 only by being more emphatic. The unregenerate nature is here described as the very element in which they live. **Cannot please God.** For, as long as his law is antagonized, God cannot be pleased. Before He be pleased, the demands of His law must be satisfied.

Ver. 9. **But ye are not in the flesh.** Life in the flesh and in the Spirit having been contrasted, this verse is an admonition to self-examination. **But in the spirit.** The American revisers seem to us right in urging again, as in ver. 4, that Spirit be spelled with a capital. The Holy Spirit is the very element in which they live. **If so be** suggests the importance of self-examination. **Dwell** indicates a permanent state, and not occasional raptures of enthusiasm and zeal. **Spirit of God.** This only serves to explain "Spirit" in the preceding clause. The Spirit is your life-element, because the Spirit dwells in you. **Of God** is added to intensify the thought of his Omnipresent Omnipotence. "Ye must assuredly be in the Spirit, if it be the Spirit of God that dwells in you. For this Spirit always transforms those whom He inhabits into the image of Himself, and pervades them with His own ever efficacious life. **Spirit of Christ.** A climax. There are three gradations, Spirit, Spirit of God, Spirit of Christ. "Spirit of Christ" means the Holy Spirit, as the Mediator and Applier of the grace and mercy acquired by Christ. We have here a testimony to the divinity of Christ, and a proof of the Church's doctrine of the Procession of the Holy Spirit from both the Father and the Son; since His relation here to both Persons is the same. The

Holy Spirit is called the Spirit of Christ in Gal. 4 : 6; Phil. 1 : 19; 1 Pet. 1 : 11. **He is none of his.** For Christ gives the Holy Spirit to all who are His, and none come to Christ except by the Holy Spirit. "The possession of the Spirit of Christ, is the characteristic note of those belonging to Him (1 John 4 : 13)" (PHIL.). "He who has the Spirit, has Christ; he who has Christ, has God" (BENGEL).

Ver. 10. **If Christ is in you.** We have another suggestion of the Trinity. As ver. 9 speaks of the Spirit of Christ within the believer, so here Christ Himself is said to be in him. (Comp. Gal. 2 : 20.) Wherever Christ is, there is the Spirit; wherever the Spirit is, there is Christ. **The body is dead,** i. e. the natural body, as ver. 11 clearly shows. It is "dead," because within it the processes of death are already working. Daily it is dying, and, except to those who will be alive at Christ's Second Coming, its death is a certainty. **Because of sin** (Rom. 5 : 12; 6 : 23). Even regeneration does not free from bodily death, to the regenerate no longer a punishment, but only a trial to enhance his blessedness (1 Cor. 3 : 22). This entire clause is concessive. The meaning is: Although the body is dead because of sin, nevertheless **the spirit is life.** Here spirit is the human spirit regenerated, as the contrast with "body" shows. "Life" means more than living; it means also life-imparting, quickening. The regenerate human spirit is so pervaded by the Holy Spirit, that through it the Spirit performs His active work in quickening and transforming man. **Because of righteousness.** Christ's righteousness, which, in justification, became the believers, is the ground and source of the gift of the Holy Spirit. Thus the presence of the ever living, ever active Spirit of God, is the proof of our righteousness and acceptance with God (Eph. 1 : 13).

Ver. 11. **But of the Spirit of him,** etc. The Apostle, in the preceding verse, had conceded that one part of the believer's nature is still left beneath the power of death. Now he proceeds to show how even this mortal part of human nature must be overcome by the quickening power of the Holy Spirit. That in which the Holy Spirit dwells, has within it resurrection-power, that must rise superior to death. The same Spirit that dwelt in Jesus, dwells also in all who belong to Him (ver. 9), and that, too, in their bodies, as well as their souls. Can a temple of the Holy Ghost be consigned to perpetual ruin? The presence of the Spirit is, therefore, a pledge of the resurrection. How carefully every word must be studied, in order to learn the meaning of the thought becomes manifest from what is involved in a variation not ordinarily noticeable to the reader. **Raised up Jesus** is followed by **Raised up Christ Jesus.** "The name *Jesus* refers to Himself; the name *Christ*, to us. The former title, as a proper name, belongs to the person; the latter, as an appellation, to the office." " The personal resurrection of Jesus merely assures us that God *can* raise us; but His resurrection, regarded as that *of the Christ*, assures us that *He will do so* actually" (HOFMANN). **Raised up** is applied to Christ's body; **shall quicken**, to the bodies of believers. The latter word indicates that the quickening of the soul by the indwelling Spirit of God is also in the Apostle's mind. The quickening process is to extend from the soul to the body. The regenerated human spirit, being now, in a new and higher sense, life, the body, to which such spirit belongs, cannot be exempt from the same quickening. **Through his Spirit.** The Holy Spirit is thus said to raise the dead, just as in John 5 : 21; 6 : 40; 10 : 17, 18; 2 Cor. 4 : 14, the same office is assigned to the Father and the Son. Attention should be given to the fact that strong manuscript evidence can be found for another reading, which changes the case of the word "spirit," and gives the preposition (*dia*) the force of "because of." So LUTHER. This seems to be more in harmony with the argument. The point of the argument here seems to be that the resurrection from the dead is the highest assurance of the renewal. Nothing can withstand the resurrection-power belonging to the new life. If it even quickens the body after it has returned to earth, how must it not quicken and energize the soul!

(*b.*) *The Obligations of the Regenerate* (vers. 12–30).

(*aa.*) *The nature of the obligation. It is one that arises from sonship* (vers. 12–17).

12–17. So then, brethren, we are debtors, not to the flesh, to live after the flesh: for if ye live after the flesh, ye must die; but if by the spirit ye mortify the deeds of the body, ye shall live. For as many as are led by the Spirit of God, these are sons of God. For ye received not the spirit of bondage again unto fear; but ye received the spirit of adoption, whereby we cry, Abba, Father. The Spirit himself beareth witness with our spirit, that we are children of God: and if children, then heirs; heirs of God, and joint-heirs with Christ; if so be that we suffer with *him*, that we may be also glorified with *him*.

Ver. 12. **We are debtors.** "Thus he answers those who misunderstand the liberty of the Gospel, which frees us from the accusation of the law, but not from obedience to it. For it remains God's eternal and immutable ordinance, that we obey God; the Gospel not only begins, but also subjects us to obedience towards God" (MEL.). The thought is: "We are debtors;" but not to the flesh. Our allegiance and obedience are to a higher law than we find in our members. (Comp. vers. 4, 5.) We owe nothing to the flesh; we owe everything to the Spirit."

Ver. 13. **For if ye live after the flesh.** This gives a reason why the flesh can exact no obedience. Instead of granting favors that entail an obligation, it has nothing but death to bestow. Life "according to the flesh" designates not merely the grosser sensual sins, but everything proceeding from unregenerate human nature. The sin of Thomas no less than that of David, the errors at Pergamos no less than the incest at Corinth, were sins of the flesh. In the Gospel for the eighth Sunday after Trinity, the false prophets warned against fall under the condemnation of this statement, which is found in the Epistle for the same day. **Ye must die.** The original is emphatic. Death is inevitable. It follows according to a law of God, whose action is as certain as that of gravitation. The "death" indicated is spiritual death and all its consequences. **But if by the Spirit.** As in ver. 11, the Holy Spirit. **Ye mortify.** The tense is present, indicating a progressive act or process, i. e. "Ye are mortifying." The work is not accomplished, once for all, at a single moment or by one act. **The deeds.** Not "works," but, as in the margin: "doings," "practices." **Of the body,** considered as the organ of sin. The Christian must not yield to bodily impulses and appetites, except as he finds in them that which conforms to the law, and is pleasing to God. His eating and drinking must be regulated by a regard for God's glory (1 Cor. 10 : 31). The "body," however, is put by synechdoche for the entire class of temptations of which those to sensuality are the most easily recognized. On the entire verse, "The death of sin is the life of man; the life of man is the death of sin" (CALVIN).

Ver. 14. **For as many as are led by the Spirit.** This connects with "Spirit" in ver. 13. They who mortify the deeds of the body, are led by the Spirit. (Comp. Gal.

5 : 18.) The leading ("are being led") is not that of momentary impulse; it is a steady habitual influence of the Spirit, both as a guide and as an impelling power. The FORMULA OF CONCORD, commenting on this text, says: "This impulse of the Holy Ghost is not a coercion, but the converted man does good spontaneously. . . . The converted man does good to such an extent and as long as God, by His Holy Spirit, rules, guides and leads him" (pp. 564 sq.). **These are sons of God.** The word for son ($vios$) emphasizes the legal side of the relation, while $τέκνον$, in the next verse refers to the identity and community of nature. The next verse shows that the word is contrasted with "servants" or "slaves," as in Gal. 3 : 26 ; 4 : 1-8. "As long as man lives under the law, he is a slave, and, as such, seeks, by works, to earn for himself reward, though reaping only wrath and curse, and stands before God his Lord and Judge, with fear and trembling. As a slave, he has no part in the inheritance. Not life, but death awaits him. But, by justifying faith, man passes from a state of slavery to sonship. Instead of the Judge's wrath and curse, the Father's love now rests upon him. Instead of the fear of a slave, he has the trust and confidence of a child, and free access to the Father's heart" (PHIL.). Recalling the connection with ver. 13, the inference is that to be a Son of God is true life or truly to live.

Ver. 15. This true and real life stated in "Ye shall live," is next described in its present condition, as a present communion with God. **For ye have not received the spirit of bondage.** This means: The spirit which you have received is not one of bondage. If you have a spirit of bondage (comp. "spirit of meekness," 1 Cor. 4 : 21, "spirit of fearfulness," 2 Tim. 1 : 7), it belongs to the natural man, who regards God as a tyrannical master, dreads His presence, hates His commands, and gives Him no cordial inner obedience. "This is not the Spirit that prevails among Christians" (Comp. Heb. 2 : 14, 15 ; 1 John 4 : 18). **Again,** implying a relapse into the state in which they lived before becoming believers. If the Spirit of God, with His life and love, dwell in you, you have received the Spirit, assuring you that instead of being slaves, you are sons and heirs, i. e. **the Spirit of adoption,** the Spirit belonging to the state of adoption. Filled therewith, you regard God no longer as a tyrant, but as a Father (Gal. 4 : 5 ; Eph. 1 : 5). **Abba, Father.** Thus conscious of our sonship, our access to God is immediate and direct, and we address Him in the most familiar way consistent with reverence. **Abba,** used in the Aramaic, spoken in Palestine in the time of Christ, became a usual term in prayer for addressing God with love and tenderness. As such it was used by Christ (Mark 14 : 36), and again by Paul in Gal. 4 : 6. It was natural for those using another language to add to it the name current in that language. On the thought, MELANCHTHON : " As long as conscience is without faith, despairing in its fears, it flees from God, and doubts whether God hears or cares. It does not call upon God. For this reason Paul unites consolation and prayer, and ascribes it only to those who already through the Gospel are encouraged by faith. For when he says: We cry Abba Father, the meaning is : We acknowledge that God is our Father, and truly hears us, and with this faith we receive consolation, and call upon God. This faith and knowledge of God's mercy properly make the distinction between Christians and the godless, since in the latter there are always doubt and indignation against God. But in believers, faith is a new recognition of God's mercy, and contends against doubt, and affirms that, for Christ's sake, we are truly heard." With much beauty, LUTHER adds : " The word *Abba* is one which a young child makes from simple and filial confidence in his father, crying 'Ab, Ab.' For it is the easiest word which a child can learn to make. Such a simple filial word faith uses, when addressing God through the Holy Spirit."

Ver. 16. **The Spirit himself beareth witness with our spirit.** The addressing of God as Father results from the reception of the Spirit of adoption. This cry, "Abba Father," is the testimony of our spirits; for when we call God Father, we declare **that we are children of God.** But this our testimony depends upon evidence. This evidence comes to us from the Holy Spirit. "As no man can say Jesus is Lord but in the Holy Spirit" (1 Cor. 12 : 3), so no man can call God Father except in the same Spirit. This confession and this prayer are inseparable from a state of regeneration. The assurance of God's forgiveness meets us through the voice of the Holy Spirit in the Word of God, and, through that word, as sealed to us in the sacraments. The general assurance and promise of the Gospel are then applied to every individual not repelling them. The general assurances are: "God loved the world," "Christ died for all men," "God has towards sinners only thoughts of love." The Holy Spirit applies these assurances so that we read them : "God loves me," "Christ died for me," etc. Thus the Holy Spirit says: "Thou art a son of God, and on the basis of this assurance, the regenerate spirit declares: "I am a son of God. Thou, O God, art my Father." The testimony of the Spirit, therefore, is the expression of the Christian's self-consciousness, awakened by the testimony of God's word applied to man by the Holy Spirit.

In much weakness is this testimony of our spirits uttered. Hence the voice of the Holy Spirit does more than precede. It must be constantly repeated, or the testimony of our spirits would cease. It is not enough, then, that the spirit once bore witness. The testimony is present and continuous. "The Spirit *beareth* witness."

"That we are God's children, and may certainly regard ourselves such, we have not of ourselves or of the law; but it is the testimony of the Holy Ghost who, against the law and the feeling of our unworthiness, gives us, in our weakness, such testimony and assures us of it. The testimony is of such a nature that we also feel and experience the power of the Holy Ghost which He works in us through the Word, and our experience agrees with the Word or preaching. For when in need and sorrow you receive consolation from the Gospel, you can feel this in you and thereby you overcome such doubt and terror, so that your heart firmly concludes that you have a gracious God, and that you no more flee from Him, but, in such faith, can joyfully call upon Him and expect aid from Him. . . Such is the true inner witness whereby you learn to know that the Holy Ghost is working in you. Beside, you have also external signs and marks, that He gives you especial gifts, a spiritual understanding, grace and success in your calling, etc., that you have pleasure and love for His Word, and confess the same, even with danger of body and life, before all the world, also that you are an enemy to all godless ways and sins and oppose them. All these things, those who are not Christians, i. e. those who are without the Holy Ghost, cannot do, true though it is that even in saints this occurs in great weakness" (LUTHER).

No stronger testimony to the certainty of faith and the assurance of personal salvation than that of this verse is possible. It completely overthrows the doctrine of the Roman Catholic Church, which teaches that doubt concerning personal salvation is a virtue. On this, see the argument of CHEMNITZ in his *Examen*, chapter "*De Fide Justificante.*"

Ver. 17. **And if children, then heirs.** Sonship and heirship go together. Adoption implies the setting aside of an inheritance for the person adopted. This inheritance differs, however, from others, in that its enjoyment is not dependent upon the death of the father. (Comp. Heb. 9: 16, 17.) **Heirs of God and joint-heirs with Christ.** The contrast here is not between the Father and the Son, but between God as unincarnate, and God incarnate in Jesus of Nazareth. We become heirs to all the merits of the mediatorial work of the Son of God, and through them to all the glory and blessedness of Father, Son and Spirit, that existed before the foundations of the world (John 17:5). Thus heirs to all God is and has, we partake of all the glory that the humanity of Christ receives (Phil. 2:5-11). But what is the inheritance? Answer: **That we may be also glorified with him.** This identity of lot, both in suffering and in glory, is taught in John 12:24-26; Matt. 16:24 sq.; 2 Tim. 2:12.

(*bb.*) *The end of the obligation, viz., man's highest blessedness in the completion of his renewal in everlasting life* (ver. 18-30).

18-30. For I reckon that the sufferings of this present time are not worthy to be compared with the glory which shall be revealed to usward. For the earnest expectation of the creation waiteth for the revealing of the sons of God. For the creation was subjected to vanity, not of its own will, but by reason of him who subjected it, in hope that the creation itself also shall be delivered from the bondage of corruption into the liberty of the glory of the children of God. For we know that the whole creation groaneth and travaileth in pain together until now. And not only so, but ourselves also, which have the first-fruits of the Spirit, even we ourselves groan within ourselves, waiting for *our* adoption, *to wit*, the redemption of our body. For by hope were we saved: but hope that is seen is not hope:

for who hopeth for that which he seeth? But if we hope for that which we see not, *then* do we with patience wait for it.

And in like manner the Spirit also helpeth our infirmity: for we know not how to pray as we ought; but the Spirit himself maketh intercession for *us* with groanings which cannot be uttered; and he that searcheth the hearts knoweth what is the mind of the Spirit, because he maketh intercession for the saints according to *the will of* God. And we know that to them that love God all things work together for good, *even* to them that are called according to *his* purpose. For whom he foreknew, he also foreordained *to be* conformed to the image of his Son, that he might be the firstborn among many brethren: and whom he foreordained, them he also called: and whom he called, them he also justified: and whom he justified, them he also glorified.

Ver. 18. **For I reckon.** This verse shows how, notwithstanding the sufferings required by fidelity to the obligation of children of God, their salvation is assured. The judgment here given arises from the certainty of God's promises and the testimony of the Holy Spirit. **That the sufferings.** The connection with ver. 17 shows clearly that the reference is to those sufferings that belonged to their calling as Christians. (Comp. 1 Pet. 4; 16.) "What he had already suffered when he wrote this Epistle, all the marks of the Crucified in His body (Gal. 6 : 17), all pains of soul because of enemies of the Cross of Christ (9 : 2 ; Phil. 3 : 18), together with all the sufferings that still await him, up to the time of his decapitation (Col. 1 : 24), all put together, he regards of no account when contrasted with the glory that is to be his" (BESSER). **Of this present time.** More limited than "this world." A very brief and transitory period in this world's history. (Comp. 2 Cor. 4 : 17.) ! **With the glory that shall be revealed.** Emphatic in the original, whose revelation is inevitable. The time is at the second coming of Christ. **To usward** shows that what is revealed is not something already existing within. The glory has been provided ; its revelation will occur when brought to us from without (1 Pet. 1 : 4, 5 ; John 17 : 24 ; 14 : 3).

Ver. 19. For the earnest expectation. All consolation is found in the intention of heart and mind upon the goal towards which the eager gaze of even the irrational creation is directed. The word here used means literally: "watching with outstretched head," "to wait with the head raised and the eye fixed on that point of the horizon from which the expected object is to come." **Of the creation.** This cannot mean, as in 1 : 20, the act of creation; or, as in 1 : 25, a single creature. Nor can it refer to all created objects. Angels are beyond the need of redemption, and are not burdened by man's sin. The children of God are directly contrasted, in vers. 19, 21, 23, with this "creation." Unbelieving men have no hope in this revelation and will not share in its glories. The visible irrational creation, Nature animate and inanimate as contrasted with man. The figure by which Nature is referred to as conscious and sentient, is not unusual. (Comp. Deut. 32 : 1; Is. 35 : 1; Hos. 2 : 21, 22.) This interpretation is confirmed not only by O. T. predictions, as Is. 11 : 1–9; 65 : 17; Ps. 102 : 26. 27, but also by the N. T. passages referring to the restoration or renovation of Nature (Acts 3 : 21; Rev. 21 : 1; Matt. 19 : 28). **Waiteth for.** "What foolish words to men of the world! The Romans, lords of the earth, were treading all kingdoms of the world beneath their iron feet. The Church had, as its associates, besides the dogs of Lazarus, the wild beasts which tore to pieces the bodies of the martyrs. Only the ear of the Christian could hear the voice of creation in its waiting and sighing for revelation" (BESSER). **The revealing of the sons of God,** i. e. the manifestation of the entire work of redeeming grace in all its fullness (Col. 3 : 4; 1 John 3 : 2). The hour of man's complete deliverance from sin will be that also of the deliverance of creation that has been made to suffer for his sin.

Ver. 20. **For the creation was subjected.** The tense in the original indicates a particular time when this was done, viz. at the Fall. Evidences of suffering and death at preceding periods, if established by Geology, must be explained, either upon the supposition of another order of things, with which the present creation has nothing to do, or, that in the sight of God, even though preceding the Fall, they were connected with the entrance of sin. The Holy Scriptures record the history only of the present order of things. As the sin of the soul affects the body, so the sin of man brought consequences that pervaded all the world about him. When man, the centre of creation, was turned from his true course, the entire sphere of which he was the centre was necessarily affected. **To vanity,** i. e. nothingness, emptiness, failure. The curse of man's sin fell upon the earth (Gen. 3 : 17, 18). " Everywhere our eyes meet images of decay and death ; the scourge of barrenness, the fury of the elements, the destructive instincts of beasts, the very laws which govern vegetation, everywhere give Nature a sombre hue " (REUSS). " Everything hideous, wild, malignant, ravenous, murderous, destructive, within the sphere of the creature, is a shadow which man's sin has cast upon the elements, animals, plants and all his domain " (BESSER). Nor only this. Even in its nearest approach to its ideal, it is still subjected to vanity. As Luther most forcibly remarks, the sun shines upon scarcely one godly man among a hundred, and the earth does not nourish one who receives its fruits with thanksgiving to one who returns for it no thanks. The good creature of God is thus made the servant of the sin of godless men. **Not of its own will.** In contrast with man, who had the choice between the service of God and that of vanity. "The redemption of humanity is grace; the redemption of Nature, justice; for the fall of humanity is voluntary guilt, the fall of Nature, involuntary suffering" (PHILIPPI). Hence Nature's constant struggle against this vanity to which it has been involuntarily subjected. "Every animal, every plant struggles to get beyond itself, to realize an idea, in the realization of which it has freedom, but the nothingness, pervading its nature, lets no created thing attain its aim; every individual of the species begins the circle of its course again. Nature cannot rest in itself" (OLSHAUSEN). **By reason of him who subjected it,** viz. God. It was God's will, that this subjection of the creature to vanity should occur, in order that His wise plans of bringing thereby greater good, for both man and creation, might be attained. (Comp. 2 Tim. 2 : 26.)

Ver. 21. **In hope that the creation itself also shall be delivered,** i. e. was made subject in hope. The purpose of God is figuratively described as the hope of the creation; just as in Acts 2 : 16 the flesh is said to hope. There is a goal towards which this subjection of creation inevitably tends. The creature was made for man. In its original state, it was adapted to administer to the blessedness of a sinless man. When man fell, creation changed, so as to be adapted to man's changed conditions, and to serve the plans of redemption. The house had to correspond with its tenant. Paradise was lost. The vanity of creation becomes an incentive to the exertion of man's moral and physical powers. If the field had not been cursed, the prodigal would not have been driven by the pains of hunger and the humiliation of his abode with swine, back to his father's house. All the miseries of creation are thus both means and prophecies of approaching deliverance. **The bondage of corruption.** Not an appositional, but a subjective genitive, meaning "the bondage exercised by corruption." The corrupt condition, resulting from the Fall, and pervading creation, prevents it from attaining its true end. Struggle as it may, it is powerless. **Into the liberty.** The goal of creation. The bondage of corruption over, it will enter upon that perfectly free course, which it was designed to fulfil. No death, no suffering, no defilement, no service of vanity. **Of the glory of the children of God.** Creation shares the lot of God's children. Here and now, it participates in their humiliation; there and then, it will partake of their glory. When the children of God shall be glorified, creation shall attain its complete liberty. The world is not merely an abode—and to a glorified man belongs also a glorified abode—but it exists in reciprocal and essential union with the glorified child of God. The body borne by the glorified is not a gift from Heaven, although the giver is the Lord from Heaven, but it is, so to say, the morning gift of the glorified earth to the child of God in his glory; for what is here sown in corruption, shall at last be raised in incorruption (1 Cor. 15 : 42)" (NEBE.). "The sun has never been as fair, bright and clear, as at the beginning when it was made, but on man's account, is half dim, decayed and soiled, but on that day, God will again purge and purify it by fire (2 Pet. 3 : 10), so that it shall be brighter and clearer than it was at the beginning" (LUTHER, 8 : 106). Hence the beautiful application of DELITZSCH: "I rejoice always when I find the cross, which stands on our altars, also planted upon the hills, or anywhere else under the open heaven. For the cross is not only the standard of redemption for us men, but also for all creatures that surround us. The blood which flowed down therefrom, not only extinguished the anger upon us sinners, but has also broken the power of the curse upon the earth. When thou, then, standing on the mountain top, kindled with the view which is presented around, criest out: How marvelous is God's earth! do not forget how infinitely more marvellous it will be, when it has wholly become the reflection of God's love, which the Crucified One has won back again for us" (*Bibl. Psychol.*, Transl. p. 562).

Ver. 22. **For we know.** An appeal to the experience of all Christians in their observation of the world. **That the whole creation.** Nature in its entirety is regarded as one body. "The entire creation sets up a grand symphony of sighs" (PHILIPPI). This, however, is exclusive of the children of God. Their sufferings are introduced as an additional factor in ver. 23. **Travaileth together,** indicating hope, as well as suffering. Not the pains of destruction, but of birth; effort, as well as sorrow (John 16:21). Only the believer, with the open Scriptures in his hands, can interpret the mystery of sorrow which the history of the world discloses. **Until now.** Even though redemption has been provided, it has not been appropriated; humanity, and, with it, the world, have not come within the sphere of its complete application.

Ver. 23. **And not only so,** i. e. It is not only the whole creation that is in travail, **But ourselves also.** All Christians; not, as some have suggested, only the Apostles, or the early church. **Which have the first-fruits of the Spirit.** The beginning of the gift of the Holy Spirit, as the pledge of the bestowal of His fulness (2 Cor. 5:5; Eph. 1:14). The gift of the Spirit is also a first-fruit and pledge of the other blessings attending this gift. Since we have but "the first-fruits," sanctification has been only begun. **Within ourselves,** i. e. individually, as every one is brought face to face with the contrasts and contradictions in his own life. "With the perpetual Abba cry of the children of God, is blended a perpetual *Kyrie eleison* " (PHILIPPI). Every assurance of God's grace calls forth a corresponding sigh for what is yet lacking. Besser applies this in detail to the explanation of the Third Article of the Creed. " I believe " calls forth the sigh of Mark 9 : 24 ; " Of my own reason or strength," that of Rom. 7 : 14; " Called me by the Gospel," meets the response of Phil. 3 : 12, 39; " Enlightened me by his gifts," 1 Cor. 13 : 12 ; " Sanctified and preserved me," etc., Ps. 116 : 10; 42 : 1–3, etc. **Waiting for.** " This is the paradox of the Christian life, that we wait for what we have, or that, at the same time, we are and are not what we become. Righteous and sinful ; holy and impure ; kings and slaves ; free and bound ; living and dead : saved and condemned. The former, all, outside of ourselves in Christ ; the latter, all, in ourselves and outside of Christ " (BESSER). " Every gift of the Gospel, while already present, is at the same time future. The germ is the plant, and yet is not the plant " (PHIL.). **Our adoption.** The full realization of adoption, for adoption itself is present (Gal. 4 : 6). The Apostle refers to the time when this adoption will be fully recognized, as in ver. 19 it is called " the revealing of the sons of God." This full realization of adoption will coincide with **the redemption of our body,** i. e. at the resurrection, the complete deliverance of the body from the dominion of corruption (1 Cor. 15 : 42–44 ; Phil. 3 : 21). Death indeed separates the soul from our sinful body ; but it is only the Second Coming of Christ that shall deliver the body, a part of our nature, from sin and corruption. " Not incorporeity, but corporeity, is the end of God's way " (NEBE.). (Comp. 2 Cor. 5 : 4.)

Ver. 24. **For by hope we were saved.** The preposition is supplied by the translators. Luther renders it : " For we are saved indeed, yet in hope." An excellent paraphrase. Not hope, but faith is the instrument that apprehends and appropriates salvation. But hope is inseparable from faith. "Faith and hope are as inseparably united as the arms of Simeon which embraced the Christ-child, and the eyes of Simeon which looked through the wrappings of the Christ-child into Christ's glorious Kingdom" (BESSER). The thought here is that when by faith man becomes a child of God, he may be said to be saved. But this salvation has only been begun. It looks forward towards the future. Its glory consists in its assurance of a deliverance still to come, salvation for body as well as for soul. The incompleteness of salvation is presupposed in the word "hope." **Hope that is seen,** i. e. when what has been hoped for at last stands before the eyes, hope becomes a matter of the past.

Ver. 25. **Then do we with patience wait for it.** This brings into prominence the close connection between hope and patience. Hope regards a future good; patience, a present evil, that threatens the future good.

Ver. 26. But this perseverance under trial is attained, not simply by the influence of the blessing offered and reserved for us in the future. Within us, there is a direct agency of the Holy Spirit. Not only does the new life have the Spirit as its source, but He sustains this life with ever new supplies from the life-giving fountain. **Helpeth our infirmities.** The infirmity is not removed. We are left to contend with it. But He gives us strength to overcome it (2 Cor. 12 : 8, 9). Infirmity comprises everything collectively that opposes and obstructs the hope and persevering endurance mentioned. **For we know not how to pray as we ought.** Prayer being a means whereby we appropriate to ourselves God's promises and obtain from Him their realization, we are strengthened by the Holy Spirit's work in enkindling within us true prayers. Even from the basis of the new life imparted in regeneration, the child of God is not able to make prayers, which, in their various details, are right and best for him. "What we should pray for is not absolutely and in general unknown to us, since this is manifestly the completion of salvation, but we know not what it is needful for us to pray according to the relation in which we stand, in order, by the sufferings of the present time, to reach the longed-for goal" (WEISS). Besides Paul's prayer in 2 Cor. 12:8, that of Monica, the mother of Augustine has been cited as an illustration, where the prayer that her son might not visit Italy was not answered, while, by his conversion, under the preaching of Ambrose, the Lord "denied her special, to grant her life-long request." **But the Spirit himself maketh intercession for us.** This He does by praying in and for the believer. "The Holy Spirit is an intercessor by moving us to prayer, according to Rom. 8:15; Zach. 12:10" (MEL.). "He is said to pray, when He makes us pray; when He excites, forms and directs these prayers and groans within us; enkindles our heart and love for prayer, and gives confidence to the end, while we pray" (HUNNIUS). So AUGUSTINE: "He groans in us, because He makes us groan" (Tract VI. on John, § 2). (Comp. Matt. 10:20; Gal. 4:6.) All true prayer is inspired. **With groanings which cannot be uttered.** Words only feebly express these divinely inspired petitions. Their substance cannot be contained in any form. The most adequate moulds of human language only declare the presence of the prayer, but cannot present it as it is. The Spirit Himself must interpret His own prayers. As every true prayer rests upon and embraces a promise, we can know what the prayer means only when we fully comprehend and know the complete contents of the promise.

Ver. 27. **And he that searcheth the hearts,** i. e. God. (Comp. 1 Sam. 16 : 7; 1 Kings 8 : 39; Jer. 17 : 10; Acts 1 : 24; Rev. 2 : 23.) **Knoweth what is the mind of the Spirit,** i. e. the real prayer of the heart, even though the words should contradict or fail to express it. **Maketh intercession . . . according to the will of God.** " For the groanings which he excites within us are according to God's will, and on that account please God, through Christ in whose name they are offered " (BALDWIN). " If, then, we want our prayers to be accepted of God, He should be asked to direct them according to His will " (CALVIN).

Having answered the difficulties suggested by the infirmities of the Christian life, he looks, through all the trials before him, towards the ultimate end, and triumphs in view of the permanence of the workings of divine grace for his salvation.

Ver. 28. **To them that love God.** Used to describe those who are true Christians. (Comp. 1 Cor. 2 : 9; 8 : 3; Eph. 6 : 24.) That they love God is a proof of God's love to them, and of His divine working for their salvation. For the love of God must come to man, and enter man's heart, before man can love God (1 John 4 : 19); just as the Holy Spirit must pray in man, if man is himself to pray (ver. 26). **All things.** The allusion is to the afflictions of this present time (ver. 18), but not to the exclusion of other things (1 Cor. 3 : 21, 29). **Work together for good.** Thus there is one point in which the conflicts and discords of earth all blend. However warring with one another and hostile to him they seem, they are, by God's guidance, directed towards the good of the child of God. (Comp. Gen. 50 : 20.) **Even to them that**

are called. This shows the mode in which this love of God has entered their hearts. It has come in and through the call. The call is the preaching of the Gospel, accompanied, as it always is, by the applying grace of the Holy Spirit. **According to his purpose.** This traces the origin of the call. The love of God comes from the call, but the call comes from the purpose. This must not be understood as though there were a call that is not according to the purpose. That would be only the semblance of a call, and no true call. The call is the revelation of God's purpose. We cannot distinguish between an efficacious and an inefficacious call. An inefficacious call is not sincere, and, therefore, is no call. That the call is not in all cases followed by its acceptance, is explained by the freedom of man's will to oppose and shut out the grace extended towards him. That the efficacy of the call is in other cases manifested in changed lives, is due to the workings of divine grace in overcoming man's natural resistance. Man's comfort and hope rest not, however, upon aught that is in him, but in that which is outside of and beyond himself, viz. in God's call, expressive, as it is, of God's purpose, ages before the one called came into being. As the call is the fruit of the purpose, so faith is the fruit of the call, and love the fruit of faith. To those in whom this order may be traced all things conspire for good. In the Epistles, where Christians are treated of, and the call is particularly emphasized as the ground of consolation, " the called " always mean those in whom the call has reached its end, those who through the call have been brought to faith. It is otherwise in Matt. 22 : 14.

Thus Paul introduces the doctrine of Predestination. As to the place where it occurs in the argument, see FORMULA OF CONCORD, p. 526 : " To him who is really concerned about the revealed will of God, and proceeds according to the order which St. Paul has observed in the Epistle to the Romans, who, first, directs men to repentance, knowledge of sins, to faith in Christ, to divine obedience, before he speaks of the mystery of the eternal election of God, this doctrine is useful and consolatory." This is simply the application of a suggestion made by LUTHER in his Introduction, which TYNDALE has paraphrased and expanded so well, that its consideration here is of importance:

" Follow thou the order of this epistle, and nosel thyself with Christ, and learn to understand what the Law and the Gospel mean and the office of both the two. . . . After that, when thou art come to the eighth chapter, and art under the cross and suffering of tribulation, the necessity of predestination will wax sweet, and thou shalt well feel how precious a thing it is. For except thou have borne the cross of adversity and temptation, and hast felt thyself brought unto the very brim of desperation, and unto hell-gates, thou canst never meddle with the sentence of predestination, without thine own harm, and without secret wrath and grudging inwardly against God; for otherwise, it shall not be possible for thee to think that God is righteous and just. Therefore must Adam be well mortified, and the fleshly wit brought utterly to naught, ere that thou mayest away with this thing, and drink so strong wine. Take heed therefore unto thyself, that thou drink not wine, while thou art but a suckling. For every learning hath its time, measure and age; and in Christ is there a certain childhood, in which a man must be content with milk for a season, until he wax strong and grow unto a perfect man in Christ, and be able to eat of more strong meat."

Ver. 29. **For whom he foreknew, he also foreordained.**

A statement of the Order of Salvation. The Apostle gives the history of a saved soul. To be glorified, one must first be justified; to be justified, one must first be called (for "how shall they believe in him of whom they have not heard?" Rom. 10:16); to have the call reach its end in faith, as the word "called" means according to our interpretation above of ver. 29, one must be predestinated; and to be predestinated, one must first be foreknown. But there is no history given here of the approaches of divine grace towards those who repel it, and are ultimately lost. The Apostle is writing here for a practical end, and not to give a complete exposition, on its various sides, of the doctrine of Predestination. He wants to comfort the afflicted people of God with the assurance that their salvation rests in God's hands, and that it is in process of accomplishment according to God's purpose; and this is enough. Treating the subject anthropopathically, he first traces the existence of the individual Christian in God's mind before he had an existence in time. John, Paul and David were to the omniscient God actual entities and objects of His thought from all eternity. He foreknew them. But they were not only comprised in His foreknowledge, but in His forelove. Foreknowing them, and foreseeing their sin and death, His gracious and merciful love formed the purpose to bring them salvation, and devised the various acts of redemption by the Son of God and the applying grace of the Spirit. At one glance, their final glorification was seen and determined as the ultimate end, together with all the intermediate stages—calling, faith, justification—in the Christian course through which they were to pass. They were foreordained to glorification through the call and justification, with all that follows the call, and conditions justification. But it is not meant here that *all* whom He foreknew were foreordained, or all whom He called were justified, or all who were at some time in their lives justified were or shall be glorified. Together with the universality of divine grace and the utter helplessness of man's own powers for salvation, provision was made at every stage for the entire freedom of man's will in the rejection of the proffered mercy. Man, if saved, must be saved wholly by God's grace; nevertheless, this grace is always resistible, and, from all eternity, the Divine Foreknowledge has recorded this resistance.

In this place the emphasis lies on the call, i. e. the preaching of the Gospel as the revelation of God's purpose of love. This purpose no power on earth or in hell can thwart. It can fail only through God's determination not to save men against their wills; and, in this regard too, the result is eternally foreknown. The call itself, considered independently of our possibility of resistance, bears us onward towards eternal life. Only by opposing our own determination to resist can we be lost. Only as the grace of God overcomes our resistance does the stream of Divine Love carry us along from the foreordination of eternity to our glorification in eternity. Then will the application of 2 Tim. 2 : 19 be understood.

A reference may be made to several interpretations which seem untenable: 1. One school of interpreters attaches to the word "foreknow" the ideas of affection and choice. This is contrary to the usage of the language and occasions tautology. 2. The opposite school insists on inserting the thought of faith into the foreknowledge, i. e. "Whom he foreknew as believing," etc. This interpretation we cannot accept. Repeating the explanation above given, we guard it against both extremes: 1. A man—e. g. Paul—is present to God's foreknowledge before the world was created, as a fallen, sinful and justly condemned child of wrath. 2. God, out of infinite mercy, determines to save him by forgiving his sins and bringing him to everlasting life; i. e. he is foreordained. 3. After Paul is born, God comes to Paul with the call, to which Paul yields. 4. The Holy Spirit works in Paul faith, and Paul is justified. 5. By the grace of the Holy Spirit, Paul is preserved in faith until the end of life, and at death his soul is glorified. 6. His body awaits glorification at the resurrection, when soul and body will together enjoy life eternal. True, as it is, that no one who is foreordained to glorification will ever be without faith at death, the consideration of the relation of faith to either predestination or justification is a matter entirely outside of the scope of this passage. It belongs elsewhere.

To be conformed to the image of his son. So intent are most who treat of this passage upon the settlement of the controversy concerning the relation of foreordination to salvation or to faith, that the intensely practical point of this verse is often overlooked. The end of the foreordination is that true Christians be conformed to the image of Christ. This occurs: 1. By the union of the divine and human. As the Son took upon Him a human nature, so Christians become the temples of the Holy Ghost, and Christ lives in them. The mystical union is a reflection of the personal union. The Christian becomes partaker of the Divine Nature (2 Pet. 1 : 4). 2. By the holiness of life proceeding from the indwelling Spirit, and after the example of Christ (Phil. 2 : 5). 3. By the patient endurance of suffering (1 Pet. 2 : 21–24). 4. By final glorification (1 Cor. 15 : 49; 2 Cor. 3 : 18; Phil. 3 : 21; 1 John 3 : 2). **That he might be the first-born.** The glorification of the child of God has as its end the glorification of the Son (Col. 1 : 15, 18). " What comes out, as the end of the divine decree, is the creation of a great family of men, made partakers of the divine existence and action, in the midst of which the glorified Jesus shines as the prototype" (GODET).

Ver. 30. **And whom he foreordained, them he also called.** (See notes on ver. 28.) **And whom he called them he also justified.** "Since, however, not all who are called obey, but some oppose the Word, and reject God's counsel concerning themselves, we must understand that the Apostle is here speaking of that call which reaches the purposed end; for he is treating of those who are also justified and glorified, whom he also describes elsewhere (2 Tim. 1 : 9). These are the same as the predestinated; the only difference is, that predestination occurs from eternity, while calling occurs in time. Justification is nothing but the temporal carrying out of the predestination that occurred from eternity" (BALDWIN). "Paul does not make the number of those who are called, justified, glorified to be absolutely equal; he does not deny that the believer may fail between the special call and the glorification (11 : 22); nor does he deny that there are also persons called who may not be justified; but he shows that so far as God is concerned, He conducts His people from step to step" (BENGEL). **Them he also glorified.** Completing the history of a saved soul, he uses the past tense, and looks back over its entire course. "Concerning all these acts, he speaks in the past, partly, on account of the certainty of the subject, because God's election makes no mistakes, and they who have been predestinated to glory assuredly will attain it: and, partly, because the process occurs *à posteriori*, and, in this passage, nothing is treated of except the justification, call and predestination of the glorified" (BALDWIN).

It should be remembered that this chain of argument

is in explanation of what is meant by the call, and the love of God proceeding therefrom.

Ver. 31-39 contain one of the most sublime passages in all literature, "a dithyrambic of faith equal to any of the most sublime creations of human language" (OLSHAUSEN), "a hymn of the assurance of faith." ERASMUS asks: "What did Cicero ever say that was grander?"

31-39. What then shall we say to these things? If God *is* for us, who *is* against us? He that spared not his own Son, but delivered him up for us all, how shall he not also with him freely give us all things? Who shall lay anything to the charge of God's elect? It is God that justifieth; who is he that shall condemn? It is Christ Jesus that died, yea rather, that was raised from the dead, who is at the right hand of God, who also maketh intercession for us. Who shall separate us from the love of Christ? shall tribulation, or anguish, or persecution, or famine, or nakedness, or peril, or sword? Even as it is written,

> For thy sake we are killed all the day long;
> We were accounted as sheep for the slaughter.

Nay, in all these things we are more than conquerors through him that loved us. For I am persuaded, that neither death, nor life, nor angels, nor principalities, nor things present, nor things to come, nor powers, nor height, nor depth, nor any other creature, shall be able to separate us from the love of God, which is in Christ Jesus our Lord.

Ver. 31. **To these things**, viz. In view of all that has been said, not only concerning God's purpose, but in the argument concerning justification, that has preceded. "What shall we say? Will we lament as though the condition of Christians were one of certain sorrow and uncertain joy? Far from it! Let us murmur and complain because of our unbelief, and be ashamed of our distrust" (BESSER). **If God is for us.** A positive statement, strengthened by a hypothetical form. An echo of Ps. 27 : 1; 118 : 6. (Comp. Ps. 56 : 5, 11.) "For what are Emperor, Pope, Kings, Princes, all the world, against God? So long as the Lord be with us, we abide, and even though they should slay us, they do not thereby slay the Lord, who is with us. But if He abide, wherever He abides, there also shall we, as He says (John 14 : 19), 'Because I live, ye shall live also'" (LUTHER on Ps. 118 : 6).

Ver. 32. The thought is: "What can be denied those for whom the Son of God has been given?" **Spared not.** The best interpretation is found in Gen. 22 : 12. "The Father's Eternal Love did a certain violence to Itself in the surrender of His Son" (LIDDON). **His own Son.** Literally "his peculiar," "his proper" (*idios*) Son, distinguished from angels, who are sons by creation, and believers, who are sons by adoption. **For us all.** This neither teaches nor denies the universality of the atonement, which must be decided by other passages. The meaning here is that all believers share equally in all the blessings brought by Christ. **With him.** The argument is from the greater to the less. If He would not deny His Son, what is there that He could deny? **Freely give** in the original is one word, "gratify," "favor us in all things." Whatever comes as a consequence of Redemption is gratuitous. **All things.** This Paul himself explains more fully in 1 Cor. 3 : 21–23. (Comp. ver. 28.)

Ver. 33. **Who shall lay anything to the charge?** A technical legal term, meaning "come forward as a prosecutor," "prosecute." "Paul is not ignorant how many accusers every believer has : Conscience, the Law, Satan, the persons we have offended or scandalized by our faults; all so many voices rising against us. Did Paul himself, when writing these words, not think of the cries of pain uttered by the Christians whom he had cast into prison and scourged, and especially of the blood of Stephen? All these charges are only too real" (GODET). **God's elect.** Those whom God has determined to save, and in whom the work of grace described in vers. 29, 30, is in progress. **It is.** Some urge here the interrogative: "Is it God that justifieth?" i. e. Can God who acquits be the prosecutor? But this is less forcible than the Indicative, which is supported by Is. 50 : 8, 9—the same thought in its O. T. and less clear form. Luther's paraphrase brings out the meaning: "God is here that justifies." "Here, in the Church, where all sins are forgiven; here in His Word, the Word of all grace, and in the sacraments of His precious oath; here we meet God, but nowhere else" (BESSER). If God then is here, who justifies, all other voices must be silent. If the judge is himself the surety, what has the one arraigned before him to dread? Were there no other, this passage alone would establish the forensic character of justification. To "justify" is the reverse of to "lay to the charge of."

Ver. 34. **Who is he that shall condemn?** or "Who shall be the condemning one?" In the Greek, the change of grammatical structure is very apparent, showing that while many may accuse, there is but one Judge (Acts 10 : 42; 17 : 31; Rom. 14 : 10). **It is Christ Jesus that died.** The Judge Himself appears as our Advocate. He offers what He Himself has paid as the price for our sins. Again Luther's paraphrase: "Christ is here, who died." "Under His wings our Saviour covers us, and we must be uninjured, even though Satan be intent on devouring us" (BESSER). **Yea rather, that was raised from the dead.** Christ is no longer in the grave. We preach not a dead, but a risen and ever-living Christ. The resurrection is the pledge of the completion and efficacy of His redemption. (Comp. on 4 : 25.) **At the right hand of God,** declaring the full participation of the humanity of Christ in the omnipresent divine dominion over the Universe. Here the reference is to Christ's omnipotent power in behalf of His elect. **Who also maketh inter-**

cession for us, i. e. Can He who acts as our Mediator, and prays for us to the Father, be persuaded to condemn us? He who wants to ruin God's elect appears before the wrong court for such a procedure. On the intercession of Christ, see Luke 22 : 31 seq.; Hebr. 4 : 14-16; 7 : 25; 9 : 11, 12, 24; 1 John 2 : 1.

Ver. 35. Preserving the strictly logical coherence in this rhapsody, Paul comes to the application to the thought from which he started in ver. 18. "The Apostle has defied accusers; their voice is silenced by the sentence of justification which covers believers. He has asked whether at the last day the Judge will not condemn, and he has seen sin, the object of condemnation, disappear from the believer's life before the work of the crucified and glorified Christ. It remains to be known whether some hostile power will not succeed in violently breaking the bond which unites us to the Lord" (GODET).

Who shall separate us? The objects referred to are regarded as though they were persons. The ardor of feeling assumes poetic phraseology. **From the love of Christ,** i. e. From Christ's love to us. What shall turn aside Christ's love from us? (Comp. notes on 5 : 5.) It is the love of Him who died and who is interceding for us (ver. 34). That the meaning cannot be our love to Christ, is manifest from the fact that we cannot be separated from our own love to an object. "It is not my imperfect love to Him, but His perfect love to me that brings me comfort." **Tribulation or anguish,** etc. Often found together, as in 2 : 9; 2 Cor. 6 : 4. The latter is more intense, and brings out more the inner side of suffering. (See TRENCH, Synonyms, 2 : 20 seq.) The entire catalogue is explained by 2 Cor. 11 : 23-27.

It seems almost as though, with prophetic insight, Paul looked forward through his future course, until his death by the sword. All these things only test love. He who flees when calamity comes upon one whom he professes to love, has not loved him really, or, if really, only very feebly. Can it then be thought that Christ who died for us, loves us no more than to forsake us when tribulation, anguish, persecution, etc. come? (Comp. John 10:11, 12.)

Ver. 36. **Even as it is written,** viz. in Ps. 44:22. By these words, Paul shows that the experience of Christians is nothing new. As in chapters three and four he shows that the Old is a continuation of the New Testament, so he here further confirms this by declaring that their experience is precisely the same as that of the O. T. saints. The verse is quoted from the LXX. "But there is this remarkable difference between the tone of the Psalmist and the tone of the Apostle. The former cannot understand the chastening, complains that God's heavy hand has been laid without cause upon His people; the latter can rejoice in persecution also, and exclaim: 'Nay, in all these things we are more than conquerors'" (PEROWNE on Ps. 44). **We are killed,** "being killed"; some, at one time; others, at another. **All the day long.** Without regard to any particular hours. Persecution, like death, has all seasons for its own. At any moment, some may fall. **Accounted as sheep.** A type of the animals given man for food (Ps. 44:11); whose death is, therefore, in accord with God's will. The thought is that their enemies treated them precisely as though God desired that they should be slaughtered. The Apostle derives especial consolation from the words: "For Thy sake."

Ver. 37. **Nay, in all these things.** Unlike the Psalmist, this causes the Apostle no despondency, but only increases his triumph. "Nay"="but," i. e. notwithstanding these afflictions. **We are more than conquerors.** Not only are our enemies repelled, but we profit by their attack. We drive them from the field; and, at the same time, every act of violence on their part becomes only a means of enhancing our blessedness. (Comp. 1 John 4:4.) **Through him that loved us,** viz. Christ (ver. 37). The aorist is used, because His death is present to the writer's mind, as the great proof of His love (5:8). "The love of Christ, is not simply a thought, but a force" (GODET). Christ, who loved and loves us, works in and through us (Gal. 2:20; Rev. 1:5). "A Christian is thus a king, i. e. lord over all, and to him all creatures must be obedient, but spiritually. Externally, life and its possessions may be taken from him, but he labors for and does what is commanded him. And even though everything were taken from him, yet he is always benefitted thereby, and his faith is ever growing and ruling in his heart; so that neither riches nor poverty trouble him, or make him either sadder or more joyful (Phil. 4:12). Whether he be maligned or praised, it is all the same. This is accomplished by the mind which he has, i. e. the joyful, firm faith whereby he cleaves to God. Such a lord is a Christian heart, which no one can change or trouble; it always retains its self-possession. Such lords faith makes of us. But where are such Christians? St. Paul was one of them" (LUTHER).

Ver. 38. **For I am persuaded.** He has no doubt whatever. **That neither death nor life,** i. e. Whether we die or live, we remain in the love of Christ. Death comes first, because it has just been in mind in ver. 36. There is nothing either in this world or the world to come that can turn the love of God away from us. **Nor angels, nor principalities.** A contrast between good and bad angels. The former refers, as in Gal. 1:8, to a hypothetical case. Even though the good angels should attempt—as they will not—to divert the love of Christ from him, they could not do it! (For "principalities," comp. Eph. 6:12.) **Nor things present.** All that is already about us. **Nor things to come.** The inevitable future and all that it contains. **Nor powers.** This seems here to be general and to apply to what immediately follows in next verse; i. e. Let all the powers in heaven and hell combine; they cannot wrest our Saviour's love from us.

Ver. 39. **Nor height, nor depth.** In partitative apposition with "powers," i. e. "powers above and below," "powers in heaven and in hell." **Nor any other creature.** Nothing outside of God. **Love of God which is in Christ Jesus.** This is generally interpreted of the love of the Father in sending His Son. Not inconsistent with this is the thought that it refers to the love of God going forth towards man in his foreseen sin through all eternity, which found historical realization in the death of the incarnate Son of God, and which has entered our lives as a new life-force.

PART IV.

EXCURSUS: THE RELATION OF JUDAISM TO THE DOCTRINE OF THE UNIVERSALITY OF GRACE (9 : 1—11 : 36).

THE argument of the entire Epistle ought to be reviewed before proceeding to this appendix to what may be called the doctrinal portion of the Epistle. The Universality of Grace has been established: 1. From the universal need of justification: 2. From the universal provision of justification : 3. From the failure of the argument that such a doctrine must encourage sin.

This doctrine is so strange to a Jew, that it may be expected to excite many questions, with respect to matters that have heretofore been closely connected with his religious experience. St. Paul knows well what these questions are. There can be no such conflict through which he himself has not passed. He is ready with the answers, since they are those which he has repeatedly given himself. He tells what God's grace has made him and what he had been without it. From all these privileges, his unbelieving countrymen have cut themselves off. Undoubtedly this entire argument is directed towards the Judaistic portion of the church at Rome, which felt a peculiar sympathy for their non-Christian kinsmen. He lets them know that their sympathy cannot exceed his own.

Section I.—The Apostle's Sorrow for the Jews (9 : 1–5).

1–5. I say the truth in Christ, I lie not, my conscience bearing witness with me in the Holy Ghost, that I have great sorrow and unceasing pain in my heart. For I could wish that I myself were anathema from Christ for my brethren's sake, my kinsmen according to the flesh : who are Israelites; whose is the adoption, and the glory, and the covenants, and the giving of the law, and the service *of God*, and the promises ; whose are the fathers, and of whom is Christ as concerning the flesh, who is over all, God blessed for ever. Amen.

Ver. 1. **I say the truth in Christ**, i. e. as one who speaks not as a natural man, but as a regenerate Christian (Eph. 4 : 17; 1 Thess. 4 : 1 ; 2 Cor. 2 : 17; 12 : 19). Thus he prepares the way for declaring the final rejection of Israel, which if foretold, without some such statement, might excite indignation. He disclaims all personal and partisan animosity. **My conscience bearing witness.** Conscience as the faculty whereby we discriminate good from evil may be perverted or obscured, so as not to be an infallible guide. But in this case his conscience is entirely under the illumination and control of the Holy Spirit. **In the Holy Ghost** qualifies " bearing witness." When one is " in Christ," all the actions of his life, and, therefore, even those of his conscience, proceed from the Holy Ghost.

Ver. 2. **I have great sorrow.** Contrast this with the close of the preceding chapter. " In spiritual things, the extremes of grief and joy may exist together " (BENGEL).

Ver. 3. **For I could wish.** Not " I once wished," but, " I could wish, if it were so permitted," " if it were God's will." To wish this unconditionally would be to display more love for his kinsmen than for God. **I myself were**

anathema. In spite of all efforts to soften this expression, anathema cannot mean simply excommunication, but must mean as A. V. translates it, "accursed" or "a curse," "devoted to everlasting destruction from God's presence." For argument, see PHILIPPI'S exhaustive note, and LIGHTFOOT on Gal. 1 : 8. The wish can be explained only by the devotion of the Apostle in winning souls to Christ. "Such expressions we cannot comprehend, because we are so remote from such love as that which moved the Apostle" (CHRYSOSTOM). Moses made a similar prayer (Ex. 32 : 32). HODGE refutes the use of this passage to prove that willingness to be damned, for Christ's sake, must be required as an evidence of a truly Christian spirit. "Paul does not teach that we should be willing to be damned for the glory of God. 1. His very language implies that such a wish would be improper. 2. If it is wrong to do evil that good may come, how can it be right to wish to be evil that good may come? 3. Can one love God so much as to wish to hate Him? Can he be so good as to desire to be bad? We must be willing to give up houses and lands, parents and brethren, and our life also, for Christ and His Kingdom, but we are never required to give up holiness for His sake, for this would be a contradiction." **For my brethren's sake.** Not "in their stead," but "for their good."

Ver. 4. **Who are Israelites.** The Greek means clearly : "Inasmuch as they are." Beyond the ties of the flesh, is the fact that they are "Israelites." He calls them not Hebrews, for that would designate them rather by their language, nor Jews, for that would mark their race, but "Israelites," with respect to their position as the chosen people of God (Gen. 32 : 28). (Comp. 2 Cor. 11 : 22.) **Whose is the adoption.** They were distinguished from all other nations, by being in a peculiar sense the children of God (Ex. 4 : 22, 23; Deut. 14 : 1, 2 ; 32 : 6; Hos. 11 : 1). **And the glory.** The visible symbol of the divine presence, as in the pillar of cloud and fire in the wilderness, the lightnings of Sinai, the Shecinah (Ex. 25 : 22; Lev. 16 : 2; Ps. 80 : 1). **The covenant.** The covenant made with Abraham (Gen. 15 : 18; 17 : 17). Sometimes designated "his," i. e. God's covenant, Ps. 25 : 10; 111 : 5, 9, was often repeated. Hence the plural, as in Eph. 2 : 12. This covenant was before the law (Gal. 3 : 17). **And the giving of the law.** They had not been left to the light of nature, but were the possessors of a divine revelation (Deut. 4 : 8; Neh. 9 : 13). (Comp. Acts 7 : 53; Gal. 3 : 19; Heb. 2 : 2.) **And the service,** viz. the entire O. T. worship Heb. 9 : 1, 6. **And the promises,** i. e. those concerning the Messiah. "The promises flow from the covenants, and the service of God was instituted by the giving of the law" (BENGEL).

Ver. 5. **Whose are the fathers.** Their descent from eminent servants of God is a matter of no small importance. In a special sense, Abraham, Isaac and Jacob are meant (Ex. 3 : 13–16; 4 : 5; Matt. 22 : 32; Acts 3 : 13; 7 : 32). **Of whom is Christ, as concerning the flesh.** (See chap. 1 : 3.) Thus the humanity of our Lord is designated. **Who is over all God blessed.** Thus the divinity of Christ is designated. "Who" clearly refers to Christ. For similar testimonials to the divinity of Christ by Paul, see 2 Cor. 5 : 19; Col. 2 : 9; 1 Tim. 3 : 16; Phil. 2 : 6; Tit. 2 : 13, etc.; by other writers, John 1 : 1; 1 John 5 : 20; Heb. 1 : 8. Some regard this clause as disjoined from what precedes, and make it a doxology. This would be extremely abrupt.

Section II.—Vindication of God's Attributes Against Objections Arising from the Rejection of Israel (9 : 6–29).

(*a.*) *The Truth of God* (vers. 6–13).

6–13. But *it is* not as though the word of God hath come to naught. For they are not all Israel which are of Israel: neither, because they are Abraham's seed, are they all children: but, in Isaac shall thy seed be called. That is, it is not the children of the flesh that are children of God; but the children of the promise are reckoned for a seed. For this is a word of promise, According to this season will I come, and Sarah shall have a son. And not only so; but Rebecca also having conceived by one, *even* by our father Isaac—for *the children* being not yet born, neither having done anything good or bad, that the purpose of God according to election might stand, not of works, but of him that calleth, it was said unto her, The elder shall serve the younger. Even as it is written, Jacob I loved, but Esau I hated.

Ver. 6. **Not as though the word of God,** viz. God's promise (Gen. 12 : 3). The fact that many who have sprung from the chosen people have renounced their faith, and disavowed the promises, does not prove these promises void. From the very beginning, the promise was not transmitted by natural descent, but by divine election. **They are not all Israel, which are of Israel,** i. e. they are not all spiritual children of Israel, who are his descendants according to the flesh. The first Israel here designates the people, i. e. the true children of God, and the second, the patriarch.

Ver. 7. **Neither because they are Abraham's seed.** Surely this should be nothing strange to devout Jews who remembered the promise. They must remember that these covenant privileges did not pertain to all descendants of Abraham, but only to descendants of Israel. Ishmael was excluded. Thus the divine election is maintained even in the Old Testament. "Seed" designates descent according to the flesh: "children," spiritual as well as carnal descent. **In Isaac shall thy seed be called**, i. e. be acknowledged or recognized as such. The descendants of Isaac are to be recognized as true children. A quotation from Gen. 21 : 12. "As, therefore, Isaac and Ishmael, according to the flesh, were sons of Abraham, and, nevertheless, Isaac only was the heir of the promise; so believing and unbelieving Jews were both descendants of Abraham, and, nevertheless, the promise pertained only to the believing, with whom it was never in vain. As both also were from the loins of Abraham, and, nevertheless, only Isaac was heir to the land of Canaan, Ishmael being rejected; so all the Jews are of the posterity of Abraham, and, nevertheless, only the believing are heirs of the eternal blessings, which the promise especially embraced" (BALDWIN).

Ver. 8. **It is not the children of the flesh**, etc., i. e. Spiritual blessings do not descend by natural inheritance. **But the children of the promise.** The antithesis to "children of the flesh" is most emphatic and exclusive. Children of the promise are those who become children in virtue of God's promise. Isaac was not a child of the flesh, since Abraham and Sarah had passed the period when they could naturally have had a child. It was the power of God's promise that enabled them to become parents of Isaac, supernaturally and contrary to the law that operated in the flesh. **Are reckoned for a seed**, i. e. even though they can lay no claim to natural descent. (Comp. Gal. 4 : 23.)

Ver. 9 shows what the word of promise was, to which Isaac owed his origin. A quotation from Gen. 18 : 10, 14. **According to this season**, i. e. "At this time, next year." (See DELITZSCH on Gen. 18 : 10.) Emphasis is placed upon Sarah, the mother of the child of the promise, as Hagar was mother of the child of the flesh.

Ver. 10. **And not only so.** The Apostle continues, that, even leaving Ishmael, and confining attention to the descendants of Isaac, the same principle obtains. Natural descent determines nothing. If Ishmael and Isaac were descendants of the same father, but of different mothers, Esau and Jacob were sons of the same father and mother. If the attempt should be made to explain the inequality between Ishmael and Isaac by the fact that the mother of the one was a slave and that of the other was free; the origin of Esau and Isaac, being absolutely identical, could not be explained in this way. Rebecca, not Isaac, is mentioned, since it was to her and not to Isaac that the prophecy mentioned in ver. 12 was addressed (Gen. 25 : 23). Rebecca is subject to a verb understood, such as "fared likewise," "had the same experience."

Vers. 11–13. Many of the difficulties connected with the exposition of these verses disappear, when we remember:

1. That it is foreign to the Apostle's argument to introduce here a discussion of the entire doctrine of Predestination. His object is to declare that spiritual privileges do not come by natural descent, but through God's promises as the declarations of His sovereign and eternal purposes. The blessings offered to Israel were not for all, but only for those within Israel, who, beside natural descent, were heirs also of the promises (ver. 8).

2. That the discussion presupposes a world of sin. The illustration here introduced cannot be understood as determining the sinfulness or absence of sin of those mentioned; but describes God's relations to those of the same sinful stock.

3. That Esau and Jacob are not referred to as individ-

uals. As in ver. 6, Israel stands for descendants of Israel, so here Esau and Jacob represent their descendants. This is proved by the passages quoted. The reference in Gen. 25 : 23 is explicitly to "two nations" and "two manner of people." In Mal. 3 : 2, 3, the word "hated" of ver. 13 is shown to be fulfilled in the Edomites. Esau never served Jacob (2 Sam. 8 : 14 ; 2 Kings 8 : 20).

4. That the **election** here described is not election to salvation. Otherwise, no descendant of Esau would be saved, and none of Jacob be lost. " Even Ishmael is not left without promise (Gen. 16 : 10; 17 : 20), and is preserved by divine providence (21 : 17, sqq.). Esau also receives his blessing (Gen. 27 : 39 sq.), while the life of Israel and Jacob is fertile in peculiar trials and sorrows " (PHIL.). If election here were election to salvation, the rejection of Esau must refer to his being consigned to eternal punishment ; if this rejection be meant here, it would teach the doctrine that, without regard to their merits, men are eternally condemned—a doctrine contrary to the entire tenor of God's Word.

5. That the word **" hated "** does not denote here to dislike or abhor. It simply expresses the preference shown to one who is loved, when his claims or interests come into conflict with the other, so that, even though love to him may exist, the conduct is such that it would seem, to one who looked at it externally, as though he were hated (Luke 14 : 26; John 12 : 25; Prov. 13 : 24). " When a Hebrew compares a less with a greater love, he is wont to call the former hatred " (Gen. 29 : 30, 31 ; Deut. 21 : 15, etc.). (THOLUCK.)

Ver. 11. **That the purpose of God according to election.** Election first, the purpose afterward. The reference is to God's purposes of love made with respect to those whom He had chosen for a special mission in the development of His Kingdom. "The purpose which is quite free is founded on election alone" (BENGEL). God raises up and trains those who are to fit into peculiar places in His great world-plan. These places are filled without regard to the merits of individuals, but solely from God's own choice. **Not of works, but of him that calleth.** This defines the purpose. God's purpose "is not the result of the presence or absence of conduct in conformity with the law, but has its ground in the will of God" (LIDDON). Nevertheless, this will of God is not arbitrary or capricious. God places limitations upon Himself, whenever He establishes an order of agencies, as, for example, in the Gospel. The will of God never acts in violation of this revealed order.

Ver. 12. **The elder shall serve the younger.** Literally: "The greater shall serve the less." So LUTHER. "In all worldly things Esau surpassed Jacob. But, before God, the greater was subject to the less, as the mighty Emperor Augustus served the small Christ-child in Bethlehem; or the Edomite King Herod, the small Jesus who fled from him into Egypt; or the great mass of unbelieving Jews, and worldly-renowned heathen, the little flock of Christians, who are for awhile despised and weak, but whom all things must serve, in order that they may inherit the promise of everlasting dominion in the Kingdom of God" (BESSER).

Ver. 13. **Even as it is written.** The passage in Malachi clearly refers to the bestowal of temporal blessings. The descendants of Jacob are, in this respect, so signally favored, that it might almost seem as though the descendants of Esau were hated. These earthly blessings, however, are a type of the higher privileges of the theocracy. These prerogatives of the Jews have been already described in this Epistle (3 : 1, 2), and even in this chapter (vers. 4, 5). The application of the argument has been already described in this Epistle (3 : 1, 2). The application of the argument here is to enforce the question, whether God, who had so signally blessed the Jews above others, without regard to their merits or works, but solely by His sovereign grace, were not free, in His own time and way, to extend the same grace, so that it may comprehend others also. But this cannot be used to support the theory of any irresistible grace, or that God had such personal feeling against Esau, as to withhold from him or his descendants grace sufficient for salvation. This would contradict Tit. 2 : 14.

(b.) The Justice of God (vers. 14–21).

14–22. What shall we say then? Is there unrighteousness with God? God forbid. For he saith to Moses, I will have mercy on whom I have mercy, and I will have compassion on whom I have compassion. So then it is not of him that willeth, nor of him that runneth, but of God that hath mercy. For the scripture saith unto Pharaoh, For this very purpose did I raise thee up, that I might shew in thee my power, and that my name might be published abroad in all the earth. So then he hath mercy on whom he will, and whom he will he hardeneth.

Thou wilt say then unto me, Why doth he still find fault? For who withstandeth his will? Nay but, O man, who art thou that repliest against God? Shall the thing formed say to him that formed it, Why didst thou make me thus? Or hath not the potter a right over the clay, from the same lump to make one part a vessel unto honour, and another unto dishonour?

Ver. 14. **Is there unrighteousness with God?** Paul anticipates here the turn which he foresees that the opponent of his argument will give to the use of the passages just cited. As GODET remarks, the Jewish thought is that man's doings regulate those of God, and that any variation from this would be a violation of justice.

Ver. 15. **For he saith to Moses.** The force of this is

not appreciated, unless it be remembered that the emphatic point lies in the fact that this is a quotation from the Old Testament, which the objecting Jew most highly revered. Every Jew must be struck dumb, when in the midst of such a charge against the New Testament conception of divine grace, he hears these words from his own Holy Scriptures (Ex. 33 : 19). If these views of the sovereignty of God's grace and its total independence of human deserts be wrong, says Paul, what will you do with such a sweeping text from your own law? And yet you correctly acknowledge the law as the standard of right! **I will have mercy on whom I have mercy.** God has His own reasons for showing mercy that He declines to reveal to man. Man must be satisfied with the simple assurance that God has so willed it. This is enough. Outside of and beyond God there is no standard of right, according to which God's revelation is to be judged. " His mercy is unconditioned by any human right or title, and is conditioned by nothing but His own unfettered will " (PHILIPPI). As originally spoken to Moses, these words were intended to remind him that God's condescension in making him, in a peculiar way, the organ of revelation, could not be attributed to any merit or worthiness of his, but solely to God's mercy. At the same time the comprehensiveness of this mercy was revealed (Ex. 34 : 7).

Ver. 16. **So then it is not of him that willeth.** Man's will can oppose, obstruct and prevent the work of divine grace from attaining its end (Matt. 23 : 37; John 5 : 40). Where man becomes the channel of divine grace, his will is active, and accomplishes that towards which it is directed. But this activity of man's will is originated, maintained and constantly energized by that of God (Phil. 2 : 12, 13). Instead of God's purposes being dependent upon man's doing, man's doing is dependent upon God's gracious will towards man. **Nor of him that runneth.** That man may obtain God's blessings, he must "run" (1 Cor. 9 : 26; Phil. 3 : 14; 2 Tim. 4 : 7). This favorite figure of St. Paul refers to the ardent, earnest, energetic endeavor, in response to God's offer; but this comes also from the divinely-impelled will. From first to last, all the activity of the child of God is explained by 1 Cor. 15 : 10; Heb. 13 : 21. This is illustrated even by the concurrence of God in natural things (Ps. 128 : 1), although what is here said belongs to a higher sphere, where the divine activity is more than concurrence. If all, then, come **of God that hath mercy,** what complaint can man justly make, because of God's unequal distribution of what is absolutely and entirely His own? God's sovereignty controlled even the hostility of Pharaoh. Much more was it to be regarded as supreme in all arrangements for the diffusion of the Gospel and the extension of the Kingdom of God. These words are found in Ex. 9 : 16. **Did I raise thee up**=prepared and appointed him to an office in which his enmity to God might be conspicuous, and might be allowed to exercise itself to the fullest extent. Pharaoh, whose character was well foreknown to God, might have cherished his enmity in obscurity. God advanced him to power, although a bitter enemy, for a great purpose. **I might shew in thee my power.** For it must not be supposed that God was thwarted by Pharaoh's long-continued resistance of God's will. Pharaoh was allowed to go to the farthest extreme; that the power of each being put to the test, it might be manifest as to which was the stronger. Had there been no Pharaoh, there would have been no such triumphs in leaving Egypt as those which the children of Israel for generations celebrated, as the proofs of God's signal favor. A Pharaoh was a necessary prerequisite to their Psalms of thanksgiving and victory. **And that my name might be published abroad.** The name of God is God, so far as He is known or revealed. As we learn to know an object from its contrasts, and the brightest objects stand forth most conspicuously upon a dark background, so what God is would be most clearly seen in His conflict with Pharaoh. **Throughout** all the earth. Wherever the Book of Exodus is read, this is fulfilled. (Comp. Matt. 26 : 13.) The entire tenor of Scripture forbids any interpretation of this verse which would teach either that God instigated Pharaoh to sin, or that He regarded his offences with indifference.

Ver. 18. **So then he hath mercy on whom he will,** etc. A repetition of ver. 15. **Whom he will, he hardeneth.** A further statement of what had been treated already in ver. 17. To "harden" is to withhold or withdraw that grace whereby men are led to recognize their true relations to God, i. e. to see their sins and to surrender to the work of the Holy Spirit. The history of Pharaoh shows that men first harden themselves, i. e. by continued resistance, they render themselves insensible to the approaches of divine grace, before God is said to harden them. Five times Pharaoh is said to have hardened his heart (Ex. 7 : 13, 14, 22 ; 8 : 15, 32 ; 9 : 7. See the Hebrew or the R. V.) before God is said to harden him ; "and even after that, as if a remnant of liberty still remained, it is said for the last time that he hardened himself" (Ex. 9 : 34, 35). (GODET.) "God Himself is said to do that which results from a misuse of the laws of Nature which He has given; and yet, so far as God is concerned, this result is always a judgment for man's neglect of God's merciful calls and warnings" (LIDDON). God's sovereignty, however, controls and determines the very laws by which men, persistently opposing known truth and duty, become absolutely callous, and irresponsive to His first approaches. "He had refused to glorify God actively, he must glorify Him passively" (GODET). Pharaoh being a Gentile, the Jews willingly acknowledged God's justice in this. Paul here shows that the same principle applies within Israel. Those among them who persistently oppose the clear light of the Gospel and harden themselves to the truth, must expect the fate of Pharaoh, even though they be members of God's chosen people.

Ver. 19. **Thou wilt say, then, unto me,** etc. Objection after objection is placed upon the lips of an imaginary adversary, as they had occurred to the mind of Paul himself. We can see the proud Pharisee of his unregenerate nature arguing with the new man enlightened by the grace of the Gospel. To this Pharisee within, Paul gives no quarter. He does not attempt to argue with him, or to show how this doctrine of Divine sovereignty must be interpreted by that of Divine love. The justice of God has been questioned, and that justice in all its strictness and severity must be set forth. If the objector were a sincere inquirer, ready to bow before the Divine justice, the mysteries of the Divine love would have been disclosed. But the Law comes before the Gospel; and the mercy of the Gospel belongs only to those who have recognized the justice of the Law. **For who withstandeth his will?** The objector says: If all this be so, there is no place for human accountability, and man cannot do otherwise than the results show. Paul might have proved that there are spheres within which a resistance of God's will is possible (Matt. 23 : 37; Acts 7 : 51); but this was not the place to proclaim this doctrine, which even conscience, in its assertion of man's responsibility, teaches.

Men must be humbled before they are qualified to learn the law of Divine love pervading that of justice.

Ver. 20. **Nay, but, O man, who art thou?** An emphatic contrast between "man" and "God" is here made. He makes man feel his complete nothingness before God. A slight irony pervades the question, which exposes the absurdity of any criticisms of God that man has to offer. He does not reply to the question asked, but to the spirit which prompted it. The thought is: Even assuming your premises, where would be the injustice? Arguing on the ground of justice, you must acknowledge that God could make whatever disposition of men He pleased. God's actions are not regulated by the norm of man's judgment. **Shall the thing formed say to him that formed it?** This is enforced by a question, containing allusions well understood by his Jewish opponents to Is. 29:16; 64:8; Jer. 18:6. "What makes the Prophet's language so exactly appropriate to the Apostle's argument is, that they are both dealing with the same subject, namely, God's formation of Israel as a nation, and His consequent unquestionable right to deal with it as seems good to Him" (GIFFORD).

Ver. 21. **Or hath not the potter a right over the clay?** But it is foreign to his argument to explain how this right is exercised. The entire discussion has reference to absolute justice, not to the revealed mercy of God. "The power of God is one thing; the exercise of this power is another thing. Thus the human race having fallen into sin, God had the power to absolutely reprobate all as vessels of wrath; but He did not use this right, but, having compassion on the human race, He willed that they only who to the end would be unbelieving should be reprobate" (CALOVIUS). "The potter does not make the clay, but digs it; God makes man; therefore, He has greater power than the potter. But absolute power and liberty do not imply an absolute will and decree. Had God left the whole human race under sin and death, He would not have acted unjustly, but He did not use that right" (BENGEL). "The potter, by his efficacious will, prepares both vessels. God, however, does not make vessels of wrath, but, finding us all by nature the children of wrath, He most justly allows those who obey not the Gospel to be further hardened by the devil, and, in this way, to be prepared for destruction. Hence it is clear that the figure of the potter and the clay was not proposed by Paul, with the intention that all its members should apply; but, that the difference between the potter and God being shown, the justice of God might be still more effectually vindicated from the wicked murmur of men. They err, therefore, who attempt to apply this figure to the purpose of the Apostle, so as to say that God, by His efficacious will, and that, too, absolute, destines, forms and prepares some men for dishonor and destruction. That this explanation is most foreign from the mind of Paul, the very context shows" (HUNNIUS). The figure of the vessels is repeated in 2 Tim. 2 : 20, 21.

(*c.*) *The Mercy of God* (vers. 22-24).

23-24. What if God, willing to shew his wrath, and to make his power known, endured with much longsuffering vessels of wrath fitted unto destruction : and that he might make known the riches of his glory upon vessels of mercy which he afore prepared unto glory, *even* us, whom he also called, not from the Jews only, but also from the Gentiles?

Vers. 22, 23. The incompleteness of the sentence renders the construction somewhat difficult. There is an ellipsis of the conclusion of the conditional sentence. There is also in ver. 23 a change of construction that renders the dependence of the clause of purpose ambiguous. Of the three explanations proposed, that adopted by both of the English versions seems by far the best. The thought is: "What reply can you make, if you find that God endures with longsuffering vessels of wrath?" So also: "What reply can you make, in case you learn that, in order that He might make known the riches of His glory, He so determined?" **If** belongs to endured. **God willing** is a concessive clause. The thought is: "What, if God, although willing, i. e. purposing, to show His wrath, endured with much longsuffering," etc. The problem here presented is the contrast between God's wrath and His longsuffering. **To show his wrath.** "God's wrath is no perturbation of His mind, but the judgment by which punishment is inflicted upon sin" (AUGUSTINE). The wrath of God always implies guilt in the object upon which the wrath descends. God created nothing in wrath, or to be the object of His wrath. It becomes an object of wrath by its departure from the end for which God created it. **His power known.** Literally: "That which it is possible for Him to do." **Endured with much longsuffering,** i. e. It is a great problem to reconcile God's justice with His protracted forbearance. Why, if He is just, was the descent of His wrath so long deferred, when He intended all along that it should be shown? The past tense refers primarily to Pharaoh, but it suggests also the unbelieving Israelites who, in Paul's day, were, in like manner, hardening their hearts, by resisting the plainest evidence of the truth. "Longsuffering" implies that the infliction of punishment is delayed, with a view to the possible repentance of the sinner (Rom. 2:4; 2 Pet. 3:9). **Vessels of wrath,** either as devoted to wrath, or into which the wrath of God is to be poured. **Fitted unto destruction.**

But God is not said to fit them for destruction, as in the next verse He is said to prepare vessels of mercy unto glory. Man's agency in fitting himself for destruction is thus recognized. "The two factors, the human and the divine, concur in the tragical development of such a moral state" (GODET). "The world is full of vessels of wrath, fitted for destruction, but God waits until the Last Day with a longsuffering that is inconceivable even to the saints" (Rev. 6 : 10). (BESSER.) **That he might make known the riches of his glory.** The glory of God is the sum of His attributes. (See note on 1 : 23.) The meaning here is "the inexhaustible fulness of His divine perfections." **Upon vessels of mercy,** i. e. those upon which the divine mercy is shed in such abundance that they are regarded simply as vessels. The receptive side of the Christian life is here brought into prominence. **Which he afore prepared.** (Comp. 8 : 29 sqq.) **Unto glory.** The display of His power and wrath is subordinate to that of His mercy. Compare Collect for tenth Sunday after Trinity: "O God, who declareth Thine Almighty Power chiefly in showing mercy and pity." "There are, therefore, three purposes which the Apostle produces why God bears with the vessels of wrath : 1. To display His wrath in punishing them. 2. To declare His power in destroying them. 3. To manifest the riches of His glory towards the vessels of mercy. For since they are of the same mass which is by nature damnable, it is apparent from the perdition of the vessels of wrath what, by divine mercy, has been granted them " (BALDWIN).

Ver. 24. **Even us.** The argument being complete, he ends it with the personal application. **Whom he also called.** The salvation was not only prepared for us, but, in time, it has been revealed, and we have been called to accept it. **Not from the Jews only.** Thus the key-note of the Epistle, the universality of divine grace as over against Jewish particularism, sounds throughout the Epistle. No one is called and saved because he is a Jew, but from the number of the Jews.

(*d.*) *Old Testament Proofs of the Adoption of some of the Gentiles, and the Rejection of some of the Israelites.*

25-33. As he saith also in Hosea,
    I will call that my people, which was not my people;
    And her beloved, which was not beloved.
    And it shall be, *that* in the place where it was said unto them, Ye are not my people,
There shall they be called sons of the living God.
And Isaiah crieth concerning Israel, If the number of the children of Israel be as the sand of the sea, it is the remnant that shall be saved: for the Lord will execute *his* word upon the earth, finishing it and cutting it short. And, as Isaiah hath said before,
    Except the Lord of Sabaoth had left us a seed,
    We had become as Sodom, and had been made like unto Gomorrah.
    What shall we say then? That the Gentiles, which followed not after righteousness, attained to righteousness, even the righteousness which is of faith: but Israel, following after a law of righteousness, did not arrive at *that* law. Wherefore? Because *they sought it* not by faith, but as it were by works. They stumbled at the stone of stumbling; even as it is written:
    Behold, I lay in Zion a stone of stumbling and a rock of offence:
    And he that believeth on him shall not be put to shame.

Vers. 25, 26. For this inclusion of Gentiles in the covenant-promises made to Israel, the Apostle next cites proof-texts from the Old Testament. The first passages are from Hosea, three passages being combined, and their order intentionally changed, for the purpose of bringing out the full force of the prophecy. The first part of ver. 25 is the last clause of Hos. 2 : 23; the second part is the second clause of the same verse in Hosea. **I will call that my people,** etc. This is the thought, but not the exact words of the prophet. Lit. in Hosea: " I will have pity on the not-pitied one, and I will say to the not my people, My people art thou."

Ver. 26 is from Hos. 1 : 10. **In the place where it was said unto them.** This was, according to the prophecy, the land of their exile. (See Hos. 1 : 11.) It is applied here to all Gentile lands, the Gentile Christians being regarded as the extension of the ten tribes (1 Pet. 2 : 10).

Ver. 27. As Hosea had taught that Gentiles were to share in the covenant, so Isaiah declares that the larger part of Israel will be excluded (Is. 10 : 22, 23; 1 : 9). **Isaiah crieth,** indicating the intensity of his earnestness. The quotation is from the LXX. R. V. reads: "Though thy people Israel shall be as the sand of the sea, only a remnant of them shall return." Two things are here indicated: First, a remnant shall be saved, i. e. however numerous those lost, nevertheless some shall still remain who shall escape the all but universal destruction, and in whom God's purposes shall assuredly be accomplished. Secondly, it is, however, only a few, "a remnant," that shall be saved. "'If the number of the children of Israel be as the sand of the sea,' i. e. if the Jews were so many that their number could not be computed, but their multitude exceeded all reckoning, like the sand, 'a remnant shall be saved,' i. e. they whom the Lord shall leave for Himself, when He will reject the rest. Or if their number were sterile and heavy, like the sand, a remnant which shall be resplendent and shall be fixed, like the stars in heaven, shall be saved. For both were promised Abraham" (Gen. 22 : 17). (ANSELM.) "He is speaking of the remnant and the most despised (i. e. of the holy apostles and martyrs) who have forsaken the ancient synagogue, and by faith have been regenerated so as to become a new people" (LUTHER). "St. Paul adopted nearly the words of the LXX.; again (as in ver. 25, and very often) developing a second and deeper fulfilment where the first fulfilment lay in past events of Israel's history; e. g. here, in the comparatively *small* return of the exiles, under Zerubbabel and Ezra. The return, in the Second Fulfilment, is a return to Christ, and thus equivalent to 'salvation.'"

Ver. 28. **The Lord will execute his word.** Again the LXX. text is followed, which is a paraphrase rather than a quotation of the Hebrew text. The latter reads according to the R. V.: "For a consummation, and that determined, shall the Lord, the Lord of hosts make in all the earth." The LXX. reads: "Finishing the word and cutting it short in righteousness, because a cut-short word will the Lord make in the whole world." The thought is that of the certainty of impending judgment, like that taught by Peter's sermon in Acts 2 : 19-21. **Cutting it short,** i. e. going the shortest way to accomplish it. A vivid description of its speedy fulfilment. "The verse seems to contain two things: 1. The manner of the thing, viz. that, in rejecting His people, God will use a certain cutting off, and, as it were, an abbreviation. For unless the days were shortened, not even the remnant would be saved. 2. The fruit or result. For when this cutting off of the people would be accomplished, he says that righteousness shall abound. For since the rejection of the Israelitic people has been accomplished, the Gospel of Christ, in which the righteousness of God is revealed from faith to faith, has been propagated throughout the whole world, not by the slender channel of rivulets, but with the great rush of torrents" (MYLIUS, quoted by CALOVIUS).

Ver. 29. **And as Isaiah hath said before.** R. V. of Is. 1 : 9 reads : " Except the Lord of hosts had left unto us a very small remnant." **Seed,** taken from the LXX., expresses not only the fewness of those who remained faithful, but also the promise of the future to be unfolded from them. However corrupt the teaching, obscure the church or few her true members, God always preserves for Himself a holy seed, a perpetual line of witnesses; and from this seed will spring, and in due time be manifest, a great harvest. But the idea that is here prominent is, that it is only the remnant that survives; the great mass of Israel is lost. **He had become as Sodom,** etc. To be like them means to be given wholly to destruction. None of their inhabitants, except Lot's family, who were not citizens, but sojourners remained. There is a climax here, Lot and his family escaped from Sodom; but not a soul remained of all who lived in Gomorrah. No seed or remnant was left.

Vers. 30, 31. **What shall we say then?** viz. concerning this admission of the Gentiles, and exclusion of many of Israel. Now comes the explanation, previously withheld by the Apostle, when urging the doctrine of God's sovereignty, and arguing from the standpoint of absolute justice. **That the Gentiles,** or merely "Gentiles," not referring to them as a whole, but indicating that the great mass of those actually receiving the promises are Gentiles. **Which followed not.** The original is emphatic, "pursued not," "made no earnest and persevering efforts to reach." **Righteousness** is attainable only as the divine standard of right, the Law, is in view. But the Gentiles were without the revealed knowledge of God, and the natural knowledge was so obscured and perverted, that the love and desire of righteousness could not be excited. The morality of heathenism was not, in the proper sense, righteousness. Three times the word is used, each repetition making it all the more forcible. A great parodox; a wonder of wonders, to associate

Gentiles with all their carelessness and indifference to the Law, with righteousness, while **Israel did not arrive at that law,** i. e. did not fulfil what the Law required, or attain righteousness, and this, notwithstanding all its painstaking efforts, and its boast of the Law! "These words are an authoritative commentary on ver. 16. All the willing and running of the Jews were unavailing. Thus, then, all depends on God's having mercy. Positively, man cannot produce the least of what is good; he must, therefore, always place himself in a passive position towards God, never in an active; his whole productive power is negative, and its fruit evil, of which the essence is opposition to the will of God. Hence no sin is so difficult to cure as self-righteousness; for this is want of love; and love alone is the fulfilling of the law" (OLSHAUSEN).

Ver. 32. **Wherefore,** i. e. How is the difference between the Gentiles and Israel to be explained? The answer is: By the faith of the one and the unbelief of the other. The cause of Israel's rejection is to be found, not in God, but in Israel itself. They failed to attain righteousness, **because they sought it not by faith.**[1] Their unbelief cannot be understood as the result of God's foreordination, even though God would not have been unjust, had He so foreordained (ver. 20 sqq.). Besides, if their unbelief is thus the cause of their rejection, God must have made faith possible to them. Remembering that faith is not determined by man's own powers, but is the work of God, the charge of unbelief as the cause of man's rejection clearly implies a persistent attitude of resistance on

---

[1] "Here he expressly states the cause of reprobation, viz. that the godless are unwilling to believe the Gospel; for this reason, I have above said that the illustration concerning the clay must not be understood as though the cause of reprobation did not lie in the will itself of men." (MELANCHTHON.)

their part to God's efforts to give them faith. Thus the difference may be thus stated: The cause of the Gentiles' acceptance is alone the grace of God; the cause of Israel's rejection is alone their will not to accept salvation upon the terms offered by God. "While man's salvation is not his own merit, but Christ's merit and God's choice, his destruction is only his own fault and his own choice" (PHILIPPI). "They sought it, where it could not be found, viz. by the works of the law; they did not seek it where it could be found, viz. by faith. They were like those who, in making a journey, hasten much, and bear heavy burdens, but enter upon a course leading away from the place whither they want to go. For just as the more rapidly they run, the farther do they recede from it; so do they wander farther and farther from the goal of salvation, who prefer to seek righteousness by the deeds of the law rather than by faith" (MYLIUS in CALOVIUS).

Ver. 33. **Stone of stumbling.** A combination of Is. 28 : 16 and 8 : 14. The thought of Isaiah (chap. viii.) is that of the two-fold relation to the Lord, corresponding to the two-fold attitude of man. To the one class, he is a sanctuary, "a place of peace and comfort and spiritual refreshment"; to the other, only the occasion for utter failure and ruin. "We break ourselves struggling against the Messiah, rather than break Him" (GODET). Is. 28 : 16 is directed against those who, despairing of the strength of Israel to resist its enemies, favored an alliance with Egypt against Assyria. In answer to such proposals, the Lord declares that Israel has within it a firmer foundation than that belonging to any earthly government or human plan. The reference is to the Messiah. **Shall not be put to shame.** The LXX. is again followed here. The Hebrew is, as in R. V., "shall not make haste," or, as Delitzsch renders it: "Will not have to move." Haste implies insecurity. The LXX is a paraphrase: "shall not be put to shame," expressing the idea underlying the original. The application is that the stumbling of Israel should be no discouragement on the part of Christians; this had been long foretold.

Section III.—How the Jews Misunderstood the Design of the Law (Ch. 10).

(*a.*) *Their Rejection based upon no Fatalistic Determination, but on their own Hostility to the Gospel.*

1-4. Brethren, my heart's desire and my supplication to God is for them, that they may be saved. For I bear them witness that they have a zeal for God, but not according to knowledge. For being ignorant of God's righteousness, and seeking to establish their own, they did not subject themselves to the righteousness of God. For Christ is the end of the law unto righteousness to every one that believeth.

Ver. 1. **Brethren.** An appeal prompted by the apprehension that what has just been said may have the appearance of severity and harshness. **My heart's desire.** Marg.: "Good pleasure." **And my supplication.** Every holy desire in the Christian heart leads to prayer. Bengel adds significantly: "Paul would not have prayed, had they been reprobate." **That they may be saved.** Lit.: "Unto salvation," i. e. that which is directed towards their salvation.

Ver. 2. **For they have a zeal for God.** Their deep religious character especially moves his sympathy and urges him to pray for them. "The Apostle declares that notwithstanding their unbelief, he cannot but in a certain respect love the Jews more than the unbelieving heathen. It could not be questioned that the Jews, even during their disbelief of the Gospel, were anxiously concerned for their salvation" (THOLUCK). **Not according to knowledge**, and therefore misdirected and erroneous. The word here used (*epignosis*) means a deep and thorough knowledge; one, as a rule, that is grounded upon experience, an experimental knowledge. The question may be asked: Which is the worse: "zeal without knowledge," or "knowledge without zeal"? This text is an effectual answer to the frequent statement, that it is a matter of indifference what religion one have, if he have only some form of religion, or the kindred statement that everything depends upon one's sincerity. Paul does not question the sincerity of the Jews. "Let us learn from this whither our good intentions carry us if we obey them. It is commonly regarded the very best and a sufficiently valid excuse when one against whom a charge is made replies that he has not done the act with a bad intention. But none of us would attempt to excuse the Jews for crucifying Christ, or for raging cruelly against the apostles, or for endeavoring to destroy and extinguish the Gospel; all their defence is the very same in which we securely glory. Let these vain evasions concerning a good intention cease; if we seek God sincerely, let us follow the only course that leads to Him. 'For it is better to limp on the road, than to run eagerly outside of it,' as Augustine says. If we want to be religious, let us see to it that we have the true religion; and that only is the true religion which rests upon the Word of God" (CALVIN).

Ver. 3. **For being ignorant of God's righteousness.** Righteousness is conformity with the will of God. No other righteousness than that of God can, therefore, exist. To be ignorant of God's righteousness is, therefore, to be ignorant of all righteousness. What greater ignorance than to regard phantoms as realities and realities as phantoms? to neglect what one can have—righteousness in Christ—and to spend all life in the quest for what one can never attain—one's own righteousness? **Seeking to establish their own.** Explained by Paul in Phil. 3 : 9, as "righteousness of the law," i. e. justification by the complete fulfilment of all the law's requirements. How vain are such attempts, is shown in the first part of this epistle. An *ignis fatuus*. **Did not subject themselves.** It is not, then, a mere intellectual infirmity from which they are suffering! It is partly also a matter of the will. They are unwilling to submit to the will of God. The essence of unbelief is disobedience. "This is his commandment, that we should believe in the name of His Son Jesus Christ" (1 John 3 : 23). Their unwillingness to accept clear evidence, their persistent hostility to truth, is the cause, not only of their ignorance, but also of their rejection.

Ver. 4. **For Christ is the end of the law,** i. e. at once the object, the fulfilment and the termination of the law (Gal. 1 : 24). "The law was given for the purpose of leading us by the hand to another righteousness; yea, whatever the law teaches, commands, promises, has always Christ as its aim" (CALVIN). 2. But, Christ is its aim also, because He is its fulfilment, by doing all that the law required (Matt. 5 : 17). 3. Since Christ is its aim and its fulfilment, He is also its termination. The way of salvation by works no longer has place, since Christ has fulfilled the law for us. "The law pursues a man until he takes refuge in Christ; then it says, Thou hast found thine asylum; I shall trouble thee no more; now thou art wise, now thou art safe" (BENGEL). We need not trouble ourselves as to which of these three meanings is intended; they all belong together. **The law.** The Moral, as well as the Ceremonial and Forensic. **To**

every one that believeth. The emphasis is on "believeth," bringing out the condition of faith, as contrasted with the condition of works, under the old dispensation (ch. 4 : 4, 5).

The Apostle then shows the two matters pertaining to salvation of which the Jews were ignorant.

(*b.*) *The Freeness of Salvation.*

5-11. For Moses writeth that the man that doeth the righteousness which is of the law, shall live thereby. But the righteousness which is of faith saith thus, Say not in thy heart, Who shall ascend into heaven ? (that is, to bring Christ down:) or, Who shall descend into the abyss ? (that is, to bring Christ up from the dead.) But what saith it ? The word is nigh thee, in thy mouth, and in thy heart : that is, the word of faith, which we preach : because if thou shalt confess with thy mouth Jesus *as* Lord, and shalt believe in thy heart that God raised him from the dead, thou shalt be saved : for with the heart man believeth unto righteousness; and with the mouth confession is made unto salvation.

Ver. 5. **For Moses writeth . . . that the man that doeth.** An emphatic contrast is here made between "doeth" and "believing" in ver. 9. The law is here described as demanding perfect obedience. If salvation be sought according to the law, it must be kept to the very letter. There is no grace or mercy ; there can be no palliation or excuse for any error or mistake (Deut. 27 : 26; James 2 : 10). No compromise with the way of salvation under the Gospel can be regarded. All that law demands must be done, or there is no salvation. (See Gal. 3 : 10–13.)

Vers. 6–9 present, in contrast with the impossible condition of ver. 5, what is not only possible, but even what may be easily attained. Under the Gospel the way of salvation is so simple and direct, that it is surprising that men would prefer any other. The doctrine is unfolded on the basis of Deut. 30 : 11–14. A comparison shows considerable variation both from the Hebrew and the LXX.

The R. V. of Deut. 30 : 11-14 reads :

"For this commandment which I command thee this day, it is not too hard for thee, neither is it far off. It is not in heaven that thou shouldest say, who shall go up for us to heaven, and bring it unto us, and make us hear it, that we may do it? Neither is it beyond the sea, that thou shouldest say, who shall go over the sea for us, and make us to hear it, that we may do it? But the word is very nigh unto thee, in thy mouth and in thy heart, that thou mayest do it."

Paul does not attempt a formal quotation. Nor does he simply take the Old Testament text as a model, upon which to construct a paragraph treating of something entirely different. The words in Deuteronomy have a wider application than the subject to which they, at first, directly referred. The intersecting lines are the same; but their relation is now read on the arc of a vaster circle. When the O. T. passage is applied to N. T. times, the interpretation is Rom. 10 : 6-9.[1]

Ver. 6. **The righteousness of faith.** If Paul had meant to quote directly, he would have said as before: "For Moses also writeth." But the contrast is very significant: First, between "Moses" (ver. 5), and "the righteousness of faith" (ver. 6). The implication is, since "the righteousness of faith" is here referred to as belonging to the O. T., that even the O. T. contains two elements, law and Gospel. The former is designated by Moses (ver. 5); and the latter by "the righteousness of faith," as the Gospel promise accompanying the law, and found even in Moses, although not belonging to the peculiar sphere

---

[1] Comp. LUTHER on Deuteronomy xxx.: *Exegetica Opera Latina* (ERLANGEN), xiii. 328.

of Moses. Turning then to Deuteronomy, he finds, in the passage quoted, the germs of the Gospel, and shows how it unfolds in the light of the facts of the New Testament.

Saith thus. This is contrasted with "writeth" of ver. 5, indicating the greater freedom of Spirit, as opposed to the bondage of the mere letter. It is by this freedom that he enters into the spirit of the Deuteronomic passage, and, in the language of another time and place, explains its greater depth and more extensive range.

The main thought of the passage in Deuteronomy is that the word of God is not difficult to learn; God has made a revelation: and the contents of that revelation are before the children of Israel. As to what has not been revealed, they are to have no concern. The amount of what has already been revealed must always be the test of obedience and of the self-surrender of the will to God. But Paul goes farther, and applies this thought to the ampler and clearer revelation that had been made in Christ. He teaches two things, viz. where the righteousness of faith is to be sought for, and what the righteousness of faith is. **Say not in thy heart:** Think not. **Who shall ascend into heaven?** i. e. We are not to anxiously speculate concerning the secret will of God, or with great efforts to search for this revelation, as though it were out of ordinary reach. **That is to bring Christ down;** i. e. Such inquiries and efforts amount to the denial that Christ actually became incarnate and revealed to men God's will. For if man must rise to heaven to learn this, Christ did not reveal it; and the incarnation remains a necessity for the race to be realized in the future. To so think is therefore to deny the entire doctrine concerning Christ. Or if the object be the attainment of righteousness, the result is the same. An incarnate, suffering, risen and ascended Christ is the pledge of righteousness procured for us; to seek this righteousness by our own efforts, is to deny that Christ has ascended. It is to bring Him down to the level of ordinary mortals.

Ver. 7. **Who shall descend into the abyss?** The opposite of heaven (Job 11:8; Ps. 139:8; Am. 9:2; Matt. 11:23). Another expression for the great difficulty of the task. The enduring of sorrows, sufferings, dangers, **cares,** with the expectation of gaining righteousness thereby, or learning God's will, are descents into the abyss. They amount to a practical denial of the doctrine that Christ was raised for our justification (4:25). **That is, to bring Christ up from the dead,** means here to treat His redemptive work as though it were incomplete and He were still held captive by death. But the incarnation and ascension of Christ being incontrovertible realities, away with all such questions!

Ver. 8. **But what saith it?** That is, What does the righteousness of faith say? **The word,** lit.: "utterance," i. e. revelation. **Is nigh thee.** The word of the righteousness of faith is constantly at hand; but that of the righteousness of the law is as far removed as heaven or the abyss; for it is an impossibility. This was relatively true when the declaration was made in Deuteronomy; but, since the coming of Christ, it is true in a far higher and more efficacious way. "The believer so far regards neither heaven, nor the abyss, since he has what he desires as near to him as he is to himself. But unbelief fluctuates; it is always wishing it knows not what; it is always seeking, and finds nothing. Hence it looks into the deep with giddiness; nor can it look joyfully up to heaven" (BENGEL). **In thy mouth and in thy heart.** " The former means: Easy to be learned and repeated;

the latter, easy to be loved" (GODET). **The word of faith,** i. e. the doctrine concerning faith, or concerning the promise offered faith, viz. the Gospel; for the law or the doctrine of works cannot be meant.

"He teaches, first, where the righteousness of faith is to be sought, viz. not above us, or beneath us, not in any secret will of God, for this would be to bring Christ down from heaven, as a new interpreter of the divine will, or to recall Him from the dead, as though He had not previously made a sufficient revelation of all things; but by us, in the revealed word, which is preached among us and heard by us, and, on that account, is called the word of faith, because in it faith in Christ is declared to us, and through it faith is brought us, and only by faith can it be understood" (BALDWIN).

Ver. 9. **That,** as in A. V., is preferable to "because" of R. V. It designates, therefore, the contents of the Word that is preached. **If thou shalt confess with thy mouth** comes first, because "mouth" is first in ver. 8. Faith of the heart always precedes, and invariably leads to confession. The confession is not only the expression of the faith, but also the means for diffusing it. **Jesus as Lord.** Jesus is the name of our Lord as a man. This means, therefore, to confess and believe in the reality of the incarnation, i. e. that Jesus is true God begotten of the Father. It is the reverse of the unbelief implied in the questions of vers. 6, 7. "He who confesses that Jesus is Lord no longer tries to bring Him down from heaven" (BENGEL). But that such confession be made, the Holy Spirit must first take possession of the heart (1 Cor. 12 : 3). **Believe in thy heart.** Corresponding to ver. 8. This condition of the Gospel is contrasted with that of the Law of ver. 5. **That God raised him from the dead.** Our salvation depends on no abstractions, but on clearly ascertained historical facts; neither on what we are to do, but on our acceptance of what God has done. Faith in the resurrection implies faith in the death of Christ. The resurrection declares the completion of Christ's sacrificial work. If our faith in Christ ended with His death, we must then regard His atonement insufficient, and would still be under the bondage of sin. But "he who believes Jesus' resurrection, no longer tries to bring Him from the dead" (BENGEL). His eye rests upon a definite point in the past. Towards this he points, and says: There and then, everything needful for my salvation was done.

Ver. 10. **For with the heart,** "The seat of faith is not in the brain, but in the heart" (CALVIN). Faith is not mere intellectual assent. It is the attitude of the entire heart towards God, the heart being the centre of man's being, determining all his impulses and movements. **Believeth unto righteousness,** i. e. with the result that we receive the righteousness provided for us in the death and resurrection of Christ. **And with the mouth confession is made unto salvation.** "Faith without confession is not faith of the right kind, just as confession without faith is not confession of the right kind" (BESSER). Not that the confession is a cause of salvation, or means of receiving salvation, as faith is a means of receiving righteousness. "The righteousness obtained by faith would be lost, and would not attain salvation, if faith had not the life-force to produce confession of the mouth, which speaks out of the fulness of the heart. See Matt. 10: 32; comp. 2 Cor. 4: 13" (MEYER). A description of the way of salvation: 1. Faith. 2. The reception of righteousness. 3. Confession. 4. Salvation in eternal life. "The question why St. Paul connects righteousness with the faith of the heart, and salvation with the confession of the lips in ver. 10, is to be answered (as at Rom. 4 : 25), at least in part, by reference to the parallelism of Hebrew poetry, the rhythm of which sometimes shapes the Apostle's prose. And yet the distribution of his thought is not wholly or chiefly to be accounted for thus. He conceives of a righteousness which may not issue in salvation, since righteousness may be forfeited by the moral cowardice of the believer, who does not venture to avow his faith before men. If faith does not grow with confession, it dies back, first, into mere 'opinion,' and then into unbelief" (LIDDON).

Ver. 11. **For the Scripture saith.** Thus he recurs to the same quotation from Isaiah with which chapter nine closes, and which has been the basis of this section of his argument (See on 9 : 33.) Under divine inspiration, however, he introduces the word "whosoever," not found in Isaiah, or as he cited it above, and thus makes a transition from the discussion of the freeness to that of the universality of divine grace.

(c.) *The Universality of the Offers of Salvation.*

12-21. For there is no distinction between Jew and Greek: for the same *Lord* is Lord of all, and is rich unto all that call upon him : for, Whosoever shall call upon the name of the Lord shall be saved. How then shall they call on him in whom they have not believed? and how shall they believe in him whom they have not heard? and how shall they hear without a preacher? and how shall they preach, except they be sent? even as it is written, How beautiful are the feet of them that bring glad tidings of good things!

But they did not all hearken to the glad tidings. For Isaiah saith, Lord, who hath believed our report ? So belief *cometh* of hearing, and hearing by the word of Christ. But I say, Did they not hear? Yea, verily,
  Their sound went out into all the earth,
  And their words unto the ends of the world.
But I say, Did Israel not know? First Moses saith,
  I will provoke you to jealousy with that which is no nation,
  With a nation void of understanding will I anger you.

And Isaiah is very bold, and saith,
> I was found of them that sought me not;
> I became manifest unto them that asked not of me.
> But as to Israel he saith, All the day long did I spread out my hands unto a disobedient and gainsaying people.

Ver. 12. The sole condition of righteousness and salvation being faith, all national, class, social and individual distinctions vanish. (Comp. ch. 3 : 22.) The proposition which is the great theme of the Epistle, viz. the universality of the grace of God in Christ, as opposed to Jewish particularism, is here again repeated. The Apostle first denies the observance by God of national or racial lines, and then in the **over all** and **whosoever** applies this same principle to individuals. **The same Lord**; i. e. : As all have the same Lord, and His resources are unlimited, every one receives from this Lord's bounty all that he needs, without in any way diminishing the amount which that Lord has for others. All motives for envy are thus removed. "He is never compelled to retrench" (BENGEL). But He does not give unasked, even though He offers unasked: He "is rich **unto all that call upon him**." Calling upon God, as well as the confession of Christ, is an expression of faith (ver. 14).

Ver. 13. **For whosoever shall call**, etc. A quotation from Joel 2 : 32. (Comp. Acts 2 : 21 for the N. T. application of the passage.) **The name of the Lord.** The reference is not to God the Father, but to Christ. The passage in Joel is Messianic. The application here is the same as that of the pronoun "him" in ver. 11; but this manifestly refers to Christ, as may be seen by comparing it with ver. 14.[1] (Comp. 9 : 33.) If, then, the reference

---

[1] "In the Gospels, κύριος usually designates God (the O. T. *Lord*), and in the Epistles, especially Paul's (in accordance with the growth of Christian phraseology), most frequently *Christ*, the Lord (Phil. 2 : 11; cf. 1 Cor. 15 : 24 ff." *Winer's Grammar of N. T. Greek*, p. 124).

be to Christ, the Jews in rejecting Christ must fail of salvation, even upon the testimony of their Old Testament Scriptures. Such is the inference which Paul draws in the next verse.

Ver. 14. The Apostle here uses the figure called by logicians *sorites* or chain-argument, to prove that as the Lord wants men everywhere to call upon Him, so it is His will that men be sent everywhere to preach the Gospel. No calling upon the Lord, without faith; no faith, without the hearing of the Word; no hearing of the Word, without a preacher; no preaching, except there be a sending forth of men and an Apostolic office. **How then shall they call on him in whom they have not believed?** For there is no true prayer or invocation of God, unless it be the expression of faith (Heb. 11:6. Comp. 8:15, 26). Until God open our lips to pray, we are dumb. **How shall they believe him whom they have not heard?** God's call must precede man's response. Man has no knowledge of Christ, except through revelation. He cannot gain it by reflection upon himself or consideration of the works of nature, or the acquisition of earthly knowledge. He must hear it, and, as R. V. correctly indicates, he must hear this from Christ Himself. It is not "Him of whom," but "Him whom they have not heard." **How, without a preacher?** Thus all ideas concerning an inner word or direct testimony of the Holy Spirit, outside of the preached Word, are confounded. Neither is the mere reading of the Word, or diffusion of the influences of Christianity, sufficient. The Word must be heard from the living witness of its power. It makes its conquests through the sanctified personal influence of those within whose hearts it is treasured, and who preach it from the depths of an intense conviction of its truths. "No people ever has been or can be converted, nor can a church be formed by means of the Holy Scriptures alone, without an interpreter and the living word of preaching" (OLSHAUSEN).

Ver. 15. **And how shall they preach except they be sent ?** The thought is : If the Gospel is preached anywhere, this occurs because it has been sent thither by God. " As faith depends entirely on God's Word, no one can preach God's Word unless he be sent by God" (LUTHER). According to ver. 14, it is Christ whose voice they must hear ; this is possible only when He calls and commissions men to preach in His stead (Luke 10: 16 ; 2 Cor. 5 : 20). " The Gospel does not rain down fortuitously from the clouds, but is carried by men's hands whithersoever it is divinely sent " (CALVIN). The original, however, in its use of the word for " sent," implies the Apostolic office, which was universal, and, not like that of other ministers, local in its scope. The special function of an apostle, besides being a witness of the resurrection, was to proclaim the universality of God's grace, and to carry it to all people (John 17: 18; Matt. 28: 19; Mark 16: 16). **As it is written,** viz. Is. 52 : 7. **How beautiful are the feet.** By metonymy for " coming " or " approach." " Feet at a distance ; how much more their lips close by " (BENGEL). **Glad tidings of good things,** viz. those of the Messianic Kingdom, the blessings of the Gospel. " Isaiah describes the sending forth of the Apostles into all the world ; for they were not stationed in one place, but, as messengers of God, they were sent everywhere, and with great speed passed over lands and seas. Their doctrine was not properly the Mosaic law, for this had been known before, but ' the Gospel of peace.' They were good messengers, proclaiming peace, not of body, but of soul, viz. the peace with God and with conscience, which Christ procured by His death. They preached good things, viz. not transitory and temporal, but heavenly and eternal things—the forgiveness of sins and eternal life and salvation" (BALDWIN).

Ver. 16. **But they did not all hearken.** Thus he declares that the enjoyment of the blessings of the Gospel is not as universal as the call. Faith does not necessarily follow in all who hear the preaching of the Gospel. " Not all " ("a tragic *litotes*," LIDDON) refers here to the Jews. This statement he supports by an appeal to Is. 53: 1, **Lord, who hath believed our report,** which, immediately following the description of the blessings attending the preaching of the Gospel, declares that those who accept the gracious offers of salvation are relatively few. (Comp. notes on 9: 27.)

Ver. 17. **So belief cometh of hearing.** The word "hearing" is identical with "report," which closes ver. 16. It is put for that which is heard. **And hearing by the word of Christ,** i. e. All the efficacy of the preaching lies in the word of Christ which it contains. It is only another way of saying that faith is the result of the heard word of Christ. A return to the thought of ver. 14. The whole discussion turns here on the bringing of the word of Christ to the hearts of men. " Hearing " is mentioned as the ordinary mode whereby this occurs; but it is not exclusive. The deaf, for example, learn the Gospel, not, strictly speaking, by hearing, but by learning the word communicated in signs, or watching attentively the lips. So belief comes from reading the Bible. These are manifestly included by synechdoche in the hearing. In the same way, the work of the Holy Spirit in the sacraments is also included. " The Word of God is the only power that works sacramentally and orally to the creation and nourishment of faith. ' Where the bodily, external word is not preached, there we must not imagine that the

Holy Spirit works. The sun has two qualities, light and heat. Whither its light goes, thither also goes its heat; and where its light is excluded, there its heat does not come. So with the external word and the Holy Ghost. The Holy Ghost works nowhere unless He first enter the heart through the Word as a channel." (LUTHER, Walch ed. XI. 3098). The Apostle is contending here not against enthusiasts and fanatics, who despise the outward, oral word, and make a miserable distinction between 'spirit' and 'word,' but he speaks thus in order to put to shame the unbelieving hearers of the efficacious and living Word of divine preaching" (BESSER). Nevertheless this was a favorite text with the theologians of the period of the Reformation, whereby they effectually answered the assumptions of a false mysticism. "God the Holy Ghost effects conversion, not without the use of means, but uses for this purpose the preaching and hearing of God's Word (Rom. 1 : 16; 10 : 17). And it is God's will that his Word should be heard, and that man's ears should not be closed. With this Word the Holy Ghost is present and opens hearts, so that they are attentive to it, and are thus converted through the grace and power of the Holy Ghost" (FORMULA OF CONCORD, p. 497 sq.).

Ver. 18. **Did they not hear?** The subject is the "not all" of ver. 16, viz. the unbelieving Jews. Can they offer as an excuse that they did not hear the Gospel? **Their sound went out into all the earth**, etc. A quotation from the LXX. of Ps. 19 : 4, adapted to the theme, in a manner like that of the quotation in vers. 6–8. The psalm does not refer to the preaching of the Gospel, but to God's manifestation of Himself in Nature. But this is regarded as an illustration of the universality of God's manifestation of His grace in the Gospel. "As the heavens and their hosts proclaim God's existence and perfections to the whole universe, and, mute as they are, make their voice re-echo in the hearts of all men; so, says St. Paul, with a sort of enthusiasm at the memory of his own ministry, the voice of the preachers of the Gospel has sounded in all countries and in all the cities of the known world. There is not a synagogue which has not been filled with it; not a Jew in the world who can justly plead ignorance on the subject" (GODET). (Comp. Col. 1 : 6, 23.) It has been suggested that Paul's great prominence in this work deterred him from describing here the spread of the Gospel in his own language. That this language is to be understood relatively, is clear from ch. 15 : 20, 24, 28, where he declares that the Gospel has not been preached as yet in Spain. The argument is intended to prove no more than that no Israelite can excuse himself upon the plea of not having heard it.

Ver. 19. **But I say, Did not Israel know?** Know what? Both the entire context and the passages from the O. T. that answer this question make the explanation preferable which supplies the words, "the universality of the preaching of the Gospel," or "the calling of the Gentiles and their own rejection." The Apostle answers that if they did not know, it was not because the O. T. Scriptures had not clearly predicted it. **First Moses saith.** (See Deut. 32 : 21.) This is contrasted with the quotation from Isaiah, and indicates that from the very beginning of their national life this had been distinctly foretold. **That which is no nation,** i. e. no nation of any account. " A not-people; for only the people of God was the real one, the people corresponding to the divine idea of a people; every other is the negation of this idea. Comp. 9 : 25; 1 Pet. 2 : 10" (MEYER). As Israel regarded itself as a nation that was a nation, so they regarded others as nations that were not nations. "The heathen, being without the true bond which unites individuals into a nation, viz. the recognition of the Divine Will that rules all things harmoniously (comp. Deut. 4 : 6-8), every aggregation of heathen with the Israelitic nation is no nation (comp. 9 : 25), just as the gods of the heathen contrasted with the God of Israel are no-gods" (BESSER).

Vers. 20, 21. **And Isaiah is very bold,** i. e. He speaks still more clearly and pointedly. Most expositors of Isaiah urge that these words, quoted from Is. 65 : 1, refer not to the Gentiles, as Paul here declares, but to apostate Jews. (See especially DELITZSCH). But this involves no contradiction. The apostate Israelites who were brought back were a type of the straying Gentiles. The prophet declares in these words a principle which Israel should have laid to heart, that God often bestows His grace upon those who have wandered farthest from Him, while the seemingly most devout are forsaken and rejected. Paul follows the LXX. inverting the sentences. **All the day long,** thus showing the patience and persistence of His love. **A disobedient and gainsaying people,** i. e. contradicting. Those who answer back God's messages of love by saying, "We will not" (Matt. 23 : 37). Thus he shows that the cause of the rejection of the Jews lies not in God, but in their own abuse of their free will, in resisting and antagonizing Him (Prov. 1 : 24-26).

SECTION IV.—CONSOLATION CONNECTED WITH ISRAEL'S REJECTION (Ch. 11.).

(*a.*) *The Rejection not Total, but Partial.*

1-10. I say then, Did God cast off his people? God forbid. For I also am an Israelite, of the seed of Abraham, of the tribe of Benjamin. God did not cast off his people which he foreknew. Or wot ye not what the scripture saith of Elijah? how he pleadeth with God against Israel, Lord, they have killed thy prophets, they have digged down thine altars : and I am left alone, and they seek my life. But what saith the answer of God unto him? I have left for myself seven thousand men, who have not bowed the knee to Baal. Even so then at this present time also there is a remnant according to the election of grace. But if it is by grace, it is no more of works : otherwise grace is no more grace. What then? That which Israel seeketh for, that he obtained not : but the election obtained it, and the rest were hardened : according as it is written, God gave them a spirit of stupor, eyes that they should not see, and ears that they should not hear, unto this very day. And David saith,

> Let their table be made a snare, and a trap,
> And a stumblingblock, and a recompense unto them :
> Let their eyes be darkened, that they may not see,
> And bow thou down their back alway.

Ver. 1. **Did God cast off his people.** Does this rejection involve the entire Israelitic nation? **God forbid.** (Comp. vers. 3 : 4.) **For I also am an Israelite.** It cannot be, he says, that all are rejected; for he knows by experience that the promised blessings belong to him, and, since he is an Israelite and is thus an object of the divine mercy, not all of the people have been rejected. **Of the tribe of Benjamin.** The tribe of Benjamin having been united with that of Judah, Paul here affirms that he comes from the very core of the nation.

Ver. 2. **God did not cast off his people whom he foreknew,** i. e. those whom He foreknew to be His people. Those who imagine that the entire nation could be rejected forget the omniscience and foreknowledge of God. (Comp. 2 Tim. 2 : 19.) God has not been thwarted. In spite of the resistance of His will by the great mass, and their consequent rejection, He has still His purposes to accomplish through the nation. All this He foreknew before He called Israel. Through its experience of shame, Israel is yet to reach its final glory. "It is certain, therefore, that God still has those who are His among the

Jews (2 Tim. 2 : 19), and those given to Christ by the Father (John 17), as are all the faithful and elect. Whence it follows that the Apostle is treating here not of absolute and pure foreknowledge, but of the foreknowledge whereby God saw the men who would believe in the Son, and would follow the order of election, of whom, undoubtedly, there were some in the midst of the rebellious Jews" (BALDWIN). **Of Elijah.** Literally: "In Elijah," i. e. in that part of Scripture that tells of Elijah. 1 Kings 19 : 10, 14, 18 are the verses referred to. **Pleadeth with God** against Israel, i. e. "protest before God against their conduct" (GODET).

Ver. 3. **I am left alone.** Not the only prophet, but the only worshipper of the true God, that remains. An historical parallel to the conditions in the Apostle's time. The lesson is that no human eye can tell how many there may be faithful, even where appearances are the most discouraging.

Ver. 4. **I have left to myself,** i. e. for my property and worship. **Seven thousand.** Man's view, even though it be that of one who, like Elijah, from its superior penetration, is called a seer, is very contracted and uncertain, and leads to sweeping conclusions and indiscriminate judgments. However open to criticism their lack of courage, and however indeterminate their merely negative position, there was still a considerable number within whom the sparks of faith were not entirely extinct. **Who have not bowed the knee to Baal.** In the Greek Baal has here the feminine article, while in most places it is masculine. An ingenious and possible explanation has recently been given by DILLMAN (quoted by SANDAY). Just as the Hebrews substituted Adonai for Jehovah in reading the Hebrew text, and even pointed Jehovah with the vowel sounds of Adonai, so in reading the Greek text of the LXX. it became usual to substitute ἡ αἰσχύνη, "the disgrace" for Baal, even where the latter was retained in the written text. It thus became a very easy matter for Baal to have the feminine article, belonging to the word which so often replaced it. This suggestion seems more plausible than the conjecture that Baal was regarded as androgynous or that it refers to his idol.

Ver. 5. **A remnant,** implying that the great majority have been rejected. This remnant is composed of those of the Jews who have been converted to Christianity. (Comp. ch. 9 : 27.) **According to the election of grace.** The specific reference is not to the election of individuals, as in 8 : 29, 30, although that is of course implied, but to God's election of Israel as His chosen people, and His purpose to attain His end through those still left, when the majority of the chosen people proves unfaithful. This is established by the connection with ver. 3. It is called "election of grace," because determined by no excellence of Jewish character, or no conformity by them with law, but solely by the free will of God.

Ver. 6. **But if it is by grace,** etc. The thought developed in ch. 4. Its application here is to show that the remnant of Israel, while saved, were saved on no other terms than the Gentiles, since the latter also were saved not by works, but by grace. **Otherwise grace is no more grace.** As in Gal. 5 : 4, the two ways of salvation are in uncompromising antagonism. He who chooses salvation by works, excludes himself from grace; he who chooses salvation by grace, cannot add works to enhance the merit of grace, without excluding himself from the benefits both of works and grace. In order to guard against such perversions of the conception of grace, the Reformers sometimes speak of "the purely gratuitous grace of God." But there is no other grace than that which is purely gratuitous; for just in so far as man's works are introduced, the need of the merits of Christ as the ground of salvation is removed. We are saved altogether by grace, because it is only by grace that we receive Christ. The alternative is: "Nothing but Christ," or "No Christ." There is no intermediate position.

Ver. 7. **What then?** This connects with ver. 5, viz.: What inference is to be drawn from the fact that there is a remnant according to the election of grace? **That which Israel seeketh for.** Note the tense, indicating that this search is now in progress. The object sought for is righteousness (9:31), which is not obtained because it is not sought for in the right way. **But the election,** i. e. the elect, the remnant in Israel. **The rest were hardened.** This is a stronger word than that used in 9:18. Literally: "Grew callous," the first application of the word being to a petrifaction, or the formation of a hard substance at the joints, when bones have been fractured. (See note on 9:18.) "A penal judgment for a prolonged indifference to grace and light."

Ver. 8. **According as it is written.** The hardening of those who persistently oppose themselves to divine grace is illustrated and proved by passages from the O. T. This verse consists of a combination of Is. 29:10 with Deut. 29:4. **God gave them a spirit of stupor.** This phrase is from Is. 29:10: "The Lord hath poured out upon you the spirit of deep sleep." In order that man may understand and feel and know, God's enlightening grace is needed. God not only presents the object, but creates the spiritual capacity by which it is received. Man's natural condition is one of spiritual insensibility. God, by His grace, seeks to remove this, while He urges upon man the truths pertaining to his salvation. But when man persistently repels this grace, God leaves him to his native stupor. Hence God can be said to give the spirit of stupor, when, as a punishment for man's obstinacy, He deserts man to the natural consequences of his sins. As God creates darkness by withdrawing the light, so He gives the spirit of stupor by withdrawing His grace. **Eyes that they should not see,** etc. Deut. 29: 4: "The Lord hath not given eyes to see." By the withdrawal or withholding of grace, the spiritual faculty to discern spiritual things is lacking (1 Cor. 2: 14). They have not such eyes as are able to see or such ears as are able to hear. The objects may stand before their open eyes; the sounds may strike their ears, but no distinct idea is conveyed. "It is indicated that they had been able both to see and to hear, but that, as a punishment of preceding sin, they were unable in divine things to use either their eyes or ears; for when God withdraws His hand, man is both blind and deaf, and, at last, must altogether fall" (BALDWIN).

Ver. 9. **And David saith** (Ps. 69: 22, 23). The Davidic origin of the psalm is not settled by this statement. Paul is not dealing with questions of criticism. It is sufficient to quote from an inspired composition, mentioned, according to its title, as the words of David. **Let their table.** The figure is that of those who, in careless security, are enjoying the good things of this life, unarmed, unsuspecting. Even the prosperity bestowed as a blessing by God may be turned into a curse, when it is used in forgetfulness of the claims of God. **A snare and a trap.** A means of their capture and ruin. **And a recompense,** i. e. the retributive justice of God will be displayed in the manner in which the choicest gifts of God, when improperly used, bring only injury. The application is to the law. See 7: 10-13, where the reference is general. Here it is particularly applied to Israel.

Ver 10. **Let their eyes be darkened.** So that Israel, with its possession of the Law and the Prophets, is ignorant of their real meaning, while this is known to the Gentiles. **And bow down their back alway.** The Hebrew of the psalm says: " Make their loins continually to shake." Both are images of servile fear. They know nothing of the freedom of a Christian man, in which they can look joyfully to God as their loving Father, but are in bondage to their laws, the interpreters of these laws, and even to God. (See Acts 15 : 10, 28 ; 2 Cor. 3 : 16, 17 ; Gal. 4 : 24.)

(B.) THIS PARTIAL REJECTION OF ISRAEL, NOT ETERNAL, BUT TEMPORARY (vers. 11-33).

(a.) *The Conversion of the Gentiles through this Rejection of Israel, and the Ultimate Conversion of Israel through the Gentiles.*

11-15. I say then, Did they stumble that they might fall? God forbid: but by their fall salvation *is come* unto the Gentiles, for to provoke them to jealousy. Now if their fall is the riches of the world, and their loss the riches of the Gentiles ; how much more their fulness?

But I speak to you that are Gentiles. Inasmuch then as I am an apostle of Gentiles, I glorify my ministry : if by any means I may provoke to jealousy *them that are* my flesh, and may save some of them. For if the casting away of them *is* the reconciling of the world, what *shall* the receiving *of them be*, but life from the dead?

Ver. 11. **Did they stumble, that they might fall?** Was their fall, asks the objector, the ultimate end for which God allowed them to stumble? As in Heb. 4 : 11, to fall means "everlasting destruction." **God forbid.** (Comp. 3 : 4.) **By their fall, salvation to the Gentiles.** The best comment on this clause is Acts 13 : 46. (Comp. Matt. 21 : 43 ; 22 : 9 ; Acts 28 : 28.) The rejection of the Gospel by the Jews was the occasion for its being preached to the Gentiles. Had the Jews accepted Christ, God would doubtless have brought the Gospel to the Gentiles in some other way. But such being the case, this is the mode in which the conversion of the Gentiles was accomplished. "Not that God willed that the Israelites should fall, but because, as they were to fall by their own fault, He directed this calamity of theirs to good, partly, so far as the Gentiles were concerned, to their salvation, and, partly, so far as the Jews were concerned, to wrest them from ruin by their emulation of the Gentiles" (CALOVIUS). **For to provoke them to jealousy.** (Comp. 10:19.) "Jealousy," in a good sense. The knowledge that the Gentiles enjoy the exalted spiritual blessings, intended originally for the Jews, will fill them with the desire, previously absent, to obtain their gifts. (Comp. Rev. 3:9). This, then, is the very reason of "that they might fall."

Ver. 12. **If their fall is the riches of the world,** i. e. the cause of riches. The world is enriched by their fall, since their rejection of Christ is the means for preaching His unsearchable riches to the world (Eph. 3:5; 1 Tim. 3:16). **Their loss.** God's loss, or the Church's loss of the Jews. Lit.: "The diminution" of the number of true children of God among the Jews. Some understand the word quantitatively, as though the meaning were: "If the few Jews who remain faithful enrich the Gentiles." But this seems contrary to the general use of the word. **The riches of the Gentiles.** Since when the Jews reject the Gospel, one nation after another becomes the subject of its power and grace. **How much more their fulness,** i. e. the repair of this loss, that which fills up the gap, made the apostasy of some, their complement, their full number. CALVIN and CALOVIUS understand the application as past, viz.: "If they had received the Gospel, their faith would have produced far more fruit than did their unbelief." But the reference must be future. The argument shows that the fall of the Jews brings a blessing to the world; then, indirectly through the conversion of the Gentiles, to the Jews themselves; and then further reacts, through the final conversion of the Jews, again upon the Gentiles.

Ver. 13. **But I speak to you that are Gentiles.** Paul had been contending against Jewish particularism. Now he anticipates, with his answer, the opposite extreme of Gentile particularism. The Gentiles could readily regard the privileges of the Gospel almost exclusively theirs, since the Jews had rejected them. They might be disposed to censure Paul, "the apostle of the Gentiles," for his assertion of the claims, and proclamation of the future of Israel. He answers: **I glorify my ministry.** No narrow and contracted view, adapted simply to present relations, does he take. The sweep of his vision is far-reaching. Looking far into the future, he sees that the greatest blessings will come to the Gentiles by the conversion of Israel. Hence, as the Apostle to the Gentiles, he labors for the conversion also of Israelites, since God's purposes of love for the Gentiles cannot be completed, until the promises concerning the Jews be fulfilled.

Ver. 14. **If I may provoke to jealousy,** i. e. If I may infuse into any of my kinsmen the desire to enjoy the blessings, that were first offered them, but are now possessed chiefly by the Gentiles—God's second choice. (See ver. 11.) **And may save some.** He does not expect the conversion of the entire nation during his lifetime, but he wants to make the beginning. Men are converted not in mass, but as individuals. He can save his countrymen by bringing them the Gospel (Rom.

1 : 16). Men are said also in 1 Cor. 7 : 16; 9 : 22; 1 Tim. 4 : 16, to save other men. This saving of some is simply a portion of the preparation for the ultimate "fulness" or complement of ver. 12.

Ver. 15. A repetition and interpretation of ver. 12. **If the casting away is the reconciling of the world**, i. e. If, through their being rejected, the world comes to know Christ, and thus large numbers be reconciled to God. **What shall the receiving of them be?** What will not the effect be, when they are converted in mass, and acknowledged by God as His children? . **But life from the dead.** The return of the Jews will infuse new life into Christianity, then in such a state of spiritual torpor, that it might be regarded dead; just as Paul's conversion brought new life to the Apostolic Church, and the conversion of the German tribes brought new life to Mediæval Christianity. We cannot find here, however, as some have done, the prophecy that the conversion of the Jews will immediately precede the resurrection from the dead. Luther's interpretation is that "the dead Jews shall be raised to life by the example of the heathen." But the protasis of this sentence seems clearly to require that the effect described in the second clause is one upon the world, "life from the dead, for the world."

(*b.*) *Warnings to the Converted Gentiles, because of the Spiritual Privileges they have Received.*

16–24. And if the firstfruit is holy, so is the lump: and if the root is holy, so are the branches. But if some of the branches were broken off, and thou, being a wild olive, wast grafted in among them, and didst become partaker with them of the root of the fatness of the olive tree; glory not over the branches: but if thou gloriest, it is not thou that bearest the root, but the root thee. Thou wilt say then, Branches were broken off, that I might be grafted in. Well; by their unbelief they were broken off, and thou standest by thy faith. Be not highminded, but fear: for if God spared not the natural branches, neither will he spare thee. Behold then the goodness and severity of God: toward them that fell, severity; but toward thee, God's goodness, if thou continue in his goodness: otherwise thou also shalt be cut off. And they also, if they continue not in their unbelief, shall be grafted in: for God is able to graft them in again. For if thou wast cut out of that which is by nature a wild olive tree, and wast grafted contrary to nature into a good olive tree: how much more shall these, which are the natural *branches*, be grafted into their own olive tree?

Ver. 16. **And if the firstfruit is holy.** A declaration concerning how well grounded is the view of the final conversion of Israel. The seed of the Word may encounter many calamities which seem to defer all prospects of the ultimate harvest, but through them all the life, inherent in it, is preserved and forces its way, until the end is at last reached. The illustration here is from the heave-offering of Numb. 15:19-21. The firstfruits of dough, not of grain, are referred to. Of every baking, a portion was to be set aside; and from this a cake was to be baked for the priests. This act consecrated the entire mass of dough. The firstfruits stand for the patriarchs. This is determined by the fact that in the second figure here used, **the root** must have this meaning; and the connection makes it clear, that "firstfruits" and "root" must designate the same thing. **The lump,** then, refers to all the chosen people. **Holy,** with respect to the patriarchs, both externally and internally, but with respect to Israel not primarily by internal, but by external holiness, as in 1 Cor. 1:24, i. e. they are brought within the sphere in which the means of grace are administered; and these means are never without some saving fruit (Is. 55:11). "The firstfruits or patriarchs he calls holy, not by nature, but by grace, because they believed the promise concerning the Messiah, and, by faith, served God in righteousness and holiness. To these patriarchs, the promise was made: 'I will be thy God and of thy seed after thee.' Wherefore the posterity of these patriarchs he calls holy in the same way; since it has not been altogether rejected, without a holy remnant being left, i. e. some believing Jews, however few, in whom the promise, made to the fathers, is fulfilled" (HUNNIUS). **If the root is holy.** The figure is changed, because that of "the firstfruits" is not adequate. An additional thought is to be presented in the succeeding verse, which the figure of "firstfruits" will not supply. The Jews who rejected Christ separated themselves from the root, i. e. from the patriarchs, all whose aspirations in life and death were directed to the coming Messiah. **So are the branches,** viz. as long as they are united with the root (ver. 17). All this shows that the mission of Israel has not been a failure, and that there is no reason for despising it. Even to-day, the Jews should not be objects of the scorn and contempt of Christians. While their predominantly mercenary character and spirit truly show the work-righteousness that pervades their religious life, God is constantly preserving from those called out from them a seed for a future harvest.

Ver. 17. **But if some of the branches were broken off.** The reference is to the Jews who, in rejecting Christ, separated themselves from the promises made to their ancestors and the religious life that had been sustained thereby. **Thou wast grafted in.** Even though shoots from another source be grafted in, these shoots live not from their native strength, but from the life of the plant into which they have been grafted. The meaning is that the spiritual life of Gentile Christians is dependent upon their organic connection by faith with the promises made to the patriarchs, and the plan of salvation prepared by God through Israel. The very root which produced the branches that have fallen off, sustains the engrafted branches. The Apostle was not ignorant that the shoot, grafted upon a new stock, retains the peculiarities of the stock whence it has been cut; but it was foreign to his purpose to enter into all the details of the process of grafting. No illustration dare be pressed to all possible applications. All that he desires to show is that the branch that is grafted must derive all its nourishment from the root of the plant upon which it is grafted. **Root of the fatness,** i. e. root which is the source of the fatness; that whence all the blessings of salvation come. **Glory not over the branches,** i. e. It is altogether out of place for you, who owe all that you have to the blessings of salvation provided through the Jews, to boast even over those among them who have fallen, especially as it is a matter of pure grace that you are found in their place.

Ver. 18. **But if thou gloriest.** The thought is: "Suppose you do glory. How foolish! You act as though Judaism were indebted to you, and in utter forgetfulness of how much you owe to Judaism. You act as though grace and salvation were rooted in you, and the salvation of the patriarchs were in some way dependent upon their relation to you. You forget the root which sustains your own life. You have been admitted into the fellowship of the patriarchs, and owe all that you have and are to what has come to you through the Jews." "The Gentiles become God's people by means of the Jews, not the Jews by the instrumentality of the Gentiles. In view of this fact, the contempt of the latter becomes absurd, and even perilous" (GODET).

Ver. 19. Intensely ironical. **Thou wilt say they.** The thought is: "Pray do not think that these branches were broken off for the express purpose of making room for you!"

Ver. 20. **By their unbelief, they were broken off.** This

verse declares that it is not by God's will that these branches were broken off. They separated themselves from the root. The cause lies not in God, but in themselves. But the cause of the converted Gentiles' enjoyment of the blessings of divine grace is ascribed altogether to God. **Thou standest by thy faith ;** and this faith is a gift of God (5 : 2 ; Eph. 2 : 8). God did not break off the natural branches, to make room for you ; but when they broke off, through man's abuse of his freedom, you were placed there by God's grace, and alone, by this same grace, you remain.

Ver. 21. **If God spared not the natural branches.** If the natural branches were broken off by their separation of themselves from the root out of which they grew, the danger of such separation on the part of the engrafted branches seems still more imminent. The loss of faith is possible. The example of the broken-off branches should, therefore, only stimulate to earnestness, lest their high privileges be lost.

Ver. 22. **Behold then the goodness and severity.** Of these two attributes of God, "goodness" (lit. "mildness") comes first. " Severity," that which cuts off, that which is inflexible in its rigor. Towards **them that fell,** i. e. the disbelieving and rejected Jews. God deals with them according to the full measure of His retributive justice. **Towards thee, God's goodness.** It is not, therefore, a matter of justice that the believing Gentile enjoys such privileges. In ascribing it to God's "mildness," all man's merit is excluded. Nothing is left, on account of which the recipient of this goodness may exalt himself over others. **If thou continue.** Thus we are clearly taught the possibility of a fall from grace. Men can turn themselves away from God's goodness, and thus **be cut off.** This cannot be referred to any hypocritical or merely professed faith; for these branches actually, and not merely seemingly, were grafted into the olive tree, and made partakers of the root (ver. 17). Inasmuch as what happened to the natural branches will be repeated also in those that are engrafted, when their circumstances are the same, i. e. when the grace of God is persistently opposed, no one can justly glory; there is nothing in him that has determined the favor of God. He can boast of nothing but the tender mercy of God in Christ.

Ver. 23. **And they also.** The Jews who reject Christ. This cannot refer to all individuals. The Apostle is speaking of the nation. Individuals perish; but the race continues. The identity of the "they" who rejected Christ, then, and of those who would be grafted in, must, therefore, be that of the race. **If they continue not in their unbelief,** i. e. Whenever Jews yield to the pleadings of divine grace and accept Christ as their Saviour. This does not necessarily exclude the return of individuals to the faith they had once held, but the scope of time involved is so vast, that this may be regarded here as exceptional. **For God is able to graft them in again.** The appeal to the Divine Omnipotence implies the great difficulty connected with their return. It also declares that man's return is all of God. But man's will can at any stage oppose an effectual bar to this work of God. Thus vers. 22, 23 teach the three doctrines of the amissibility, the recoverableness and the resistibility of God's grace. "It may, indeed, be alleged, that the Apostle is here dealing not so much with particular individuals, as with the people collectively. But, at all events, he expected, in his own day, to see a partial fulfilment of his hopes in the case of fallen individuals, ver. 14; and, besides, we are warranted in drawing inferences from the course of history in a nation collectively to that of particular individuals" (PHILIPPI).

Ver. 24. **How much more shall these,** i. e. How much more natural is it for the Jews to be converted to Christianity, than for Gentiles to enter into the communion of the Church. The antagonism of Judaism to Christianity is entirely contrary to God's order. The Jewish foe of Christianity cuts himself off from everything glorious in the past history of the nation, and, on returning, enters, by becoming a Christian, into the full inheritance of all that is promised in the O. T. He only is faithful to the Scriptures he has ever professed to revere. But the Gentile Christian breaks with his entire past, and, for a long time, his heathen prejudices and habits color and modify his conception of Christianity. **Their own olive tree.** The Patriarchal, which has now become the Christian Religion. "Since, therefore, Gentiles have been brought into the Church, who will doubt concerning the restoration of the Jews?" (BALDWIN).

(*c.*) *The Final Conversion of Israel* (vers. 25-30).

25-30. For I would not, brethren, have you ignorant of this mystery, lest ye be wise in your own conceits, that a hardening in part hath befallen Israel, until the fulness of the Gentiles be come in; and so all Israel shall be saved: even as it is written,
　　　　There shall come out of Zion the Deliverer;
　　　　He shall turn away ungodliness from Jacob:
　　　　And this is my covenant unto them,
　　　　When I shall take away their sins.
As touching the gospel, they are enemies for your sake: but as touching the election, they are beloved for the fathers' sake. For the gifts and the calling of God are without repentance.

Ver. 25. The words, **For I would not have you ignorant,** introduces a statement of particular importance

(1 : 13; 1 Cor. 10 : 1; 12 : 1; 2 Cor. 1 : 8; 1 Thess. 4 : 13). **Of this mystery.** The New Testament use of the word "mystery" should be noted, as that which, while of itself unable to be known, has been proclaimed in divine revelation. As such it is often applied to the mystery of redemption through Christ (Rom. 16 : 25; 1 Cor. 2 : 7-10; Eph. 3 : 3-5). **That a hardening.** (See v. 7; 9 : 8.) **Lest ye be wise,** viz. by your conjectures concerning the future of Israel, and God's purposes with reference to it. **In part,** i. e. Not all have believed, and, therefore, a portion have been hardened. **Hath befallen Israel until.** The effects of the hardening are to continue, i. e. the great mass of the Israelitic people will remain hardened until the time mentioned. **The fullness of the Gentiles.** (See note on ver. 12.) The Gentiles who are to fill up the gap that has been made by the loss of so many of the chosen people. "It might be said that when once the rent made in God's kingdom by Israel's apostasy is repaired by the supplement from the Gentiles, there will then be no room for all Israel (ver. 26), and that, too, as a supplement to enter. But here also we must not press the figure too strictly. In one aspect, the Gentiles are admitted to Israel's place, and, in the other, Israel itself returns to its former place" (PHILIPPI). **Be come in,** viz. into that communion of the people of God which has been symbolized by the olive tree.

Vers. 26, 27. **And so all Israel shall be saved.** The entire context (vers. 12, 23, 30, 32) forbids us to interpret this as the spiritual Israel, or even the comparatively small number of Israelites who, from time to time, will be converted to Christ. This argument of Paul loses all point in that way. It means that the Jewish nation will become a Christian nation, like others among whom the Gospel of Christ is externally revered and brings forth saving fruit in individual lives of a large multitude. This, then, does not necessarily mean that, at the time in prospect, every Jew will be brought to Christ; but the hostility of the race to Christ will cease, and large numbers of them become Christians both in profession and at heart. There seems to be no obscurity whatever about the prophecy. " These words of the Apostle are not received in a uniform sense by expositors. Some understand, by the name of Israel, not the Jewish people, but all believers without distinction. There are others who think that, by this mystery, the Apostle wants to indicate that, before the day of judgment, a great multitude of Jews will be converted to the Christian faith. While neither interpretation is impious, yet when the entire context of the Apostle is more carefully examined, the latter explanation, I think, is more in harmony with the words and present purpose of Paul. For since what immediately precedes treats expressly of the Jewish people, and the Apostle himself so comprises this mystery concerning the salvation of Israel, as in what follows he clearly shows he is speaking of the Jews, the intermediate words seem also such as should be interpreted of the Jews. This is seen, besides, from the fact that the Apostle calls it a mystery. But if the sense had been that all believers of every nation would be saved, this certainly was already known to the Roman Christians, and was not a new mystery. Furthermore, it is certain that these words are connected by the causal conjunction with those which are before, and depend upon them, and are the reason or cause of the preceding assertion why the Jews could be inserted anew into their own olive tree" (HUNNIUS). "He calls what he had said and was about to say concerning the conversion of the Jews 'a mystery'; for on account of the extreme obstinacy of that people such conversion seemed to the Gentiles very difficult, and to many altogether incredible. Hence he calls it a mystery. For he presents this mystery, in order that the Gentiles might not seem to themselves to be wise, i. e. as a remedy for their pride, lest they might exalt themselves above the Jews, whom God, nevertheless, in His own time, will call back again into the Church. . . . As the fulness of the Gentiles does not denote each and every nation, but a great part of their number, so we are not to hope for the conversion and salvation of each and every Jew. It is apparent, therefore, that Paul is prophesying concerning a peculiar conversion of the Jews, the greater part of whom, before the last day, will acknowledge the Messiah, and be brought to the faith of Christians. Although this prophecy has not yet been fulfilled, nevertheless we doubt not that it shall certainly occur; the time is known only to God, and, hence, it is a mystery also to us" (BALDWIN).

LUTHARDT has correctly said that the history of the interpretation of this passage in the Lutheran Church is a warning concerning allowing Exegesis to be dominated by Dogmatics.[1] Luther's earlier position is that which is above given. Thus, in 1521, he says: "It is certain that the Jews will yet say to Christ: 'Blessed be He that cometh in the name of the Lord.' This is prophesied by Moses (Deut. 9 : 30, 31), also by Hosea (3 : 4, 5), and Azariah (2 Chron. 15 : 2–5). . . . But this passage cannot be understood of the Jews of to-day. St. Paul says: 'Blindness in part has come upon Israel, until,' etc. God grant that this time may be near, Amen."[2] In 1523, he expresses the hope that the new light of the Gospel will bring many to Christ. That

---

[1] *Die Lehre von den letzten Dingen*, Leipzig, 1861, p. 111.
[2] WORKS, *Erl. Ed.* (1st ed.) 10 : 231 sq.; (2d ed.) 10 : 244 sq.

hitherto they had not been converted, he ascribes as due, in large measure, not to their own obstinacy, but to the manner in which they had seen and heard Christianity represented to them by the Papists. But from 1538 there is a change. In 1543, the renunciation of Christianity by some fanatics and their transfer to Judaism, and the visits of several Rabbis to Luther to persuade him to become a Jew, excited his indignation, so that it found expression in a little book, " Of the Jews and their Lies."[1] Henceforth he has no hopes of the Jews. This verse he says means something quite different. But, as LUTHARDT notes, he attempts no explanation of it. It is a mystery still. Lutheran theologians, with some few exceptions, as HUNNIUS and BALDWIN above noted, and HUTTER, GESNER, MYLIUS, MEISNER, HAFENREFFER, etc., followed LUTHER. GERHARD, with great caution and discrimination, citing and weighing the arguments on both sides, returns to the older exposition, guarding against chiliasm, limiting the " universality " to a very great number, and maintaining that the details of the prophecy can only faintly be understood in advance.

It is interesting to note the chief arguments which GERHARD quotes as used against the literal interpretation. They are briefly : " Such a universal conversion of the Jews before the last day cannot be expected : 1. On account of the threefold curse under which they rest : the general (Deut. 27 : 15) ; the peculiar (Matt. 27 : 25) ; the words of Christ through David (Ps. 69 : 22, 23). 2. On account of their obstinate rejection of the means of conversion and salvation. 3. On account of Paul's prediction that the revelation of Anti-Christ will be the last especially memorable work of God before the end of the

[1] *Erl. Ed.* 32 : 99–274.

world (1 Thess. 2 : 8). [But these theologians, with Luther, regarded the Pope as Anti-Christ, and found, therefore, no room for so important an event as the conversion of the Jews.] 4. On account of the duration of the call to the Gentiles, which, according to Luke 21 : 24 sq., is extended to the end of the world. . . . 5. On account of the uniformity to be expected in the conversion of the Jews, and of the fulness of the Gentiles. For as the conversion of Gentiles was not made at once, but successively, so the Jews, it would seem, should be converted here and there, and successively. . . . 6. On account of the prediction of Christ and the Apostles concerning the paucity of believers, and the multitude of heresies about the end of the world." [1]

Among Lutheran interpreters of the present century, BESSER is almost alone in his long argument to prove that no universal or even relatively universal conversion of the Jews to Christ before the end of the world can be meant. His argument is briefly: 1. The use of "thus," not of "then," at the beginning of ver. 26. 2. The application of "all Israel" to the great body of Israelites at a certain period in this world's history does not satisfy the comprehensiveness of the expression "all"; and, besides, contradicts the New Testament conception of the gifts of God's grace being independent of descent according to the flesh. 3. It implies a change in the plan of salvation, if God at one period hardens one portion of Israel, and at another period saves all Israel through faith, and conflicts with the warning of Heb. 3 : 8. 4. It conflicts with the idea of ver. 15 of the new life that is to enter the Church with the event here mentioned. For if the number of the Gentiles that are to be saved is completed, and "all Israel" is saved there can be no future develop-

[1] *Loci Theologici* (Preuss), ix. 108 seq.

ment of the Church. 5. It conflicts with the second sentence of 9:6.

Against all these objections, we ask only the careful reading of the entire argument of this Epistle, and especially of this chapter. The *first* of Besser's arguments we believe is completely answered by " until " of ver. 25. ; the *second* by a comparison with 1 Kings 12:1 ; 2 Chron. 12 : 1 ; Dan. 9 : 11, and the remembrance that this is simply an unfolding of God's plans in bringing His grace to all men of all nations; the *third*, by the fact that the hardening of Israel has been by their own fault, and not from any lack of God's grace (10: 3), and that in the period prophesied there can be no change in the way of salvation, and even then every Israelite will have the same power, as his kinsmen to-day, to resist God's grace— God's prophecies in no way annul the freedom of man's will in antagonizing His purposes; the *fourth*, that the external conversion of Israel, and even the inner conversion of all who are to be saved—which is not stated or meant—would still leave enough for the activity of the Church in the development of the Christian life of its members, and the work of their sanctification ; and the *fifth*, by the consideration that 9:6 clearly refers to "Israel" in a different sense, since the meaning must be determined by the argument of the two chapters.

We add the judgments of a few modern expositors: " A survey of the entire line of argument shows incontrovertibly that here the discourse is concerning Israel only in the national and proper, and not in the figurative sense ; for, throughout, the contrast between Israel and the Gentile world is maintained " (LUTHARDT).[1] " ' All Israel,' in contrast with ' in part ' of ver. 25, can be understood of nothing else than the entire sum of the

[1] *Die lehre von dem letzten Dingen*, p. 113.

people of Israel. Its application to the spiritual Israel (Gal. 6:16) is just as arbitrary as its application to the believing elect portion of the Jews. Such explanations merely show to what violent exegetical shifts interpreters can be led by preconceived opinions" (PHILIPPI). "'All Israel' designates the totality of the people, as it is constituted by descent from the patriarchs,—the people as such, i. e. as a popular unit, which, however, does not exclude the abiding of some individuals in unbelief. The reference to all individual Israelites (MEYER) is just as much in violation of the test, as arbitrary limitations, e. g. 'the spiritual Israel' (Gal. 6:16), as Augustine, Theodoret, Luther, Calvin, Grotius, etc., interpret, or a select portion of the Jews (CALOVIUS, BENGEL, OLSHAUSEN), or to regard 'all' as comparative, and referring only to the greater number ((ECUMENIUS, WETSTEIN, RÜCKERT, FRITZSCHE, CALVIN)" (WEISS). "Israel, here, from the context, must mean the Jewish people, and 'all Israel,' the whole nation. The Jews, as a people, are now rejected; as a people, they are to be restored. As their rejection, although national, did not include the rejection of every individual; so their restoration, although in like manner national, need not be assumed to include the salvation of every individual Jew" (HODGE). "Paul, in expressing himself as he does, does not mean to suppress individual liberty in the Israelites who shall live at that epoch. He speaks of a collective movement which shall take hold of the nation in general, and bring them as such to the feet of their Messiah. Individual resistance remains possible" (GODET). "The context requires the literal Israel; considering (1) what is meant by 'their fulness' (ver. 12); (2) the subject of 'if they continue not in their unbelief, they shall be grafted in' (ver. 23); (3) the parallel instituted between the Jews and the Heathen, in vers. 30, 31; and 'that He might have mercy upon all' (ver. 32). Israel's entrance as a nation into the Church of Christ, although contrary to all present probabilities, is a climax of the 'mystery' disclosed by the Apostle in vers. 25, 26" (LIDDON). "The whole context shows clearly that it is the actual Israel of history that is referred to" (SANDAY). "Clearly the meaning here is, *The Israelitish nation at large.* To understand this great statement, as some still do, merely of such a gradual inbringing of *individual* Jews, that there shall at length none remain in unbelief, is to do manifest violence to it and to the context. It can only mean the ultimate ingathering of Israel as a *nation*, in contrast with the present remnant" (BROWN).

PHILIPPI notes here that the idea, entertained by some, that the end of the world is to immediately follow this conversion of the Jewish nation, arises from a misunderstanding of ver. 15, as though it referred to the "resurrection." (Comp. notes on above passage.)

Even as it is written. A combination of Is. 59:20 with 27:9, following in general the LXX. **The Deliverer.** Hebr. *Goel* = the Redeemer. The variations in the quotation do not affect the application of the passage, whose thought is that Zion shall be delivered from its oppression by taking away the iniquity of the entire people, **Jacob,** or, what is the same, by leading the entire people to turn from their transgression, and that then (ver. 27) the broken covenant with them shall be renewed.

Ver. 28. **As touching the Gospel,** i. e. on account of their rejection of the Gospel. **They are enemies.** God is hostile to them. **For your sake.** (See on ver. 11.) **As touching the election.** (See ver. 5.) There is among them a small number of elect, preserving the seed of the truth, until the promise of ver. 26 is fulfilled. **For the fathers' sake** (Luke 1:55; Acts 3:25). (Cf. ver. 16.)

Ver. 29. **For the gifts,** the charisms. (See on 1 Cor. 12.) "The Greeks, the Romans, the Phœnicians had their special gifts in the different domains of science and art, law and politics, industry and commerce. Israel, without being destitute of the powers related to those spheres of mundane activity, have received a higher gift, the organ for the divine and the intuition of holiness" (GODET). These gifts are simply exponents of the **calling, without repentance.** God's purpose and call are sure to be realized. Individuals may reject the call; but it ultimately reaches its end in the race. No gift of God can be absolutely wasted; no call of God can in the end be thwarted. "God will let unbelieving generations succeed one another as long as shall be necessary, until that generation come which shall at length open its eyes, and freely return to Him" (GODET), i. e. shall use these gifts and yield to the call despised by those who preceded them. Generations come and go, but call and gifts remain until they are at last appropriated.

(d.) *Review of the Divine Plan.*

30–32. For as ye in time past were disobedient to God, but now have obtained mercy by their disobedience, even so have these also now been disobedient, that by the mercy shewn to you they also may now obtain mercy. For God hath shut up all unto disobedience, that he might have mercy upon all.

Vers. 30–32 have as their one theme the mercy of God as exercised both towards Jew and Gentile. Salvation comes to all alike through mercy. First, we find the thought repeated that the occasion of the mercy shown to the Gentiles is the disbelief of the Jews, as in vers. 12,

15, 28, in order to show that this very mercy shown the Gentiles leads to the conversion of Israel. That is, the very disobedience of the Jews leads, by the wonderful scheme of Divine Providence, to the ultimate conversion of the nation. The Kingdom of God progresses, and the very opposition which it encounters, becomes the means for its greater triumph. **God hath shut up.** This is to be understood as a penal act, just as God is said to harden men. The disobedience or unbelief of men is not willed by God; but when it is present, God knows how to arrange His scheme of world-government in such a way as to produce the highest good. Even the disobedience of the unbelieving is directed towards the attainment of the purposes of Divine Mercy. Boast as he may of his freedom, man's path is shut up by God's power. "In the religious development of humanity, the divine ordination is the warp, human freedom is the woof of the web. The direction of the latter is determined by the former; but the web itself only comes into existence by the interlacing of the two" (PHILIPPI). **All,** viz. all nations, Jews and Gentiles. **That he might have mercy.** But this does not teach that these purposes of mercy will be realized in absolutely all. Even at the end, the will of the individual will be free to resist and reject, however sure it be that all nations shall be converted.

(c.) *Concluding Doxology.*

33-36. O the depth of the riches both of the wisdom and the knowledge of God! how unsearchable are his judgements, and his ways past tracing out! For who hath known the mind of the Lord? or who hath been his counsellor? or who hath first given to him, and it shall be recompensed unto him again? For of him, and through him, and unto him, are all things. To him *be* the glory for ever. Amen.

Ver. 33. "Paul in Chapter IX. had been sailing, as it were, on a strait; he is now on the ocean" (BENGEL). "Like a traveller who has reached the summit of an Alpine ascent, the Apostle turns and contemplates. Depths are at his feet; but waves of light illumine them, and there spreads all around an immense horizon which his eye commands. The plan of God in the government of mankind spreads out before him, and he expresses the feelings of admiration and gratitude with which the prospect fills his heart" (GODET). **Depth** expresses the fulness of that which is denoted by the three genitives that follow. **Of the riches.** The marginal reading of R. V. gives the preferable interpretation, viz. that which make the three genitives that followed co-ordinate. "Depth of the riches and of the wisdom and of the knowledge." (So CHRYSOSTOM, THEODORET, BENGEL, THOLUCK, ALFORD, HODGE, WEISS, LIDDON, GIFFORD, SANDAY.) **Riches** denote the inexhaustible divine goodness (Phil. 4 : 19, ch. 10 : 2) and power (Eph. 3 : 20). **Wisdom** refers to the wonderful adjustment of means to ends, as this has just been traced; the abandonment of the Gentiles, the election of the Jews, and, then, the rejection of the Jews, and the conversion of the Gentiles, and, finally, the ultimate triumph in the conversion also of the Jews, and how, in this plan, every apparent defeat only enhances the final victory. **And of the knowledge.** This looks forward to the future, and considers the varied details of the plan not revealed, concerning which we are not to conjecture, but which we must be satisfied to let rest in God's loving heart. **Judgments** judicial decisions, verdicts. (Comp. 2 : 2 sq.; 3 : 8; 5 : 16; Ps. 36 : 6; 119 : 75.) However severe, His mercy underlies and pervades them all. **Ways** modes of effecting His purposes. **Past tracing out.** "We may as well attempt to mark the path of a ship through the sea, or of an eagle through the air" (STARKE).

Ver. 34. **For who hath known.** The words are taken from Isai. 40 : 13, but not directly quoted. So well known were they to those to whom Paul is writing, that they become a proof of what has just been said. **The mind** refers to the depths of God's knowledge. **Who hath been his counsellor?** refers to the depths of God's wisdom.

Ver. 35. **Or who hath first given.** A quotation from Job 41 : 11. An illustration of the depth of God's riches (ver. 33). All that man receives must be solely of God's grace and mercy; for God cannot gain aught by any work, gift or service.

He ends this part of the Epistle with the key-note that runs through the complicated argument, viz. that man is saved alone by God's mercy, without any merit of worthiness in man. He clinches the argument by an appropriate and forcible Old Testament text.

Then comes the Doxology, properly so called.

Ver. 36. **Of him,** as the source. **Through him,** as the means. **To him,** as the ultimate end. He is the beginning, the middle and end of all things. All things were created by Him; all created things owe all their activity to His concurrence with them, and efficiency in them; and all things are directed towards the working out of His purposes, and the glory of His name. " To him " belongs to the Father and Son equally with the Holy Spirit. But if this be used as a Trinitarian formula, the application must be that all things, even the forces of nature and the opposition of men, are employed in the service of the work of the Holy Spirit in applying Redemption to the race. Beyond this, there is a still more distant goal, which belongs to other persons of the Trinity.

PART V.

PRACTICAL EXHORTATIONS.—THE LIFE OF THE JUSTIFIED (12 : 1—15 : 13).

1. *General Obligations* (12 : 1—13 : 7).

(*a*.) *With Respect to Man's Two-fold Nature* (12 : 1, 2).

1-2. I beseech you therefore, brethren, by the mercies of God, to present your bodies a living sacrifice, holy, acceptable to God, *which is* your reasonable service. And be not fashioned according to this world: but be ye transformed by the renewing of your mind, that ye may prove what is the good and acceptable and perfect will of God.

Therefore. This connects, first of all, with what has just been declared. Chapter 11 : 33-36 contains an exclamation and reflection of the Apostle upon the wonders of the plan of Divine Mercy which he had been unfolding, and which he had summed up in vers. 29-32. **By the mercies of God.** Only count the Apostle's use of the word mercy in the immediate context :—ver. 30 : " Obtained *mercy ;* " ver. 31 : " By the *mercy* shown to you," " May now obtain *mercy ;* " ver. 31 : " That he might have *mercy*,"—four times in three verses. But, while thus immediately connected with the context, it is also a conclusion drawn from the entire doctrinal part of the Epistle. " Since in what precedes the Apostle had taught how the sum of religion had been transferred from the Jews to the Gentiles, from circumcision to faith, from the letter to the spirit, from the shadow to the truth, from a carnal to a spiritual observance" (ANSELM). **beseech you.** "Moses commands; the Apostle exhorts" (BENGEL). **Brethren:** "What I ask, our mutual brotherhood requires" (ANSELM), i. e. it is the necessary result of that grace which has now made of us who were hitherto strangers one family in Christ Jesus. **Your bodies.** Paul avoids saying "yourselves" for a purpose. The emphasis of the bodily side of man's nature seems to be connected with the preceding argument, which was to the effect that, throughout all the vicissitudes of Israel's history, God was preserving for Himself within the nation a holy seed, and that in the line of carnal descent from the patriarchs the covenant promises were being handed down which ultimately would be acknowledged when "all Israel shall be saved" (Rom. 11 : 26). The bodily descent becomes, therefore, an insignificant factor, only when it is separated from the spiritual factor, and is urged to the neglect of the higher claims of God. To warn against this, Paul says: "Present your bodies **a living sacrifice.** A paradox. The Levitical sacrifices had as their end the destruction of the victim. Here the victim dies, in order to live, i. e. to live as it has never lived before (Gal. 2 : 20). But since the victim lives, the sacrifice is not over in a moment. It is continuous. The body is always dying to the world and to sin ; the believer is constantly suppressing his carnal appetites and desires, in order that Christ may reign in him. "Sacrifice" refers to the earthly object that is constantly falling : "living," to the heavenly and divine spirit that, as the earthly object falls, rises towards God. The dead offerings of the Levitical sacrifices testified to their incompleteness. That to which they testify has its full realization in a sacrifice which, though dying, still lives. **Holy,** not only as faultless, and without blemish, but because of their spiritual nature, as proceeding from the Holy Spirit, dwelling in the heart, and, therefore, readily contrasted with the purely external services of the O. T. **Reasonable service** is in opposition to "Present your bodies." The meaning is that it is only such a disposition of the external, bodily life, that is in harmony with their Christian profession. Starting with the premises laid down in the preceding chapters, this must be the "logical" result. A man who does otherwise has not thoroughly and sincerely apprehended these truths. There is an opposition here to the false estimate placed upon mere carnal descent by the Jews, as well as to the entire tendency of pure externalism of which this estimate was only an exponent, so that their worship consisted in the offering of dead sacrifices and in conformity to ritual observances without faith in Him around whom they all centred.

Ver. 2. Assumes the danger that, in the estimate of the body, false standards are very likely to be followed. This false standard pervades both the Judaic and the Heathen thought and life, and is at the root of all differences among Christians. **Be not fashioned.** The reference is to the external life. **According to this world,** i. e. the standards followed by those who are not Christians, the world of sight and sense, as contrasted with that of faith. The thought is found in an expanded form in Hebrews xi. **Be ye transformed.** Note the contrast with "fashioned." Here the inner life is regarded ("$\mu o \rho \phi \acute{\eta}$, organic form, $\sigma \chi \tilde{\eta} \mu \alpha$, external form," LIDDON). "Fashioned" indicates also what is more transient and temporary, as the occasion of the hour requires an expression, adapted to its changing circumstances; "transformed," which is permanent and habitual. **Renewing of your mind,** as the source of the transformation (comp. Tit. 3 : 5; also 2 Cor. 4 : 16; Col. 3 : 16), referring to the progressive change in man's entire way of looking at things, and his disposition towards them, produced by the indwelling of the Holy Spirit. The "mind" here is the faculty that discriminates between the right and the wrong, the true and the false. Not only the doctrine of the training of man's moral faculties is here taught, but that also of the radical nature of the work, since the external is reached only through the internal life. **Prove** = "to determine what is" God's will. By the renewing of his mind, the believer is enlightened, amidst many perplexing courses of conduct that are offered, to know what God would have him do. (Cf. on 1 : 28; Phil. 1 : 10.) **The good and acceptable and perfect.** Either adjectives giving the three characteristics of God's will, or nouns in opposition with "will," indicating what that will is. The distinction is unessential. "Acceptable" means what if followed will surely please God, and, at the same time, must in the end approve itself to the consciences of men (2 Cor. 4 : 2).

(b.) As a Member of the Body of Christ. The Christian's Duties to the Church (12 : 3–8).

3–8. For I say, through the grace that was given me, to every man that is among you, not to think of himself more highly than he ought to think; but so to think as to think soberly, according as God hath dealt to each man a measure of faith. For even as we have many members in one body and all the members have not the same office: so we, who are many, are one body in Christ, and severally members one of another. And having gifts differing according to the grace that was given to us, whether prophecy, *let us prophesy* according to the proportion of our faith; or ministry, *let us give ourselves* to our ministry; or he that teacheth, to his teaching; or he that exhorteth, to his exhorting: he that giveth, *let him do it* with liberality; he that ruleth, with diligence; he that sheweth mercy, with cheerfulness.

Ver. 3. **For** shows the connection between humility

and the self-surrender to God described in the preceding verses. **Through the grace given me.** Not that common to all believers, but the special grace bestowed upon him for his Apostolic office (Ch. 1 : 5 ; Eph. 3 : 7, 8 ; 1 Cor. 15 : 9, 10). This points forward to the latter part of the verse. **To every one,** however high his attainments or office. **Not to think,** etc. In the original, there is a play upon words (*paronomasia*) which cannot be reproduced in a translation. **To think soberly,** i. e. with a sound mind, modestly. **Measure of faith.** Faith is God's gift. Here the different degrees of faith are not regarded with respect to faith's apprehension of Christ and salvation, but with respect to the activity of faith in the service of love. The degrees of faith given by God in this sphere, have respect to the different callings each is appointed to serve. "The measure or range assigned for the exercise of faith" (CREMER). With the call to some difficult labor, comes the faith from God to properly respond to it. Men without the divine call have not the faith to perform the allotted work; and hence must not be judged according to the higher standard. Responsibility rises with the measure of faith, and, as it is recognized as God's gift, self is more and more depreciated, instead of being exalted (1 Cor. 4 : 7). On the contrary, the entire effort of the world is directed towards making the impression that one is actually greater than he really is ; he exalts himself above his measure.

Vers. 4, 5. A motive for this sober estimate. The comparison with respect to civil life was not unusual in the classics. It is given a new application here. The best comment on these verses is the entire Twelfth Chapter of 1 Cor. **In Christ;** i. e. The union of each member with Christ gives the entire body unity. As the union with Christ of the individual is sundered, the unity of the body is destroyed; it falls to pieces, like the natural body, when the breath is gone, immediately dissolves, by being resolved into its constituent atoms. For the expression, see on ch. 8 : 1. **Members one of another.** Each member belongs not only to the entire body, but to every other member. Thus the argument is passing from the assertion of the common interest that all men have in Christ, to that of the common interest that all in Christ have in one another.

Vers. 6. Such being the case with individuals, it is true also with respect to classes and offices within the Church. Paul, therefore, begins an analysis of the Body of Christ into its various members. The list is not exhaustive, but only suggestive. Some have the gift of prophecy; that is one member. Others that of administration; that is another member, etc. **Gifts.** Lit. *Charisms*, the gifts of grace bestowed for special service in the Church. Of these gifts, some were temporary, belonging to the Apostolic period, before the N. T. Scriptures were complete, and others permanent. (See on 1 Cor. 12.) Even those that were temporary corresponded, however, to permanent endowments of the Church, differing chiefly in degree or form. **According to the Grace.** (See on ver. 3.) **Prophecy.** Inspired utterance. Not to be limited to the foretelling of future events, or even to the interpretation of the O. T. " He who prophesies declares what he knows by revelation of God's counsel and will; whether it be the hidden future which he unveils (1 Pet. 1 : 10), or the unintelligible present which he explains (Luke 1 : 6, 7 sq.); whether it be the secret decree of God which he proclaims (Eph. 3 : 5), or the secrets of man's heart which he discloses (1 Cor. 14 : 24, 25), or whether it be that, with power of conviction which God gives, he proclaims the great deeds of God and preaches the way of salvation" (BESSER). Every sermon that is the product of Holy Scripture, as its truths have entered into the experience of the preacher and have constrained him to testify to others of their power, is a form of prophecy. But in the Apostolic Church, there was a higher degree of such prophecy, just as the inspired writers wrote under the inspiration of the Holy Spirit. **According to the proportion of our faith.** "Proportion" means "right relation to" (CREMER). There must be a standard to which even the inspired prophet must conform. This standard is **faith.** Thus we understand that in his prophecies, he must beware of exceeding the sphere of faith. It is only in so far as he complies with the measure of faith (ver. 3) that his speech is true prophecy. The exhortation of the Apostle here means that each class in the Church must be careful to observe the bounds of its calling. This is the proof passage for the doctrine of "the analogy of the faith." This affirms that all doctrines of Revelation harmonize, and all obscure passages of Scripture must consequently be interpreted according to this principle, in order that all parts may be consistent. But this is rather the proper application of the exhortation to the present period of the Church, with the N. T. Scriptures completed and in our hands, than what the Apostle directly means.[1] Undoubtedly to preachers of to-day, the Holy Scriptures must ever be the norm, as well as the source of all true preaching.

Ver. 7. **Ministry.** While sometimes used, in general, for all forms of Christian activity (11 : 13; 1 Cor. 12 : 5; Eph. 4 : 12), yet when contrasted with other forms of

---

[1] Philippi, Hodge and Liddon, among more recent expositors, however, defend the analogy of the faith as Paul's meaning.

service, it refers to the administration of the various matters pertaining to the temporal wants of the Church, such as the care of the poor, the sick, the strangers, etc. (1 Cor. 12 : 28; Acts 6 : 1 sqq; Phil. 1 : 1; 1 Tim. 3 : 8, 12; 1 Pet. 4 : 11; Rom. 16 : 1). **Teaching.** A more calm, comprehensive and systematic form of instilling truth, than that of prophecy. The prophet impresses truth upon the heart; the teacher, upon the intellect. (Comp. Acts 13 : 1; Eph. 4 : 11.)

Ver. 8. **He that exhorteth,** i. e. one who has a special gift for stimulating men to action, or comforting them under affliction. (Comp. Acts 13 : 15.) **That giveth** distribution of his own possessions. As PHILIPPI shows, a different word would be used to indicate one who was simply an almoner of funds entrusted to his distribution by others. The *charism* of giving implies first a certain amount of property or wealth. **With liberality.** The A. V. translates literally "with simplicity," i. e. without any selfish motives prompting or accompanying the gift. R. V. obtains "liberality" by a derived meaning, supported by a passage in Josephus, from the open hand being "without a fold" (*sine plica, simplex*), then "open-handed," "liberal." But this does not seem as satisfactory as in the older translation. **That ruleth.** One who is placed over others, whether in the Church, the family, or the State. **With diligence.** Lit. "with zeal," throwing his whole soul into the work, "with laborious and minute attention to duty." **With cheerfulness.** Not simply willingly, but with gladness and joy, "with hilarity," that he is able to relieve suffering and dispel sorrow. Never can we forget the jubilant greeting of a theological student in the service of the Christian Commission in the rear of the battle-field of the Wilderness, as he passed us in his mission of administering to the wounded and dying: "Oh, this is blessed work." Nothing, we are sure, could have torn him from his ministry of love. All these graces come from special charisms or graces of the Spirit. The implication, then, is that those who are specially endowed with gifts for the one sphere, should not seek to obtrude into those of another.

(*c.*) *As a Member of Human Society. The Christian's Duties to his Fellow-men* (12 : 9–21).

9–21. Let love be without hypocrisy. Abhor that which is evil; cleave to that which is good. In love of the brethren be tenderly affectioned one to another; in honour preferring one another; in diligence not slothful; fervent in spirit; serving the Lord; rejoicing in hope; patient in tribulation; continuing stedfastly in prayer; communicating to the necessities of the saints; given to hospitality. Bless them that persecute you; bless, and curse not. Rejoice with them that rejoice; weep with them that weep. Be of the same mind one toward another. Set not your mind on high things, but condescend to things that are lowly. Be not wise in your own conceits. Render to no man evil for evil. Take thought for things honourable in the sight of all men. If it be possible, as much as in you lieth, be at peace with all men. Avenge not yourselves, beloved, but give place unto wrath: for it is written, Vengeance belongeth unto me; I will recompense saith the Lord. But if thine enemy hunger, feed him; if he thirst, give him to drink: for in so doing thou shalt heap coals of fire upon his head. Be not overcome of evil, but overcome evil with good.

Ver. 9. **Without hypocrisy,** i. e. perfectly open and candid. **Abhor that which is evil,** etc., viz. in the object loved. Love which does otherwise is hypocritical. "They who do not meet evil with hatred, but calmly smile upon the crimes committed by others, show that they have no Christian zeal" (OSIANDER). "It is a feigned love, when one loves his brother, and does not admonish or correct him, if he find him erring" (ANSELM).

Ver. 10. **In love of the brethren.** "Love" (*agape*) of the preceding verse is universal. "Love" as used here (*philadelphia*) is love towards fellow-Christians (1 Thess. 4 : 9; Heb. 13 : 1; 1 Pet. 1 : 22; 2 Pet. 1 : 7). The relation between the two is described in Gal. 6 : 10. **Be tenderly affectioned.** In the original the word is very expressive, denoting the affection between parents and children. **Preferring one another.** Lit. " taking the lead," i. e. allowing no one to surpass you in the respect you feel and the honor you show one another (John 13 : 14).

Ver. 11. **In diligence, not slothful.** Whatever you do, throw your whole heart into it (Col. 3 : 23). Be energetic and enthusiastic in attending to all the duties of the Christian calling. (Comp. " with diligence," ver. 8.) **Fervent in Spirit.** Lit. " boiling," with your interest in your work always kept at the boiling point. " We see the believer hastening with his heart on fire wherever there is any good to be done " (GODET). **Serving the Lord.** Some manuscripts give the reading, " serving the time," and Luther has followed them in the translation : " Adapt yourselves to the times." But the external evidence is against it, as well as the use of the Greek word for " serve " (" to be in bondage to ") here used. The clause has its place as a limitation and warning concerning what precedes. The thought is: Let all your activity and fervor be regulated by the constant presence in your mind of the fact that it is the Lord, and not yourself, whom you serve. This will be an effectual guard against the fanaticism, which otherwise might enter. Thus also the full emphasis of the word used for serve is brought out. Every thought must be brought into obedience to Christ (2 Cor. 10 : 5).

Ver. 12. **Rejoicing in hope,** by looking not at the things that are seen, but at the unseen, not at the temporal, but the eternal (1 Cor. 4 : 16–16). **Patient in tribulation.**

Zeal, such as described in the preceding verse, soon encounters opposition and brings trouble. But, with the hope of God's glory before him, he is not disturbed by wrath towards his persecutors or by murmurs against God. He calmly abides at his post in spite of the trials it involves. **Continuing steadfastly in prayer.** The sure remedy against all impatience. The believer's life must be sustained by constant communion with God, the source of all light, and strength, and courage.

Ver. 13. **Communicating to the necessities.** Lit. "Sharing in," i. e. treating them as though they are our own, making them our own. This is far more than almsgiving. (See Phil. 4 : 14.) **Of saints.** They should have especial care (Gal. 6 : 10). **Given to hospitality.** GODET suggests translation: "Eager to show hospitality." (Comp. Heb. 13 : 3; 1 Pet. 4 : 9.) A virtue especially important, in view of the numbers of journeying and persecuted Christians. This exhortation, be it noted, is addressed to Christians living in the world's capital, whither strangers thronged from all quarters. "The Christians looked upon themselves, as a body of men, scattered throughout the world, living as aliens among strange people, and, therefore, bound together as the members of a body, as the brethren of one family. The practical realization of this idea would demand that whenever a Christian went from one place to another, he should find a home among the Christians in each town he visited" (SANDAY).

Ver. 14. **Bless them that persecute you.** As ver. 13 is occupied with their treatment of their friends, this verse indicates their treatment of their enemies. We bless them when we pray for their good (Matt. 5 : 44; Luke 6 : 28). The motive is given in 1 Pet. 3 : 9.

Ver. 15. **Rejoice . . . weep.** The two forms of sympathy are enjoined. Their opposites are the envy which regards the good fortunes of others with pain, and the malice which is gratified with their misfortunes. The reference, here again, must be to sympathy with everything that pertains to members of the Christian brotherhood. (Comp. 1 Cor. 12 : 26, 27.) This sympathy has to do only with that which is a real and proper source of joy or sorrow. The Christian cannot rejoice in such temporal pleasures of his brother, as may imply great temptations or lack of fidelity to God. The reference is to joys that come to him as a divine blessing.

Ver. 16. **Be of the same mind.** Refers to more than simply harmony, but rather: " Having the same aspirations for one another." A beautiful picture of the unity of the Christian brotherhood where each one desires for every other member the same rich blessings which he himself enjoys. (Comp. 15 : 5; 2 Cor. 13 : 11; Phil. 2 : 2; 4 : 2.) Where this prevails, there can be no church parties or cliques. **Set not your mind on high things,** i. e. riches, honors, high positions. A warning against any aristocratic spirit in the Church. **But condescend.** See marginal reading for what is literal: " Be carried away with," indicating the intense interest felt. **Things that are lowly.** " The lower circumstances, conditions and occupations of life " (PHIL.). " Humble tasks, interests, relations in life " (LIDDON). " Self-withdrawal and exclusiveness belong to the religion of the Old Testament ; that of the New Testament bids us remain in communion even with those in whom the life of Christ dominates not yet. The Son of God teaches the duty to consort with publicans and sinners, in order to win them for His kingdom " (OLSHAUSEN). **Be not wise in your own conceit.** (Comp. Is. 5 : 21 ; Prov. 3 : 7.) This is an offence against

Christian love, since it implies the despising of the opinions of others.

Ver. 17. **Recompense to no man.** (Comp. ver. 14.) The reference is to the Christian in his private capacity. As charged by God's call, with public duties, he is bound to administer justice. (See Matt. 5 : 39; 1 Thess. 4 : 15; 1 Pet. 2 : 23; 3 : 9.) **Take thought for things honorable.** Lit. " Providing beforehand." " Preoccupied with." The Christian is to be so preoccupied with schemes of doing good to his fellow-men, that the thought of evil cannot enter. **In the sight of all men.** Except where a matter of principle is involved, he is not indifferent to public opinion ; then 1 Cor. 4 : 3 applies.

Ver. 18. **If it be possible.** This implies that there are circumstances where peace cannot be entertained. **As much as in you lieth.** Even where peace is impossible, this command can be observed, so far as we are concerned ; for the peace must then be broken on the other side. " Not so much an absolute keeping of the peace, or rather an absolute seeking of the peace, is enjoined. Consequently, the apostolic utterance cannot be thrown in the teeth of the witnesses of the truth, who stand prepared for conflict " (PHILIPPI). The divine rule is that of James 3 : 17 : " First pure, then peaceable." CALVIN gives the warning: " A double caution must be employed here : lest we affect to be so gracious, as to decline to assume the hatred of some for Christ's sake, as often as is necessary. Then lest readiness to assent degenerate, so that, for the sake of peace, we flatter the vices of men. Since, therefore, it is impossible always to have peace with all men, he has introduced these two particles of exception. Hence it is becoming that, for the purpose of promoting peace, we bear with many things, pardon offences, and courteously relax the rigor of the law, so that, as often as necessity demand, we may be ready to wage war zealously. For it cannot be that the soldiers of Christ should have eternal peace with the world whose prince is Satan."

Ver. 19. **Give place unto wrath**, i. e. Do not anticipate God's wrath. Let it take its own time to descend on the guilty, and to vindicate your cause. To avenge oneself is practically to deny faith in the justice of God. "This wrath of God will descend in various ways, viz. through the magistrate, through the devil, through sickness, famine, etc.; for all creatures are God's rod" (LUTHER). **It is written** (Deut. 32 : 35).

Ver. 20. A quotation from Prov. 25 : 21, 22. **Thou shalt heap coals of fire.** This cannot mean to bring down God's judgment, or to inflict severer pain than by any direct act of vengeance. AUGUSTINE well says: "How can any one really love a person to whom he gives food and drink for the purpose of heaping coals of fire on his head, if coals of fire mean any grievous punishment?" Hence ANSELM: "Either glowing coals of repentance, since he will grieve that he has injured you from whom he has received only good . . . or 'You will pour into his heart love glowing with the fire of the Holy Spirit,' i. e. just as glowing coals kindle the body on which they fall, so your good deeds will influence the heart of your persecutor to love, and by your example you will provoke him to well-doing by the fervor of the Holy Spirit." CALVIN finds here a two-fold effect, viz. the winning over of one class of enemies, and the pains of conscience that result in those too hardened to be won over. LUTHER understands the meaning to be that, in this way, the enemy is led to become angry with himself for his unjust conduct.

Ver. 21. **Be not overcome of evil.** For every attempt

we make to resent a wrong, indicates that we have been worsted in the battle. **But overcome evil with good.** " When by our calmness, we make even the enemy calm " (THOLUCK).

(*d.*) *The Christian's Relations to the Civil Government, even though Pagan.*

1-7. Let every soul be in subjection to the higher powers : for there is no power but of God ; and the *powers* that be are ordained of God. Therefore he that resisteth the power, withstandeth the ordinance of God : and they that withstand shall receive to themselves judgement. For rulers are not a terror to the good work, but to the evil. And wouldest thou have no fear of the power ? do that which is good, and thou shalt have praise from the same : for he is a minister of God to thee for good. But if thou do that which is evil, be afraid; for he beareth not the sword in vain : for he is a minister of God, an avenger for wrath to him that doeth evil. Wherefore ye must needs be in subjection, not only because of the wrath, but also for conscience' sake. For for this cause ye pay tribute also ; for they are ministers of God's service, attending continually upon this very thing. Render to all their dues : tribute to whom tribute *is due* ; custom to whom custom; fear to whom fear; honour to whom honour.

The importance of treating of duties pertaining to the Civil Magistrate might be inferred from the oppressive tyranny of the government, and the repeated efforts, made by legal persecution, to exterminate Christianity. Paul is writing during the reign of Nero. The Jews regarded the theocracy the only legitimate form. The Ebionites ascribed the exercise of civil government to the control of the devil.

Ver. 1. **Let every soul.** This teaches that a man's relation to his government is an individual matter. It cannot be delegated to cliques or parties or trades-unions or political bosses. **Be in subjection.** Lit. : " Subject itself," indicating that this subjection is to be rendered by the free will of the subject. **To the higher powers,** i. e.

rulers in an eminent position. This is not to allow of disobedience to those of lower rank, but to direct attention to the imperial government, with all the injustice by which it was established, and all the wrongs which it perpetrated. **No power but of God.** "What subsists *jure divine* certainly subsists not simply *gratia humana* or *voluntate populi*" (PHILIPPI). The private Christian has not to ask by what right these rulers have attained their authority. He has simply to submit himself to the government that exists. The hand of God has been beneath the forces that have raised them to their present power. **The powers that be,** i. e. the mere *de facto* existence of the government, not necessarily its rightful existence, establishes its claim to obedience. "Christianity gives its sanction, not exclusively to *one* definite form of government, but to the form of government actually subsisting at any time, and guards it against the attempts of revolutionary subversiveness" (PHILIPPI).

Ver. 2. **He that resisteth,** i. e. in matters, where obedience to a magistrate is not otherwise contrary to a law of God (Acts 4 : 19 ; 5 : 29). This resistance is not confined to open violence ; it occurs also where fraud is employed to defeat the ends of government. **Withstandeth the ordinance of God**—an offence, therefore, greatly to be condemned in one who makes a Christian profession. **Shall receive to themselves judgment.** Thus the utter uselessness of this resistance is declared. There can be only one result—failure and punishment. The word "judgment" refers to divine retribution which may be inflicted through the magistrate (ver. 4) or otherwise.

Ver. 3. **For** refers to the thought of the preceding verse. Such resistance can bring only injury to themselves, "for," etc. **Are not a terror,** i. e. are not to be dreaded, except when wrong is done. The distinction, however, must be made between the office and the persons who administrate it. The office itself is to bring security to the good, and punishment to the wicked; but it may be abused by the persons so that the directly contrary result is attained. **The good work.** "The ruler has to do only with the work: of the intention he knows nothing" (LIDDON). **Thou shalt have praise.** This is the rule. The worst of governments is better than anarchy. Even where there are despots who abuse their power, the benefits the government brings, corrupt though it be, are greater than its evils.

Ver. 4. **For he is a minister of God.** This denies all abitrary power in the ruler. He has no other rights than those to which God has called and appointed him. He is not to rule for his personal aggrandizement, but for the public good. He is a debtor both to God and to his subjects. **He beareth not the sword in vain,** i. e. The sword is not only to be borne, but to be used where necessity requires. The sword of the magistracy is not intended merely for parade, but for death. A clear proof of the right and duty of inflicting, in extreme cases, capital punishment.

Ver. 5. **Not only because of the wrath,** i. e. from fear of punishment, **but also for conscience' sake,** i. e. because of the Christian's conviction as to what God commands and what his duty is. "A Christian, so far as he is flesh, is to obey, 'because of the wrath;' but, so far as he is spirit, he obeys 'for conscience' sake'" (PHILIPPI).

Ver. 6. **For this cause,** viz. in order that the magistrates may be enabled to administer the laws. **Pay ye tribute.** Particularly galling and offensive to the Jews was the payment of taxes to Gentiles (Matt. 22 : 17). The Christianized Jews readily retained this prejudice. They needed the warning of the Master, not only to keep them in the right, but also to anticipate the false charges made against the new religion (Matt. 17 : 24-27 ; Luke 23 : 22). **They are ministers of God's service.** A different word for "minister" is here used from that found in ver. 4. The word here used (*leitourgoi*) is found in our English word *liturgy*. In Heb. 1 : 7, it is applied to the angels. Indicating first any one rendering a public official service, it was soon transferred to acts of worship. Here then we find the official holiness of their service declared. Those contributing to their support shared this in their divine service. The effect of such teaching of Paul concerning paying taxes as an act of worship, is seen in TERTULLIAN (*Apologeticus*, § 42), where he declares that whatever the Romans lost, by the spread of Christianity, in revenue from temple-dues, they fully made up by the more conscientious payment of taxes.

Ver. 7. **Tribute**=taxes on property or income ; **custom** -duties, tolls or taxes on merchandise purchased. The former is a direct, the latter, an indirect tax (Matt. 17 : 25). **Fear,** not in the sense of dread, but in the sense of " reverence " of the respect to be shown judges, military authorities, policemen—officials with whom we stand in closer contact, and whom our duties frequently cause us to meet ; and **honor,** probably to those above them, the Emperor, the Procurator, etc.

(b.) The Motives of the Christian Life (13 : 8-14).

8-14. Owe no man anything, save to love one another: for he that loveth his neighbour hath fulfilled the law. For this, Thou shalt not commit adultery, Thou shalt not kill, Thou shalt not steal, Thou shalt not covet, and if there be any other commandment, it is summed up in this word, namely, Thou shalt love thy neighbour as thyself. Love worketh no ill to his neighbour : love therefore is the fulfilment of the law.

And this, knowing the season, that now it is high time for you to awake out of sleep: for now is salvation nearer to us than when we *first* believed. The night is far spent, and the day is at hand: let us therefore cast off the works of darkness, and let us put on the armour of light. Let us walk honestly, as in the day; not in revelling and drunkenness, not in chambering and wantonness, not in strife and jealousy. But put ye on the Lord Jesus Christ, and make not provision for the flesh, to *fulfil* the lusts *thereof*.

Ver. 8. **Owe no man anything** enjoins the discharge of every obligation. Neglect the payment of nothing due any of your fellow-men. Including undoubtedly the prohibition of protracted debts of money, it is, nevertheless, far more extensive. The state or habit of debt is forbidden. Transient debts underlie all commercial enterprises. The debt forbidden is that which is unpaid when due. But so far, we are touching only the surface of these words. LUTHER enters into their depths, when he says: "You should not be in debt as *men*, but as *Christians:* so that your debt should be a *free* debt *of love*, not a debt of necessity, arising from the law. Paul teaches Christians here that they should so conduct themselves to magistrates and every one, that no one could make any complaint against them with respect to the outward law and government; but he urges that they should do more than such obligation requires, and even when it is not demanded of them, should make themselves debtors, and serve those who have no claims upon them." (Comp. what Paul says, 1 : 14.) **But to love one another.** Because he cannot truly love his neighbor, who tries by loving him once for all to rid himself of the obligation to love him any more. **He that loveth his neighbor, hath fulfilled the law**, i. e. the law concerning his neighbor (Gal. 5 : 14; Matt. 22 : 39, 40; 1 Tim. 1 : 5; James 2 : 8). But as the debt of love is always due, the law is never perfectly fulfilled. *Amare est libertas* (BENGEL). "Holy Scripture gives many and various laws, but comprehends all in love. (Comp. Matt.

12 : 3-5.) "If the law be taught and urged without love and beyond love, there can be no greater misfortune or injustice or calamity upon earth. Then the proverb *Summum jus, summa injuria*, actually becomes true. . . . Laws should be given and observed solely for the sake of love. . . . When it is seen that a law is of no use to our neighbor, it should be annulled. . . . But here the question arises, as to how it is that love fulfils the law, while love is only a fruit of faith, and faith in Christ blots out sin and justifies and satisfies the law. Answer: Faith and love must be distinguished in such a way that faith refers to the *person*, and love to the *works*. When the person (through faith) is accepted of God and justified, the Holy Spirit and love are bestowed, so that he does good with pleasure. Love, therefore, fulfils the law, by being itself the fulfilment of the law; but faith fulfils the law by affording that whereby the law is fulfilled (Gal. 5: 6). Faith, therefore, remains the doer; and love remains the deed" (LUTHER).

Ver. 9 gives a summary of the Second Table. (Comp. Mark 10: 19; Luke 18: 20.) The omission of the Fourth Commandment is due probably to the fact that vers. 1–7 contain a full explanation and enforcement of it. The order is changed and corresponds with that found in some manuscripts of the LXX. Similar changes are found also in Mark and Luke. **If there be any other.** Lit. "any different," i. e. If there be any other relation in which the rights of our neighbor are protected. **It is summed up**—" recapitulated." The same word occurs in Eph. 1 : 10. This doctrine is taught also in Matt. 22 : 39; Mark 12 : 31; Luke 10 : 27; Gal. 5 : 14; James 2 : 8. **Thou shalt love thy neighbor as thyself.** "Note in how masterly a way this commandment has been framed. It treats of four things. First, the person who is to love, 'thou,' '*thou*,' 'THOU.' Not: 'let some one else love for thee' (Gal. 5:5; 2 Cor. 5:10). The second is the noblest of virtues, love. For He says not: 'Thou shalt feed thy neighbor, give him drink, clothe him,' etc.—all precious and good works—but thou shalt *love* him. Love is the head, the fountain and the common virtue of all virtues. The third is the noblest work-room and the dearest friend who is to be loved, i. e. thy neighbor. Carnal and worldly love regards the person, and loves as long as it has use and hope for him; but the commandment requires free love to every one; it is most active and effectual towards the poor, the needy, the wicked, sinners, fools and enemies, for there it finds those whom it has to bear, to suffer, to endure, to serve. The fourth is the noblest example or model. This commandment gives a living example, when it says '*as thyself.*' This is a better example than that of all saints; for they have passed away and are dead; but this example lives perpetually. For every one must acknowledge that he feels how he loves himself" (LUTHER).

Ver. 10. **Love worketh no ill**, etc. "Love endures much wrong; it does no wrong. If one meet thee maliciously and seek, by a wrong, to lead thee to do a wrong (12:17, 21), he still is thy neighbor, and appeals for thy sympathy. It *works* no ill; for it does not fulfil, but checks the lust of the flesh (Gal. 5:16), and where we allow the evil to come to act, we check and deny love. **Love, therefore, is the fulfilment of the law.** It is not only the deed required by the law, but is itself the fulness of the entire law. The various commandments of the law are the various forms and expressions of love, which unfolds the richness of its blessing in a beautiful variety of fruits—every fruit according to the nature and form which God has prescribed in His commandments, all of which are comprised under the chief commandment of love" (BESSER).

Ver. 11. **And this,** i. e. "and this too," introducing an additional motive for the diligent cultivation of spiritual life, and the discharge of all Christian duties, prescribed in the section beginning with chapter xii., all of which have been summed up in ver. 10. **Knowing the season,** i. e. Because we know the time of night, or day at which we are now living, and what is immediately impending. The rays of the morning are already brightening the sky. **To awake out of sleep.** Indifference, carelessness, forgetfulness (Matt. 24:42; 25:13), subjection to the illusion of dreams (Is. 29:8; Job 20:8). **For now is our salvation,** i. e. the completion of our salvation. The second coming of Christ, which the Apostles believed to be near, is in mind (Phil. 4:5; 1 Pet. 4:7; 1 Thess. 5:4-6). The same motive is urged in Heb. 10:25, 37; 1 Cor. 7:29; 1 Pet. 4:7. **Than when we first believed,** i. e. when we first became Christians.

The entire Christian life and the entire course of the Church in this world are marked by successions of day and night, summer and winter. All point to one Great Day in which completed salvation shall be attained. But this day is reached through a succession of eras, both in the experience of the individual and of the Church. Growing from grace to grace, the cry constantly comes: "Our salvation is nearer than when we believed." We are constantly standing on the very verge of some new discovery of the riches of divine grace, in the light of which all that preceded may seem to be only darkness. Hence the text may well be applied to the higher revelations of the New, as contrasted with those of the Old Testament, to the preaching of Christ Crucified and Risen, as contrasted with that of a Coming Christ, and to the universal spread of the Gospel, as contrasted with the narrow particularism of Judaism. "God's promise made to Abraham is no longer to be expected in the future; it has been fulfilled. Faith, therefore, is not to be surrendered, but is rather established; we believe now that the promise has been fulfilled. But this declaration should be understood, not of the nearness of the having, or the *possession;* for the fathers had the same faith and the very same Christ, and He was just as near them as He is to us (Heb. 13:8). But Paul speaks here of the nearness of the *revelation.* (Comp. Tit. 2:11.)" (LUTHER.)

But this must not be regarded as the only application; for a large portion of the church at Rome was composed of Gentiles. Paul declares to them that their salvation is nearer than at the hour of their conversion. "Gradually the doctrine is made clearer, our religion is more widely diffused, our experience in divine and spiritual things is increased, and finally other gifts grow and are multiplied; and, therefore, although when we believed our salvation was sure, nevertheless, we may say, all have become to us clearer and more certain. Some not inaptly apply a metaphor, taken from those who run in a course,—the farther they go, the nearer they approach the goal. So the beginning of our conversion is like an entrance upon the race, the continuance and increase of our faith like the course, and heavenly glory like the goal" (FLACIUS, quoted by CALOVIUS).

Ver. 12. **The night is far spent.** The figure is that of a long winter night. The comparison is that of the present state as contrasted with the still clearer and brighter light of the Gospel that is yet to shine. **The works of darkness,** viz. those which men are ashamed to do in open daylight. **Armour of light.** Either the weapons of a soldier of the light, or the tools of an honest laborer who does his work in the daytime.

Ver. 13. **As in the day**, i e. "as though all the world saw what we do" (LUTHER). Three classes of sins are then arranged in pairs: **Not in revelling and drunkenness**, i. e. excesses in eating and drinking—gluttony. But this does not teach the asceticism which prohibits us from deriving pleasure from what God has created not only for use, but also for enjoyment (1 Tim. 6:17). It is the abuse of these sources of enjoyment, without regard to the claims of God or the higher interests of our spiritual nature, that is here prohibited. All eating and drinking that prevents the energetic discharge of the duties of our callings, that shortens life or impairs health, and above all that chills or dulls the spirit of devotion and interferes with prayer, is meant. **Not in chambering and wantonness.** Licentious deeds and impurity of speech and conduct. A frequent result of sins of the class before mentioned. "If these be so disgraceful that even carnal men are ashamed to commit them before the eyes of their fellow-men, we ought to refrain from them perpetually, as those who live in God's light, even when we are withdrawn from men's sight" (CALVIN). **Not in strife and jealousy.** Often following the other two forms of sin, but here more comprehensive. Men are guilty of the last mentioned, viz. the wrangling and jealousies of personal and partisan quarrels, who are free from charges of the other classes. All, however, belong together, as various forms of wordliness.

Ver. 14. **But put ye on**, i. e. Let your lives be a true expression of your inner communion with Christ. The reference here is to sanctification, not to justification. In Baptism, the Christ puts on Christ (Gal. 3:27); "but in the further development of the baptized one, each new advance of his moral life (comp. ver. 11) is to be a new putting-on of Christ; like the putting on of the new man, it is, therefore, always enjoined afresh" (MEYER). **Make not provision for the flesh.** Lit. "And provision for the flesh do not make unto lusts." Provision for the body must be made, but it is not to be made the tool or instrument of lust, but of righteousness (Rom. 6: 12, 13). The word provision implies forethought, "being preoccupied with," and suggests the pains and time often consumed in planning for the gratification of sensual lusts. "All natural human desires (ambition, as well as the appetite for food and sex) are not in themselves sinful, but by a perverse use, in which they are not subordinated to the service of a higher moral end, they are changed into sinful desires" (WEISS). This verse is forever connected in the mind of the Church with the crisis in the spiritual life of Augustine, which he thus relates: "I heard from a neighboring house a voice, as of boy or girl, I know not, chanting and oft repeating 'Take up and read;' 'Take up and read.' Instantly, my countenance altered. I began to think most intently, whether children were wont in any kind of play to sing such words; nor could I remember ever to have heard the like. So checking the torrent of my tears, I arose; interpreting it to be no other than a command from God to open the book, and read the first chapter I should find. Eagerly then I returned to the place where Alypius was sitting; for there I had laid the volume of the Apostle, when I arose thence. I seized, opened, and in silence read that passage on which my eyes first fell: 'Not in violating and drunkenness, not in chambering and wantonness, not in strife and envying, but put ye on the Lord Jesus Christ, and make not provision for the flesh in concupiscence.' No further would I read ; nor needed I : for instantly at the end of this sentence, by a light as it were of serenity infused into my heart, all the darkness of doubt vanished away" (*Confessions*, Book VIII. § 30).

(B.) *Principles involved in the Settlement of a Pending Controversy* (14 : 1—15 : 13).

(*a*.) *Address to both the Strong and the Weak.*

1-12. But him that is weak in faith receive ye, *yet* not to doubtful disputations. One man hath faith to eat all things : but he that is weak eateth herbs. Let not him that eateth set at nought him that eateth not; and let not him that eateth not judge him that eateth : for God hath received him. Who art thou that judgest the servant of another ? to his own lord he standeth or falleth. Yea, he shall be made to stand; for the Lord hath power to make him stand. One man esteemeth one day above another : another esteemeth every day *alike*. Let each man be fully assured in his own mind. He that regardeth the day, regardeth it unto the Lord : and he that eateth, eateth unto the Lord, for he giveth God thanks ; and he that eateth not, unto the Lord he eateth not, and giveth God thanks. For none of us liveth to himself, and none dieth to himself. For whether we live, we live unto the Lord ; or whether we die, we die unto the Lord : whether we live therefore, or die, we are the Lord's. For to this end Christ died, and lived *again*, that he might be Lord of both the dead and the living. But thou, why dost thou judge thy brother? or thou again, why dost thou set at nought thy brother ? for we shall all stand before the judgement-seat of God. For it is written,

As I live, saith the Lord, to me every knee shall bow,
And every tongue shall confess to God.
So then each one of us shall give account of himself to God.

Ver. 1. "**Him that is weak in faith**," i. e. "in his faith." The reference is to members of an ascetic party in the Roman Church, evidently of Jewish origin, who regarded themselves under obligation to abstain from meat and wine, and to observe the Jewish fasts and festivals. Possibly they were members of the sect of Essenes who had been converted to Christianity. At all events, they represented kindred views. The injunction here given clearly shows that they formed a very small minority of the Christians at Rome. This asceticism, Paul here declares, is inconsistent with a proper knowledge of Christianity, and indicates a weak faith. It is consistent with faith, but not with strong faith. **Receive ye:** take to yourselves, admit to your confidence. **Doubtful disputations.** Better the marginal R. V.: "Decisions of doubt," or "Criticism of scruples." The advice is that, when recognized as a brother, the effort be not zealously made to at once force from him his scruples and inconsistencies. Time must be allowed for his principles to work out their proper solution. "In the fourteenth chapter, he teaches that we should deal gently with consciences weak in faith and forbear with them, so that we use our Christian freedom, not to the injury, but to the advancement of the weak. Where this is not done, dissent and a despising of the Gospel follow. It is better to yield a little to the weak, until they become stronger, than that the doctrine of the Gospel be entirely suppressed" (LUTHER). "As many of the Jews still adhered tenaciously to the shadows of the law, he confesses that this is a fault in them. But, for the time being, he asks that indulgence be given; since to urge them more severely would be to undermine their faith. Doubtful disputations, therefore, he calls those which disturb a mind not sufficiently settled, or involve it in doubts" (CALVIN).

Ver. 2. **Hath faith to eat all things,** i. e. to make no distinction in his food. His faith has raised him above all such scruples. Knowing that all creatures of God are good, and nothing to be refused (1 Tim. 4:4), he knows that sin or holiness does not depend upon the sort of food that is eaten or is not eaten. **Eateth herbs,** i. e. nothing but herbs. Copious illustrations both among heathen and Christians are given by GROTIUS. "A Christian knows no distinction of days; he knows no Friday or fast day. But when he comes to a place where this is not understood, and the day is still observed, he conforms thereto" (LUTHER).

Ver. 3. **Set at naught.** Those of stronger faith would naturally be liable to look with contempt upon the narrowness of the vegetarian Christians, and to regard them as of no account. Of course this would show, that, strong as they were, their own faith was still deficient, and their strength was only relative. **Judge him** describes the censorious judgment which is the characteristic of a religiousness that lays its chief stress upon the fulfilment of external requirements. **God hath received him,** viz. the stronger brother who has no scruples about eating meat. If God has forgiven him his sins and accepted him as his child, and his life in other respects manifests the presence of the Holy Spirit, all such criticism is out of place.

Ver. 4. **Who art thou?** This is addressed to the weaker brother. **That judgest.** And, too, by laws of your own making! **The servant of another.** He belongs to God's house, not to yours. **He shall be made to stand.** The weak Christian thinks the stronger one in great danger by disregard of the ascetic warnings of the former. Paul ironically suggests that whatever the danger, he has a powerful Lord at hand who can defend him from the spiritual peril of eating meat! "Received of" God (ver. 3), God will uphold him.

Ver. 5. **One day above another.** He refers to the observance by Jewish Christians of the fasts and feasts of the Jews (Col. 2 : 16). **Esteemeth every day alike.**

Not by secularizing holy days, but by sanctifying all secular days, from the conviction that all our time belongs to God, and every energy of the Christian's life is to be directed to God's glory (1 Cor. 10:31). This conception does not forbid a distinction between days, but it makes such distinction for the sake of order, and not as though one day in itself were holier, or the devotion of one day above another to religious worship implied or brought a higher degree of holiness. **Let each man be fully assured in his own mind.** These differences do not justify a suspension of judgment concerning what each one ought to think or do. On the contrary, every one is exhorted to come to a clear and definite conclusion. He is to take sides, but, at the same time, to do so with charity towards those who reach another conclusion.

Ver. 6. **Unto the Lord.** As they are believers, the Lord is the end of all their thoughts, purposes and acts. The motive of the one, in claiming the perpetual obligation of the day, is to glorify his Lord; as such, his devotion to his conviction, is to be respected by the other. The motive of the other, in regarding all days as alike holy, is to claim for his Lord the entire devotion of all our time, and as such must be respected by the one who makes a difference in days. This is implied, even if not expressed as in A. V. So in regard to difference of foods. The one thanks God for all things, and partakes of them to the glory of God (1 Cor. 10:31). The other thanks God for only vegetables, and to the glory of God eats only vegetables. His motive for abstaining from meats is the same as that of the other for eating them. In this both unite and co-operate. **God.** The alternation of "Lord" and "God" shows that Lord applies to Christ, as in ver. 9, and makes a distinction between the persons of the Trinity.

Vers. 7, 8. Using and abstaining, acting and refraining from acting, are to the Christian not arbitrary matters, determined by his own caprice, but they are determined by his conviction as to what the will of the Lord is. The Christian in all things realizes the fact that he is not his own, but belongs to Christ. Even his death cannot be by his own act (hence suicide implies a renunciation of Christ), but comes only as Christ wills (Phil. 1 : 21–24).

"We not only live unto the Lord and are the Lord's, but we ourselves are also lords. For if, when we die and live, we are the Lord's, we truly lord it over life and death" (LUTHER).

Ver. 9. For to this end, Christ died and lived again. It is not Christ's life upon earth that made Him Lord of His people, but His death and resurrection. Death and resurrection belong together. He did not become Lord of the dead by His death, and of the living by His resurrection. His death purchased for Him a people; His resurrection delivered those whom He had purchased (Ch. 4 : 25). **Lord of both the dead and the living.** His relation is the same to those who have departed as to those now on earth. BENGEL correctly notes that these words exclude all theories of soul-sleeping. (Comp. Luke 20 : 38). Death then only transfers us from one sphere of conscious service to another.

Ver. 10. Dost thou judge, addressed to the weak (ver. 3). **Set at naught,** addressed to the strong composing the majority of the Roman Church. Such judging he declares is to usurp a prerogative of God (Comp. 1 Cor. 4 : 5). **Of God** is supported as the reading by the best MSS. Elsewhere, as in A. V., "Of Christ." So in 1 Cor. 5 : 10. God the Father will judge the world through Christ (Acts 17 : 31 ; Ch. 2 : 16).

Ver. 11. A free quotation from Is. 45 : 23 to sustain the statement that God's judgment must be awaited. The emphasis rests on **to me** and **to God**. Ver. 12 is a direct inference, **each one of us** corresponding to "every knee" and "every tongue."

(b.) *Appeal to the Strong.*

13–23. Let us not therefore judge one another any more: but judge ye this rather, that no man put a stumbling-block in his brother's way, or an occasion of falling. I know, and am persuaded in the Lord Jesus, that nothing is unclean of itself: save that to him who accounteth anything to be unclean, to him it is unclean. For if because of meat thy brother is grieved, thou walkest no longer in love. Destroy not with thy meat him for whom Christ died. Let not then your good be evil spoken of: for the kingdom of God is not eating and drinking, but righteousness and peace and joy in the Holy Ghost. For he that herein serveth Christ is well-pleasing to God, and approved of men. So then let us follow after things which make for peace, and things whereby we may edify one another. Overthrow not for meat's sake the work of God. All things indeed are clean; howbeit it is evil for that man who eateth with offence. It is good not to eat flesh, nor to drink wine, nor *to do anything* whereby thy brother stumbleth. The faith which thou hast, have thou to thyself before God. Happy is he that judgeth not himself in that which he approveth. But he that doubteth is condemned if he eat, because *he eateth* not of faith; and whatsoever is not of faith is sin.

Ver. 13. **Judge this rather.** An elliptical expression for "Judge ourselves according to the rule that no one," etc. **Stumbling-block, or occasion of falling.** To distinguish the two words here used is difficult. Most commentators maintain there is no difference. GODET suggests " shock or stumbling-block."

Ver. 14. **I know.** Paul here takes sides. The strong are right. **In the Lord Jesus.** He thus declares the depth of his conviction on the subject. It springs from his life-communion with Christ. The Ceremonial Law is abolished, and with it all such distinctions (Acts 11 : 9;

1 Tim. 4 : 4). **To him who accounteth.** What is of itself an adiaphoron or matter of indifference may not continue to be such when applied to an individual case, or in the practice of an individual. Right though a course may be, one sins if he follow it while he regards it wrong (ver. 23).

Ver. 15. **Because of meat.** Any article of food. **Is grieved.** His conscience is burdened or distressed. Not applicable to where obstinate prejudice may ask that something allowed by Christian Liberty be not indulged in, to avoid pain to the self-will of the one making the demand. This would be to sustain him in that judging which has just been rebuked. But it does mean that liberty is not to be used, where any practice touches the sensibility of true children of God in regard to what is more precious to them than life, unless by refraining from such exercise we are hampered in our testimony to the truth, or in our discharge of the duties of our callings. **Destroy not him.** A very small sacrifice is asked of you contrasted with what Christ gave. Christ gave His life; and are you unwilling to forego the pleasure of a single object of meat or drink? We are taught here that it is possible for those who have been redeemed by Christ to fall and perish.

Ver. 16. **Your good** —The Christian Liberty of the strong (1 Cor. 8 : 9–11).

Ver. 17. **Not eating and drinking,** i. e. Your eating and drinking whatever you please does not make you a Christian ; you will lose nothing of importance, therefore, by your self-denial. These matters are trifling and insignificant, when mentioned alongside of those in which the Kingdom of God actually consists. **Righteousness,** i. e. the righteousness which comes by faith, and the **peace** and **joy** that follow. " Righteousness, as respects God ;

peace, as respects our neighbor; joy, as respects ourselves" (BENGEL). But external peace, to which Bengel refers, is rather a consequence and mark, than a constituent element of this Kingdom. "Peace does not denote here harmony or external peace with others, but internal peace of conscience, or tranquillity, of which the Apostle had treated, as that which flows forth from justification by faith immediately into the hearts of believers, and which alone can keep in Christ Jesus unto everlasting life (Phil. 4 : 7), and in which we have firm and true joy in the Holy Ghost (Rom. 5 : 1 sqq.), because we are sure of the grace of God and of our heavenly inheritance. These three, 'the righteousness of Christ' which we apprehend by faith, 'peace with God the Father,' which the justified enjoy for Christ's sake, and 'joy in the Holy Ghost,' which arises from our justification and peace of conscience, are truly the Kingdom of God" (CALOVIUS). "The Kingdom of God begun in this life, and to be completed in the world to come, is not dependent upon these external matters, food and drink, but is defined by far greater and necessary matters, viz. righteousness, which we obtain by faith in Christ, and then, peace of conscience, and joy, that is not earthly, but spiritual, and as Peter says, inexpressible and full of glory, whereby the regenerate, in consideration of the blessings of Christ, exult in their hearts through the Holy Ghost" (HUNNIUS). "The Kingdom of God is considered either as the kingdom of grace in this life, or the kingdom of glory in the life to come. On either side, there is no profit from the use of the food formerly forbidden in the law; for as Christ says elsewhere: 'The Kingdom of God cometh not with observation' (Luke 17 : 20). But there are matters of far greater importance in which the Kingdom of God consists, three of which are here mentioned:

1. The righteousness whereby, in God's judgment, we are accounted righteous, and which we obtain only by faith in Christ. 2. Peace, which we have before God through Christ. 3. Joy, by which he understands tranquillity of conscience. This is the beginning of eternal life, and results from the former. Our zeal should be occupied, therefore, in retaining these three things, and this will render us more grateful to God, and more acceptable to men, than if, without respect to the weak, we use all food indifferently" (BALDWIN).

" It is a doctrine of the Pope, that to avoid eating meat is a good work and atones for sin. This is foolish and senseless; for neither eating nor drinking, neither hunger nor thirst, but only the blood of Christ does that. If, then, such obedience do not efface sin, disobedience also can be no sin. It is, therefore, no sin before God to eat meat or fish on whatever day I please. The external mode of life, even though we can dispense with it as little as with eating and drinking, does not help us before God; it is only faith that does that. The Kingdom of God is spiritual, and does not consist of external things, but only of justification, tranquillity and comfort of man's heart and conscience. It is produced or regulated by no law, even not by that of God, and, therefore, much less by human ordinances, but alone by the Gospel and faith in God, whereby hearts are purified, consoled and tranquillized. The enactment of many laws withdraws men from the Kingdom of God to the kingdom of sin; wherein there is nothing but disquietude, anxiety and sorrow of conscience; just as in the Kingdom and knowledge of God, there is nothing but peace, joy and consolation of heart" (LUTHER).

Ver. 18. **He that herein serveth Christ**, i. e. The Christian who, under these circumstances and with these motives, is willing to forego his liberty. **Is well-pleasing to God.** The good works of believers are well-pleasing to God. **Approved of men.** Even those whose approval he does not seek. The Christian constantly meets opposition and every now and then calls forth their hostility. He is often the object of slander and abuse. But in the end this rule prevails. He is esteemed as a man true to his convictions and thoroughly in earnest. Public opinion is fickle and uncertain; but when all is told, the man who makes every sacrifice to do what is right is not forgotten (Ps. 23 : 5 : 2 Cor. 4 : 2). There is a strong implication here that the person who constantly endeavors to display his liberty without regard to the consciences of his brethren will not be approved of men. Even his truly Christian character will not be understood or acknowledged.

Ver. 19. **So then,** i. e. Since the Kingdom of God does not consist of those matters on which these controversies have existed, and the favor of God is gained neither by the use of these outward things, nor by abstracting from them. **The things which make for peace,** viz. the peace of the Church. Even in the use of those things which by themselves are innocent, the peace of the Church may be destroyed to no good end. **Things whereby we may edify.** Those by which faith is strengthened, sanctification promoted, influence and usefulness advanced. (See Jud. ver. 20.)

Ver. 20. **The work of God,** i. e. the Christian life, begun in him. **It is evil.** The reckless use of Christian liberty becomes an offence; and yet it may be difficult for the strong brother to learn how his use of that which in itself is innocent and free, can bring spiritual injury to others.

Ver. 21. **Good.** That which is externally honorable (*Kalon*), which appears well. **Drink wine.** PHIL.,

Hodge, etc., think that wine offered to idols is meant. Baldwin says: "He wants to teach that we should abstain from all flesh and all wine, rather than, in any way, offer an occasion for a fall to one who is weak." Everything should be done to prevent God's work from being destroyed. We must eat, if by this our brother is edified; and we must not eat, if by this the work of God decreases. We must drink, if thereby the faith of our brother be advanced; and we must not drink if thereby his faith suffer loss" (Anselm).

Ver. 22. **The faith which thou hast.** Addressed to the strong. Its meaning is: Do not make a parade of thy faith. Seek not by thy free use of all God's creatures to show that thy faith is strong. If so, it is enough that God knows it. **Happy is he.** Be content with knowing that your free use of God's gifts is not contrary to what you have learned that God desires.

Ver. 23. **But he that doubteth.** Also an admonition to the strong. Their example may lead the weak to act contrary to their convictions of duty, and thus to do what does not come from faith. They have compared their conduct with the conscience of another, instead of being guided by their own consciences as enlightened by the Holy Ghost. **Faith** here means their persuasion of duty. But to the Christian, this persuasion of duty must spring from faith in Christ, the centre of his spiritual life and all its activities. "The confidence of salvation grounded upon Christ, upon which all his activity must depend; since it is sinful, as soon as he even doubts whether it be compatible with the continuance of his possession of salvation" (Weiss).

"To wish to serve God, and yet to be ignorant whether the service be pleasing to Him or not, is not a service that is grateful to God, but a work especially displeasing to Him. He lays down this rule as a foundation for all others. For it is necessary that faith or the firm persuasion of mind derived from the word of God must precede, if anything ought to be done in accord with the free use of Christian liberty, and without a hesitating conscience. . . . This passage does not speak directly concerning justifying faith, but concerning the sure persuasion of heart that what is done is not displeasing to God; nevertheless the argument is valid that the works of those who do not believe in Christ do not please God. For if those things are sin, which are done without the faith whereby we believe that something is conceded in adiaphora, much more will those be sins which are done without the sure confidence of the heart in Christ. The general aphorism concerning every kind of faith is true: 'Whatsoever is done without faith, is sin,' whether this be understood as historical faith, or faith of conscience, or faith in Christ. There is no reason, therefore, why this declaration cannot be applied to justifying faith, although here it is applied to faith of another form" (BALDWIN). "There is evidently a sinful disregard of the divine authority, on the part of a man who does anything which he supposes God has forbidden, or which he is not certain He has allowed" (HODGE).

(c.) *The Union of all in Christ, the End of all Controversies* (15: 1–13).

(aa.) *Christ as an Example.*

1–7. Now we that are strong ought to bear the infirmities of the weak, and not to please ourselves. Let each one of us please his neighbour for that which is good, unto edifying. For Christ also pleased not himself; but, as it is written, The reproaches of them that reproached thee fell upon me. For whatsoever things were written aforetime were written for our learning, that through patience and through comfort of the scriptures we might have hope.

Now the God of patience and of comfort grant you to be of the same mind one with another according to Christ Jesus: that with one accord ye may with one mouth glorify the God and Father of our Lord Jesus Christ. Wherefore receive ye one another, even as Christ also received you, to the glory of God.

Ver. 1. Another motive than that of injury threatened to the weak is introduced. It is the regard which every believer has for his Lord and Saviour, and the example the latter has left us of self-denying and condescending love and patience. **The strong** are those who have been properly instructed concerning the use of matters of indifference. **The weak** are those who find matters of sin in external usages, the use of foods, the observance or non-observance of days, etc. **Not to please ourselves,** i. e. not to make our own pleasure the rule and guide. Instead of making a display of our Christian liberty, and demanding its rights, and exercising it to the fullest extent, we should subordinate it to helpfulness to our brethren, however weak and prejudiced they be. For Paul's personal application of this principle, see 1 Cor. 9 : 20 sqq.

Ver. 2. **Please . . . for that which is good.** (Comp. 14 : 19.) The limitation and motive must always be the highest good and edification of our neighbor; we are not to please him to his injury, but must even displease him, if this be necessary for his good. (See Gal. 4 : 16.)

Ver. 3. **For Christ also pleased not himself.** A strange servant he must be who deems himself too exalted to condescend as his Master has done. The same thought is expressed as in Phil. 2 : 5 sqq.; 1 Pet. 2 : 21 sqq. Christ did not use his prerogatives—to which our much vaunted Christian liberty is nothing—but gladly forbore their use in order to effect our salvation. **The reproaches of them,** etc. (Ps. 69 : 9).

Ver. 4 declares why the Apostle uses an O. T. text to enforce the doctrine of the self-denial of Christ. The coming of Christ has not abolished the O. T. scriptures. The religion of the O. T. and of the N. T. are the same only at different stages. (See Ch. 1 : 2.) **Our learning** implies that the full force and benefit of the O. T. cannot be obtained, until the times of the N. T. (Comp. 2 Tim. 2 : 16.) **Patience and comfort of the scriptures.** The patience and comfort derived from the devout study of the scriptures. **Hope** is always prospective. Here it reaches forward towards the future blessings that are to be attained in life eternal. The reference here is to the specifically Christian hope (5 : 4, 5).

Ver. 5. **Now the God of patience and of comfort,** i. e. The patience and comfort of the scriptures cannot be obtained simply by reading them. God is their author, and our reading must, therefore, be constantly accompanied by devout and earnest prayer. "Lest any one presume, by his own powers, to obtain patience and comfort of the scriptures, he indicates by his entreaty that these gifts of God are to be obtained by humble prayer" (LUTHER). The connection between this clause and the preceding is very well brought out in the collect, probably by CRANMER, which is prescribed by the *Book of Common Prayer* for the Second Sunday in Advent, and is found in the Lutheran *Common Service* (No. 49): "Blessed Lord, who hast caused all Scripture to be written for our learning; grant that we may in such wise hear them, read, mark, learn and inwardly digest them, that by patience and comfort of Thy holy word, we may embrace and ever hold fast the blessed hope of everlasting life, which Thou hast given us in our Saviour Jesus Christ." **Grant you to be of the same mind.** Something we do not have by nature. Such harmony cannot be obtained, until we have patience and comfort, and these gifts, we have seen, must come from above. **According to Christ Jesus**, i. e. not according to Christ, as a model, but according to His will. (Comp. 8 : 27.) Peace at the sacrifice of truth or principle is repudiated. We may allow weaknesses of our Christian brethren, but, for the sake of peace, we must not be asked to adopt or defend them.

Ver. 6. **That with one accord, ye may with one mouth.** "The hymn of saved humanity" (GODET). Jews and Gentiles, strong and weak, unite as one choir in one song of praise. PHILIPPI suggests: "Oneness of mind has oneness of speech as its consequence." But the thought is rather, that, when they come together for public worship, they use not only the same words, which is assumed, but that there be but one heart back of these words, and they be filled with the spirit of mutual love. (Comp. Acts 2 : 46.) **God and Father.** "He who, according to the humanity of Christ, is His God, according to His divinity, is His Father" (ANSELM). But the word translated **and** may be epexegetical or explicative, as A. V. renders it, "God, even the Father" (see 2 Cor. 1 : 3; 11 : 31; Eph. 1 : 3; Col. 1 : 3), and passages where "of Jesus Christ" is not added (1 Cor. 15 : 24: Eph. 5 : 20; Col. 3 : 17; James 1 : 27; 39). So MEYER, PHILIPPI, LIDDON, STUART, WEISS, BESSER. The article in the original does not decide the meaning. If the latter be right, God is first considered abstractly, as the object of worship; then He comes before us in His Trinitarian relations. "As there is one God, who has called you, and you all have obtained the same mercy. He who has called the strong, has called also the weak, and made no distinction between any; so then, without being distracted by such illusions into diverse interests, you should with one accord, recognizing this grace as common to all, glorify God. As the grace of the call has not made a distinction, neither ought diversity of strength or weakness to do so" (LUTHER).

Ver. 7. **Receive ye one another.** (Comp. 14 : 1.) This admonition is addressed to both the strong and the weak. **As Christ received you,** i. e. without any merit or worthiness, without any strength or fitness in you, out of pure mercy, only as sinners (Luke 5 : 32 ; 15 : 2). The strength of the strongest without Christ is weaker than the weakness of the weakest. This suggests also what is next introduced and commented on, viz. that in thus receiving them, there was no preference made of race or nationality. Jew and Gentile were treated alike. **To the glory of God,** i. e. that God may be glorified, viz. that His truth (ver. 8) and His mercy (ver. 9) may be declared.

(*bb.*) *The two diverse Manifestations and Relations of the one, all-embracing Love of Christ.*

8–13. For I say that Christ hath been made a minister of the circumcision for the truth of God, that he might confirm the promises *given* unto the fathers, and that the Gentiles might glorify God for his mercy; as it is written,
    Therefore will I give praise unto thee among the Gentiles,
        And sing unto thy name.
And again he saith,
        Rejoice, ye Gentiles, with his people.
And again,
        Praise the Lord, all ye Gentiles ;
        And let all the peoples praise him.
And again Isaiah saith,
        There shall be the root of Jesse,
        And he that ariseth to rule over the Gentiles ;
        On him shall the Gentiles hope.
Now the God of hope fill you with all joy and peace in believing, that ye may abound in hope, in the power of the Holy Ghost.

"If Christ has received with equal goodness, there has yet been a difference in the mode of this receiving. Unity in the works of God is never uniformity. Rather harmony implies variety" (GODET).

Ver. 8. God's dealings with the Jews declare the glory of His **truth. Christ, a minister of the circumcision.** "Circumcision" is used here, as in 3:30; 4:12; Gal. 2:7 sqq.; Eph. 2:11, etc., for the Jews. Jesus came, first of all to minister to the Jews (Matt. 15:24). He ministered by giving His life a ransom (Matt. 20:28). **That he might confirm the promises,** viz. by fulfilling them (1:2).

Ver. 9. God's dealings with the Gentiles declare the glory of His **mercy. That the Gentiles might glorify God.** The construction is difficult. Both English versions regard "glorify" as in the same construction as "confirm" in ver. 8. This appears the most satisfactory explanation. The thought then is: "He was the minister of the circumcision: 1. That He might confirm the promises. 2. That the Gentiles might glorify God," i. e. His fulfilment of the promises and manifestation of God's truth in serving the Jews, is the foundation of His mercy to the Gentiles. He was the minister of the circumcision, in order that the Gentiles might be saved. **Therefore will I give praise,** Ps. 18:49.

Ver. 10. **Rejoice ye Gentiles,** etc., Deut. 32:43. Ver. 11. **Praise the Lord,** etc., Ps. 117:1. Ver. 12. **There shall be a root,** etc., Ps. 11:10. All these O. T. texts in most explicit terms declare that salvation is not confined to the Jews, and prophesy the world-wide mission of Christianity.

Ver. 13. **Now the God of hope,** etc. Doxology to the entire argument of the Epistle, which has just ended with its key-note, viz. "The universality of the grace of

God in Christ;" "The brotherhood of Jew and Gentile in Christ." "Hope" is the final word of ver. 13. The doxology dwells upon it. God is its author. As before, the reference is to the specifically Christian hope (5 : 2-5; 15 : 4). **Joy and peace.** (Comp. on 14 : 17.) Where these are found, mutual concord among Christians will prevail. The spirit of strife and controversy springs from the failure of Christians to completely appropriate to themselves the divine blessings provided and offered in Christ. They are always involved in strife without, because, within, there is no "joy and peace in believing."

Epilogue (15 : 14-33).

This corresponds to the introduction (1 : 8-16), and comprises two parts, viz. an apology for the manner in which he has written (vers. 14-22), and a statement concerning the plans he has in view for his journeys (vers. 23-33).

1. *Apology.*

14-23. And I myself also am persuaded of you, my brethren, that ye yourselves are full of goodness, filled with all knowledge, able also to admonish one another. But I write the more boldly unto you in some measure, as putting you again in remembrance, because of the grace that was given me of God, that I should be a minister of Christ Jesus unto the Gentiles, ministering the gospel of God, that the offering up of the Gentiles might be made acceptable, being sanctified by the Holy Ghost. I have therefore my glorying in Christ Jesus in things pertaining to God. For I will not dare to speak of any things save those which Christ wrought through me, for the obedience of the Gentiles, by word and deed, in the power of signs and wonders, in the power of the Holy Ghost; so that from Jerusalem, and round about even unto Illyricum, I have fully preached the gospel of Christ; yea, making it my aim so to preach the gospel, not where Christ was *already* named, that I might not build upon another man's foundation; but, as it is written,

    They shall see, to whom no tidings of him came,
    And they who have not heard shall understand.

Wherefore also I was hindered these many times from coming to you.

Vers. 14, 15 state his motives for writing. It was not because of any lack of ordinary knowledge on the part of the Church at Rome, but because Paul had been entrusted with Apostolic grace for teaching the Gentiles. **Ye are full of goodness,** i. e. of a kind and benevolent disposition, which would prompt to a proper course towards fellow-Christians, whoever they may be, and to the settlement of variances. "Full of goodness," as they are, he wants to enlarge their capacity. The Epistle shows that he knew that there were faults among the Christians at Rome; but this does not deter him from commending that in them that was praiseworthy. His praise and his censure are always discriminating. **I write the more boldly,** i. e. with considerable boldness. **In some measure.** Lit.: "In part," i. e. in some portions of the letter, where he speaks sharply, as 6 : 19–21 ; 11 : 19–22, etc. **As putting you again in remembrance.** He writes nothing new, or unknown. Often have they heard these things before. **The grace that was given me.** As in 1 : 5 ; 12 : 3, for the grace of the Apostolic office.

Ver. 16. **A minister.** Not the same word as in ver. 8, but the word (*leitourgos*) used in ch. 13 : 6 ; Heb. 1 : 7 ; 8 : 2. (Comp. on 13 : 6.) One who conducts a public worship. **Of Christ Jesus,** i. e. appointed by Him. **Ministering.** Margin is exact : " Ministering in sacrifice." The preaching of the Gospel is regarded as a sacrificial act. The Gentiles are offered; the Gospel is the instrument by which the sacrifice is made. The sacrifice here is a eucharistic one. The Gentiles as brought to God, through the preaching of Christ, and sacrified by the Holy Spirit, are presented as an acceptable offering. "As the sacrifice of the N. T., he designates the hearts of the Gentiles so prepared and furnished by the preaching of the Gospel, that they can please God, since by faith in Christ the Holy Spirit purifies their hearts (Acts 15: 7–9). Undoubtedly the Apostle has Mal. 1: 11 in mind" (BALDWIN). (See also Is. 66: 19, 20.)

Ver. 17. **I have.** These words are emphatic. It is actually true that I, humble though I be, have reason for boasting. **Therefore,** viz. because by the exercise of the grace given me (ver. 15), I have brought so many Gentiles to Christ. (Comp. 1 Cor. 15: 10.) **In things pertaining to God,** i. e. in extending the kingdom of God, and especially in the conversion of the Gentiles.

Ver. 18. **Any things save those which Christ wrought through me,** i. e. Christ is the author of all his actions that afford ground for glorying. All his glorying is, therefore, only the recognition of what belongs to Christ, and the confession of Christ's name, and the vindication of Christ's claims before men. **By word,** i. e. through his sermons, and other testimonies to a Crucified and Risen Christ. **By deed,** i. e. such as are recounted in 1 Cor. 11: 23–28.

Ver. 19. **In the power of signs and wonders.** These words, often conjoined, refer to the same objects, as designated in two diverse relations, the former referring to them as sealing the truth by manifest evidences of God's approval, and the latter indicating their supernatural character, and the effects which they produced upon men. The thought here is that a public miraculous power accompanied and wrought through his words and deeds, and that back of this power and working through it was a special activity of the Holy Spirit. "He ascribes power to the signs, i. e. efficacy and work in the minds of spectators, who, in this way, were the more readily brought to faith in Christ" (BALDWIN). **So that from Jerusalem.** Paul began to preach at Damascus (Acts 9: 20). But Jerusalem is mentioned as the centre of his preaching in the S. E., as Illyricum on the N. E. shore of the Adriatic marks its N. W. boundary. That nothing of St. Paul's preaching in Illyricum is mentioned in Acts, is not significant. His abode in Arabia (Gal. 1 : 17), is not alluded to in Acts. The time may have been that described in Acts 20 : 1-3. **I have fully preached.** Completely fulfilled my commission to preach the Gospel. "It is clear that Paul was not claiming to have finished the work of preaching in relation to the small towns and country districts of the lands he had evangelized. He regarded his Apostolic task as entirely fulfilled, when he had lighted the torch in the great centres, such as Thessalonica, Corinth and Ephesus. That done, he had reckoned on the churches founded in those capitals continuing the evangelization of the provinces" (GODET).

Ver. 20. **Making it my aim.** See marginal reading: "Being ambitious." **Upon another man's foundation.** It was the office of an Apostle to lay the foundation and begin the work; it was the less difficult office of a pastor to carry on what an Apostle had begun (1 Cor. 3 : 10). He appeals to the establishment of new congregations as a proof of his Apostolic office (1 Cor. 9 : 2).

Ver. 21. Is quoted from Is. 52 : 15, as giving the one great thought pervading his entire ministry.. As usual, he supports this assertion which he has just made with a text from the O. T.

Ver. 22. **Wherefore,** viz. because he wanted everywhere to break ground for the Gospel. **I was hindered,** viz. by calls from places where previously nothing had been done. **Coming to you.** See Acts 19 : 21 for his purpose.

2. His Plans for the Future.

24-33. But now, having no more any place in these regions, and having these many years a longing to come unto you, whensoever I go unto Spain (for I hope to see you in my journey, and to be brought on my way thitherward by you, if first in some measure I shall have been satisfied with your company)—but now, *I say*, I go unto Jerusalem, ministering unto the saints. For it hath been the good pleasure of Macedonia and Achaia to make a certain contribution for the poor among the saints that are at Jerusalem. Yea, it hath been their good pleasure; and their debtors they are. For if the Gentiles have been made partakers of their spiritual things, they owe it *to them* also to minister unto them in carnal things. When therefore I have accomplished this, and have sealed to them this fruit, I will go on by you unto Spain. And I know that, when I come unto you, I shall come in the fulness of the blessing of Christ.

Now I beseech you, brethren, by our Lord Jesus Christ, and by the love of the Spirit, that ye strive together with me in your prayers to God for me; that I may be delivered from them that are disobedient in Judæa, and *that* my ministration which *I have* for Jerusalem may be acceptable to the saints; that I may come unto you in joy through the will of God, and together with you find rest. Now the God of peace be with you all. Amen.

Ver. 23. **No more place in these regions.** The opportunities of preaching the Gospel in new places have ceased in the regions in which he has hitherto been occupied, viz. East of the Adriatic.

Ver. 24. **Spain.** The word as then used stood for the entire Pyrenæan peninsula. This journey was probably taken after Paul's first imprisonment. Those who deny a second imprisonment deny that this journey was ever made.

Ver. 25. **Unto Jerusalem.** Nevertheless, in God's Providence, the ultimate end of this journey was Rome. **Ministering.** Not merely "to minister," but the journey was itself a ministry. **Saints,** ch. 1:7.

Ver. 26. **Macedonia and Achaia.** The two sections of Greece, North and South, of that time. He might have written: N. and S. Greece. **Contribution.** How that contribution was gathered, and Paul's plans as a Church financier may be learned from 1 Cor. 16 : 1-4. Further details in 2 Cor. 8, 9.

Ver. 27. **Their good-pleasure . . . debtors** express the two motives prompting the contribution. First, the pleasure of the Christian in relieving the necessities of his brethren; secondly, the sense of obligation. **If Gentiles partakers.** The congregation at Jerusalem was the mother church, from which were sent forth the influences by which the Gentiles were brought to Christ. There is contained here a suggestion to the Roman Christians as to their duty in regard to this same contribution. Why should not the Roman Christians—mainly Gentiles—share in the zeal of those of Macedonia and Achaia? The debt to the mother church was in both cases the same. **To minister unto them,** as an act of worship. The word is of same root, as ver. 16; ch. 13 : 6, and means " to make a sacrificial service." The money gathered for this purpose becomes a eucharistic sacrifice.

Ver. 28. **Have sealed to them** =have securely and in due form delivered it. The Apostle was the bearer of the alms, in order to inspire confidence in the collection. Hence the necessity of a public and official transfer. While no one could have doubted his integrity, had he handed it over privately, the importance and value of the undertaking were enhanced by its publicity. The money was more than a relief for the necessities of the Christians; it was a testimonial of the love of those making the contribution.

Ver. 29. **The fulness of the blessing.** He will bring with him all the gifts and graces connected with the Apostolic office. (Comp. 1 : 11.) They will not be without rich fruit in the life of the congregation. " Fulness of blessing is a Hebraism for abundant or full blessing, consisting in growth in doctrine, in a better constitution of the church, in the obtaining from God of greater gifts, in being incited to the pursuit of godliness, and the like, all of which he promises that he will bring with him" (BALDWIN).

Ver. 30. **By the love of the spirit**, viz. that which is enkindled by the Holy Spirit. **Strive together.** Lit. "Agonize together with," indicating the earnestness and perseverance of the prayer that is asked for. Even one endowed with the special gifts of an Apostle, "the fulness of the blessing," craves for the prayers of the humblest believers (2 Cor. 1 : 11 ; Eph. 6 : 18, 19 ; Col. 4 : 3 ; 1 Thess. 5 : 25 ; 2 Thess. 3 : 1, 2).

Ver. 31. **That I may be delivered.** The Apostle apprehends open hostility on the part of the Jews, and the prejudices and secret distrust instilled by Judaizers in the church (Acts 21 : 20, 21). **That my ministrations may be acceptable.** He has, therefore, some doubts whether, after all his pains and dangers, the Jewish Christians at Jerusalem will appreciate his services, and accept his offices as their benefactor.

Ver. 32. **And together with you find rest.** A. V.: "With you, be refreshed," i. e. find his rest in the anticipated mutual intercourse between him and the Roman Christians. All came to pass ; but how differently from what was expected ! He came to Rome "in joy," but as a prisoner. He found at Rome his rest; but it was by the sword of the executioner.

Ver. 33. **The God of peace**, i. e. the God who brings peace. The thought is suggested from vers. 31, 32.

CONCLUSION.

(A.) *Commendation of Phoebe* (16 : 1, 2).

1-2. I commend unto you Phœbe our sister, who is a servant of the church that is at Cenchreæ : that ye receive her in the Lord, worthily of the saints, and that ye assist her in whatsoever matter she may have need of you : for she herself also hath been a succourer of many, and of mine own self.

Ver. 1. **Phœbe.** According to the subscription to the Epistle, she carried it to Rome. **A servant.** Undoubtedly " a deaconess." Not that the office was fully developed at this time, but that the Roman Church had women deacons, as well as men deacons. This is the plain meaning of 1 Tim. 3 : 11, where violence is done to the entire context, either by the rendering " wives " of A. V., or " women " of R. V. The deaconesses were charged especially with the care of the sick, of strangers, of catechumens among the women, of the younger female members and children of the Church, and all other duties in which they could execute diaconal functions as women, more readily than they could be attended to by men. This office, however, was not identical with the institution of widows of 1 Tim. 5 : 9 sqq., whose members had reached an age beyond that at which the active and laborious duties of the female diaconate were possible."[1] **Cenchreæ,** the sea-port of Corinth.

Ver. 2. **Worthily of saints.** i. e. as saints ought to receive a person in her office, on her errand, and with her endorsements. **Assist her.** Lit. " stand by her." **She may have need.** Official business may have taken

---

[1] See my " Female Diaconate of the N. T.", Philadelphia, 1892, and *Lutheran Church Review,* January, 1892; also Uhlhorn's *Christian Charity in the Early Church.*

her to Rome, to look after female members of the Cenchræan and Corinthian churches who had removed to the capital of the world, or to discharge some special commissions belonging to the Achaian churches, that could be best secured through such a representative woman. **Succourer.** "One who stood before," or "anticipated the wants" of many and of the Apostle himself, "a patroness."

(B.) *Greetings.*

3-16. Salute Prisca and Aquila my fellow-workers in Christ Jesus, who for my life laid down their own necks; unto whom not only I give thanks, but also all the churches of the Gentiles: and *salute* the church that is in their house. Salute Epænetus my beloved, who is the first fruits of Asia unto Christ. Salute Mary, who bestowed much labour on you. Salute Andronicus and Junias, my kinsmen, and my fellow-prisoners, who are of note among the apostles, who also have been in Christ before me. Salute Ampliatus my beloved in the Lord. Salute Urbanus our fellow-worker in Christ, and Stachys my beloved. Salute Apelles the approved in Christ. Salute them which are of the *household* of Aristobulus. Salute Herodion my kinsman. Salute them of the *household* of Narcissus, which are in the Lord. Salute Tryphæna and Tryphosa, who labour in the Lord. Salute Persis the beloved, which laboured much in the Lord. Salute Rufus the chosen in the Lord, and his mother and mine. Salute Asyncritus, Phlegon, Hermes, Patrobas, Hermas, and the brethren that are with them. Salute Philologus and Julia, Nereus and his sister, and Olympas, and all the saints that are with them. Salute one another with a holy kiss. All the churches of Christ salute you.

Ver. 3. **Prisca and Aquila.** Aquila, a native of Pontus, and his wife, Prisca or Priscilla, makers, like Paul, of tent-cloth, went to Corinth from Rome, to Ephesus from Corinth, to Rome as here shown from Ephesus, and are found once more in Ephesus (2 Tim. 4 : 19). They appear first in Acts 18 : 2, 26. Prisca is mentioned first, probably because of her greater interest, energy and activity. HORT has suggested that her priority is due to the fact that she was of noble birth.

Ver. 4. Laid down their own necks. At some particular time, not mentioned in the Book of Acts or the Epistles, they exposed themselves to an especial peril for the sake of Paul. **All the churches,** because the labors of the Apostles to the Gentiles were thus prolonged.

Ver. 5. Church that is in their house. (Comp. 1 Cor. 16:19; Col. 4:15; Phil. 2.) In the large cities, Christians, having as yet no church buildings, and being too numerous to assemble in one place, met in groups, in the houses of various members. Those in better circumstances, having larger houses, were in this way able to do an especial service to the brotherhood. Such were Aquilla and Priscilla. **Epænetus.** Not elsewhere mentioned. **First-fruits of Asia.** The first convert from the Roman province of Asia, of which Asia was the capital. The reading "Achaia" followed by A. V. seems inconsistent with 1 Cor. 16:15.

Ver. 6. Mary. The only Hebrew name in the entire list. **Bestowed much labor.** Unknown the labor, its record remains her perpetual memorial (Matt. 26:13). It may have been as a deaconess in some especial calamity that had befallen the Roman Church. The Roman Christians knew what it was, as well as Paul.

Ver. 7. Andronicus and Junias. It is impossible to know whether "Junia" of A. V. or "Junias" of R. V. be correct. The accusative case of both is the same. If Junia be correct, the reference is to a woman; if Junias to a man. **My kinsmen.** We read in ver. 11 of Herodion, and in ver. 21 of Lucius, Jason and Sosipater, as other kinsmen. His sister's son is mentioned in Acts 23:16. The wider meaning "countrymen" is contrary to Mark 6:4 and Acts 10:24. **Fellow-prisoners.** The word means "prisoners of war," i. e. They shared with

Paul at some time not mentioned imprisonment for the sake of the Gospel. According to 2 Cor. 6:5; 11:23, he suffered a number of imprisonments. **Among the Apostles,** i. e. The Apostles knew well their devotion. **Before me.** A touching tribute. So he elsewhere calls himself the last of the Apostles (1 Cor. 15:8).

Ver. 8. **My beloved** is applied to Ampliatus and Stachys in absence of any special public activity for which they were noted. They were tenderly cherished by Paul for their personal excellences.

Ver. 9. **Our fellow-worker** applied to Urbanus, indicates that his activity in the Church at Rome was in a cause that was one with that to which the Apostle was devoting his life.

Vers. 10, 11. **Approved in Christ**—the tested Christian. Through special afflictions and trials, the faith of Apelles had remained firm. **Which are of the household** Most probably believing slaves belonging to Aristobulus; so also **of Narcissus.**

Ver. 12. **Tryphæna and Tryphosa,** probably like Phœbe (ver. 1), deaconesses. (Cf. "Mary," ver. 7.) While the former are laboring, **Persis labored,** either referring to some crisis, when her service was particularly important, or to the fact, that, as an aged woman, her period of activity was over, but what had been accomplished, while she had the strength, was worthy of commemoration. It has been noted that Paul's delicate sense of propriety is shown here in speaking of Persis, not as " my beloved," as in vers. 8, 9, but simply as " the beloved."

Ver. 13. **Rufus.** As the Gospel of Mark was written at Rome, and the names of the children of Simon of Cyrene are there mentioned (15 : 21), as though well known, there is a strong probability that the same Rufus is here meant. He would then be the son of the man who bore the cross of Christ. The family had moved from Jerusalem to Rome. **Chosen in the Lord,** i. e. preeminently. He was a distinguished Christian. **His mother and mine.** There is nothing to contradict the supposition that Paul refers to kindness shown him in this household, when he was a boy going to school at Jerusalem.

Vers. 14, 15 refer possibly to two different groups of believers, members of two house-congregations, like that of ver. 5, or to those closely connected in their trades or business pursuits. They may not have been personally known to Paul, and, hence, the designation is not more specific.

Ver. 16. **With a holy kiss.** After sending his greetings to all prominent members of the Church, and those best known to him, he reaches the rest in this way. Each one is to receive an individual pledge of Paul's interest. Each individual believer is to have this seal of the interest of each member in him. All inequalities of rank and condition were thus lost in the assemblies of Christians. The kiss was an ordinary Oriental mode of greeting. The adjective refers to the manner in which it was to be given and received. " Not a feigned, treacherous or lascivious, but a holy, religious and chaste kiss " (ANSELM). (Comp. 1 Cor. 16:20; 2 Cor. 13:12; 1 Thess. 5:26; 1 Pet. 5:14.) "This custom has been abolished. In the Gospel, we read clearly that Christ received His disciples with the kiss. This was the usage in those lands. Paul often speaks of the kiss " (LUTHER on 1 Pet. 5:19). But, as used in the early Church, the adjective "holy" shows that it had a Christian consecration. It was embodied in the eucharistic service at an early date: " Let the bishop salute the Church, and say:

The peace of God be with you all. And let the people answer, And with thy spirit; and let the deacon say to all, Salute ye one another with the holy kiss. And let the clergy salute the bishop, the men of the laity salute the men, and the women the women" (*Apostolic Constitutions*, 8 : 12). **All the churches.** Paul, as an Apostle, and, therefore, officially connected with every congregation, could present the assurances of the interest and sympathy of all.

"Saints are not stoics, or inhuman; but courteous, affable, kind, compassionate, sympathetic. Among Christians, the salutation is not a mere civil custom; but a true prayer whereby we beseech God for blessings of all kinds for our fellow-Christian. This prayer, too, is never in vain, if received by a faithful heart" (HUNNIUS).

(*c.*) *Warnings against False Teachers.*

17-20. Now I beseech you, brethren, mark them which are causing the divisions and occasions of stumbling, contrary to the doctrine which ye learned: and turn away from them. For they that are such serve not our Lord Christ, but their own belly; and by their smooth and fair speech they beguile the hearts of the innocent. For your obedience is come abroad unto all men. I rejoice therefore over you: but I would have you wise unto that which is good, and simple unto that which is evil. And the God of peace shall bruise Satan under your feet shortly.

The grace of our Lord Jesus Christ be with you.

Ver. 17. The unity of the Church presented in the greetings suggests the hindrances that mar it elsewhere; and this leads to the consideration of perils that threaten the future, near or remote, of every church, however harmonious and prosperous (Acts 20 : 29). The beginnings of these troubles Paul indicates are already present; and against them, effectual measures must be at once taken. **Mark them, he says, which are causing the divisions and occasions of stumbling.** The "divisions" refer to the interposition of anything interfering with brotherly fellowship, leading to the formation of cliques and parties within the Church, and finally to external separations or schisms (Gal 5:20). The article indicates that these divisions were well known to the Roman Christians. **Occasions of stumbling.** (Comp. 14:13.) **Contrary to the doctrine.** As in Gal. 1:8. This does not imply necessarily an open contradiction of the doctrine, but may mean also that which is offered to supplement it—something "alongside of the doctrine." **Ye learned,** i. e. when you became Christians. The reference is probably to Judaistic teachers who endeavored to overthrow or supplement the Pauline type of doctrine. **Turn away from them.** Have nothing to do with them. Do not listen to them, or attempt to refute them (Tit. 3:10; 1 Thess. 3:14).

Ver. 18. **Serve their own belly.** Their underlying motive is that they may spend in self-indulgence the fruits of their schismatic and sectarian leadership. (Comp. 3:19.) **By their smooth and fair speech.** The former adjective designates their manner as mild, kind, mellow; the latter, the matter, as abounding in benedictions, and praises—flattery, and deceitful promises. Of such men, says Paul, beware. **Innocent,** i. e. guileless.

Ver. 19. **Your obedience,** etc. The mild reproof, at the close of this verse, sustains the view that regards the first part as teaching that, since their docility was widely known, it rendered them peculiarly exposed to the danger indicated. **Wise unto that which is good.** With faculties sharpened to discern and receive everything good wherever found. This implies fidelity and zeal for the pure Gospel. **Simple unto that which is evil.** Lit.

"unmixed with." So wise with respect to the good as to avoid all contamination by and compromise with evil. The Lord's words in Matt. 10 : 16 are in his mind. "We notice here what the simplicity is which is commended in Christians; in order that they may not claim the title who to-day regard stupid ignorance of God's word the highest virtue. For although he approves the courtesy and affability displayed by the Romans, nevertheless he wants prudence and discrimination to be exercised, so that their credulity may not subject them to imposition."

Ver. 20. **God of peace.** (Comp. on ch. 15 : 33.) **Shall bruise Satan.** He looks forward to the final victory predicted in Gen. 3 : 15, and which according to 13 : 11 is not now far off. Yet this ultimate triumph is again and again foreshadowed in the victory of the church of particular times and places over its adversaries. Their rage can never last long. **The grace,** etc. Benediction, with which it was evidently Paul's intention to conclude. But he finds it advisable afterwards—possibly days or weeks later—to add what follows in vers. 21–27. (See on ch. 1 : 7.)

(d.) Greetings Conveyed.

21–23. Timothy my fellow-worker saluteth you: and Lucius and Jason and Sosipater, my kinsmen. I Tertius, who write the epistle, salute you in the Lord. Gaius my host, and of the whole church, saluteth you. Erastus the treasurer of the city saluteth you, and Quartus the brother.

Ver. 21. **Timothy** is mentioned in all of Paul's Epistles except Ephesians, Galatians and Titus.

Ver. 22. **Tertius, who write,** viz. as Paul's amanuensis. When Paul wrote with his own hands, the failure of his eyes rendered very large characters necessary (Gal. 6 : 11).

Ver. 23. **Gaius.** Baptized by Paul (1 Cor. 1 : 14). The

name is the same as the Latin Caius, and was common. Hence those of the name mentioned in Acts and 3 John may belong elsewhere. **Erastus, the treasurer.** A man, therefore, in high social and official position. Some regard him as ex-treasurer (comp. 2 Tim. 4 : 20), where the reference is clearly to the same person. **The brother.** Simply " our Christian brother."

(c.) Concluding Doxology.

25-27. Now to him that is able to stablish you according to my gospel and the preaching of Jesus Christ, according to the revelation of the mystery which hath been kept in silence through times eternal, but now is manifested and by the scriptures of the prophets, according to the commandment of the eternal God, is made known unto all the nations unto obedience of faith ; to the only wise God, through Jesus Christ, to whom be the glory for ever. Amen.

Ver. 25. **To stablish you:** to keep you steadfast. **According to my gospel:** " In my Gospel," i. e. the word of God's grace as he had taught it (Rom. 2 : 16 ; 2 Tim. 2 : 8), and as distinguished from that of Judaism. **The preaching of Jesus Christ.** The thought is the same as though this were in apposition with Gospel. The Gospel is the doctrine of Jesus Christ and Him Crucified. **According to.** The expression is not co-ordinate with those that precede, nor is the meaning identical. Paul's preaching was in accordance with the revelation that had been made (Eph. 3 : 3-5).

Ver. 26. **By the scriptures of the prophets.** This revelation contained in the O. T. could not be read until Christ came ; but, as this Epistle shows, since He has come, the O. T. Scriptures in this new light become the clearest proofs of what He teaches. **According to the commandment.** Since the Apostles were divinely commissioned teachers. **Unto all the nations.** The leading thought of the Epistle. **Unto obedience:** To make them obedient (ver. 27). **Only wise.** Since in the whole plan of Redemption and its entire administration, this wisdom is so wondrously manifest (Ch. 11 : 33).

EXCURSUS.

LUTHER'S INTRODUCTION TO THE EPISTLE (1522).

THIS Epistle is actually the chief part of the New Testament. It is the absolutely pure Gospel. A Christian should not only commit it word for word, but he should daily feed upon it, as the daily bread of his soul. For it never can be read too often or be studied too well. The more it is studied, the more precious it becomes, and the better it tastes. By this preface, therefore, I will endeavor to prepare a way into it, so far as God shall give me grace, that it may be understood in the best way by every one. For, hitherto, it has been greatly obscured by glosses and aimless comments of various kinds, although, in itself, it is a bright light, almost sufficient to illumine all the Scriptures.

First, we must carefully note the language, and learn what St. Paul means by the words, law, sin, grace, faith, flesh, spirit, etc. For otherwise, there is no use to read it.

WHAT IS LAW?

The word "law" must not be understood in a human way, viz. as teaching what works are to be done, and what to be left undone; as in human laws, where the law is fulfilled by outward works, even though the heart be not in them. God judges according to the ground of the heart. His law requires, therefore, the ground of the heart, and is not satisfied with works wrought without the heart, but rather reproves them as hypocrisy and lies.

In Ps. 116 : 11, all men are called liars, because no one from the ground of his heart can hold or keep God's law; since every one finds in himself displeasure with the good and pleasure in what is evil. Where there is no free pleasure to do good, there the ground of the heart is not according to the law of God; and there is no doubt that before God, there is sin, and that His wrath is deserved, even though externally many good works, and an honorable life be manifest.

For this cause, Paul concludes in the Second Chapter (vers. 12, 13) that the Jews are all sinners, and declares that only the doers of the law are righteous before God. He means, thereby, that no one is, by his works, a doer of the law, but says rather to them: "Thou teachest a man should not commit adultery, and yet thou thyself committest adultery" (ver. 22); and also: "Wherein thou judgest another, thou condemnest thyself, because thou doest the same things that thou judgest" (ver. 1). This is the same as saying: Thou livest outwardly in the works of the law, and judgest them that live not so. Thou knowest how to teach others, and seest the mote in another's eye, but art not aware of the beam in thine own eye.

For although, by thy works, thou outwardly observest the law, from fear of punishment or love of reward; thou doest all this without free pleasure or love to the law, but with displeasure and constraint. Thou wouldst greatly prefer that there should be no law. Hence the conclusion is plain that, from the ground of thy heart, thou art an enemy of God. Of what avail, then, is it that thou teachest others not to steal, if, in thy heart, thou art a thief, and wouldst like to steal externally, if only thou darest? Nevertheless such hypocrites are not able always to suppress the outward work. Thou teachest another man, but teachest not thyself; yea, thou knowest not what thou teachest, for thou understandest not the law aright. Aye, the law increaseth sin, as he says (5 : 20); for the more it commands that man cannot do, the greater is man's hostility to it increased.

He says, therefore (7 : 14), that the law is spiritual. What does this mean? If the law were a bodily thing, we would fulfil it by our works. But it is spiritual. No one satisfies it, unless all that is done, be done from the bottom of the heart. But such a heart is given only by the Spirit of God, who makes man like the law, so that in his heart he has pleasure in the law, and henceforth does nothing from fear or constraint. The law, therefore, is spiritual, which will be loved and fulfilled with such a spiritual heart, and demands such a spirit. Where the spirit is not in the heart, there is sin, displeasure and hatred to the law, which, nevertheless, is good, righteous and holy.

Acquaint thyself, therefore, with the Apostle's mode of speaking, that to do the works of the law and to fulfil the law are entirely different things. The work of the law is all of the law that a man can do from his own free will and his own powers. But since, beneath and along with such works, there are in men's hearts displeasure and constraint with respect to the law, such works are all lost and of no use. This is what St. Paul means in 3 : 20, when he says: "By the deeds of the law, shall no flesh be justified in His sight." You see, then, that the sophists and scholastics are deceivers when they teach us by our works to prepare ourselves for grace. How can one by his works prepare himself for that which is good, when he can do no good work without displeasure and unwillingness? How can a work, proceeding from a displeased and rebellious heart, please God?

To fulfil the law is with pleasure and delight to do its work, and to live a good and godly life freely and without constraint of the law, just as though there were no law or punishment. Such pleasure and unconstrained love comes only by the work of the Holy Spirit in the heart, as he says (5 : 5). But the Spirit is not given, except only in, with and through faith in Jesus Christ. This faith comes not, except through God's Word or the Gospel, proclaiming Christ, as God's Son and Man, who died and rose again for us, as he says (3 : 25 ; 4 : 25 ; 10 : 9).

Hence it is, that only faith justifies, or fulfils the law; for, by Christ's merits, it brings the Spirit. The Spirit makes the heart joyful and free, as the law demands; and then good works proceed from faith itself. This is what he means in 3 : 31, after he has rejected the works of the law, so that it sounds as though he intended, by means of faith, to abolish the law. No, he says, we do not destroy the law, but only fulfil it by faith.

What is Sin?

Sin is in the Scriptures not only an outward bodily work, but also everything that incites to the outward work, viz. even though it pertains only to the centre of the heart with all its powers. When the little word "commit" is used, we mean that the man is altogether carried away into sin. For no outward act of sin is committed except when man is entirely carried away into sin, both in body and in soul. Scripture looks particularly into the heart and to the root and fountainhead of all sins, which is unbelief in the bottom of the heart. As faith, therefore, alone justifies, and brings the Spirit and pleasure to good outward works, so unbelief alone sins and provokes the flesh and pleasure to wicked outward works, as happened to Adam and Eve in Paradise (Gen. 3 : 6).

For this cause, Christ calls unbelief alone sin in John 16 : 8, 9. Before, therefore, good or bad deeds are done, as good or bad fruits, there must first be in the heart either faith [as the source of all virtues], or unbelief as the root, sap and chief strength of all sins. This unbelief is called in Scripture the head of the serpent or of the old dragon, which the seed of the woman, Christ, must tread under foot, as was promised Adam (Gen. 3 : 15).

What is Grace?

Grace and gift differ. Grace properly means God's favor or good-pleasure, which He bears towards us of Himself [i. e. without our having deserved it], and from which He is inclined to shed abroad Christ and the Spirit, with His gifts, in us, as is seen in 5 : 15. Although the gifts of the Spirit increase in us daily, and are not yet perfect, so that wicked lusts and sins still remain in us, which fight against the Spirit, as he says (Rom. 7 : 14 and Gal. 5 : 17), and as was previously prophesied (Gen. 3 : 15); nevertheless so great is God's grace, that we are regarded as though we were entirely righteous before God. For God's grace is not divided,[1] like the gifts, but receives us entirely into favor, for the sake of Christ, our Advocate and Mediator, and because in us the gifts of the Spirit have been begun.

---

[1] Luther refers here to the grace of justification. For justification is never divided, increased or diminished. One is either entirely forgiven all his sins, or is forgiven none whatever. We have either perfect and complete justification, or none whatever.

This, then, explains why, in the seventh chapter, Paul accuses himself of being a sinner, and, nevertheless, in 8 : 1 says that there is no condemnation to them that are in Christ Jesus, because of the imperfect gifts of the Spirit, and because of the Spirit Himself. Because of the flesh not being as yet entirely killed, we are still sinners; but because we believe in Christ and have the beginning of the Spirit, God is so kind and gracious, that He will not regard or judge such sin, but will deal with us according to our faith in Christ, until our sin be completely dead.

WHAT IS FAITH?

Faith is not man's opinion and dream, which some take to be faith. When they see that no amendment of the life or good works follow, although they hear and can talk much of faith, they fall into error and say: Faith is not enough; good works must be done, if one is to be righteous and to be saved. The reason is that, when they hear the Gospel, they immediately devise, from their own powers, the imagination in their hearts, to which they give expression in the words: "I believe." This they regard as right faith. Nevertheless it is nothing but man's thought and imagination, which is never experienced in the bottom of the heart; hence it accomplishes nothing, and no amendment follows.

But faith is a divine work in us, which transforms us, and begets us anew of God (John 1 : 13). It puts to death the old Adam. It makes us entirely different men, in heart, mind, sense and all powers, and brings with it the Holy Spirit. Oh, it is a living, active, busy, efficient thing that we have in faith! It is impossible for one who has faith to do otherwise than incessantly to do good. He asks not whether good works are to be done, but, before such a question can be asked, he has done them, and is always busy. But he who does not such works is an unbeliever, who gropes and looks around after faith and good works, and knows neither what faith is, nor what good works are, although he has many words to say of both faith and good works.

Faith is a living, wide-awake confidence in God's grace, that is so certain, that one who has it is ready to die a thousand times for it. Such confidence and knowledge of God's grace makes one joyful and brave before God and all creatures. Such a disposition is wrought by the Holy Spirit through faith. Willingly and without compulsion, it is ready to do good to every man, to serve every man, to suffer all things from love to God and to the glory of God who has bestowed such grace. As impossible, therefore, is it to separate works from faith, as to separate heat and light from fire. Consider, then, thy false notions and wild talk, which make a great pretence of knowledge with respect to faith and good works, and yet are the very extreme of folly. Pray God to work faith in thee; otherwise thou shalt remain eternally without faith, though thou thinkest and doest whatever thou wilt or canst.

What is Righteousness?

Righteousness is just such faith, and is called God's righteousness, or the righteousness that avails before God, because God gives it, and reckons it as righteousness for the sake of Christ, our Mediator. It makes man pay every one his due. For through faith man is without sin, and loves God's commandments, whereby he gives God honor and pays Him what is His due; and to men also he does willing service, and, so far as he can, pays also his due to every one. Such righteousness can never be wrought by nature, free will or our own strength. For as no one can give himself faith, so no one can remove his own unbelief; how then can he remove even the very smallest sin? Wherefore all is false hypocrisy and sin that is done without faith, or in unbelief (Rom. 14:23), whatever be the appearances.

Flesh and Spirit.

Flesh and Spirit must not be understood here in such a way as though flesh were only that which has to do with unchastity, and Spirit, that which inwardly pertains to the heart. But here Paul, like Christ in John 3:6, calls all that is born of the flesh, flesh, viz. the entire man, with body and soul, with reason and all senses. All that, therefore, is to be called flesh which is thought, taught or talked about, in regard even to exalted spiritual things, as may be learned from Gal. 5:20, where heresy and envy are called works of the flesh. In Rom. 8:3, he says that, by reason of the flesh, the law is weak; which is not understood of unchastity only, but of all sins, and chiefly of unbelief, which is a most spiritual vice. That, on the other hand, is called spiritual, which has to do with the most external works of all; as the work of Christ, when He washed his disciples' feet, and of Peter, when he guided his ship and fished.

Flesh, therefore, is a man who inwardly and outwardly lives and works, so as to serve the use of the flesh and of this temporal life. But spirit is one who inwardly and outwardly lives and works, so as to serve the Spirit and the world to come.

Without such interpretation of these words, thou wilt never understand this Epistle of St. Paul, nor any other book of the Holy Scriptures. Beware, then, of all teachers who understand these words otherwise, be they who they may, even though Jerome, Augustine, Ambrose, Origen, and the like, or even higher. Now we will consider the Epistle.

The Argument.

Forasmuch as it becomes a preacher of the Gospel, first, through the revelation of the law, and of sin, to rebuke and prove all things as sin, which proceed not from the Spirit of God and faith in Christ, to the end that men may be led to the knowledge of sin and to sorrow therefor, so as to be humbled and to desire aid; even so does St. Paul. In *the first chapter*, he reproves the gross sins and the unbelief which all men see, such as were and still are the sins of the heathen who live without God's grace. He says: "The wrath of God is revealed, through the Gospel, from heaven upon all men, for their ungodliness and unholy living." For though they know and daily recognize that there is a God, yet nature in itself, without grace, is so wicked, that they neither thank, nor worship Him, but blind themselves and constantly deteriorate, until they come to idolatry and the most shameful sins, and allow them to pass unrebuked in others,

In *the second chapter*, he extends his rebuke still farther to those who are outwardly godly, or secretly sin; such as the Jews were, and the hypocrites of to-day, who live well without love [to God and man], and in their hearts are God's enemies, while they freely censure other people. For it is the nature of all dissemblers to judge themselves pure, and yet to be full of covetousness, hatred, pride and every abomination (Matt. 23:25).

They despise God's goodness, and, according to the hardness of their hearts, heap up for themselves the wrath of God. Paul, therefore, as a true interpreter of the law, permits no one to be without sin, but proclaims the wrath of God against all who wish to live well from nature or their free will, and rates them as no better than open sinners. He says that they are hard-hearted, and that they cannot repent.

In *the third chapter*, he mingles all together, and says that the one is as the other, all sinners before God, except that the Jews had God's Word. Even though many of them believed not, yet God's faith and truth are not made void. He quotes a declaration from Ps. 51:4 that God may be justified when He speaks. After that, he returns and proves also by Scripture that all are sinners, and that, by the deeds of the law, no one is justified, but that the law was given only in order that sin should be made known.

Then he begins and teaches the right way to live a godly life, and to be saved. He says, that they must all be sinners and without praise before God, but that they are justified without merit through faith in Christ, who has merited this for us by His blood, and has become unto us a Mercy Seat before God, for the remission of sins that are past. In this way He proves that the righteousness which He gives in faith alone helps us. This righteousness was revealed to us in time through the Gospel, and was previously witnessed by the law and the prophets. Thus the law is established by faith, although the works of the law, with all their glory, are thereby overthrown.

In *the fourth chapter*, since sin has been revealed in the first three chapters, and the way of faith to righteousness taught, he begins to answer certain objections and claims. First, he considers those which they commonly make, who hear that faith, only, without works, justifies. They say: "Are men, then, not to do good works?" He holds Abraham up to them, as an example, and says: "Was all in vain that Abraham did with his works? Were his works of no use?" He concludes that Abraham, without all works, was justified alone by faith, inasmuch as, before the work of circumcision, he was praised of the Scripture and called righteous only by his faith (Gen. 15:6). The work of circumcision he did, not to be made righteous, and yet God commanded it, and it was a good work of obedience. So, undoubtedly, no other good work contributes anything to righteousness; but, as the circumcision of Abraham was an external sign, whereby he proved his righteousness in faith, so all good works are only outward signs which, as good fruits, follow faith, and prove that man is already justified before God.

Hereby, as with a cogent example from Scripture, Paul proves the doctrine previously stated in Chapter III., concerning faith, and adduces besides the testimony of David in Ps. xxxii., who also says that man is justified without works, although he remains not without works when he is justified. After that, he extends his example against all other good works of the law, and concludes that the Jews cannot be Abraham's heirs merely because of their blood, and, much less, because of the works of the law; but if they be true heirs, they inherit Abraham's faith; since Abraham before the law, both of Moses and of circumcision, was justified by faith, and was called a father of all believers. Besides the law rather causes wrath than grace, since no one fulfils it out of love and from pleasure, so that God's displeasure rather than His favor comes of the law. Hence it is only faith that receives the grace promised Abraham. For such examples were written for our sakes, that we also should believe.

In *the fifth chapter*, he comes to the fruits and works of faith, such as peace, joy, love to God and every man; moreover assurance, trust, confidence, courage and hope in trouble and sorrow. For all this follows where the faith is right, because of abundant blessings God has given us in Christ, in that He gave Christ to die for us before we could pray to Him, aye, while we were still His enemies. Thus it is proved that faith justifies without any works whatever, and, nevertheless, from this it does not follow, that no good works should be done; but the proper works should not be omitted, of which those who follow work-righteousness know nothing. For such persons devise works of their own, which have neither peace, joy, assurance, love, hope or confidence; nor do they have the nature of true Christian works or faith.

He makes, then, a long digression, and shows whence both sin and righteousness, death and life come, and contrasts the two, Adam and Christ. He means to say: Christ must needs come as a Second Adam, to make us heirs of His righteousness through a new spiritual birth in faith; just as the First Adam made us heirs of sin through the old birth of the flesh.

Thereby it is proclaimed and established that no one, by means of his works, can deliver himself from sin, so as to attain to righteousness, any more than he can prevent himself from being born bodily. It is likewise proved hereby that the divine law, which should have helped if anything could have helped, not only brought no help, but has even increased sin, because the corrupt nature has become only the more hostile, and seeks only the more to fulfil its lusts, as the law forbids it. The law, therefore, makes Christ the more necessary, and requires more grace with which to aid nature.

In *the sixth chapter*, he considers the peculiar work of faith, viz. the conflict of the Spirit with the flesh, as the former seeks to kill the sins and lusts remaining in the flesh after our justification. He teaches us that we are not so set free from sin through faith, that we should thereafter be idle, careless and secure of ourselves, as though sin were no longer in us. Sin is still present; but it is not reckoned to our condemnation, because of faith which fights against it. We have enough to do with ourselves our whole life long, in taming our bodies, putting to death its lusts, and compelling its members to obey the Spirit and not lusts, that we may be like the death and resurrection of Christ, and may fulfil our baptism, which signifies the death of sin and the new life of grace, until entirely free from sin with Christ we rise bodily and live eternally.

This we can do, he says, seeing we are under grace, and not under the law. What it is, not to be under the law, he himself expounds. It is not to be understood as though there were to be no laws, and every one might do as he pleased; but to be under the law, is when, without grace, we are occupied with the deeds of the law. For so long undoubtedly sin reigns through the law; since no one by nature is favorable to the law—and this natural dislike and aversion to the law, is of itself sin. But grace makes us love the law, so that sin no longer is present, and the law is no longer against us, but is at one with us.

But this is the right freedom from sin and from the law, of which he writes at the close of this chapter, that it is a freedom to do only good with pleasure, and to live well without compulsion of the law. Wherefore this freedom is a spiritual freedom, which does not destroy the law, but offers what the law demands, viz. pleasure and love, whereby the law is stilled, and has no more to urge or demand. It is as though thou wert in debt, and wert not able to pay. In two ways, thou mightest be freed: One, if thy creditor would require nothing of thee, and would erase the entry against thee; another, if some good man were to pay for thee, and give thee what would satisfy the account. In this way, Christ hath freed thee from the law; this, therefore, is no wild, carnal liberty, that is under no obligation, but it is one that does much and in all directions, and yet is free from the demands and debt of the law.

In *the seventh chapter*, he establishes this by an illustration from married life. As when the husband dies, the wife is at liberty, and thus the one is free from the other. Not as though the woman may or should not take another man, but rather now first of all is she free to marry another; which she could not do before she was freed from her first husband.

Even so our consciences are bound to the law under the sinful old Adam; but when he is killed by the Spirit, the conscience is free. Not as though the conscience should not do anything, but now first of all it cleaves to Christ, as the second husband, and brings forth the fruits of life.

Then he declares still more fully the nature of sin and of the law, how that, through the law, sin revives and gathers strength. For the old man becomes the more hostile to the law, since he cannot pay what the law demands. For sin is his nature, and, of himself, he cannot do otherwise; hence the law is death, torment and martyrdom to him. Not that the law is evil, but that the evil nature cannot endure what is good, and that what is good is demanded of it; just as a sick man cannot bear that he should be required to run, to leap, and other deeds of a sound man.

For this cause, Paul concludes that where the law is understood and perceived in the best way, it does no more than remind us of our sins, and thereby slays us, and subjects us unto eternal wrath: all of which he feels and understands, whose conscience is truly touched by the law. Man, therefore, must have something more than the law, to make him godly and save him. They, however, who understand not the law are blind, and act presumptuously, when they imagine that, by their works, they will satisfy it. For they know not how much the law requires, viz. a free and cheerful heart. They do not look Moses straight into the eyes; the veil hangs between and covers them.

Furthermore he shows how the spirit and the flesh fight together in one man, and he gives himself as an example in order that we may learn to know how to work aright, viz. to kill sin within us. He calls both the Spirit and the flesh a law; because, just as it is the nature of God's law to impel and to demand; so also the flesh impels, demands and rages against the Spirit, and will have its lust satisfied. On the other hand, the Spirit fighteth against the flesh, and will have His desire satisfied. Their strife continues in us, as long as we live; in one, more, in others, less, as the Spirit or the flesh is stronger. The entire man is both Spirit and flesh, who fights with himself until he becomes entirely spiritual.

In *the eighth chapter*, he comforts such fighters, that they do not condemn such flesh, and he shows farther what is the nature of flesh and Spirit, and how the Spirit comes from Christ who has given us the Holy Spirit, that makes us spiritual, and represses the flesh, and assures us that we are still God's children, although sin rages in us, as long as we follow the Spirit and resist sin to the death. Because nothing is so good for mortifying the flesh as the cross and suffering, he comforts us in afflictions by the assistance of the Holy Spirit, and the sympathy of all creatures, viz. that both the Spirit groans in us, and creatures long with us, that we may be delivered from the flesh and sin. So we see that these three chapters, viz. the sixth, seventh and eighth, drive us to the only work of faith, which is called killing the old Adam and curbing the flesh.

In *chapters nine, ten and eleven*, he treats of the eternal Predestination of God, whence it originally proceeds, as to who shall or who shall not believe, and who can and who cannot be freed from sin. By this predestination, that we are godly is taken altogether out of our own, and is placed in God's hands. This is also most highly necessary. For we are so weak and uncertain, that if it depended upon us, no man whatever would be saved, and the devil would certainly prevail over all. But now God is sure that His foreknowledge does not deceive Him, nor can any one withstand him; and, therefore, we have hope against sin.

But here a limit must be set to those presumptuous and ambitious spirits, who bring hither their reason, and begin from above to investigate the abyss of God's predestination, and in vain torment themselves with the question as to whether they be of the elect or not. They must, then, cast themselves headlong, so as either to despair, or to commit themselves to free chance. But follow thou the order of this Epistle and concern thyself with Christ and the Gospel, that thou mayst recognize thy sins and His grace; then fight with sins, as Chapters I.–VIII. have taught. After that, when thou hast come to the eighth chapter, and art under the cross and suffering, thou wilt learn right well in Chapters IX.–XI. how comforting predestination is. For unless one have experienced suffering, the cross and the sorrows of death, he cannot meddle with predestination, without injury and secret wrath against God. Adam must, therefore, be well killed, ere thou canst bear this, and drink such strong wine. See to it, then, that thou drink not wine, while thou art still a suckling. Every doctrine has its measure, time and age.

In *the twelfth chapter*, he teaches the true worship of God, and makes all Christians priests, to offer neither gold nor beasts, as in the law, but their own bodies, with the killing of their lusts. Then he describes the outward lives of Christians, in their spiritual government, how they should teach, preach, rule, serve, give, suffer, love, live and act towards friend and foe and every one. These are works that a Christian does. For, as it is said, faith does not keep holiday.

In *the thirteenth chapter*, he teaches us to honor and be obedient to the worldly government. Although this does not make men righteous before God, yet it has been established in order that the godly may have external peace and protection, and the wicked may not be free to do evil with impunity. Therefore even the godly, though they need it not, should honor it. Finally he comprehends all in love, and concludes with the example of Christ, that, as He hath done to us, even so should we do to one another.

In *the fourteenth chapter*, he teaches that the consciences that are weak in faith should be tenderly dealt with, and that the freedom of Christians should be used, not to their injury, but to their profit. For where this is not done, dissensions and a despising of the Gospel follow. It is better, therefore, to yield a little to the weak in faith, until they become stronger, than that the doctrine of the

Gospel be entirely suppressed. Such work is a peculiar work of love, that is necessary even now, where, without any need, men treat others with harshness with respect to the eating of flesh and other matters of Christian liberty, so as to disturb weak consciences, before they know the truth.

In *the fifteenth chapter*, he sets forth Christ as an example, that we should bear with the weak otherwise than with those who are guilty of open sins and of immoral life. These we should not reject, but bear with them, until they become better. For thus Christ has done and is now doing with us every day, so that He bears in us many faults and bad habits, with many imperfections, and, nevertheless, constantly aids us.

Then, at the close, he prays for them, praises them and commends them to God, proclaims his office, and urges them to be liberal in their contributions to the poor at Jerusalem; it is all pure love of which he speaks, and with which he deals.

The last chapter is one of greetings: but with these he mingles an excellent warning against the doctrines of men propounded as supplementary to the Gospel and that cause offence: just as though he had seen that, from Rome and through the Romans, the notorious Canons and Decrees would proceed, together with the ulcers and vermin of human laws and ordinances, which have corrupted all the world and abolished this Epistle and all Scripture, the Holy Spirit and faith. From these may God deliver us. Amen.

We find, then, in this Epistle a most ample presentation of what a Christian should know, viz. what Law, Gospel, Sin, Punishment, Grace, Faith, Righteousness, Christ,

God, Good Works, Love, Hope and the Cross are, and how we should conduct ourselves towards every one, be he godly or sinner, strong or weak, friend or foe, as well as towards ourselves. All this is most thoroughly grounded upon Scripture, and so illustrated by examples of his own experience, and of the prophets, that nothing more can be desired. It seems, therefore, as though St. Paul intended in this Epistle to comprise in a summary the entire Christian and evangelical doctrine, and to prepare an introduction to the entire Old Testament. For, without doubt, whosoever has this Epistle perfectly in his heart has the light and force of the Old Testament in him. Let every Christian, then, without exception, exercise himself constantly therein. For this may God grant His grace. Amen.

ANNOTATIONS

ON THE

FIRST EPISTLE OF ST. PAUL

TO THE

CORINTHIANS.

CHAPTERS I.—VI.

By HENRY E. JACOBS.

INTRODUCTION.

On the isthmus connecting the Peloponnesus (now the Morea) with the main land of Greece, there stood, in the life of St. Paul, the most important city of the country. With three seaports, Lechæum on the Corinthian Gulf, and Schœnus and Cenchræa on the Saronic Gulf, it enjoyed exceptionable commercial advantages. Situated on a ledge two hundred feet high, behind it rose, to the height of 1886 feet, the precipitous mass of rock, on which the Acrocorinthus, or citadel of Corinth, was built. From the summit, in favorable weather, the country around Athens, forty miles or more distant, was clearly discernible across the Saronic Gulf. Ancient Corinth, known in Grecian History, had been completely destroyed B. C. 146. On its side, one hundred years later, Julius Cæsar founded a second Corinth, which soon vied with its predecessor in population and trade, enterprise and wealth, luxury and licentiousness.

The Eighteenth Chapter of Acts tells the story of Paul's introduction to Corinth, and the founding there of a Christian church during his eighteen months' stay. Leaving Corinth to spend the feast (probably Pentecost) at Jerusalem, he went from Jerusalem to Ephesus, where he remained for three years. During the close of his stay there, he heard various rumors concerning irregularities that had arisen in the Church at Corinth. Unable to proceed at once thither he sent first Timothy (1 Cor. 4 : 17 ; 16 : 10), and, as Timothy had commissions to attend to in Macedonia (Acts 19 : 22), Titus and a companion afterwards, more directly (2 Cor. 12 : 18 ; 8 : 6, 22, 23). They most probably carried this Epistle (written in A. D. 57), as Titus afterwards reported to Paul the results that followed its reception (2 Cor. 7 : 6-15).

Like the Epistle to the Romans, the Second Epistle to the Corinthians, and that to the Galatians, this Epistle has never had its genuineness seriously questioned. The most hostile critics accept it. It is attested by both external and internal evidence.

It is occupied with the consideration of the divisions and disorders in the Corinthian Church, and answers to questions concerning which Paul's judgment had been asked. The order of the Epistle is very readily followed:

I. Introduction (I. 1-9).
II. The Divisions in the Corinthian Church, I. 10—IV.
III. The Moral Disorders in the Corinthian Church, V.—VII.
IV. Social and Ecclesiastical Disorders in the Corinthian Church, VIII.—XIV.
V. The Doctrine of the Resurrection, XV.
VI. Conclusion, XVI.

[NOTE.—The literature of the Epistle will be noticed at the close of this exposition.]

I. INTRODUCTION (1 : 1-9).

(A.) *Salutation.*

1-3. Paul, called *to be* an apostle of Jesus Christ through the will of God, and Sosthenes our brother, unto the church of God which is at Corinth, *even* them that are sanctified in Christ Jesus, called *to be* saints, with all that call upon the name of our Lord Jesus Christ in every place, their *Lord* and ours: Grace to you and peace from God our Father and Lord Jesus Christ.

Ver. 1. **Called to be an apostle.** The assertion of his official position is called forth here by the attempts to question his authority, current in the Corinthian Church (compare Ch. IX.); just as in Romans it was used because he had not personally met the members of that congregation. LIGHTFOOT'S suggestion that, if any polemical reference were intended, the words would be stronger, as in Gal. 1 : 1, is not decisive, as the polemical reference here is not designed to be particularly prominent. **Sosthenes.** In Acts 18 : 17, one by this name is mentioned as the ruler of the synagogue at Corinth, who was beaten by the Jews before the tribunal of Gallio. We see no reason why this may not have been the same man as the one mentioned in this address to the Corinthians as a person well known to them. "At the time when St. Paul was brought before Gallio, he had either actually declared himself a Christian, or at least shown such leaning to Christianity, as to incur the anger of his fellow-countrymen, who set upon him and beat him" (LIGHTFOOT). So CALVIN, HUNNIUS, BALDWIN and CALOVIUS. The mention of Sosthenes indicates that this is a joint-letter of the Apostle, and of a member or former member of the Corinthian congregation who is with Paul at Ephesus.

Ver. 2. **The church of God.** In the five earliest of St. Paul's Epistles, 1, 2 Thessalonians, 1, 2 Corinthians, Galatians, he uses this form of address. **Them that are sanctified.** In apposition with "Church of God." Notwithstanding the disorders and abuses in the Corinthian Church that merit his severest censures, he recognizes it as a "Church of God," and a "communion of saints." **Called to be saints.** Literally "the called saints," also in apposition to "Church of God." "The ascription of 'holiness' to a community guilty of such irregularities, is strikingly significant of St. Paul's view of the Christian Church. All who are brought within the circle of Christian influences are in a special manner Christ's; all who have put on Christ in baptism are called, are sanctified, are holy. Let them not act unworthily of their calling. Let them not dishonor and defile the sanctity which attaches to them" (LIGHTFOOT). **All that call upon the name,** viz. All Christians, wherever or whoever they may be, into whose hands this Epistle may fall. **Their Lord and ours.** A rhetorical correction. "Our Lord," the Apostle had said, and then pauses to add: "But not simply ours, their Lord also."

Ver. 3. See on Rom. 1 : 7.

(B.) *Thanksgiving.*

4–9. I thank my God always concerning you, for the grace of God which was given you in Christ Jesus : that in everything ye were enriched in him, in all utterance and all knowledge; even as the testimony of Christ was confirmed in you: so that ye come behind in no gift : waiting for the revelation of our Lord Jesus Christ; who shall also confirm you unto the end, *that ye be* unreproveable in the day of our Lord Jesus Christ. God is faithful, through whom ye were called into the fellowship of his Son Jesus Christ our Lord.

Ver. 4. **I thank,** etc. (Comp. Rom. 1:8; 1 Thess. 1:2; 2 Thess. 2:3.) **The grace.** Here put for the gifts of grace particularized in ver. 5. **In Christ Jesus.** It was while they abode in mystical union with Christ that these gifts were bestowed.

Ver. 5. **In all utterance and all knowledge.** The former refers to the gift of giving clear and correct expression to the contents of their faith, and the confession of the truth before friends and foes. Literally: "In every word." The latter indicates their clear apprehension, and saving appropriation of this truth. "Utterance" is mentioned first, as that which distinguishes them, above others, to external observation. "Knowledge" traces the confession of the faith to its source, and declares how sincere and genuine such confession is.

Ver. 6. **The testimony of Christ,** i. e. the Apostolic testimony concerning Christ, the Gospel. (Comp. 2 Tim. 1:8; Rev. 1:2, 9.) **Was confirmed in you.** To others they were living evidence to the truth of the Gospel, while within them the witness of the Spirit (Rom. 8:16), to the reality and preciousness of the Christian faith, was enjoyed. Whatever might be the faults of the Corinthian Church, there was an immeasurable difference between its members and their Christless neighbors. Paul wishes to have this clearly kept in view throughout the reproofs that are to follow.

Ver. 7. **Ye come behind in no gift** refers to a present condition. The divine rule, according to which they who receive what God offers have more given to them in ever increasing measure (Matt. 25:29), had been fulfilled in their case. No other Christian Church had received more gifts of God's grace. The comparison with other churches is obvious. If the meaning were simply: "Ye are lacking no gift," the genitive without a preposition would be used. The gifts here refer both to those which are ordinary and those which are extraordinary. **Waiting for the revelation.** A connection between their progress in the Christian Life and their eager expectation of the future coming of the Lord in glory is clearly indicated. (See 1 John 3:2, 3; 2 Pet. 3:11, 12.)

Ver. 8. **Who shall also confirm you.** Having declared what he thinks now of the Corinthians, he proceeds to state his faith in their future. "Who" refers to Christ. At His appearing, the Lord will bestow upon them the full realization of all their hopes; what they now believe they shall then see. **Unto the end.** As in Matt. 28:20, the end of the world. **That ye may be unreproveable.** "He calls them faultless, because in this life the sins of believers are covered by the blood of Christ, and they live a faultless life by the power of the Holy Spirit, and are free from grosser sins which Paul calls works of the flesh. But at last, on the day of the Lord Jesus Christ, they will be entirely blameless, clad in the most perfect habit of inherent righteousness" (HUNNIUS). But being unreproveable at the last day is conditioned upon perseverance in faith in Christ, and the consequent completion of sanctification. In this expression, there seems to be the suggestion which is afterwards developed in the Epistle, that the Corinthians have not yet reached the stage in which they are unreproveable. The Apostle, however, prefaces his letter of often severe censure by an expression of the confidence that his reproofs will be certainly laid to heart and those who are erring be completely restored.

Ver. 9. **God is faithful.** If the end, described in ver. 8, be not reached, it will not then be through any defect on God's part. " Three foundations of divine preservation unto the end are here given: 1. God's faithfulness (Deut. 32 : 4 ; Ps. 37 : 23–25 ; 1 Cor. 10 : 13). 2. The purpose of the call (1 Pet. 1 : 11 ; Rom. 11 : 29). 3. Fellowship with Christ, since those who partake thereof are sons and heirs of God, and coheirs with Christ (Rom. 8 : 16, 17), provided they depart not by their own fault from the faith (Heb. 3 : 14; 1 Pet. 1 : 9; Is. 54: 10)" (CALOVIUS).

II. THE DIVISIONS IN THE CORINTHIAN CHURCH
(1 : 10—Chap. 4).

(A.) *The Factions Described.*

10-17. Now I beseech you, brethren, through the name of our Lord Jesus Christ, that ye all speak the same thing, and *that* there be no divisions among you; but *that* ye be perfected together in the same mind and in the same judgment. For it hath been signified unto me concerning you, my brethren, by them *which are of the household* of Chloe, that there are contentions among you. Now this I mean, that each one of you saith, I am of Paul; and I of Apollos; and I of Cephas; and I of Christ. Is Christ divided? was Paul crucified for you? or were ye baptized into the name of Paul? I thank God that I baptized none of you, save Crispus and Gaius; lest any man should say that ye were baptized into my name. And I baptized also the household of Stephanas : besides, I know not whether I baptized any other. For Christ sent me not to baptize, but to preach the gospel: not in wisdom of words, lest the cross of Christ should be made void.

Ver. 10. **Brethren.** When St. Paul uses this term, we may be prepared for a mild, but earnest rebuke. (See ver. 11; 7:29; 10:1: 14:20, etc.) **Through the name of the Lord Jesus.** Their common relationship to Christ should be the strongest bond of union. (Comp. Eph. 4: 1-6.) **Ye all speak the same thing.** The common faith in Christ ought to have a common confession. **No divisions.** The negative side of the preceding requirement, carrying with it, however, a reference to the inner thoughts and feelings. **Ye be perfected together.** " Fitted together as the fragments in a piece of mosaic, in which each minute portion exactly fills its proper place" (LIAS). **The same mind** refers rather to their agreement upon principles, and **the same judgment** to the application of these principles to particular cases.

Ver. 11. **Of the household of Chloe.** Whether children, members of her family, near relatives or slaves, cannot be determined. Her house may have been a place of prayer, and the persons referred to, Christians belonging to the number who statedly met there. "The position of importance occupied by women in the Christian Church, even at this early date, is a token of the great social revolution which the Gospel was already working" (LIGHTFOOT). **That there are contentions.** No open rupture had as yet occurred.

Ver. 12. **Each one of you saith,** i. e. Every one has his partisan leader and watchword. Four clearly distinguishable sections or tendencies in the Corinthian Church are enumerated, even though there was no absolutely determined line of division between them. The humility of Paul has been noticed, as he begins with himself, and then, in an ascending scale, next mentions his associate Apollos, then the most prominent of the Apostles, Peter, and then finally Christ. But it has also been remarked that he follows an historical order. Paul, being the founder of the Corinthian Church, his name naturally was first used for partisan purposes. Next came Apollos, who succeeded him at Corinth. Then the gradual introduction of Judaistic teachers brought Peter into prominence as a claimed partisan of that school of thought. Finally, there came those who affected an independence of all teachers and preachers, and claimed that they regarded Christ alone. For these party names and claims, the teachers themselves were not responsible. The teaching of Apollos differed from that of Paul in form, but not in matter. For the conversion and early ministry of Apollos, see Acts 18:24; 19:1. An Alexandrian Jew, learned and eloquent, a possible pupil of Philo, and a convert to the preaching of John the Baptist, he had been led to embrace Christianity at Ephesus by Aquila and Priscilla. A more complete conformity to classical models and more profound philosophical treatment may have distinguished his preaching from that of Paul, who labored also under the disadvantages of a not impressive personality. While the antagonism between Paulinism and Petrinism in the Apostolic Church has been greatly exaggerated, it is undoubtedly true that Peter neither rose to that wide and extensive view of the mission of Christianity, nor entered so deeply into its spiritual conceptions, as did Paul. The very limitations of Petrinism rendered it attractive to many converted Jews who still adhered tenaciously to Jewish opinions, which Paul rejected more clearly and more forcibly than did Peter. Those who claimed Christ alone as their leader, erred just as truly as the rest; since Christ teaches and rules His Church through human instruments, and no Christian can claim independence of his historical relations (3:21). For the various conjectures concerning the Christ-party, supported by much learning, but leading to no results, see MEYER, and especially SCHAFF, *History of the Apostolic Church*, pp. 285 sqq.

Ver. 13. **Is Christ divided?** The Church is the mystical body of Christ (12:12, 27; Eph. 4:4). Such divisions are therefore impossible, unless Christ Himself be regarded as divided. Even those who claim Christ as in an especial sense the leader of their party, only degrade Him to the sphere of a partisan leader. He who has Christ has also as his own all who are Christ's. He who absolutely repudiates Paul and Apollos and Cephas, repudiates also the Lord who approaches him through them.

Was Paul crucified for you? A delicate sense of propriety is shown, by taking himself as the example from which to show the untenableness of these partisan relations. While the one party erred by sinking Christ to the level of a partisan leader, the others erred by raising their leaders to what, if consistently carried out, would make them the equals of Christ. We are not to follow Christ, only as Paul or Luther has taught us; but we are to follow Paul and Luther, only as they follow Christ (1 Cor. 11:1). By His crucifixion, Christ bought us, not Paul or Luther (7:23). **Were ye baptized into the name of Paul?** Baptism did not incorporate you with Paul or Cephas or Apollos, but with Christ. "These words of Paul are sometimes inaptly used as though it were wrong to-day to call some Lutherans, others Calvinists or Schwenkfeldians. But there is a diversity. For Paul, Cephas and Apollos taught the same doctrine, but Luther, Calvin, Schwenkfeld, etc., that which is very diverse" (HUNNIUS).

Ver. 14-17. **I thank God.** A possible reference to a disposition at Corinth to lay stress upon the person who baptized. Paul traces here the Providential guidance which had prevented him from baptizing more than a very small number. He had not intentionally refrained, but the Lord, who foreknew what would happen, had determined otherwise. **Save Crispus and Gaius.** These exceptions may have been made for personal reasons. Crispus had been the ruler of one of the synagogues at Corinth (Acts 18:8), as Sosthenes had been of another (Acts 18:17). In the house of Gaius, Paul was making his home, when he wrote the Epistle to the Romans (Rom. 16:23). The commonness of the name prevents us from identifying this Gaius with those mentioned in other places. **The household of Stephanas.** A slip of memory in the preceding verse, which he here corrects. Even inspired writers were liable to ordinary limitations in regard to matters not pertaining directly to the revelation of God which they wrote. The correction may have been suggested by Sosthenes. **Christ sent me not to baptize,** i. e. The great aim of his ministry was not that he should himself administer baptism, but that he should preach. Paul was both presbyter and apostle, like Peter (1 Pet. 5 : 1). As presbyter, he baptized (vers. 14–16). But his chief work was that of the Apostolate, to give forth his Apostolic witness for all times and places. It required no peculiar spiritual endowment to baptize ; but such endowment was needful for preaching. " The preaching of the Word is preferred to the administration of Baptism : 1. By reason of necessity. The Church can never be without the Word, whether preached publicly or privately. But it can be without the administration of the sacraments, in case of necessity and when oppressed by tyranny ; as the Israelites in the desert omitted circumcision for many years, and were without the Passover, although they were not without the Word. For the Word is like a public letter ; the sacraments like a seal. Destroy the seal, and the letter is still valid ; but destroy the letter, and the seal amounts to nothing. 2. By reason of difficulty. Any minister of the Word can administer baptism ; but only one endowed with the necessary gifts can preach. 3. By reason of use. The preaching of the Word is daily to be repeated as food for the soul, without which we cannot live long ; while it is enough that baptism be received once. Nevertheless by this comparison we do not diminish aught from the worth of baptism " (BALDWIN). **Not in wisdom of words.** Apprehending that the importance that he attaches to preaching the Gospel may be misconstrued into an endorsement of a display of oratorical power or of logical acuteness,[1] he immediately makes this limitation. **The cross be made void.** Since, as self is asserted, Christ is depreciated. He is "emptied," "dwindles to nothing, vanishes, under the weight of rhetorical ornament and dialectic subtlety" (LIGHTFOOT).

(B.) *Corinthian Errors Concerning Wisdom* (1 : 18—3 : 3).

1. *Their False Search for Wisdom* (1 : 18—2 : 5).

18-31. For the word of the cross is to them that are perishing foolishness; but unto us which are being saved it is the power of God. For it is written,
        I will destroy the wisdom of the wise,
        And the prudence of the prudent will I reject.
Where is the wise? where is the scribe? where is the disputer of this world? hath not God made foolish the wisdom of the world? For seeing that in the wisdom of God the world through its wisdom knew not God, it was God's good pleasure through the foolishness of the preaching to save them that believe. Seeing that Jews ask for signs, and Greeks seek after wisdom: but we preach Christ crucified, unto Jews a stumbling-block, and unto Gentiles foolishness; but unto them that are called, both Jews and Greeks, Christ the power of God, and the wisdom of God. Because the foolishness of God is wiser than men; and the weakness of God is stronger than men.

For behold your calling, brethren, how that not many wise after the flesh, not many mighty, not many noble, *are called:* but God chose the foolish things of the world, that he might put to shame them that are wise; and God chose the weak things of the world, that he might put to shame the things that are strong; and the base things of the world, and the things that are despised, did God choose, *yea* and the things that are not, that he might bring to nought the things that are: that no flesh should glory before God. But of him are ye in Chirst Jesus, who was made unto us wisdom from God, and righteousness and sanctification, and redemption: that, according as it is written, He that glorieth, let him glory in the Lord.

[1] See HATCH's *Influence of Greek Ideas and Usages upon the Christian Church* for examples of the influence of the discourses of the Sophists upon the sermon in the Church.

II. 1-5. And I, brethren, when I came unto you, came not with excellency of speech or of wisdom, proclaiming to you, the mystery of God. For I determined not to know anything among you, save Jesus Christ, and him crucified. And I was with you in weakness, and in fear, and in much trembling. And my speech and my preaching were not in persuasive words of wisdom, but in demonstration of the Spirit and of power: that your faith should not stand in the wisdom of men, but in the power of God.

Vers. 18-19. Directly contradictory to that which is involved in the preaching of the Gospel, are the strained efforts at display belonging to human wisdom. Two classes are mentioned, viz. those who are perishing, i. e. those who are on the way that leads to destruction (Rom. 6 : 21), and those that are being saved, i. e. those now justified by faith, and in whom sanctification is progressing, which will reach its goal in everlasting life (Rom. 6 : 22). " In the language of the N. T., salvation is a thing of the past, a thing of the present and a thing of the future. St. Paul says sometimes "ye (or we) were saved" (Rom. 8 : 24), or "ye have been saved" (Eph. 2 : 5, 8), sometimes " ye are being saved " (1 Cor. 15 : 2), and sometimes "ye shall be saved " (Rom. 10 : 9, 13). It is important to observe this, because we are thus taught that salvation involves a moral condition, which must have begun already, though it will receive its final accomplishment hereafter " (LIGHTFOOT). **Foolishness.** An absurdity. (See vers. 22, 23.) **Power of God.** (See Rom. 1 : 16.) Ver. 19 is quoted from the LXX. of Is. 29 : 14, with one variation in perfect harmony with the meaning.

Ver. 20, a paraphrase of Is. 33 : 18, means simply : What do all the discussions of those who are revered for their learning in earthly things amount to, when they come to the treatment of spiritual subjects? **Hath not God made foolish,** viz. by leaving the wise to the results of their own speculations. Rom. 1 : 21-25, gives one illustration. The thoughts of this chapter were in the Apostle's mind and were given fuller elaboration in the later Epistle to the Romans.

Ver. 21. **In the wisdom of God.** God, in His wisdom, i. e. in the exercise of that attribute, whereby He adjusts means to the attainment of predetermined ends so arranged. This is the same as the Providential government of human history for the working out of His scheme of Redemption. It belonged to this scheme, that the world, by its own wisdom, was not to know God, and that, when the impotence of the world in this respect would be fully demonstrated, a new and entirely strange revelation of life would be disclosed to those who would receive it. **Through the foolishness of the preaching.** "The preaching" means what is preached. To the natural man, and according to all the standards of purely secular learning, the Gospel is nothing but foolishness. "When even the most able and learned men upon earth read or hear the Gospel of the Son of God, and the promise of eternal salvation, they cannot, from their own powers, perceive, apprehend, understand or believe and regard it true, but, the more diligence and earnestness they employ, in order to comprehend with their reason, these spiritual things, the less they understand and believe, and before they become enlightened or taught of the Holy Ghost, they regard this only as foolishness or fictions" (FORMULA OF CONCORD, p. 553). **Save them that believe.** The present participle, "that are believing," shows that faith is not properly an act but a habit, or temper, a disposition and attitude towards God. It is to the believing, whose heart turns away from self towards God, that the revelation of a Crucified Christ is made. In them the work of salvation is progressively realized (ver. 18), as they continue believing. The "being saved" and the "are believing" go together. The question is not: "When did I believe?" but "Do I now believe?" and "Will I continue to believe until the end?"

Ver. 22. **Jews ask for signs.** The world is regarded as divided into two classes, Jews and Greeks. The characteristic of the former was the love of external display, the ambition of material greatness. Not understanding the true nature of the Kingdom of God, they were constantly seeking for the visible, the tangible. Signs of Christ's divine authority were constantly offered them; but these they disregarded, and demanded others to their own liking (Matt. 12 : 38; 16 : 1; John 2 : 18; 4 : 48). Even after the Resurrection, in connection with the preaching of the Apostles, there seemed to be the calling for other signs than those afforded by the Holy Spirit. The omission of the article is significant. It is not "the Jews," but simply "Jews," as a class. **Greeks seek after wisdom.** The demand of Jews was loud and clamorous "ask for;" that of the Greeks was silent and habitual. They had a taste only for those things which they could understand, and concerning which they could philosophize.

Ver. 23. **We preach Christ crucified.** Not Christ, as a worker of miracles, to please the Jews; or Christ, as a teacher of divine wisdom, to please the Greeks. Christ was both; nevertheless, both relations were entirely subordinate to this redeeming work by His death upon the Cross. In opposition to the prejudices of men, the cross must occupy the foreground in all the Church's preaching. Not Jesus as an heroic character of supernatural birth, or as the exemplar of a holy life, or as a divine lawgiver, or as the best and greatest of this world's teachers,—nothing but the humiliated, suffering, bleeding, dying Jesus will avail as the ground and assurance of man's salvation. The penalty for the world's sin must be met by an all-sufficient Saviour, or the conscience can never find peace. "Christianity begins not with solving intellectual difficulties, but with satisfying the heart that longs for forgiveness" (FAUSSET). **Unto Jews a stumbling-block.** Because contrary to all their ideas of a victorious and triumphant Monarch for whom they looked in the Messiah. **Unto Gentiles foolishness.** Because they looked for redemption and salvation to intellectual effort and the attainment of wisdom. "How can God die," they asked; and "how can the dead be raised again" (Acts 17 : 32). Those who hold that man can be morally reclaimed by the leavening power of culture, and that education is regeneration, belong to this class.

Vers. 24-25. **That are called,** i. e. Believers. (Cf. Rom. 8 : 28.) By naming them "the called," emphasis is placed upon the fact that the ground of their salvation lies in something placed entirely outside of themselves. Even their faith has been enkindled or awakened by the call. **Christ,** repeated to make the contrast more marked. **Power of God** in opposition to the stumbling-block of the Jews. The Jews demanded signs of divine power. But they knew not what divine power was. The earthly power after which they grasped was only a shadow; that of a Crucified Christ alone has reality. "Christ Crucified" is the power of God, because, through death, He overcame death (Hebr. 2 : 14). **Wisdom of God,** in opposition to the "foolishness" of the Jews. In the Cross of Christ, the mystery of all pain and suffering is solved. Justice and mercy are reconciled. Ver. 25 is elliptical. The meaning is that the foolishness of God is stronger than all the wisdom, and the weakness of God, than all the strength of men.

Ver. 26. Paul confirms this statement by an appeal.

"Look around you," he says, "at those who constitute your Christian brotherhood of the called, and see whether my statement be not verified." **Calling** is put here for those who are called. **Not many.** "Thank God for the letter m," was the remark of a devout English lady of noble birth. The early Christians comprised very few persons of position and influence. But Erastus, the treasurer of Corinth (Rom. 16:23), was an exception. **Wise,** scholars. **Mighty,** prominent officials. **Noble,** of distinguished ancestry. "God caught orators by fishermen; not fishermen by orators" (AUGUSTINE).

Vers. 27, 28. **Foolish, weak** and **base** are the contrasts respectively with "wise," "mighty" and "noble" of ver. 26. **The things that are not,** i. e. Those which are of no account in the ordinary estimation of the world (Matt. 11:25). Thus it was at the introduction of Christianity, and thus it has been at all stages of the Church's history. This, however, does not derogate from the importance of consecrated learning, station, influence and wealth, as powerful auxiliaries for the diffusion of the kingdom of God. But when their proper subordination to Christ's cause is forgotten or ignored, then the Lord knows how to choose other instruments by which He declares His independence of their service.

Ver. 29. **That no flesh,** i. e. That every boast springing from an earthly source may be silenced.

Ver. 30. **But of him are ye in Christ Jesus.** Two thoughts are here: *First,* a contrast is made ("But") with the glorying of the flesh. Christians have something whereof to glory—a thought which reaches full expression in the next verse. *Secondly,* the declaration that Christians are what they are, viz. that they are in Christ Jesus, comes of God's work for and within them. (Comp. Eph. 2:8.)

Who was made unto us wisdom from God. Better translated: "who became," viz. by His incarnation and the obedience He rendered in His incarnate Person. **Wisdom** recurs to the thought of ver. 24. God's wisdom was revealed in a crucified Christ. **Righteousness and sanctification and redemption.** These are three factors of the wisdom from God, or rather three spheres in which it is revealed. The Greek has no conjunction between "wisdom" and "righteousness," as both English versions have. "Righteousness" refers to the wisdom of God, in its provisions for our justification—so clearly explained in the Epistle to the Romans. "Sanctification" refers to the same wisdom in its accomplishing our purification from sin and our positive, aggressive holiness, by the power of Christ in us, and the ever active agency of the Holy Spirit. "Redemption" is used here for our final glorification, our attainment of the complete enjoyment of the redemptive work of Christ. While "redemption" properly refers to the payment of the price of our sins, it sometimes, as here, denotes the full accomplishment of that for which Christ suffered (Luke 21 : 28; Rom. 8 : 23; Eph. 1 : 14 ; 4 : 30).

Ver. 31. **That** connects with "are ye" of ver. 30. The thought is : God has done for you all this, in order that you may have a true ground for boasting. What follows is an abridged quotation from the LXX. of Jer. 9 : 23, 24; 1 Sam. 2 : 10. In their full form, these passages refer to the wise, the mighty and the rich, almost the same as in ver. 26.

Chapter II.

Ver. 1. In accordance with the above explanation of the true nature of the Gospel, Paul proceeds to defend his preaching against those who questioned his authority and depreciated his influence, because he did not resort to the philosophical and oratorical mode of speaking which was so greatly admired by the Greeks. **Brethren.** (See above on 1 : 10.) **Mystery of God.** Marginal reading: "Testimony" is still preferred by some of the best critics, upon the assumption that mystery "has probably crept in from ver. 7." (See ELLICOTT, LIGHTFOOT, etc.)

Ver. 2. **I determined not to know.** Translation defective. It should be: "I did not determine to know anything," i. e. It was not my purpose, I made no effort to consider anything but a crucified Christ. But he does not say that he made the effort to exclude all other knowledge. His sole object was a positive one, to know Christ. **Save Jesus Christ, and him crucified.** Not the Son of God in His pre-existent glory with the Father, not Christ even as Risen and Ascended; not Christ within, as the power of a new life, or before us as a model; not Christ as a divine teacher. All these relations of Christ have their place in Christian teaching. But they can be profitably received, and can, therefore, be taught to edification, only when the doctrine of the cross occupies the chief place in the mind, and hearts of the hearers. More persons might have been attracted to the Corinthian congregation, if Paul had passed by this doctrine, and explained to them only the Sermon on the Mount. But he puts this most offensive doctrine in the front, and excludes all who will not accept it.

Ver. 3. **In weakness.** The consciousness of weakness produced, on the one hand, by his deep sense of the importance of his message and the vast results dependent upon its proper presentation, and, on the other, by his recognition of his own defects that seem to disqualify him for so great a work. **In fear and in much trembling.**

"The expression 'fear and trembling' (2 Cor. 7:15; Eph. 6:5; Phil. 2:12) seems always used by the Apostle to mark that anxious solicitude that feels it can never do enough" (ELLICOTT). "Each word is an advance upon the other. The sense of weakness produced fear. The fear betrayed itself in much trembling" (LIGHTFOOT).

Ver. 4. **My speech and my preaching.** The former is a general term referring to every mode in which he presented the truth, the latter refers to its more elaborate form in public addresses. **Persuasive words.** He did not seek to move men by the arts of the logician, rhetorician, philosopher, or orator. **In demonstration of the spirit and of power.** His speech abounded in proofs that reached men's hearts through the power of the Holy Spirit who spoke in and through Him.

Ver. 5. **Not in the wisdom of man.** For faith must have a firmer basis than philosophical arguments or logical clearness or oratorical force. The Apostle, with his thorough training in the schools, could have availed himself of any of these expedients; but he feels they are beneath the dignity of his subject, and in the end will retard, instead of advance the Gospel.

2. *Contrast between True and False Wisdom.*

6-16. Howbeit we speak wisdom among the perfect: yet a wisdom not of this world, nor of the rulers of this world, which are coming to nought: but we speak God's wisdom in a mystery, *even* the *wisdom* that hath been hidden, which God foreordained before the worlds unto our glory: which none of the rulers of this world knoweth: for had they known it, they would not have crucified the Lord of glory: but as it is written,

Things which eye saw not, and ear heard not,
And *which* entered not into the heart of man,
Whatsoever things God prepared for them that love him.

But unto us God revealed *them* through the Spirit: for the Spirit searcheth all things, yea, the deep things of God. For who among men knoweth the things of a man, save the spirit of the man, which is in him? even so the things of God none knoweth, save the Spirit of God. But we received, not the spirit of the world, but the spirit which is of God; that we might know the things that are freely given to us by God. Which things also we speak, not in words which man's wisdom teacheth, but which the Spirit teacheth; comparing spiritual things with spiritual. Now the natural man receiveth not the things of the Spirit of God: for they are foolishness unto him; and he cannot know them, because they are spiritually judged. But he that is spiritual judgeth all things, and he himself is judged of no man. For who hath known the mind of the Lord, that he should instruct him? But we have the mind of Christ.

Ver. 6. Is there, then, no place in Christianity for any but the most elementary doctrines? Paul answers, when he says: **We speak wisdom among the perfect,** i. e. among the full-grown or mature. (Comp. Phil. 3 : 15; Heb. 5 : 14.) The latter passage brings out most clearly this principle. It is the mark of a diseased life, if men must for years be confined to "the first principles," and be fed only with milk (Heb. 5 : 12, 13). Our Lord Himself teaches the principle of adaptation of doctrine to various stages in the Christian life in John 16 : 12. A comparison of the earlier with the later epistles of St. Paul will show how he applied it. " Such **wisdom** we have in the Epistles to the Colossians and Ephesians, and in a less degree in the Epistles to the Romans " (LIGHTFOOT). It is also found in the treatment of the doctrine of the Resurrection in Ch. XV. of this Epistle. **Rulers of this world.** All human authorities, that are held in high esteem for learning, judgment, influence, etc. **Which are coming to naught.** In the light of the wisdom taught by Christ, they are found ignorant and impotent.

Ver. 7. **God's wisdom** is contrasted with man's. **In a mystery,** i. e.: In our declaration of the mystery of the incarnation and sufferings of Christ, we proclaim God's wisdom, viz. the plan of salvation which His wisdom devised. Throughout Paul's Epistles the word " mystery" means something which had been hidden, but is now revealed. (See Rom. 11 : 25 ; 16 : 25 ; Col. 1 : 26, etc.) **Unto our glory,** i. e. so that we be brought at last to the complete enjoyment of His glory. Thus the bright hope of the humble and despised Christian is contrasted with the waning power and influence of those who now enjoy the world's favor, as described in ver. 6.

Ver. 8. **Rulers of this world.** Those who were responsible for the crucifixion of Christ, Jews and Gentiles, Scribes and Pharisees, Herod and Pilate. **The Lord of glory.** Glory is the sum of all the attributes of God. (See on Rom. 1 : 23.) The Lord of glory, therefore, is One invested with these attributes. Thus God is called in Acts 7 : 2 "The God of glory," since to Him alone belongs glory (Rev. 5 : 13; Is. 6 : 3; John 12 : 41). Whatever glory creatures attain, He imparts to them from His fulness, out of pure grace. To none but God does it belong absolutely, essentially or by right (Is. 48 : 11).

Ver. 9. **But as it is written.** This introduces a free quotation and adaptation of Is. 64 : 4. Origen says the passage occurs in the very form cited by Paul in the *Apocalypse of Elias;* but Jerome denies this. MEYER accepts Origen's view. Its original derivation from Isaiah is manifest. **Things which eye saw not.** The object of the verb " we speak " or in apposition to " wisdom " in ver. 6. The contrast is here made between the science of the world of sense, and the science of the world of faith. Even philosophy, when it enters the sphere of the intellectual, becomes nothing more than a science building upon phenomena cognizable by sense. This wisdom surpasses, however, even all the objects of human thought and imagination. **Whatsoever things God prepared.** This is also the object of " we speak."

Ver. 10. **God revealed.** However unknown they may be to others, we now know them. **To us,** being in the same person and number with "we speak," refers evidently not to Christians in general, but to the Apostles and other teachers of the Word; since this is a defence of their teaching, as contrasted with that of the philosophers of their day. **Through the Spirit.** (See Eph. 1:17; 3:3, 5.) **The Spirit searcheth all things.** "Not that He is ever ignorant of them, but because He has a precise and accurate knowledge of them; as God is said to search the hearts (Jer. 17:10), because He shines through the most remote recesses and darkness of the mind." **The deep things of God.** God's most hidden counsels; God's most profound thoughts. This passage is a most conclusive one as to the Personality of the Holy Spirit. No mere force could be represented as making such a search, and, therefore, knowing all things.

Ver. 11. **Who among men knoweth?** That is, a man's own spirit is better informed that other men are concerning his own life and doings. So the Holy Spirit knows all the things of God.

Ver. 12. **We received not the Spirit of this world,** which judges according to earthly and carnal standards, heavenly and spiritual things, and is, therefore, brought to naught within this sphere (ver. 6). **The Spirit which is of God,** viz. the Holy Spirit (John 14:17; Rom. 8:15). **That we might know.** If He who abides in God and searchest the deep things of God (ver. 10), lives and acts in us, He must undoubtedly communicate to us His hidden wisdom. His "search" indicates not only His knowledge, but His incessant activity in the exercise of His knowledge. Hence guiding believers into all truth (John 16:13, 14), they have wisdom and knowledge far exalted above the transitory speculations and glimpses of truth imparted by human science. **The things that are freely given to us by God,** or, as the clause might just as well have been translated, "the gifts of God's grace that were made ours." Such are the factors of divine wisdom enumerated in 1 : 30; or those of the kingdom of God, in Rom. 14 : 17. In this way, all that Christ said was brought to the minds of the Apostles (John 14 : 26), together with its correct application and development with respect to the ever changing wants and relations of the Church. A very clear proof of the doctrine of the inner witness of the Holy Spirit, such as is taught in Rom. 8 : 16.

Ver. 13. **Not in words which man's wisdom teaches.** The subjects of knowledge and the standard whereby they are interpreted, and the faculties whereby they are perceived, being so different, the language and style must likewise greatly vary. Here all the rules of art of heathen rhetoricians and philosophers must fail. For he in whom the Holy Spirit lives and through whom the Spirit works, lives in another world, and must speak another tongue. **But which the Spirit teacheth.** "The notion of a verbal inspiration in a certain sense is involved in the very conception of an inspiration at all, because words are at once the instruments of carrying on and the means of expressing ideas, so that the words must both lead and follow the thought" (LIGHTFOOT). The words are the correct expression of the inspired thought. Revelation comes first; then comes the communication of this revelation to others through the medium of human language. **Comparing spiritual things with spiritual.** Far better is the first marginal reading: "Combining spiritual things with spiritual." A mathematical truth is expressed in the technical language of Mathematics; a chemical truth in that of Chemistry; a logical principle in the terminology of Logic; a musical direction in the nomenclature of

Music. So spiritual thoughts seek expression in spiritual words and forms of statement; spiritual truths demand spiritual methods.

Ver. 14. **Now the natural man.** It is difficult to express the full force of this adjective in English. A contrast is made between a man with a soul (*psychical*) and a man with a spirit (*spiritual*), ver. 15. The same contrast appears in connection with the doctrine of the resurrection (15 : 44, 46). A similar contrast between the soul and the spirit is made in Heb. 4 : 12 and 1 Thess. 5 : 23. The use of "soul" and "body" (Matt. 10 : 28), and again of "spirit" and "body" (Rom. 8 : 10, 13 ; 1 Cor. 5 : 3), to designate the two parts of human nature, shows that "spirit" and "soul" cannot refer to distinct things. They designate one and the same thing in two different relations. The "soul" is the immaterial principle of human nature, so far as it is concerned with merely earthly things; the "spirit," the same principle as occupied with spiritual and heavenly things.[1] When "soul" and "spirit" are contrasted, the soul refers to man's intellectual and moral nature without the Holy Spirit, i. e. in its unregenerate state. The *psychical* man is "man devoted in his thoughts and strivings to the phenomenal world and lost in it" (MÜLLER, *Christian Doctrine of Sin*, 2 : 398). "The higher principle of life, the human spirit which he has, is not laid hold of and quickened by the Holy Spirit" (MEYER). **Receiveth not,** i. e. rejects. **The things of the Spirit of God,** i. e. the mysteries of faith. **Because they are spiritually judged.** The unregenerate man is without the faculty or organ to apprehend spiritual things. In order that a landscape be appreciated, it is not enough to lead one to an elevation that commands it; he must have eyes to see it. In order that a letter convey its message

---

[1] See my *Elements of Religion*, p. 256 sq.

to the person addressed, he must know the language in which it is written. So in order that spiritual things may reach the heart and be savingly understood and applied, the Holy Spirit must be given. Otherwise they are foolishness, like the formula stating the results of chemical discovery to one ignorant of Chemistry. That unregenerate men reject Christianity and deride its mysteries, is only what is to be expected. Men need no new revelations; but they need only to become spiritually minded in order to read what God has already revealed.

Ver. 15. **He that is spiritual**, i. e. the regenerate man, in whom the Holy Spirit dwells. **Judgeth all things.** He apprehends and appreciates divine things. "Some things we must love in order to know" (PASCAL). But besides these, even earthly things are seen and judged in a new light, in new relations and according to new standards. **Is judged of no man**, i. e. by no unregenerate and unrenewed man, since such a one is utterly incapable of understanding and appreciating what comes from the Holy Spirit. "A regenerate man cares nothing, therefore, for the perverted judgments of the unregenerate, to whom the wisdom of God seems to be foolishness. Nor do human schemes for governing the church avail, unless they be controlled by the Holy Spirit, since the Church is the spiritual kingdom of Christ, which cannot be ruled after the model of worldly governments" (BALDWIN).

Ver. 16. **Who hath known the mind of the Lord?** The line of thought is: Just as certainly as we are spiritual, do we have the Holy Spirit within us teaching us from the deep things of God which He searches. Our mind, thus pervaded by the Holy Spirit, who unites us to Christ so that Christ thinks and judges and works in and through us (Rom. 8 : 10; Gal. 2 : 20; Eph. 3 : 17), is thus the mind of Christ (Phil. 2 : 5). What weight, therefore, should we give to the opinions of an unregenerate man concerning that which we have thus learned from the Lord Himself? The first sentence is a quotation of Is. 40 : 13.

3. *Their Incapacity for a Higher Wisdom the Explanation of the Simplicity of Paul's Preaching.*

1-3. And I, brethren, could not speak unto you as unto spiritual, but as unto carnal, as unto babes in Christ. I fed you with milk, not with meat; for ye were not yet able *to bear it:* nay, not even now are ye able: for ye are yet carnal: for whereas there is among you jealousy and strife, are ye not carnal, and walk after the manner of men?

Ver. 1. So far the argument has been: Paul answers the objections to the plainness and simplicity of his preaching, by stating that this was designed. The taste and standard of the Corinthians had been perverted, so that they elevated the modes of the heathen rhetoricians about them to models of proper preaching. He shows that Christian teaching has still more profound doctrines to unfold, than those upon which he had dwelt—doctrines necessary for the advanced Christian (2 : 6); but that these doctrines could not find a place, until the more elementary doctrines were first apprehended and assimilated. Now comes the application. **Brethren.** You may generally expect a gentle rebuke, when Paul uses this word. (See on 1 : 10.) **Could not speak unto you,** etc. A touch of irony! In their imagination, Paul had been deficient, and they had elevated themselves above him as critics. This compels him to tell them, how, in accommodation to their weakness and ignorance, his gifts had been repressed and all advanced instruction been withheld. **As unto spiritual.** (See above, ver. 15.) Paul's expression is strong. He means to say that although they are " brethren," and as such regenerate Christians (even saints, 1 : 2), yet that the spiritual life in them is so feeble, that it would seem almost as though it were altogether absent, when their dissensions are considered. **As unto carnal.** Two words for "carnal" are used in this paragraph. The difference may be indicated by the two words "fleshly," having the characteristics, or partaking of the nature of flesh, of ver. 3, and "fleshy," made of flesh, as here. A very emphatic term. Until such conduct would cease, he would be necessitated to treat them as men in whom "the flesh" (see the entire seventh chapter of Romans) had the upper hand. **As unto babes in Christ.** He at once softens the expression. He would not do them the least wrong or injustice. The least spark of Christian life must be acknowledged and cherished. Beneath the outbreaks of their carnal nature, he could recognize the new man growing in much weakness; and, hence, had to direct all his efforts to its support, until it reached maturity.

Ver. 2. **I fed you with milk.** (See on ver. 6.) (Comp. Heb. 5 : 13, 14.)

Ver. 3. **Ye are yet carnal.** (See on ver. 1.) The milder form of "carnal" is here used, meaning "partaking of the nature of the flesh." **Jealousy and strife.** The former an inner feeling; the latter its external expression in words. **Walk after the manner of men**, i. e. Act as unregenerate men are in the habit of doing (Matt. 16 : 23), who are always stirring up quarrels concerning matters of little moment, and such as could readily be settled by any earnest efforts for personal conference and the disposition to make concessions.

4. *The Grounds of the Controversy Examined, and a Decision given.*

4-23. For when one saith, I am of Paul; and another, I am of Apollos;

are ye not men? What then is Apollos? and what is Paul? Ministers through whom ye believed; and each as the Lord gave to him. I planted, Apollos watered; but God gave the increase. So then neither is he that planteth any thing, neither he that watereth; but God that giveth the increase. Now he that planteth and he that watereth are one : but each shall receive his own reward according to his own labour. For we are God's fellow-workers : ye are God's husbandry, God's building.

According to the grace of God which was given unto me, as a wise masterbuilder I laid a foundation; and another buildeth thereon. But let each man take heed how he buildeth thereon. For other foundation can no man lay than that which is laid, which is Jesus Christ. But if any man buildeth on the foundation gold, silver, costly stones, wood, hay, stubble; each man's work shall be made manifest: for the day shall declare it, because it is revealed in fire; and the fire itself shall prove each man's work of what sort it is. If any man's work shall abide which he built thereon, he shall receive a reward. If any man's work shall be burned, he shall suffer loss : but he himself shall be saved; yet so as through fire.

Know ye not that ye are a temple of God, and *that* the Spirit of God dwelleth in you? If any man destroyeth the temple of God, him shall God destroy; for the temple of God is holy, which *temple* ye are.

Let no man deceive himself. If any man thinketh that he is wise among you in this world, let him become a fool, that he may become wise. For the wisdom of this world is foolishness with God. For it is written, He that taketh the wise in their craftiness : and again, The Lord knoweth the reasonings of the wise, that they are vain. Wherefore let no one glory in men. For all things are yours; whether Paul, or Apollos, or Cephas, or the world, or life, or death, or things present, or things to come; all are yours; and ye are Christ's; and Christ is God's.

Ver. 4. **Of Paul . . . Of Apollos.** Paul specified only two of the parties as examples ; and, with characteristic generosity, names that attached to himself, and to his most intimate associate. **Are ye not men,** i. e. . . . Like other men ; mere men, unregenerate and unrenewed. A stronger word than " carnal " of ver. 3, and equivalent to " carnal " of ver. 1. The whole tendency of the world without Christ is towards dismemberment and disintegration. The common interests of all work and faith in Christ, their partisan feeling denied.

Ver. 5. **What,** more emphatic than who. **Ministers,**

and, therefore, as subordinates, not to be regarded as masters. As instruments through which God brings us to faith, they are to be held in high esteem. " Equal in office, they are unequal in gifts ; and according to the inequality of their gifts, there are different grades of ministers " (BALDWIN). This diversity of gifts is expressed in the words : **Each as the Lord gave to him.**

Ver. 6. **I planted, Apollos watered.** Two different parts of one and the same work. Different portions of the labor belong to each according to their diverse gifts. Important as is the planting, what is it without the watering; important as is the watering, what is it without the planting? Acts XVIII. and XIX. will show the relation of the work of Paul to that of Apollos. Our Lord uses still another figure to describe the same relation in John 4: 37, 38. **God gave the increase.** The results of their ministry came neither from the planting or the watering, but from Him who wrought through both. (Comp. Ps. 127 : 1, 2.)

Ver. 8. **Are one.** " Not in substance or person, nor in grade, gifts, calling, authority, time, labor or reward ; but one in ministry, faith, charity, purpose ; workmen of one Lord, defenders of one faith, guides to one Heaven. They are one as they subserve one another ; for both serve the Divine Highness " (CALOVIUS after THEODORET). **Each shall receive his own reward.** Hence his friends need not be uneasy, as though justice shall not be done him, or be moved, on that account, to excite controversies. (Comp. 1 Tim. 5 : 25.) If the one actually surpass the other, this will be recognized by the impartial Judge of all. **According to his own labor.** " *Secundum laborem, non propter laborem.* According to, but not on account of his labor ; for we merit nothing before God " (CALOVIUS). The rewards are the rewards of grace, given because of God's free promise; and not because anything has been actually earned. (See my *Elements of Religion*, pp. 217 sq.)

Ver. 9. **For** connects with the assurance of the certainty of reward. There is no doubt, he says, concerning the fact that each one shall be rewarded; for it is God's co-laborers that we are, and it is in God's work that we are engaged. God is not a husbandman who forgets to pay His farm-hands; nor is He one for whom a house is built who will defraud His workmen.

Ver. 10. **According to the grace of God.** An application of "as the Lord gave" of ver. 5. Paul illustrates the principle, by elaborating the illustration of the "building" that has just been given. He makes prominent the thought, that whatever he has been able to do, he has done by the grace of God; thus excluding all boasting. **As a wise masterbuilder.** Gr.: "Architect." Even His wisdom was a gift of grace. **I laid a foundation.** That was his entire office. The Church rests not upon the persons of the Apostles, but upon the foundation which God's grace laid through them. **Another buildeth thereon.** The reference is not only to Apollos, but to each and every other teacher who followed him. It was the especial work of Paul to lay foundations. (Comp. Rom. 15: 20.) **How he buildeth,** i. e. with what materials. (See ver. 12.)

Ver. 11. **Than that which is laid.** The first thought, undoubtedly, is that the foundation, laid by Paul, is such that all who come after him can do nothing but build upon it. But the reference is still deeper. Paul himself did not, in the proper sense, lay the foundation anew, but he took a foundation that had been already laid, and made that the basis of the building. "St. Paul is here inconsistent in his language, only that he may bring out the truth the more fully. He had before asserted that he had already laid the foundation stone. Now he affirms that the foundation stone was already laid for him " (LIGHTFOOT). **Which is Jesus Christ.** The foundation which God has laid by providing an incarnate Saviour. (Comp. 1 : 30 ; also Eph. 2 : 20 ; Matt. 21 : 42 ; Acts 4 : 10 sq.; 1 Pet. 2 : 6). " Christ he calls the foundation : 1. With respect to His Person, because the salvation of the Church is found in Him, who alone could satisfy the eternal Father—which neither God alone, nor a mere man could have done. 2. With respect to His Merit, upon which our regeneration and justification, and all our hope and faith safely rest. 3. With respect to doctrine ; because whatever we ought to know of Christ, He Himself has brought us from the bosom of the Eternal Father (John 1 : 18). This foundation has been laid by God : 1. Immediately, by reason of the decree. Concerning which, see Ps. 118 : 22 ; Is. 28 : 16; Rom. 9 : 33 ; 1 Pet. 2 : 6. 2. Mediately, by the Prophetic and Apostolic doctrine, with respect to revelation and to the Church (Eph. 2 : 20). Whatever, therefore, is taught in the Christian Church, is the foundation of all other things which are necessary to be known by the Christian. For with Christ and His merit, all theological knowledge properly begins, and whatever recedes from this doctrine overthrows the Church's foundation " (BALDWIN). The relation, then, of the laying of the foundation by the Apostle, with the laying of the foundation by God, is that God provided the objective foundation, Jesus Christ, while Paul so brought this to men and brought men to this, that, by the grace attending his word, when it was accepted in the heart subjectively by faith, it became the foundation of their salvation. Neither Christ without faith nor faith without Christ avails. For while all our salvation depends on Christ, it becomes ours, only when faith receives Him; and continues ours, only as we continue to hold fast to Him. "Jesus Christ" emphasizes the personal relation implied in faith. Faith is a relation of person to person, and not the mere approval of a doctrine about a person. "Jesus" is the human name of our Lord, designating Him as a man among other men. "Christ," His official name, points to the incarnate Son of God (it belongs to neither nature apart from the other, as *logos* or "word" stands for the divine nature), and to His three-fold Mediatorial office performed for men.

Vers. 12, 13. **Gold, silver . . . hay, stubble.** Both Ephesus where this Epistle was written, and Corinth, gave abundant illustrations of the two classes of buildings, the palaces of the wealthy and the hovels of the poor. In more than one part of New York, to-day, may be seen the abodes of the richer classes, and within a few yards the huts of squatters, so mean in their appearance, and so temporary in their structure, that we are astonished that they survive the weather, even without a thought as to how they can shelter families. Oriential architecture gives many examples where not only gold and silver, but precious stones are used in lavish profusion in the adornments, such, for instance, as the Taj Mahal in Agra, India, with its exquisite mosaics of *lapis lazuli*, cornelian and jasper. Many, however, regard the "precious stones," as referring to the costlier marbles and other valuable building stones. The other structures are loosely constructed shanties, with crevices stuffed with straw, and a thatched roof above. A conflagration soon tests the relative value of the structures. Each man's work is proved. The more solid structures stand the test for a longer time; while the combustible buildings of the poor go down at once before the flames. **The day shall declare it**, viz.

primarily "the day of the Lord" (1 Thess. 5 : 2, called also in Rom. 13 : 12; Heb. 10: 25, "the day," and in 2 Thess. 1 : 10; 2 Tim. 1 : 12, 18 ; 4 : 8, "that day "). But secondarily, the testing processes of all trials and afflictions. **It shall be revealed in fire,** viz. as the ore is tested in the flames of the blow-pipe. **The fire itself shall prove,** i. e. " shall test," not " shall purge." "This passage does not sustain the fire of purgatory, but entirely extinguishes it; for only at the last day shall the fire try every man's work. The fire of purgatory, therefore, does not precede " (BENGEL).

Ver. 14. (See on ver. 8.)

Ver. 15. **He shall suffer loss.** All his work being destroyed, he shall be without any reward. **Yet so as through fire.** The figure employed is that of one who loses all his property by the flames, although he himself escapes from the conflagration by being carried through the very flames. (See Zech. 3 : 2.) This is the force of the preposition *dia* in Rom. 15 : 28. Literally: " I will go on *through* you into Spain." BALDWIN paraphrases the entire passage: "When one who has taught saving and useful things, will rejoice and enjoy his labor, as a useful workman of the Church, he who has introduced vain and useless things will see that they are of no value, and that they have no use. Hence his teachings will perish, while he himself, not overthrowing Christ the foundation, will be saved, as though snatched from threatening flames ; inasmuch as he will then discover with what peril to souls he taught those things which he formerly held in high esteem." Mal. 3 : 2, 3; 4 : 5, should be read in connection with this verse.

Ver. 16. **Ye are a temple of God.** Better: **God's temple.** The thought of a temple as an illustration connects with the building characterized by gold, silver, precious stones.

This naturally suggests the temple in all its magnificence. Paul then adapts this as an illustration. While other buildings crumble beneath the fires of the Last Day, God's temple remains secure. The reference here is not to individual believers, each one of whom is regarded as a temple, but to the Church as a whole (Eph. 2 : 21 ; 1 Tim. 3 : 15). In each particular congregation, there is the type of that which pertains to the collective Church. In amazement at the bitterness of the controversies in the Corinthian Church, he exclaims: "Don't you know that your Church is God's temple?" The Church as the communion of saints, "the sanctified in Christ Jesus," 1 : 2, has the abiding presence of the Holy Spirit. **Dwelleth in you.** Not only individually, but collectively.

Ver. 17. **If any man destroyeth the temple of God.** "In the opinion of the Jews, the temple was corrupted or 'destroyed' when any one defiled or in the slightest degree damaged anything in it, or if its guardians neglected their duties" (THAYER). God's temple, the Church, is defiled when its divinely-appointed teachers are depreciated and their influence is injured by making them only party leaders instead of the Church's common property, or when their doctrines, coming from the inspiring and enlightening Spirit of God, are degraded to the level of mere human wisdom. Personal and partisan controversy defiles and destroys the temple. **Him God shall destroy.** Death was the penalty assigned to any foreigner for entering within the precincts of the temple, as this was regarded a defilement. Paul was to learn this in his own experience (Acts 21 : 28 sq.). In applying this to the subject illustrated, we may recall the fact that our Lord warns against the sin of ascribing that which comes from the Holy Spirit, to the work of Satan, as the sin against the Holy Ghost (Matt. 12 : 32). It is a perilous thing, even in the ardor of partisan zeal, to traduce, and calumniate, and misinterpret, and misrepresent those whom God has made His witnesses. **Which temple ye are.** Both a warning and a consolation. The congregation being the temple, whatever injures it is a most grievous sin, which God will certainly punish. On the other hand, those faithful within the congregation may know that God regards every attack upon them as made against Him (Is. 54 : 17).

Ver. 18. Having shown the wrong of these partisan contests, he returns to the thought begun in 1 : 18, and makes a practical application. **In this world** limits the entire clause, and means that the person is inflated because of his imaginary attainments in earthly knowledge. **Let him become a fool,** i. e. let him learn what the Cross is and means; for this is the A B C of a higher form of wisdom, viz. that which is not of this world. **That he may be wise.** Then he will be prepared for that higher wisdom of 2 : 8, which transcends the elementary Christian instruction he now criticises.

Ver. 19. (Comp. 1 : 27.) **It is written.** (From Job 5 : 13.) "The only passage from Job in the N. T." (LIGHTFOOT). **In their craftiness.** When men endeavor to defeat the Lord by their cunning, they are caught in their own toils.

Ver. 20. From Ps: 94 : 11.

Ver. 21. **Wherefore.** Summing up the whole argument. **Let no one glory in men,** i. e. take this or that man as a party leader. (Comp. Matt. 23 : 9.) **All things are yours.** Such boasting is contrary to the universality of the Christian's heritage. So far as one is a Christian, everything and everybody belonging to Christ belongs also to him, and he also belongs to every one to whom Christ belongs. He cannot say: "Paul is mine," without saying

"Cephas is mine," or "I am Paul's," without also saying "I am Apollos' man." The very name of this series of commentaries may seem to violate this prohibition. The "Lutheran," however, does not properly stand for a party or an external organization, or for any teaching established by the authority of Luther, but for a confession of truth, and a form of a doctrine and a type of Christian life, harmonizing with Holy Scripture, of which Luther was an eminent witness and the chief instrument, under God, in bringing to clear expression. *Non doctori credendum, sed doctrinæ.* It is not the name of Athanasius that causes us to prize the doctrine of the Trinity, which he defended; but his defence of this doctrine causes us to revere the name of Athanasius. It is not the authority of Augustine which causes us to accept his doctrine of sin and grace, for we repudiate Augustine's doctrine of the Church. But we will ever revere the witness who so clearly confessed the truth in the Pelagian controversy. To maintain that Luther, or any other Church leader, is above criticism, would be contrary to this passage. Our respect for Luther is not diminished by the fact that we may admire and profit from the teaching of some who, on certain articles and under certain relations, opposed him. Calvin, and Wesley, and Pascal are ours, as well as Luther. The names of the composers of the hymns we sing, representing so many and such divers communions, tell the same story; as do also the scholars from various churches we have laid under contribution in preparing the annotations in this volume. Nor can we pledge ourselves to be the organs, or exponents, or representatives of any Church Body, however large or small, but only of the principles drawn from Holy Scripture which we believe such Body accepts and consistently maintains, and from which, nevertheless, any Church organization, like anything else wherein human infirmities abound, is liable, at some time in the future, near or far, to deviate. Our churches should be bound to Confessions of Faith, and not to the succession of bishops or professors, or to Synods and Councils, except in so far as they maintain these Confessions. The will of majorities is always variable and insecure. If the faith of Holy Scripture be clearly maintained and taught outside of our historical relations, and be denied within them, there should be no obstacle to our declaration that our sympathies must break through all partisan and sectarian barriers.

Ver. 22. **Paul or Apollos or Cephas,** i. e. : The Christian Ministry in all its forms and varied gifts. Whatever be the type of Christianity represented, all that is Christian in it belongs to us, and should be gratefully appropriated even when we testify with all emphasis against the errors which attend it. Between Paul and Apollos and Cephas, there were no such differences as those which have in later days divided Christendom. Between Paul and Apollos, the difference was as to the mode of teaching and applying the doctrine; between Paul and Cephas, it was that of the prominency given a particular article of the faith, and the emphasis laid upon a particular aspect of the mission of Christianity for the world of their day. The same principle, however, is confessed in the words of one of the most loyal sons of the Lutheran Church and confessors of the Lutheran faith of this century, Claus Harms: " The Catholic Evangelical Church is a glorious Church; it is maintained and developed chiefly by the sacraments. The Reformed Evangelical Church is a glorious Church; it is maintained and developed chiefly by the Word. The Lutheran Evangelical Church is more glorious than both; it is maintained and developed by the sacraments and by the Word of God " (Theses, 1817;

Nos. xcii.-xciv.). **Or the world.** The Christian who has appropriated the elementary instruction contained in the preaching of the Cross (1 : 21), and has been led thence to the deeper doctrines of Christianity (2 : 6), reaches a still higher stage. Everything that the world contains he now finds subserves his spiritual interests. Nature becomes an instrument to serve grace. Providence governs all things, to prepare the way for the Redemption, and to advance its application. The world's entire history; all its events, small and great, are directed towards the founding and upbuilding of the kingdom of God. All the world's philosophy, science, art, literature, government ; all its inventions and discoveries, even its recreations and enjoyments advance the spiritual welfare of the man who measures human things by divine standards and not divine things by human standards, and who thus uses this world as not abusing it (7 : 31). "The earth is the Lord's, and the fulness thereof" (Ps. 24 : 1). "Who giveth us richly all things to enjoy" (1 Tim. 6 : 17). Even the world's opposition advances the Church's progress (Rom. 8 : 37). The full realization of the declaration will come with the complete subjection of the world to Christ, and the Christian's complete participation in Christ's kingly office (Rom. 4 : 13). **Or life or death.** Antagonistic and mutually exclusive though they are, both are used for the highest good of the Christian (Phil. 1 : 21). (Comp. Rom. 8: 38 ; 14 : 8.) The child of God is the lord over death ; it is his slave, because Christ has overcome it and bound it, and delivers it to him only to work out His purposes of love. **Things present ; things to come.** While the contrast is primarily between what exists about us now, and what is in store in the future, yet BENGEL's interpretation is in general correct.

"'Things present': on the earth. 'Things to come': in heaven."

Ver. 23. **Ye are Christ's.** As belonging, therefore, to Christ, you cannot allow yourselves to be made the servants of men, or the adherents of any party so as to make its will your guide (7: 23). He traces the Christian life back to its very roots. However divided externally, he finds all united in Christ (John 17: 13). **And Christ is God's.** But who is Christ? The historical manifestation of the eternal love of God, God incarnate (John 1: 14). The independence of the Christian man is thus traced to the thoughts which God has had of him, i. e. to his existence in God's mind and God's heart, from all eternity. His relation to the incarnate Son is simply the carrying out in time of God's eternal purposes of love. The word "Christ" refers here neither to the merely human, nor the purely divine nature, but to the incarnate personality. The object is not directly to express the relation of the Son of God to the Father, but of the historical Christ, incarnate and crucified, heard and seen and looked upon and touched by many then living (1 John 1: 1), with God who dwells in light unto which man cannot approach, "whom no man hath seen, nor can see" (1 Tim. 6: 16). The Christian, as a son of God, can be the follower of no leader of a human party or faction. Party spirit destroys the consciousness of sonship with God.

5. *What Estimate should be Placed upon Christian Teachers.*

1-5. Let a man so account of us, as of ministers of Christ, and stewards of the mysteries of God. Here, moreover, it is required in stewards, that a man be found faithful. But with me it is a very small thing that I should be judged of you, or of man's judgement: yea, I judge not mine own self. For I know nothing against myself; yet am I not hereby justified:

but he that judgeth me is the Lord. Wherefore judge nothing before the time, until the Lord come, who will both bring to light the hidden things of darkness, and make manifest the counsels of the hearts; and then shall each man have his praise from God.

Ver. 1. **As of the ministers of Christ.** Not as partisan leaders, but only as those who are entirely subordinate to Christ, and are actively engaged in discharging duties which He has entrusted to them. **Stewards of the mysteries of God.** "The teachers of the revealed truths" (LIGHTFOOT). For "mystery," see 2 : 7. The Church is a large house or household. The provisions or treasures which it contains are the revealed truths. The ministers of Christ distribute and apply these truths as there is need.

Ver. 2. **Here,** not local, but "within this sphere," "in this relation." **That a man be foun dfaithful,** as a steward, is what is required, and is all that is required. He need not be a great orator, or a profound reasoner, or an entertaining converser. He is not expected to be eminent for his proficiency in the various departments of earthly learning. But he must reach the hearts and consciences of men with the truths of the Gospel. Such requirement of fidelity, however, is very comprehensive, embracing under it the various qualifications that are so fully set forth in the Pastoral Epistles.

Ver. 3. **That I should be judged,** i. e. tested, tried. LUTHER thinks that Paul here addresses the portion of the Corinthian Church that boasted of his name, and therefore, indiscriminately praised him. **Or of man's judgement.** Literally "man's day," as contrasted with the "day of the Lord," and then "man's judgment," as constrasted with God's. He does not mean that he is absolutely indifferent to their censure, or their praise, but their verdict neither decides the matter, nor in any way contributes to the decision. **I judge not.** Although a man may be presumed to be more familiar with the motives of his life than all others, nevertheless so much lies back of his own knowledge, that his own judgment must be ruled out.

Ver. 4. **I know nothing against myself.** No passage is more misunderstood as it occurs in A. V. "I know nothing by myself," as though he complains here of his inability to learn aught except by the divine assistance. It is not so much a mistranslation, as a change in the English language, since the translation was made, that leaves this impression. "The expression, 'I know nothing by him,' as equivalent to 'I know nothing against his character,' is a common one in the north of England. Instances of this expression in old English writers may be found in Davies' *Bible English*" (LIAS). LIGHTFOOT quotes from Cranmer: "I am exceedingly sorry that such faults can be proved by the queen," where he means "against the queen." We do not agree with LIGHTFOOT in interpreting this in a hypothetical sense, as though Paul meant: "Even though I were conscious of no guilt." It is not inconsistent with his confession of inherent sin marring even his most earnest efforts to do God's will, of which he complains in Rom. 7, to understand this statement literally. It means, then, that he is conscious of no neglect of his duties, as a minister of Christ. He is leaving nothing undone that fidelity requires. Beneath this fidelity, he of course ever recognizes the power of the forces of sin to withdraw and divert him from his course; and as he says in Rom. 7, sin is present with him, but he cannot detect any act in which he has wilfully yielded to its influences. **Yet am I not hereby justified.** Because the measure of his fidelity is not the measure of his knowledge. A man's guilt is not determined by his realizing that he is guilty. His innocence, therefore, cannot be established by his ignorance of his guilt (Ps. 19 : 12). **He that judgeth me is the Lord.** With no verdict should one be satisfied, except that which will stand approved before God's tribunal. Referring, as this verse does, primarily to the proper tribunal that is to decide the question of a minister's fidelity, the entire principle here set forth is entirely applicable to the question of the justification of men. Conscience cannot be satisfied with the approval or disapproval of any human court, not even with its own verdicts, for it knows its infirmities and corruption. It demands a justification that will be approved by God. The answer to the cries of the soul for such justification is given in Rom. 8 : 33.

Ver. 5. **Judge nothing.** But 2 : 15, and especially 1 John 4 : 1, appear to teach otherwise. How is this? " Paul speaks of the hasty judgment which men pass upon their teachers, in accordance with their partiality for them, or of a judgment that is based upon a slender conjecture without examination of the circumstances. This is judging ' according to the appearance ' (John 7 : 24), or, as it is here called, **before the time,** i. e. before the circumstances and causes can be properly weighed." (BALDWIN). "The time" is here "the proper time." What this is, is indicated by the next clause, viz **until the Lord come.** The final decision cannot be made until then. He who assumes more, usurps the place of the Lord Himself (Rom. 14 : 4). Facts there are in every case that cannot be known until then. **The hidden things of darkness.** Secret sins (1 John 1 : 6; 2 : 9, 11; Rom. 13 : 12; 2 Cor. 6 : 14; Eph. 5 : 11; Col. 1 : 13; 1 Peter 2 : 9). **Counsels of the heart.** The ultimate motives of all words and deeds. **Then shall each man have his praise**

from God. The praise of men is what the Corinthian aspired to obtain. Paul turns them from this, to seek for the praise which comes from God (Matt. 25 : 21. Comp. notes on 3 : 8. See also Dan. 12 : 3 ; Matt. 5 : 12 ; 2 Tim. 4 : 8 ; 1 Peter 5 : 4 ; Rev. 2 : 10). The meaning is that on that day, wherever praise will be given, it will come from God. The differences in eternal glory are also suggested, as in 3 : 8 ; 1 Cor. 15 : 41.

6. *Contrast between the Corinthians and the Apostles.*

6–21. Now these things, brethren, I have in a figure transferred to myself and Apollos for your sakes ; that in us ye might learn not *to go* beyond the things which are written ; that no one of you be puffed up for the one against the other. For who maketh thee to differ? and what hast thou that thou didst not receive? but if thou didst receive it, why dost thou glory, as if thou hadst not received it? Already are ye filled, already ye are become rich, ye have reigned without us : yea and I would that ye did reign, that we also might reign with you. For, I think, God hath set forth us the apostles last of all, as men doomed to death : for we are made a spectacle unto the world, and to angels, and to men. We are fools for Christ's sake, but ye are wise in Christ ; we are weak, but ye are strong ; ye have glory, but we have dishonour. Even unto this present hour we both hunger, and thirst, and are naked, and are buffeted, and have no certain dwellingplace ; and we toil, working with our own hands : being reviled, we bless ; being persecuted, we endure ; being defamed, we intreat : we are made as the filth of the world, the offscouring of all things, even until now.

I write not these things to shame you, but to admonish you as my beloved children. For though ye should have ten thousand tutors in Christ, yet *have ye* not many fathers : for in Christ Jesus I begat you through the gospel. I beseech you therefore, be ye imitators of me. For this cause have I sent unto you Timothy, who is my beloved and faithful child in the Lord, who shall put you in remembrance of my ways which be in Christ, even as I teach everywhere in every church. Now some are puffed up, as though I were not coming to you. But I will come to you shortly, if the Lord will ; and I will know, not the word of them which are puffed up, but the power. For the kingdom of God is not in word, but in power. What will ye? shall I come unto you with a rod, or in love and a spirit of meekness?

Ver. 6. **Have in a figure transferred.** The original is

a technical expression referring to a rhetorical expedient, whereby, under one argument, another is carried on. What has been said, he has stated with respect to himself and Apollos, who was most closely connected with him, and thus could speak with less danger of giving offence. But the principles he proves are of universal application. They rebuke every faction into which the Corinthian congregation was divided. **The things which are written,** viz. the general tenor of the O. T. Scriptures, concerning the relation of men to God. Of this we find illustrations in 1 : 31 and 3 : 19. These words also declare that in divine things no one should go beyond Scripture, as Paul himself professes in Acts 25 : 22. **For the one against the other,** i. e. elated by the esteem shown one, the other teacher is depreciated. So intense has the party spirit become, that some are gratified, when their favorite rises in relative honor, by some infirmity or defect of one whom they regard his rival.

Ver. 7. **Who maketh thee.** Changing from the plural to the singular number, he makes a personal appeal to each individual. "Suppose you do differ from others," he says, "whence does this come? Is it from any inherent excellency that you possess; or from the exercise of anything that you have apart from the gift of God? If God, then, be the source of this distinction, would it not be better for you to hesitate when you are inclined to boast?" If this be the case with respect to each individual, must it not be true also with respect to every one concerning whom they gloried?

Ver. 8. "The discourse, already in ver. 7 roused to a lively pitch, becomes now bitterly ironical, heaping stroke on stroke, even as the proud Corinthians, with their partisan conduct, needed an admonition to teach them humility" (MEYER). LIGHTFOOT condenses the thought of this section: "The Apostle bursts out in impassioned irony: 'You, it appears, are to be exalted by the Christian dispensation. You are eager to seize all the advantages, to aim at all the elevation; but you will leave to us all the hard work, all the indignities, all the sufferings. It is a very easy thing to claim all the privileges of your calling.'" **Already are ye filled.** In their imagination, there was nothing that they yet lacked. But the irony grows. "To be rich is more than to be filled, to reign is more than to be rich. It is like the boasting of the church at Laodicea (Rev. 3 : 17)" (CALOVIUS). **Without us,** i. e. without Apollos and me. **I would that ye did reign,** i. e. that all the blessings of the full enjoyment of the Messianic kingdom were already yours. Then, with cutting sarcasm, in the words **we also might reign with you,** he suggests that if such were the case, perhaps they would allow their old teachers some small share in the glories of their reign.

Ver. 9. "In your superiority, you assuredly will take pity upon us in our abasement!" **Us the Apostles last,** while it would naturally be expected from our position, as leaders of the Church, we would enjoy the highest place. The figure is that of the amphitheatre. The Apostles seem as if reserved to afford the greatest sport for a bloodthirsty audience. Not only **doomed to death,** they are to die for the amusement of their enemies. But thus it only seems; for other eyes besides are to gaze upon their sufferings. **Angels and men** limit and explain world. "The world," i. e. "both angels and men." We see no reason for limiting "angels" to bad angels. The whole universe, the good and the bad, gaze upon this spectacle. The figure was taken from the Isthmian games near Corinth. "There is, perhaps, a slight contrast intended between the Corinthians sitting by criticising, and the Apostles engaging actually in the struggle against evil—a contrast which is brought out more strikingly in the brief and emphatic sentence forming ver. 10" (SHORE). The thought then is: How easy it is for you to criticise, while we suffer all the pain and ignominy!

Ver. 10. "What very different sort of people ye are from us! Bent on knowing Christ only, and on having nothing to do with the world's wisdom, we are foolish, weak-minded men, for Christ's sake. Wise men are ye in your connection with Christ. In trembling and humility, we came forward, making little of human agency, and trusting for all success to the simple word of Christ. Ye, on the contrary, are 'men of power,' able to take up an imposing attitude, and to carry through great things!" (MEYER).

Vers. 11-13. **Even up to this present hour.** At the very time that he is writing, he and the other Apostles are enduring these privations. They lack the necessary food. On their journeys and voyages, they frequently suffer intense thirst. They are without the necessary clothing. **Are buffeted,** i. e. beaten with fists, probably intended here only to indicate in general the maltreatment inflicted upon them. **Have no certain dwelling-place,** i. e. are homeless. **We toil,** the word ordinarily used to express the painfulness of labor. **With our own hands.** As at Corinth (Acts 18:3), so also at Ephesus (Acts 20:34), Paul worked at his trade. **Being reviled, we bless.** The hard words uttered against them cannot, therefore, be accounted for by their indiscreet zeal in attacking men. The Spirit of Jesus is exhibited in their behavior under provocation (Matt. 5:44; Luke 6:27 sq.). **Filth, offscouring.** Synonymous expressions. The former refers to what is washed away when anything is cleaned : the latter what is rubbed or scoured off. The application is that the Apostles are treated as though they were the vilest objects on earth. Quite a contrast with the regal privileges some of the Corinthians thought were befitting them as Christians! (ver. 8).

Ver. 14. Paul feels now that he has gone far enough in his censures. Like a parent who has punished a child, he seems almost to recoil from his severity. With great tenderness, he begs the Corinthians to remember that, while he means every word he has written, these rebukes have been given in love. **Not to shame you.** This was not his end ; but only the means, which he employed to make them responsive to his admonitions.

Ver. 15. **Ten thousand tutors.** The Greek is "pedagogues." The pedagogue was not a teacher, but a guardian or tutor, often a slave, employed by the father, for the moral care of the child. (See SMITH's *Dictionary of Greek and Roman Antiquities*, Article *Pædagogus;* also LIGHTFOOT on Gal. 3 : 24.) The thought here is, that whoever else had exercised authority over them, their relation to the Corinthians was of an entirely different and subordinate character to that which Paul bore to them. They could have but one father ; and that father was Paul. Hence he had claims upon them that no one else had. **I begat you through the Gospel.** As a minister of Christ, he had regenerated them ; since the Holy Spirit wrought through the Word which he preached. The Word is elsewhere called the means of regeneration (1 Pet. 1 : 23 ; James 1 : 18). Here the Gospel appears as the portion of the Word that regenerates or brings faith ; since the Law brings no grace, but only leads to the knowledge of sin and makes men contrite (2 Cor. 3 : 6; John 1 : 17).

Ver. 16. **Be ye imitators of me.** "They were not

merely to be satisfied with saying they were 'of Paul,' but to do what Paul did, and bear what he bore" (ELLICOTT).

Ver. 17. **I sent Timothy.** The statement in 16 : 10 implies that he had been sent before this letter, and had either been detained, or had not expected to reach Corinth by a direct route. **My beloved son.** A comparison with ver. 5 renders it almost certain that Timothy was brought to the faith by Paul. **Into remembrance of my ways.** This means that the Corinthians had forgotten these ways.

Vers. 18–21. **Some are puffed up.** The allusion is to some of those who were unfriendly to Paul. They seem to have supposed that, since Timothy, and afterward Titus, was sent to Corinth by Paul, this indicated that the Apostle himself had given up all thoughts of coming thither at an early period. **I will come to you shortly.** But not until after Pentecost (16 : 8). **If the Lord will.** "James 4 : 15 properly censures the rashness of men in deliberating what they will do ten years hence, when they are not sure of even one hour of their life. Although we are not bound, by a perpetual necessity, to such expressions, nevertheless it is better to become accustomed to them, so that we may be exercised in the thought that all our deliberations should be subjected to the will of God" (CALVIN). **Not the word, but the power,** i. e. I will test whether there be any force back of their many and swollen words. The kingdom of God rests indeed upon the Word of God ; but this Word, unlike human words, is always efficacious (Heb. 4 : 12). "He teaches, therefore, that the Church is edified not by a mere flow of words, promoting neither a godly and happy life in this world, nor eternal salvation ; but by the true knowledge of God, by godly and ardent zeal in making confession, by true faith, patience and the like virtues, with which the power and virtue of the Holy Spirit are exercised. Where such power is found, there you have a taste of the Kingdom of God, such as the outward splendor and adornment of words lack" (CALOVIUS). **A rod, or in love.** To chastise by his severe rebukes, and even the extreme resort of Church discipline, or to freely admit them to the enjoyment of his love and confidence and approval.

III. THE MORAL DISORDERS IN THE CORINTHIAN CHURCH (Ch. 5-7).

(A.) *The Case of Incest* (5 : 1-8).

1-8. It is actually reported that there is fornication among you, and such fornication as is not even among the Gentiles, that one *of you* hath his father's wife. And ye are puffed up, and did not rather mourn, that he that had done this deed might be taken away from among you. For I verily, being absent in body but present in spirit, have already, as though I were present, judged him that hath so wrought this thing, in the name of our Lord Jesus, ye being gathered together, and my spirit, with the power of our Lord Jesus, to deliver such a one unto Satan for the destruction of the flesh, that the spirit may be saved in the day of the Lord Jesus. Your glorying is not good. Know ye not that a little leaven leaveneth the whole lump? Purge out the old leaven, that ye may be a new lump, even as ye are unleavened. For our passover also hath been sacrificed, *even* Christ : wherefore let us keep the feast, not with old leaven, neither with the leaven of malice and wickedness, but with the unleavened bread of sincerity and truth.

Ver. 1. The tendency to idealize the Apostolic Church, and regard it as, in every respect, affording a model for succeeding ages, was refuted by the account given of the disgraceful divisions of the Corinthian Church. A still more complete disproof of this idea is afforded by the instance here given of the utter neglect of Church discipline. The case is an extreme one. **Actually reported** indicates that the Apostle does not refer to indefinite rumors. He has his information from trustworthy sources concerning an offence which has become a matter of public notoriety. Any outbreak of licentiousness in a

Christian church is lamentable. But in this case it is such **as is not even among the Gentiles.** By this he means that it is such an offence against nature, that even the Gentiles are horrified when such a sin occurs among them. "It was an unspeakable crime among the Gentiles, except a few monsters" (BENGEL). Cicero, in his oration *Pro Cluentio,* refers to it as "a crime unheard of," except in the particular instance that he there notes; although some very rare cases can be found by classical students, such as Antiochus Soter and Darius, according to Plutarch, etc. (See other instances in CALOVIUS.) Hardened as was the conscience of the Gentiles, the crime of incest is so fatal to all human affection, and so overthrows the foundations of the family, that it still remained peculiarly sensitive to the very thought of such sins. One of the most celebrated of their mythological subjects is that concerning the terrible sufferings of Œdipus for his ignorant and involuntary crime of this same class, although of a different form. The sin here is evidently marriage or concubinage of a son with his stepmother (2 Cor. 7:12). The woman is not further mentioned, and must, therefore, have been an unbeliever. How such a crime, so revolting even to the Gentiles, could have occurred without rebuke in any Christian congregation, seems to us almost incredible. But the explanation is found in the place. Corinth was the Sodom of the Grecian world. Licentiousness was the prevailing sin. A thousand profligate women served as priestesses in the temple of Venus. The very atmosphere was infected by the contagion. Even those converted to Christianity retained some of their former weaknesses in apologies that would be made for wrongdoers. This offender had probably very specious excuses to offer as a cover for his vice. In other respects, he was probably a very reputable man; and the Corinthians were willing to pass by an offence, which was not probably more heinous than hundreds of others to which they were accustomed, except that it was committed by a member of the Church.

Ver. 2. **Ye are puffed up.** Why not exercise some of the zeal that expends itself in your sectarian divisions, in looking after your Church discipline? You are so earnest in attacking Paul, in order to exalt Apollos, and in attacking Apollos, in order to exalt Cephas! Would it not be better to let these ministers of the Lord Jesus alone, and to turn your attention to the matters of open scandal in the cases of your own members? You boast of your wisdom; exercise it in weighing the evidence and adjusting the penalties concerning such flagrant outrages upon the simplest principles of morality. "The more Theology is occupied with worldly wisdom, the more remote is it from the warm, living and efficacious sense of the nearness of God, and, therefore, the less is it able to comprehend the significance of Church discipline. Words take the place of deeds; ideas and definitions the place of realities, until the candlestick is taken out of its place (Rev. 2:5)" (VILMAR). **Did not rather mourn.** Every member of the Church who falls disgraces the entire Church. Every matter of offence that occurs is not limited to the individual, but affects the entire body of Christ (12:26). Achan's crime was visited upon all Israel, until the offender was punished (Joshua 7). **That he ... might be taken away from among you.** The failure to administer Church discipline in a matter of public scandal is a connivance at the offence. Its effect is to proclaim such sins as matters of relative indifference; and the perverted consciences of wicked men find in such connivance an argument by which to regard these offences as pardonable weaknesses.

Our Confessions are very clear in their statement of the necessity of Church discipline. "Excommunication is pronounced against the openly wicked, and the despisers of the sacraments" (*Apology*, 176 : 61). "The Gospel has given the command to excommunicate those whose crimes are known" (*Smalcald Articles*, 349 : 60).

Ver. 3 points out the necessity of prompt and energetic action. It shows that in the exercise of Church discipline, the co-ordinate action of the congregation and of Paul, either as its pastor, or because of his apostolate, was required. On the basis of this text, we have the general principle, that no act of discipline be determined upon, either by the congregation alone, or by the ministry alone, but by the judgment of both. The absence of Paul is provided for by his written authorization and verdict. Thus he is **present in spirit.**

Ver. 4 **In the name of our Lord Jesus Christ.** The best interpretation is to regard this clause as qualifying **to deliver.** The following paraphrase well expresses it: "I have already resolved that ye hold an assembly of the Church, in which ye shall consider me as present, furnished with the power of Christ, and in this assembly shall declare: 'Paul, in the name of Christ, with whose power he is here spiritually in the midst of us, hereby delivers over the incestuous man unto Satan'" (MEYER). The only exception that we take to this paraphrase, is that the clause **with the power of our Lord Jesus Christ**, we must regard as referring not simply to "my spirit," but to the entire gathered Church and the Apostle. The spiritual court, thus constituted, is invested with the power of Christ, Matt. 18 : 17–20, a passage that clearly shows that the power of the keys does not belong to the ministry alone, but to the Church, and to the ministry, as its divinely-appointed executive. In 2 Cor. 2 : 6, the penalty is said to have been inflicted by the majority.

Ver. 5. **To deliver unto Satan.** This has often been explained by the exercise of Apostolic power for the infliction of bodily death or disease, as in the cases of Ananias and Sapphira (Acts 5 : 5, 10) and Elymas (Acts 13 : 8). But this is not an act of the Apostle alone, but in connection with the congregation. Besides, 2 Corinthians makes no mention of any bodily, but only of spiritual suffering by sorrow for his offence, which the disciplined person endured. The act of the Church was, therefore, one of excommunication, which carried with it not only exclusion from the Word and sacraments, but also the withdrawal of all social relations (2 Thess. 3 : 14). Deprived of the means of grace, he would thus be without protection against Satan. **For the destruction of the flesh.** As frequently in Paul (see especially Rom. 7), the sinful principle in human nature. **That the spirit may be saved.** As elsewhere, for the saving of the soul. **In the day.** (See 3 : 13.) Thus even Satan may be used to advance the salvation of men and to further the progress of the kingdom of God. It is important to note the remedial end of excommunication, as in 2 Tim. 3 : 15. "Concerning no excommunicated person should we despair, but every one should take pains to deliver him from the jaws of the devil" (BALDWIN). "Had these facts been more deeply studied, there would have been a very different tone and spirit in many of the mediæval anathemas" (FARRAR).

Ver. 6. **Your glorying.** He here reverts to the thought of ver. 2. **A little leaven.** "The leaven of Scripture is always a symbol of evil, with the single exception of the parable (Matt. 13 : 33 ; Luke 13 : 20, 21), as it is for the most part also in rabbinical writers" (LIGHTFOOT on

Gal. 5 : 9). The reference does not seem to be to any future corruption, threatened by the presence of the leaven, but the known existence of the leaven as at once imparting a character to the entire mass. The world uses the vices of professed Christians, as an indication of the spirit of Christianity. A congregation permitting open scandals to occur without rebuke or punishment, is judged as though the offences were those of the congregation itself.

Ver. 7. **Purge out the old leaven.** Paul has in mind the prohibition concerning the presence of leaven in the households of the Jews during the Passover feast. " The word in Ex. 12 : 15 (LXX.) is very strong : ' Ye shall make it to vanish.' With what exactness this injunction was carried out, appears from a passage in Chrysostom : ' They even scrutinize mouse-holes, to see that no leaven is in them '" (LIGHTFOOT). To this, Paul gives here a spiritual application, " The old leaven " refers here to the remnants of the old Adam still found in them, " pride, ambition, lenity in regard to offences that should be punished," etc. (BALDWIN), " false doctrine, public vices and scandals " (CALOVIUS), " the sinful habits which still remain among you from your pre-Christian condition " (MEYER). **A new lump,** i. e. that your congregation may become partaker of all the renewing influences of the Holy Spirit. **Even as ye are unleavened,** viz. "by principle and profession " (ELLICOTT), or so far as you are regenerate. **For our passover,** etc. An additional argument for " purging out the old leaven." We have a passover of a higher kind than the Jews. We celebrate redemption, not as they did in type and figure, but perfect and complete redemption. The aorist tense is important. Literally : **Our passover was sacrificed,** viz. on the Cross.

Ver. 8. **Let us keep the feast,** i. e. Let us keep festival continually, throughout our whole lives. The former passover had to be repeated from year to year; this, as the celebration of completed redemption is never over. **Malice and wickedness;** the former, the inner disposition; the latter, its external expression. **Sincerity.** The word means that which can be judged in the full blaze of sunlight, open as noonday. **Truth,** both in words and deeds.

The selection of vers. 6–8 as the Epistle for Easter Sunday has not been without considerable criticism. Thus SOMMER (*Die Epistolischen Perikopen, Erlangen,* 1871) says: "We regard its selection as the Epistle for Easter a mistake, since it does not offer the necessary points to bring out the facts of the resurrection of Christ and its meaning. A proper sermon for the chief service on Easter should not pass by three matters: 1. That, by His resurrection, Christ proved that He was the Son of God. 2. That, by the resurrection of Christ, we are assured, with the greatest certainty, that we have forgiveness of sins through His Blood. 3. That, by Christ's resurrection, our own is pledged. But in this pericope, nothing whatever is said of Christ's resurrection; we are compelled to attach the Easter fact and its lesson to 'our passover hath been sacrificed for us, even Christ.' The sermon, however, should grow out of the text. Ranke justly regards it unliturgical, that the Epistle of a high festival, in which we expect to hear the festival fact presented in the lesson in a high tone begin with the words: 'Your glorying is not good.' The most appropriate Easter Epistle we regard that to be which is suggested by Nitzsch (1 Cor. 15: 12–20). In Würtemburg, the first Epistle is 1 Cor. 15: 1–20; the second, 1 Cor. 15: 51–58. In Saxony, 1 Pet. 1: 3–9," RANKE (*Das Kirchliche*

Pericopen system, Berlin, 1847), maintains that neither the Missals, nor other ancient documents, nor the practice of Luther, justifies the beginning of the Epistle with ver. 6. "The proper beginning is ver. 7, to which Luther added the second half of ver. 6. To me it seems best to begin with the words: 'For our passover hath also been sacrificed, etc.'"

(B.) *The Same Principles Applied to other Sins* (5. : 9–13).

9–13. I wrote unto you in my epistle to have no company with fornicators; not altogether with the fornicators of this world, or with the covetous and extortioners, or with idolaters; for then must ye needs go out of the world: but now I write unto you not to keep company, if any man that is named a brother be a fornicator, or covetous, or an idolater, or a reviler, or a drunkard, or an extortioner; with such a one no, not to eat. For what have I to do with judging them that are without? Do not ye judge them that are within, whereas them that are without God judgeth? Put away the wicked man from among yourselves.

Ver. 9. **In my epistle.** A former Epistle, of whose existence this allusion is the only trace. **To have no company.** That is, not to have them as our intimate friends and associates.

Vers. 10, 11. **Not altogether.** In these words, he guards the statement he has made against misapprehension and misapplication. It must not be interpreted, so as to prohibit the Christian absolutely from all dealings with persons of such a class. Worldly men they will necessarily be compelled to meet and be associated with, in business and political relations. Even though such persons be **covetous and extortioners or idolaters,** their duty to their calling will bring them into more or less close relations with such, as long as they are in this life. This has an especial reference to the Corinthians; "If all communication with 'fornicators' was to be forbidden, the sin was so universal, especially at Corinth, that all intercourse with Gentiles would have become impossible" (FARRAR). The distinction, however, must be made between those who, on the one hand, make no Christian profession, **fornicators of this world,** and those, on the other, who add to these sins the crime of hypocrisy, in claiming to be followers of Christ, **if any man that is called a brother be a fornicator, or,** etc. Such persons are professedly Christians, and yet their guilt, with respect to such crimes, is a matter of open scandal —the world, even, with its loose morals, knows well the flagrancy of their conduct. **An idolater.** Probably from the old leaven of heathenism which he still retained, like Laban and Rachel (Gen. 31 : 19, 32, 34). He would know well to assume, at pleasure, either his heathen or his Christian nature. An approach to this sin occurs whenever any forms of false worship are accepted, or a professed Christian, out of regard for unbelievers with whom he is associated, prays in any other name than that of Jesus, or suppresses his confession as a Christian. "I understand this to refer to those, who, although they despised idols, nevertheless, in order to gratify the godless, made a pretence of worshipping their images" (CALVIN). **Reviler, drunkard, extortioner.** Paul has probably some specific cases in view. Drunkenness is not mentioned here as an ordinary vice of the heathen. Drunkards are of little account, as business men, or in influential civil offices. Hence there was no need to express any opinion concerning intercourse with them in public life. But in the Church, such an offender could not be in any way countenanced. (See 1 Cor. 6: 10.) An interesting feature of this description is that the word used here for "drunkards" is, in classical Greek, of the feminine gender. May not this have been chosen, instead of the ordinary masculine form, in order to indicate that, with the infatuation for strong drink, all manliness perishes? **No, not to eat,** i. e.: Withdraw from all personal intimacy with any man, who, in this way, disgraces the Church. The severity of such treatment is explained by the following considerations: 1. The Church, as a divinely-appointed witness, must be clear and emphatic in its testimony, that such offences are not mere weaknesses, that may be lightly passed over, but that they are grievous sins. 2. The Church must protect itself from any inferences the world may draw concerning the representative character of such offenders. 3. The Church must seek to lead such persons to repentance, by removing from them the recognition that otherwise would comfort them, by the thought that, however self-condemned they may at times feel, they still have the esteem and confidence of Christian men.

Ver. 12 explains why professing Christians must be judged by a more rigid standard than men of the world, and why offences, which, in every-day life, we pass by in the cases of those who are not Christians, must be summarily dealt with where men profess to be brethren in Christ. **With judging,** i. e. with exercising Church discipline. **Those without.** An ordinary Jewish expression for Gentiles was used within the Church, for those who made no Christian profession (Col. 4 : 5 ; 1 Thess. 4 : 12 ; 1 Tim. 3 : 7). **Do not ye judge?** A. V. is preferable here to R. V. Interrogation should end with ver. 12. We have here an appeal in support of statement just made.

Ver. 13. **Those without God is judging.** The present tense is significant and emphatic, "serving to mark duration without reference to a beginning or ending, and thence, by a natural transition, what is changeless and unalterable" (ELLICOTT).

(C.) *How Christians should Settle their Disputes.*

1-11. Dare any of you, having a matter against his neighbor, go to law before the unrighteous, and not before the saints? Or know ye not that the saints shall judge the world? and if the world is judged by you, are ye unworthy to judge the smallest matters? Know ye not that we shall judge angels? how much more, things that pertain to this life? If then ye have to judge things pertaining to this life do ye set them to judge who are of no account in the church? I say *this* to move you to shame. Is it so, that there cannot be *found* among you one wise man, who shall be able to decide between his brethren, but brother goeth to law with brother, and that before unbelievers? Nay, already it is altogether a defect in you, that ye have lawsuits one with another. Why not rather take wrong? why not rather be defrauded? Nay, but ye yourselves do wrong, and defraud, and that *your* brethren. Or know ye not that the unrighteous shall not inherit the kingdom of God? Be not deceived: neither fornicators, not idolaters, nor adulterers, nor effeminate, nor abusers of themselves with men, nor thieves, nor covetous, nor drunkards, nor revilers, not extortioners, shall inherit the kingdom of God. And such were some of you: but ye were washed, but ye were sanctified, but ye were justified in the name of the Lord Jesus Christ, and in the Spirit of our God.

Paul has just taught that Church tribunals are not to judge those who make no Christian profession. If this be true, then it must also be true, that the members of the Church should not carry their disputes before worldly tribunals. Church courts for Church people. Worldly courts for worldly people. Christian arbitration for Christian dissensions and misunderstandings.

1. **Dare.** " The injured majesty (*læsa majestas*) of Christians is denoted by a splendid word " (BENGEL). **Before the unrighteous.** " Every unbeliever is unjust ; usually, even as a citizen " (BENGEL). **Saints.** Christians.

Ver. 2. **The saints shall judge the world.** Under Christ at the Last Day (Matt. 19 : 28 ; Luke 22 : 30 ; Acts 17 : 31 ; John 5 : 22 ; Dan. 7 : 22). The entire force of this allusion is lost, when this is interpreted in any other way, than by a real participation by Christians in the administration of the Final Judgment. In this Judgment, there can readily be such priority and subordination, that the Apostles shall have an office of especial prominence. The details of this divine arrangement are not revealed, and it is useless to speculate concerning them. Enough, that we have what is here so plainly stated. **Is judged** or " is being judged," the present tense indicating the certainty of the judgment. **The smallest matters.** Margin : " Of the smallest tribunals." The thought is : If the Lord deems Christians worthy of being associated with Him in administering justice at the Last Day, why should they regard each other disqualified to decide concerning their relatively unimportant earthly interests, and appeal to unbelievers as though among them a higher tribunal were to be found ? If they be qualified to act as judges at the highest court, why should they be disqualified from rendering a verdict at the lowest ?

Ver. 3. **We shall judge angels.** The good angels are not to be judged, as they stood the test of obedience. The bad angels are reserved for judgment (2 Pet. 2 : 4 ; Jude 6). Although fallen, nevertheless, by creation, they are highly exalted above men, and even now are endowed with superhuman powers. If the Christian is to judge those beneath whom he has been created, but above whom he has been raised by redemption, why should he be unable to judge **things that pertain to this life ?** For the latter expression see Luke 21 : 34.

Ver. 4. **Set them to judge.** The rendering of A. V. is preferable to that of R. V. **Who are of no account.** " The things pertaining to this life " being the matters of the very least account to one who understands the meaning of his Christian calling, the most insignificant persons in the Church, since even they shall judge the world and angels, are far better fitted to decide concerning them, than is any tribunal composed of unbelievers. "Here he says, with something of sarcasm: The very meanest of those who are to be exalted above angels, and to be judges of spiritual existences, is of sufficient authority to settle such matters as you are bringing before legal tribunals" (SHORE). "Those possessed of high spiritual gifts are better employed on higher matters than on settling petty wrongs among you, and thus serving tables" (LIGHTFOOT).

Ver. 5. **I say this**, etc. He has put the subject as strongly and sharply as possible, that the folly of their course may be seen; nevertheless, he deems it proper to apologize in these words, lest any one may think, that, when it would be desired, any member of the Church, however exalted, should hesitate about taking the lowest place (John 13:16; Rom. 12:16). **Is it so?** The irony continues. "I thought you boasted of your wisdom," he says. "Even the Apostles, in your opinion, could not rise to your exalted standard. How is it then that a congregation, so eminent for its wise men, could be so deficient in persons able to act as arbiters concerning worldly matters, that you must appeal to outsiders to settle your disputes? What! not even one, where there are so many wise men!"

Ver. 6. **But brother goeth to law with brother.** A complete proof that no such wise men could be found; for otherwise, he would prevent such a scandal from occurring, he would protest and advise against it, with such earnestness and persistency, that his counsels would at last be heeded. **And that before unbelievers.** As in ver. 1, with unbelievers as judges. This involved not only the making public of the weaknesses of the Church, but also the compliance, in oaths, etc., with regulations and forms that might otherwise compromise their Christianity. "It is not a question between ecclesiastical and civil courts, but between Law and Equity, Litigation and Arbitration. . . . The remedy is not more elaborate law, nor cheaper law, nor greater facility of law, but more Christianity" (ROBERTSON). If Paul were writing to the churches of the present day, can we believe that he would not in similar language condemn and censure the abuse of the religious press in the publication of reports, which, even if correct, should be presented before the proper ecclesiastical tribunals, instead of being proclaimed to the entire world? We certainly would hear the words: "Can it be that there is not one wise man among you to suggest the remedy, and to insist upon its adoption?"

Ver. 7. **A defect.** Lit.: "A falling short." **Why not rather take wrong?** Had they known nothing of our Lord's words on this subject in Matt. 5 : 40-42?

Ver. 8. **Ye do wrong and defraud.** The Christian Spirit is one of self-surrender to the good of others. The Christian Life is, in its proper conception, a continual sacrifice, that the glory of God may be advanced by the Christian's devotion to the highest interests of his fellowmen, first, of his brethren, and, then, of those without, in order that they may be made brethren (Phil. 2 : 3-5). Times come when the carrying out of this principle requires that even his life must be surrendered (1 John 3 : 16). Entirely opposite to this is the self-seeking spirit that is always sensitive as to its own rights, and is intent upon exacting from brethren the very utmost that the law allows. Besides, in every such suit before the world, the brother who has even a just claim inflicts a greater loss upon the one on the other side, than that entailed by the mere payment of what is due. The damage to reputation and character is greater than the loss of property or money. But such loss or damage pertains not to the individual alone, but to the entire church.—The words of Paul seem to indicate, however, that he actually knew of cases, where, by a legal process, some of the Corinthians, "under pretext of a legal right," had gained or were gaining possession of what justly belonged to their neighbors.

Vers. 9, 10. **The unrighteous.** In the Greek, this carries over into this verse the same word as in "do wrong" of ver. 8, and connects with it. **The kingdom of God,** i. e.: They may succeed in fraudulently gaining worldly property, and being sustained in their claims by worldly rulers, but, in the kingdom of God, they have no inheritance. **Be not deceived.** The prevalence of these sins, and their relations to those guilty of them, rendered the Corinthians too indulgent in their judgment. **Neither fornicators,** etc., specifying various current forms of wrong-doing. They are different modes of the narrowest selfishness, as contrasted with the Christian's duty of the surrender of self to the will of God and the good of his fellow-men. Some of these sins are mentioned above (5 : 10, 11). Similar lists are given in Gal. 5 : 19–21; 1 Tim. 1 : 10; Col. 3 : 5–7.

Ver. 11. He proceeds to show that the very nature of their Christian profession requires them to abhor such sins. **Such were some of you.** Among the Corinthian Christians, there were those who, in their unregenerate condition, had practised these sins. **Ye were washed.** Marginal reading: "Ye washed yourselves." "The first aorist middle cannot, by any possibility, be passive in its signification, as it is generally, for doctrinal reasons, here rendered. On the other hand, the middle sense has no doctrinal import, regarding merely the fact of their having submitted themselves to Christian baptism" (ALFORD, who suggests the translation: "Ye washed them off"). This reference to baptism may be explained by a comparison with Acts 22 : 16. "Observe the use of the middle from the conception of their self-destination for baptism" (MEYER). Man's part and act in baptism, in response to and pervaded by that of the Holy Spirit, seem intended, i. e.: "In your baptism, you not only were washed from these sins, but you yourselves renounced them and parted with them forever." **Ye were sanctified.** They were separated from the world and consecrated to God. "Sanctify" is used here in a wider sense than in technical theological use. "A fruit of regeneration whereby a Christian is externally recognized, and distinguished from unbelievers" (BALDWIN). **Justified,** in the Pauline sense, of declared or accounted righteous. For we have here the description of the Christian Life: 1. With respect to the former life of the Christian man. It is the denial, the forsaking, the putting away of its sins: "Ye washed yourselves." 2. In its present relations: A. As regarded by the world and expressed in the outward life, a consecration to God: "Ye were sanctified." B. As regarded by God, true righteousness: "Ye were justified," i. e.: Your former sins were forgiven, and God looked upon you, as though you were His very Son, Jesus Christ. Since, therefore, they have been thus justified, God expects better things of them than indifference to these sins from which He has delivered them. **In the name of the Lord Jesus.** The meritorious cause or ground. **And in the Spirit of our God,** the Divine Agent of this three-fold work. "Christ, therefore, is the source of all blessings; we obtain all things from Him; but Christ, with all His blessings, is imparted to us by the Spirit. For by faith we receive Christ, and His grace is applied to us; but the Spirit is the Author of faith" (CALVIN).

(D.) *The Religion of the Body.*

12-20. All things are lawful for me; but not all things are expedient. All things are lawful for me; but I will not be brought under the power of any. Meats for the belly, and the belly for meats: but God shall bring to nought both it and them. But the body is not for fornication, but for the Lord; and the Lord for the body: and God both raised the Lord, and will raise up us through his power. Know ye not that your bodies are members of Christ? Shall I then take away the members of Christ, and make them members of a harlot? God forbid. Or know ye not that he that is joined to a harlot is one body? for, The twain, saith he, shall become one flesh. But he that is joined unto the Lord is one spirit. Flee fornication. Every sin that a man doeth is without the body; but he that committeth fornication sinneth against his own body. Or know ye not that your body is a temple of the Holy Ghost which is in you, which ye have from God? and ye are not your own; for ye were bought with a price: glorify God therefore in your body.

The discussion in the preceding section was an episode or excursus to the main line of the Apostle's argument, which was naturally suggested by the demand for the exercise of Church discipline. Now he comes back to the subject that has engaged his attention from the beginning of the Fifth Chapter.

Ver. 12. **All things are lawful for me.** The principle of Christian Liberty, according to which the Christian is master and owner of all things, in virtue of his heirship with Christ, so forcibly asserted by the Apostle in 3:22, had been perverted and misapplied, just as Satan knew well how to quote Scripture in tempting our Lord. What gave plausibility to this misapplication was the fact that the Apostle himself had applied it to the eating of the flesh of victims, sacrificed to idols. So closely connected were these sacrifices and the licentious rites that constituted a part of the heathen worship (see Acts 15:29), that Paul's assertion of individual liberty with respect to the former was used as an authority to justify the latter. "More than one voluptuary in the Church had, as Paul was informed, actually declared that, just as satisfying the desire for food was an *adiaphoron*, so also was satisfying the desire for sensual pleasure by fornication" (MEYER). This leads him to such a complete exposition and statement of the subject in this Epistle, that his position can no longer be misinterpreted. By " all things," therefore, is meant all such things as are not *adiaphora*, or " matters of indifference." An *adiaphoron* or matter of indifference, is that which is neither commanded nor forbidden by God. It is never lawful to take God's name in vain, to kill, to commit adultery, to steal, etc. But to hold property, to take a walk, to read an entertaining book, to listen to or to furnish music, to enjoy food or drink, etc., are acts which, considered in themselves, are neither good nor wicked. They cease, however, to be *adiaphora*, whenever, whatever may be their abstract good, they are used in a manner or under conditions that God's word does not allow. I dare not hold property for which I have no moral and legal right; I dare not trespass on my neighbor's property; I dare not use time for my mere entertainment, which the duties of my calling justly require; I dare not eat or drink, so as to injure my body or do a wrong to my neighbor. **But not all things are expedient.** Two limitations, he says, must always be observed in the use of adiaphora. The first, noted by these words, is that all scandal to others must be avoided. (Comp. 8:9, 13.) **I will not be brought under the power of any.** The second limitation is that of the excessive indulgence of that which, in itself, is lawful. We must not allow ourselves to be tyrannized over by any habit. The Christian must be the complete master, and not the slave of these things. Self-discipline must not be broken down.

Ver. 13. **Meats for the belly,** etc. Another wresting of a true principle to the support of licentiousness. The adaptation of an organ of the body to the function to which it is devoted, is a current argument of those who seek physiological illustrations of Natural Theology. But those who advocated or apologized for licentious practices, argued thence that there was a similar adaptation of the body to the purposes of lust. As opposed to this, Paul declares that both the organ and the material which it digests are temporary and perishable, while the body itself has both an eternal relation, and will have an eternal existence. **The body is not for fornications, but for the Lord.** All bodily desires and appetites and gifts point towards a use of the body within spheres and limitations that the Lord has determined. My sense of taste does not justify me in appropriating for its enjoyment every object belonging to my neighbor that may subserve it, and that I can gain by craft or force. Because I have a key that unlocks my neighbor's safe, I have no right to freely use the treasures that he has stored within it. The gratification of pleasure is not the determinative end of life, or our use of either body or soul, even though, when subordinated to God's will and thus within the limits He has fixed, the teaching of Holy Scripture is clear, as to their place (1 Tim. 4 : 3-5). No one has ever rebuked asceticism more earnestly than Paul. The one guilty of the sin here mentioned, denies the Lord that sacrifice of the body which He asks (Rom. 12 : 1), and also leads or strengthens and confirms another immortal soul in sin, with whom he shares his shame and guilt. " The body is for the Lord, viz. it is His purpose that its vigor, strength, health, beauty and other gifts be consecrated to the glory and service of the Lord" (BALDWIN). **And the Lord for the body.** "How great condescension!" (BENGEL). Because the body, as well as the soul, partakes of the blessings of redemption (Rom. 8 : 23 ; Phil. 3 : 21). Christianity gives no encouragement to those who profess to despise the body, and regard it chiefly as a weight to the soul, or, as a prison, in which sin holds man's higher nature captive. "The Lord is for the body" by rendering the body "for the Lord."

Ver. 14 refers to the destiny of the body. As contrasted with what are mentioned in ver. 13, the body is to have an eternal existence after its resurrection. Of this, the resurrection of the Lord is mentioned as a pledge. (Comp. Rom. 8 : 11.) This verse shows that Paul could not have expected that the Second Coming of Christ would occur during his lifetime.

Ver. 15. **Your bodies are members of Christ.** ELLICOTT directs attention here to the contrast between the heathen and semi-heathen estimate of the body, and that which is taught by Christianity. The former says that our bodies are what we have in common with animals, the brutish side of humanity ; the latter, that our bodies are members of Christ. (Comp. Eph. 4 : 16 ; 5 : 30.) If we be Christians, then, our bodies are organically united with Christ, they are part of Christ. If a Christian could be conceived of as losing his self-respect, to such an extent, as to sin in this shameful way, is it possible that he would put what belongs to Christ, and is part of Christ, to so vile a purpose?

Ver. 16. **Is one body.** The union of any man with any woman in such relations as, by the divine appointment, belong only to husband and wife, constitute them one flesh. The sin referred to does not end with the mere act. It establishes a permanent relationship. But how can a Christian, by his sin, establish such a relation between Christ and one thus devoted to crime? The inconsistency shows that the person must lose his character as a Christian if this should occur. The members of Christ cannot be made the members of a harlot.

Ver. 17. **Is one spirit.** The closest of earthly unions makes of those thus united but one body. But the union of the Christian with his Lord not only establishes a bodily union, but above all a spiritual union, and that so close that Christ and His believing followers are one spirit. A forcible statement of the mystical union, as in John 17 : 23; Gal. 2 : 20. The inference, then, is that he who is one spirit with his Lord cannot be, at the same time, "one body with an harlot." The spirit determines and rules the body. If the Christian profession be denied by such a relation, it shows that faith has expired and the offender has made himself an outcast from Israel.

Ver. 18. **Flee fornication.** "Because, as Anselm, Cassian, etc., teach, other vices are overcome by fighting against them; lust alone, by fleeing from it, viz. by avoiding the objects and occasions of lust, and diverting eyes and mind, to see and think of other things" (CALOVIUS). **Every sin without . . . fornication against his own body.** "There is no sin that is within the body in the frightful form in which fornication is. By it the whole body, inwardly as well as outwardly, is made over to another, and is utterly separated from Christ. Such sins as intemperance or self-murder involve acts injuriously affecting the body, yet done, as it were, from without; but the sin of the one committing fornication (observe the tense) is, so to say, within the body, and using it as a direct agent and implement" (ELLICOTT). "The entire man is polluted also by other sins (Matt. 15 : 19); but not as by fornication, which enkindles within the body the impure flame of flagitious lust, and impresses the mark of its baseness upon it ; not rarely it proclaims its impurity by means of foul diseases as brands burnt into it by the preceding life" (HUNNIUS).

Ver. 19. **Your body is a temple of the Holy Ghost.** The same figure that is applied in 3 : 16 to the Church collectively, is here applied to each of its members individually. **Which is in you.** But the Holy Ghost is a Spirit of purity, before whose presence all such sensual defilement must vanish. " For the regenerate man, so far as he is regenerate, is ruled and governed, not by himself, not by the rational soul, but by the Spirit of God, who is the soul of such a soul, and who illumines and quickens it (John 6 : 63). The Holy Spirit directs the body and the members of the body in the regenerate man, uses his tongue to the glory of God and the profit of his neighbor, labors through his hands, moves his feet to serve others, suggests good thoughts into his heart, and, therefore, governs all his thoughts and decisions, that they seem to be not of man, but of the Spirit of God Himself" (BALDWIN).

Ver. 20. **For ye were bought.** The aorist, referring to a definite act in past time, shows that the price was paid once for all. **With a price,** viz. the blood of Christ (Eph. 1 : 7 ; 1 Pet. 1 : 18, 19 ; Rev. 5 : 19 ; Acts 20 : 28 ; 1 John 1 : 7). **In your body,** i. e. the sphere within which He is to be glorified. " They are in error who think that God should be only internally or only externally worshipped" (BENGEL). (Comp. Rom. 12 : 1 ; Phil. 1 : 20.)

www.ingramcontent.com/pod-product-compliance
Lightning Source LLC
Chambersburg PA
CBHW051243300426
44114CB00011B/868